GARDENING

I dedicate this book to my wife, a real plant lover for whom gardening holds no secrets.

P. P.

PAUL POULIOT

GARDENING

HABITEX BOOKS

- Cover Design by JACQUES DES ROSIERS
- Interior Design and Layout by DONALD MORENCY
- Cover Photograph by MALAK, Ottawa
- Many sections of this book have been previously published in the author's daily column in *La Presse,* Montreal
- Colour photographs from Encyclopédie du Jardinier Horticulteur by W. H. PERRON. Published in 1971 by Les Editions de l'Homme
- English language translation and production supervision by AMPERSAND PUBLISHING SERVICES INC., Toronto

Exclusive Distributor:
Collier-Macmillan Canada Ltd.
539 Collier-Macmillan Drive
Cambridge, Ontario
N1R 5W9

ISBN-0-88912-018-8

2

Bibliothèque nationale du Québec
Dépôt légal — 1er trimestre 1975

ACKNOWLEDGEMENTS

The author wishes to thank the following organizations which have graciously provided him with technical information as well as the photographs which were indispensible in the preparation of this book.

The Botanical Garden of Montreal
Le Ministère de l'Agriculture et de la Colonisation du Québec
Information Service, Canadian Ministry of Agriculture
The Institute of Vegetable Research, Ottawa
Malak Photographer, Ottawa
Lemoine Tropica, Inc., Montreal
La Semence Supérieure, St. Lambert, Québec
The F.T.D. Florists' Association
The California Redwood Association, San Francisco, California
Flora Pacifica, Honolulu, Hawaii
Association of Bulb Producers of Holland, Hillegom,
*   The Netherlands*
All-America Rose Selections, Shenandoah, Iowa
All-America Gladiolus Selections, Jeffersonville, Indiana
W.H. Perron

TABLE OF CONTENTS

INTRODUCTION

This book is intended for the amateur gardener. It is, therefore, a "popular" work, written in a simple and direct style. Nevertheless, there is information which will also be of interest to more experienced gardeners.

Gardening cannot possibly provide all the information or, indeed, answer all the questions which an amateur gardener may have. However, it does contain the solutions to many bewildering and persistent problems which the amateur as well as the professional gardener may encounter.

Although this book is primarily a practical manual of methods and procedures useful to the gardener, I have also attempted to give proper attention to the principles underlying these procedures.

Many of the species and plant varieties described in **Gardening** have been the subject of particular or specialized study in Canada — especially at the Institutes of Agricultural Research of the Experimental Farms under the jurisdiction of the Minister of Agriculture of Canada; at the Institute of Agricultural Technology of St. Hyacinthe under the jurisdiction of the Ministère de l'Agriculture et de la Colonisation du Québec; and at the Montreal Botanical Gardens.

Gardening has been written for **all** plant lovers, whether they have a vast estate or a few pots on their window still. As well as devoting attention to the cultivation of plants popular in our part of the world, the book also gives special attention to house plants.

An outstanding feature of **Gardening** is the "Calendar of Work" which at a glance shows the gardener the duties which must be performed each month throughout the year.

Paul Pouliot

CHAPTER 1

GARDENING

ITS MANY ADVANTAGES

Gardening is the favourite pastime of thousands of active people. It's the perfect way of escaping the monotony of a world in which mechanization becomes more important every day. It releases us — for a few hours, at least — from the frenzied activity that seems inevitable nowadays, and lets us forget the demands of our daily chores. Those who devote their leisure hours to the cultivation and care of plants are rewarded by a sense of well-being which they have never before known. Most people want to make the outside of their homes look attractive. During the sumer season, they also want to spend as much time as they can outdoors. Given a good lawn and a pleasing variety of plants, the garden is the perfect holiday spot — a place of peace, in which to welcome family and friends. The garden may be considered an extension of the house — a second living-room, without walls. And when it includes a kitchen garden, it's a handy source of delicious fresh vegetables as well.

A PLEASURE EVERY DAY

Of all the leisure activities of summer, gardening is the most popular and the most widely practised since it lies within everybody's reach. Young and not-so-young can devote themselves to gardening throughout the whole summer season. Whether their choice be ornamental plants or a kitchen garden, whether the scale of their activity be large, with many different varieties of plant set out in formal beds, or small, a balcony with tubs of flowers, perhaps, or even a simple window-box — all of them find gardening a pleasant hobby, a release from tension — leisure in its healthiest form.

Gardening affords its devotees a satisfaction which no other leisure activity or sport can match. No wonder its popularity keeps growing all the time!

THE BEST FORM OF EXERCISE

Gardening is a matchless aid to health. The dedicated gardener forgets all the cares of his daily life. There is nothing like concentrating on the upkeep of your plants to keep yourself in good shape!

When summer comes, the garden is a favourite spot for the whole family. It s a place to exercise and a place to relax. It is the outdoor extension of the living-room, the perfect place in which to welcome family and friends in surroundings that are both restful and attractive.

The various forms of physical exercise called for in the tending of a garden are splendid methods of getting yourself back into condition, and staying there. Weeding, hoeing, pruning, or simply pushing a roller or a wheel-barrow — all these activities help to tone up the muscles, stimulate the circulation of the blood, and keep the heart in good working order.

FOR THE WHOLE FAMILY

I must stress that gardening is an activity the whole family can enjoy. The preparation and upkeep of a garden are tasks in which every member of the family can share. The children will learn to enjoy and to respect Nature and they will be spending their spare time on something which is not merely pleasurable, but instructive and useful as well. In short, there is no sport or pastime which offers so many advantages, gives so much satisfaction — and asks so little in return. Gardening is a really splendid way to enjoy life!

ADVICE TO BEGINNERS

To help you get the most out of your gardening, there are some points which I feel are indispensable before you make a start. Beginners — such as those who have just become house-owners for the first time — should only undertake that which lies within their capabilities. They must be careful not to bite off more than they can chew. It's essential that they take into account the time and means at their disposal. Week-end golfers and those who travel frequently must plan their gardening to suit their time-table. Although most plants can get along fairly well on their own, they do need a little help against weeds and lack of water — not to mention the attacks of insects.

Those trying to grow plants for the first time need advice if they are to succeed, and so get the most out of their hobby, thus making it really enjoyable.

They are highly hopeful with their purchase of plants and seeds. Already they can see themselves surrounded by magnificent beds of perennials, or taking splendid vegetables from their kitchen garden. Too often, beginners discover that they've acted too hastily. It's essential that you keep your plans within the bounds of possibility, if you want your gardening to be a real pastime and not a sentence to hard labour.

MAKING A CHOICE

You must make a choice. If you are interested in vegetables, grow those your family likes. If you prefer flowering plants, limit yourself to a few varieties at the start. If your family's tastes are varied, I recommend plants that do not need too much attention, such as fruit trees and rose bushes. Lawns could be included here as well.

If you have young children of pre-school age, leave plenty of space for them to play in — even if it means growing fewer plants for the time being.

Plants which are chosen with care and skilfully arranged can give the exterior of a house a peaceful beauty which is always a source of pleasure to the beholder.

16

CHAPTER 2

LANDSCAPING
YOUR PROPERTY

PLANNING

To fulfil its role properly, a garden must have a welcoming atmosphere, and a peaceful, pleasant look. So a careful plan for the landscaping of your property is absolutely essential. I cannot stress this too strongly — the amateur gardener must always plan before he plants: without this elementary precaution, he will lose half the pleasure of his hobby. Gardening should always be a pleasant aid to physical and mental health, so seek the advice of experts whenever you can, and use well-designed modern tools to make your various jobs easier, thus avoiding unnecessary fatigue. Furthermore, a garden must suit the owner's taste — and his pocket too. It must also be planned with an eye to the leisure time he has available.

A BEAUTIFUL PROPERTY

To be really beautiful and attractive, and merit the name of 'home', a house should be surrounded with plants. The form of landscaping adopted should suit the style of the house. An aesthetically pleasing layout will usually require conscientious study. In a word, you must either draw up a proper plan yourself, or use a landscape gardener.

Trees are the first feature to be considered in the planning of a pleasing layout. Their positioning, their height, and their shape all have a very definite bearing on the look of a property.

Next come flowering shrubs. These impart a personal note to their beds by the intrinsic beauty of their shape, their leaves and their flowers.

And what of herbaceous plants, annuals and perennials? Their many-coloured leaves and flowers make them stand out like jewels against the green velvet of the lawn. The more care lavished on their choice, the more planning devoted to their placement — the more their beauty is enhanced.

Plants chosen with care, well arranged and carefully tended, produce an effect that changes with the seasons to give a constant atmosphere of welcome.

Renovating an old garden

The amateur gardener often finds it difficult to draw up a plan for his future garden and lay out the ground tastefully and effectively. But this problem is considerably less difficult than that posed by the rehabilitation of a property where the grounds have been allowed to become a wilderness — a situation faced by a good number of new house-owners every year.

According to Mr. A. R. Buckley of the Plant Research Institute, an acknowledged expert in the field, the first thing to recognize in such cases is that the garden was originally laid out in accordance with the require-ments of the previous owner, and that modifications and alterations to suit the taste of you and your family may well prove very difficult.

Experience has shown — and I can confirm this myself — that the best thing to do is to leave the garden as it is at the start, and just put in a few plants here and there which will fit nicely into their surroundings. At the same time, start making lists — say twice a month — of the plants in bloom: then you can decide which ones you like and want to keep.

I would also advise you to wait until mid-September before you start removing plants you want to get rid of.

And naturally, besides keeping some of the existing plants, there's nothing to stop you adding any of your own special favourites which happen to be missing.

THE NEED FOR OBSERVATION

Observation is certainly one way of remodelling a garden which allows you to get rid of the rubbish. Once that's done, let your inspiration, tastes and preferences take over, and start transforming your garden.

Use the summer to check how each plant's doing; then you'll be in a better position to see where the old garden falls short of your require-ments — and hence, how to draw up your new plan.

The commonest arrangement for an ordinary family garden is to keep the flowers close to the house, so that they can be enjoyed from the terrace and the windows.

WOODY PLANTS FIRST

As soon as spring arrives, you can make a fair start on remodelling your 'wilderness' by embarking on an intensive programme of lopping and pruning — mainly of the decidous shrubs. Don't be afraid to rip out an untidy old hedge to make your garden look less cramped and cluttered. Alternatively, you could simply cut the hedges down to ground level. The same treatment is equally satisfactory for clumps of overgrown shrubs with a lot of weak branches growing in all directions.

On the other hand, you might prefer merely to top the shrubs and thin out the lateral branches. If the shrubs are still in good condition, you can improve their appearance by cutting off a few of the old branches, or those which have become too heavy. This will provide more light and space for the younger shoots.

CONIFERS

The best thing to do with conifers — especially **cedars** and **junipers** — that have lost their shape, with the lower branches all bare and overgrown, is to get rid of them; there's little chance of their ever improving. It's quite a different story with the **yew,** however. If you prune it from early spring onwards, it will start growing again — though it will take two to four years to regain its proper shape. To get a fine healthy plant as quickly as possible, treat it with a complete commercial fertilizer (such as 6-9-6, for example) immediately after its first pruning. Then give it a second treatment with the same fertilizer the following year.

You can also use the same treatment for **rose** bushes. In the case of **climbing roses**, old branches should be pruned to let the healthiest branches develop better. This should be done at the beginning of spring, or immediately after the plant has blossomed.

DIVIDING PERENNIALS
AND HERBACEOUS PLANTS

You won't find it difficult to improve most of the perennials. All you need do is dig them up, and then divide them. In general, plants which flower in spring or early summer (for example, **peonies**) take root again very satisfactorily if they're divided in the autumn; while those that flower in the autumn should be divided in the spring. While you're at it, make sure to give your borders and flowerbeds a good spading; then work in some organic material (manure, compost, etc.) and a complete chemical fertilizer, before replanting.

NEW PLANTING

If you decide to do any new planting, don't forget that your new plants must be suited to the type of soil you have. You must also take into account the general perspective of your property, and the size and shape of your garden.

The seasons are also important. This is perhaps a good place to remind you that your own personal memories may well play a highly important part in the design of your new garden, as may tradition too. No doubt you remember the garden at your childhood home, or at some house that made an impression on you. As these memories and impressions come flooding back, you'll probably want certain plants in preference to others. But don't forget beautiful and ever-popular favourites such as **lilac, roses, clematis, peonies** and **spiraeas**.

On the other hand, you may want to steer clear of the traditional ornamental plants of your parents' garden and go in for the more modern type of plantings — something a bit out of the ordinary, perhaps?

The amateur gardener has a very wide range of interesting plants at his disposal nowadays. New cultivars for the gardens of today are continually being introduced and improved.

From **asters,** through **geraniums,** to **petunias** — you'll find a whole host of shapes, colours and textures that harmonize with modern building materials and lend a distinctive air to a garden, turning it into an oasis of freshness and beauty.

The Patio

LAYOUT

By definition, a patio is the inner courtyard of a house. It's also the area of transition between the house and the flowerbeds in the garden — an outdoor living-room, if you like, a room with walls of greenery and the sky above as its ceiling.

The essential requirement when laying out a patio is that it should harmonize with the house. Thus, the ground-plan and the materials used must suit the architecture of the building — for it's really an extension of the building. Furthermore, the patio should be a private place — a quiet, sheltered spot to which one can retire from the pressures of one's daily life. There's nothing very complicated about the choice of site. Often enough, the house itself is L-shaped, which gives you two walls of your patio. The third wall could be a fence covered with vines, or even a simple louvred fence. The fourth side is left open, naturally.

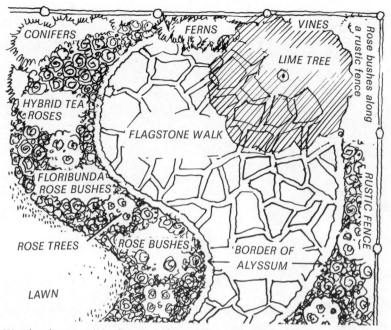

Woody plants and herbaceous perennials planted as a border add a great deal to the beauty and intimacy of this restful, relaxing terrace.

CORRECT ORIENTATION IS IMPORTANT

Since our climate in Canada tends to be fairly cold, a patio is used mainly in the summer season. The open side should face east or south — never west, unless you have some big shade trees to give you proper protection trom the evening sun.

Some shade from trees is essential. If you do not have shade, you will find that on hot summer days you simply will not be able to use the patio. This doesn't mean that you must have the trees right next to it. Furthermore, deciduous trees are preferable to conifers for once the latter have reached a certain height, they will cast unwanted shadows in winter, just when you need every ray of sunshine you can get to make you forget the rigours of a season which is often too long and cold.

Although the patio is mainly for use in the summer, it can still present an attractive appearance all year round, so that it makes a pleasant sight when seen from inside the house.

Dwarf conifers and brightly-coloured shrubs will counteract any tendency to monotony — especially if they're planted along a wall, no matter whether it's brick, stone or concrete.

This charming patio, an extension of the house itself, is decorated by a variety of plants in containers, which soften the somewhat severe straight lines of the architecture. Floor and furniture are of sequoia or "redwood", and can withstand bad weather.

You can separate your patio from your neighbour's property by a handsome redwood fence. Far from spoiling the look of your flowerbeds, such a fence gives them a well-balanced appearance and a look of permanence. At the foot of the fence above, varicoloured annuals strike a pleasant note in the background; while in the foreground some conifers contrast nicely with the reddish wood.

A PROTECTED ZONE

The house and the patio form a protective zone around the plants in that area. Thus, it's comparatively easy to grow some of the less hardy plants which would be unlikely to survive in a more exposed site or in open country. Plants in this category include various types of **box**, **azaleas** (Loiseleuria procumbens), conifers, shrubby trees such as **myrtle** (Lagerstroemia), and even some of the hardier varieties of **camellias.**

Vines such as the various types of **euonymus** and **climbing hydrangea** (Hydrangea petiolaris) also profit from the protection offered by a patio.

Nor should indoor plants be overlooked — in many cases, a spell outside will do them no harm and potted plants will enhance the general appearance of the patio and give it that "outdoor living-room" look which is so stylish.

A large variety of plants may also be planted in containers. If they were grown in a greenhouse or a hotbed, they will be in flower earlier than those in the borders and beds. The use of containers also makes it possible to establish a rotation system, and thus to have plants continuously in flower throughout the summer. **Hydrangeas, roses** and **nasturtium** plants will make a definite contribution to the appearance of a patio.

FOUNTAINS AND POOLS

The patio is the ideal place for a low wall, a fountain, an artifical waterfall and a pool. Here again, proper planning of the various components is of prime importance if an ugly, cluttered effect is to be avoided. The pool may be surrounded by plants such as **stonecrop, small-leaved ivy,** and **myrtle,** which will gradually creep over the edges of the pool, towards the water. This gives a charming natural effect, and also attracts birds to the area.

AN OASIS OF PEACE AND BEAUTY

Three questions are invariably asked by those who wish to achieve a satisfactory layout of their property: How do I lay out my patio properly? What sorts of plant should I use? Are there any set rules I should follow? Let me say at once that the same plants you use elsewhere in your garden will go very well on your patio, and that the same general principles of gardening apply there equally. However, layouts vary, and you must choose the one that gives your patio a special quality of its own.

WHY A PATIO?

What is the principal object of a patio? First and foremost, it is an outdoor rest-area where you can relax in complete quiet. Consequently, you should try to make this area as attractive as possible by the use of artistically and tastefully arranged plants.

Whether your patio be open on one, two or three sides, you must make it a pleasant spot, sheltered from the wind, where you can relax in comfort during the cool days of spring and autumn. Even more important — there must be enough shade to protect you from the burning rays of the summer sun.

A fence needn't necessarily be ugly. The important point is to choose a material which harmonizes with the surroundings to mark the boundaries of your property. Screens and fences can also be used to mark walks and pathways and to add privacy to a patio and isolate it from the activities around it. In the illustration above, redwood slats have been used to form a louvred fence to enclose a raised patio.

TREES

What sort of tree should one use for a patio? There are several which are particularly suitable for this very special part of your property. You will naturally wish to plant the tree of your choice in such a position that it will shade the paved surface of your patio. Fast-growing trees will of course produce the desired shade more quickly, but such trees tend to be short-lived, and to break easily in storms or in wintertime. You would therefore be advised to choose the more sturdy species such as **oak, linden, maple** and **ash**.

If your patio is not very large, one of the smaller shade-trees would be more suitable. Another point worth mentioning is that in addition to at least one shade-tree, any patio is improved by the presence of flowering trees. In spring, any of the following will add a touch of colour to help you forget the rigours of winter: ornamental **crab apple, chestnut, cherry, cornel, hawthorn, robinia, false acacia** and **mountain ash**. And don't overlook summer-flowering trees such as **little leaf linden, magnolia** and **catalpa**.

When planting your patio, remember the effect produced by the interplay of light and shade. Besides the lighted or shaded surfaces themselves, which can be extremely interesting and useful to your decorative scheme, you must also take into account the variations in the texture of the actual foliage.

CONIFERS are among the most essential plants in the landscaping of a property. In addition to planting a couple of major species (such as **pine** and **spruce**) to provide shade for your "outdoor living-room", some of the smaller conifers should be planted at corners or other points of vantage. **Yews, junipers** (both the **standing** and the **creeping** varieties), and **dwarf pines** can be combined with **rhododendrons** and **azaleas** with striking effect.

ESPALIERS More than anywhere else in the garden, the patio offers the perfect opportunity of showing each plant at its best. For example, you might try an espaliered fruit-tree against the wall of the house — an **apple**, say, or a **plum** or **peach**, or a flowering shrub such as **forsythia** or **jasmin**.

To break the monotony of the paved surface, raised beds may be added close to the house. They will stay full of colour right through the season, with bulbs in spring, annuals in summer and **chrysanthemums** in the autumn. Suitable bulbs for spring flowering are **jonquils, tulips, crocuses** and **grape hyacinths**. For your border hedge, you may choose evergreen or deciduous plants. Among the first group, **Korean boxwood** — a low plant with tiny evergreen leaves — is highly satisfactory. For a higher hedge, try **white spruce** which can be trimmed to a height of less than five feet. Among the deciduous group, the following are suitable for low hedges: **dwarf Siberian pea, red osier dogwood, privet** and **alpine currant.** For higher deciduous hedges try **European cotoneaster, cockspur thorn, American larch** ("tamarack"), **garden lilac, golden rose-leaved physocarpus** or **Vanhoutte's spiraea.**

Your favourite tree or flowering shrub can be planted in an empty corner of the patio to provide a contrast and break the monotony of the paved surface. You might consider giving up a little more space around this plant and creating a suitably-shaped flowerbed. Appropriate plants for this bed would be **pachysandra, pansies, hyacinths** or **tulips,** in spring, followed by **dwarf tulips** or other annuals. If there is sufficient sun, try a **coleus** or a **caladium** and **multiflora tuberous begonias.**

Nor should vines be forgotten. Because of prevailing styles in domestic architecture, vines usually occupy the place of honour at the entrance to the patio. This is the ideal spot for **climbing roses** and **hybrids of clematis.** Annual vines such as **morning glory** (Ipomoea)) always look well-placed near a patio.

In certain cases — if you want more privacy, or to increase the impression of an "outdoor room" — you can add a fence along each side of your patio, or simply at one end.

POTTED PLANTS

A patio looks incomplete without a few potted plants scattered here and there. For sunny corners choose one or two varieties of **geranium** or some annuals. Suitable plants for shady areas are **tuberous begonia, fuchsia, caladium, coleus** and **nicotiana.** A striking effect may be obtained with hanging baskets of **fuchsia** in the shade and **lantana** and **ivy geranium** in the sun.

Whatever you do, avoid overplanting around your patio. Keep it simple and attractive. Let it be an expression of your own personality and tastes and it will be a constant source of satisfaction to you and your family.

A terraced garden, or one with a patio, is an obvious centre of attraction both in summer and in autumn. The layout must therefore be chosen with care, as must the plants that are to be featured there.

A well-placed terrace becomes almost part of the house itself, and adds a value to the property far greater than the cost of its construction. In the technical sense of the word, a terraced garden is — as the word indicates — a "stepped" area, while the modern patio is usually an enclosed area open to the sky. The terms are flexible, and often both forms of layout are described as "patios", though the word "terraced" would be more accurate in the case of a garden at lawn level or a few feet higher.

HEDGES AND SHRUBS

The "walls" of your patio should be hedges or small shrubs cut low, with openings onto the garden. The garden itself need not be a complicated affair — squares of gravel or stones, surrounded by grass and bordered by simple plants, are often quite sufficient.

The hedges around the garden should be small and slow-growing. **Japanese yew** (Taxus cuspidata) or **Korean boxwood** (Buxus microphylla Koreana) are two suitable species. **Dwarf viburnum** (Viburnum opulus nanum) or **blue-leaved willow** (Salix purpurea gracilis) grow somewhat higher without becoming too thick, and their foliage gives the garden a distinctive look.

Low hedge bordering a terrace, with tubs ready for planting.

It's customary to put a narrow flowerbed in front of the hedge. Here, carpeting plants always look well, such as the **large periwinkle** (Vinca major), **Japanese spurge** (Pachysandra terminalis) or **bearberry** (Arctostaphylos uva-ursi). Among these plants, sow some small-flowered spring bulbs such as **Siberian squill, grape hyacinth** and **miniature narcissus**, if the climate is favourable.

When you build your terrace keep some space for show plants. A terrace is the perfect place for exotic plants set in tubs at strategic spots — such as **dwarf Alberta pine** (Picea glauca Albertina conica) and some of the **hostas** and the **daphnes.**

Other suitable tub plants are **blue hydrangea** and **Californian laurel.** Except in the temperate regions of British Columbia, these plants should be taken indoors and kept in a dry cellar for the winter.

If you have sandy soil on your terrace you can put little rock-plants in the cracks between the stones. They lend colour to the terrace and very often they form carpets two or three feet in diameter which will withstand a certain amount of foot traffic. Recommended species are: **sandwort** (Arenaria verna), **creeping thyme** (Thymus serpyllum) and its cultivars, **moss pink** (Phlox subulata), **speedwell** (Veronica repens) and perhaps a few little tufts of **pearlwort** (Sagina repens).

Small compact varieties such as **sweet alysum** (the **"Carpet of Snow"** variety) can be sown directly in the cracks. In warm, sunny spots, try some **annual fig-marigold** (Mesembryanthemum) and **portulaca** (either the single or the double-flowered variety).

BETWEEN THE FLAGSTONES

Should you plant between the flagstones? This is a debatable point. Efficient planting can produce a most beautiful and interesting effect. But visitors tend to find it inconvenient — they feel obliged to walk with the greatest of care in order not to crush the plants, even after being told they will withstand being trodden on. If the stones have been well laid, any grass growing in the cracks can be cropped short — though it generally tends to bunch into rather scruffy-looking tufts of varying heights.

Along a wall or a hedge I would advise low conifers mixed with well-pruned flowering shrubs. Early-flowering shrubs that bloom as the snow begins to melt make a splendid impression when the rest of the garden still looks muddy and depressing!

The beautiful waxy white flowers of **mezereon** (Daphne mezereum album) would be lost in a bushy border but on a terrace they become the focal point, even before the snow has completely disappeared from the garden. **Korean forsythia** (Forsythia ovata) gives a garden an unusual look at the beginning of spring. Follow this up with **dwarf 'Anthony Waterer' spiraea** (Spiraea bumalda 'Anthony Waterer') and **Lemoine deutzia** (Deutzia lemoinei).

A terraced garden normally begins at the kitchen door, or at a porch which affords a good view of these springs shrubs.

Planting On Slopes

It is preferable not to have steep slopes on your land, to avoid erosion during heavy rain and parching during droughts.

Try if possible to level out such slopes, and obtain a regular fall of land — not steeper than a drop of one foot per yard, then the whole surface may be grassed over. There are two ways of creating a lawn, either by laying squares of sod or by sowing grass-seed.

Laying sod is the more costly method, but it can be done at any time provided the ground is not actually frozen. However, to stop the strips of sod slipping down the slope, you must always anchor them with little bits of pointed stick or with pegs. I would also advise you to consolidate this 'carpet' with a heavy rammer as soon as you have finished laying it, and then to give it a good watering.

The other method consists of sowing a mixture of grass-seed composed of **Kentucky bluegrass, red fescue** and **perennial ryegrass** in equal proportions. After seeding. the surface should be covered with burlap which must be watered daily until the seed has sprouted. The burlap prevents both erosion and drying out. It should be left in place until the grass has come up.

STEEP SLOPES

When a considerable drop in height is inevitable a wall is generally used. This may be a stone wall or a wall planted with flowers or even a rockery. However, some cases are particlarly complicated, such as steep slopes or small ravines. Planting then becomes a problem too difficult for most amateur gardeners. This situation is often encountered in new properties located in areas where public services such as sidewalks and storm drains are not yet completed. The owners must of necessity lay their lawns on a steep slope — which means that they cannot carry out the final layout of their land for at least some time since the slope will not be flattened out until the public works have been completed.

Mowing grass on a slope is always a difficult operation. To get over the problem I suggest you plant something that needs no mowing, which grows enough to choke the weeds and which has roots that spread wide enough and deep enough to consolidate the soil, control erosion and ward off parching by the sun. This simple solution involves using a 'covering' plant which suits the general topography, the type of soil and the orientation as regards the sun. You should not forget that in certain cases it may be necessary to give the slope a smooth surface first or to add a layer of good rich loam.

A WIDE CHOICE OF PLANTS

For a slope with a north exposure, in a damp area, the solution lies in planting **periwinkle** or **creeping myrtle** (Vinca minor). This is a creeping plant with evergreen leaves of a deep, shiny green. It is particularly useful in shady areas where it forms a handsome carpet which never needs clipping, except at the edges, to stop it from spreading too far.

For a drier slope in a shady location — overlooked by a building, perhaps, or some close-leaved trees — I would advise the use of **Japanese spurge** (Pachysandra terminalis), which looks not unlike **creeping myrtle,** though without the latter's gaudy flowers.

Creeping myrtle is a very useful plant for slopes facing north or west, where a lawn is impractical. Its evergreen leaves, a beautiful deep shiny green in hue, make a magnificent carpet which never needs clipping.

On slopes exposed to the sun for several hours daily, carpeting rock-garden plants are the ideal solution. Some examples are:

Creeping thyme (Thymus serpyllum), which thrives in well-drained, sandy soil that is exposed to the sun. The typical species, with small leaves and pale pink flowers, grows to a height of four inches and spreads quite neatly.

Snow-in-summer (Cerastium tomentosum), a plant with grey leaves, which becomes covered with white flowers in June. It reaches a height of six inches. Care must be taken to cut the plants right back after flowering, otherwise they will spread too far and may stifle other less robust plants.

Moss pink or **creeping phlox** (Phlox subulata), which is particularly useful for producing masses of colour. To obtain the full advantage from this plant, you must take care to prune it in May, after flowering, to control its growth. It grows four to six inches high.

Pink (Dianthus), known as a good grower in all sound garden soils exposed to the sun. Two species are of particular interest here: **maiden pink** and **Cheddar pink**. **Maiden pink** (Dianthus deltoides) forms cushions of deep, shiny green foliage, and keeps its good looks throughout the season. It has very plentiful pink flowers and ranges between six and twelve inches in height. It flowers from June to August and makes an excellent covering — though it should not be allowed to stifle its more delicate neighbours. The **Sterns** variety of **maiden pink** grows six inches high and also flowers from June to August. Its foliage is a deep browny-green and its flowers are bright pink. This variety grows in a compact mass with sharply-defined edges. **Cheddar pink** (Dianthus gratianopolitanus) grows in handsome tufts, ranging from six to twelve inches in height. Its foliage is greyish and its pink flowers appear in July.

Stonecrop (Sedum). This plant prefers the full sun. Three species are particularly suitable for rock-gardens, and can be recommended for use on slopes: **Sedum Middendorffianum,** a very hardy species that grows very straight, six to twelve inches high. Its yellow flowers appear in June and its foliage is particularly colourful in autumn. **Sedum Sieboldii** grows to a height of six or eight inches. Its leaves are greeny-blue, and its pink flowers are seen in August and September. **Sedum spurium** has creeping stems that form a reddish-coloured network. It produces pink or white flowers in July and August.

For warm, dry locations it would be difficult to find a more suitable plant than **houseleek (Sempervivum).** Its leaves are arranged in fairly tight little rosettes; a stem bearing a cluster of flowers grows out of the centre of each rosette. The rosette dies after flowering, and is replaced by new ones which grow around the site of the old one. The plant can be made to spread very easily, merely by splitting the tufts apart.

Lawn sown
with No. 1 'Merion'
lawn-seed
mixture

Lawn sown with 'Landscaper's Special' lawn-seed mixture

African marigolds:
F-1 hybrid
'Golden Jubilee';
24" - 30"
(annual)

Zinnias:
F-1 hybrid
'Peter Pan';
All-America
gold medal 1971
(annual)

Geraniums
F-1 hybird
'Care Free';
All-America
silver medal 1968
(annual)

At back African marigolds: early dwarf 'Spun Gold'

In front Ageratums: 'Blue Mink' (annual)

China asters Carpet of Colour variety (annual)

All these plants may be used in a solid individual mass, or as a mixed bed. After planting, it's essential to remove all weeds, until your plants have formed a carpet thick enough to stifle any unwnated growths. I should also mention that these covering plants need no pruning except in early spring to remove dead stems and other rubbish.

CREEPING CONIFERS

Creeping junipers are very suitable plants for use on slopes. They vary in colour from silver-grey to deep green and their growth may take the form either of a carpet clinging closely to the ground or of a spreading, drooping mass.

There are several varieties which go well in the sort of conditions we have been discussing. Some of these are: **Waukegan juniper** (Juniperus horizontalis Douglasii), which has handsome blue-green leaves; **Silver juniper** (Juniperus horizontalis glauca), which retains its silvery foliage throughout the year; **Wilton's juniper** (Juniperus horizontalis Wiltonii), a low-growing bush which forms a thick blue carpet; and **Andorra juniper** (Juniperus horizontalis plumosa), which changes its foliage from the blue-green of the summer to a rich plum colour in September.

You could also use **cinquefoil** (Potentilla) to solve the problem of your slope. This is a plant that prefers reasonably heavy soils. There are many species: one of the more suitable is **Farrer's small-leaved potentilla** or **cinque-foil** (Potentilla parvifolia Farreri) which creates a most attractive effect with its golden flowers from spring to autumn, and with its bronzed leaves in winter.

The use of covering plants on slopes is much preferable to the laying of a lawn which risks being scorched by the sun or eaten away by erosion. Plants not only present a better appearance, but also are much easier to care for.

In areas of heavy precipitation, where rain is frequent and heavy, you should not overlook the problem of possible erosion of the soil before your plants are firmly established. The best method of guarding against this is to spread a three-inch layer of organic material over the surface to form a protective blanket against heavy rain. Chopped straw and ground peat-moss are suitable materials for this purpose.

Water Gardens

The appearance of a garden can very often be immensely improved by the intelligent use of water. Suitable application might include the installation of a lily-pond in a sunny area, a simple fountain in a pool against a background of rocks and plants, a little trickling waterfall, a series of small cascades at the outfall of a pool, a miniature lake, a fish-pond or even a simple bird-bath.

It's easy enough to include a water-area in your garden, with a pond and a waterfall or two. In fact, prefabricated waterfalls are available at garden supply shops, at reasonable prices. These are constructed of light-weight rocks and come ready equipped with small electric pumps. You may also buy plastic lily-ponds from firms that specialize in garden equipment. Alternatively, you should find no particular difficulty in building your own pond, which can be fed from the domestic water-supply system and where you will find it easy enough to grow exquisite lilies of your own.

THE SUPPLY OF WATER

When planning the installation of a pond, naturally one of the first things to be decided is the source of water-supply, nor must the overflow from the pond be forgotten. You must also decide what type of pond you want, how big it is to be, and what materials to use in its construction.

Like all other components of the landscape, your pond must fit into its surroundings. Sloping ground offers the most serious problem, because of the large amount of levelling work that must be carried out. Broken ground may allow you to form a stream, which can be given a pleasing natural look by using rocks and stones and flat slabs along its length. A small watercourse of this type should never flow in a straight line, it should be modelled on a mountain stream and include detours and bends in its course which should follow the natural lie of the land as it falls.

Every pond must be fed with a supply of fresh water: this supply may be an existing stream, or clean rain-water from the gutters, or the normal domestic water-supply. Sometimes a small continuous trickle of water from the domestic supply will be enough to keep the pool clean and attractive at small cost, and the overflow can be led to the ordinary sewer system. Alternatively, a small storage tank and an electric pump will allow the same water to be used over and over again.

Site your pond in the most attractive location available, even if it proves somewhat more difficult to supply with water than other possible alternatives. One of the special features of a pond is that its surroundings are reflected in its surface. Thus it should obviously be located facing a mass of plants; or in front of a pergola or some other attractive architectural feature.

A corner of the pool may be embellished with water plants.

To ensure the best reflection, the surface of the water should be as open as possible to the rays of the sun: and the pond must be located in such a position that whatever is reflected in it can be seen from the house or other vantage-points such as the patio or the area of the lawn used for sitting-out.

If the pool is to be of any considerable size, you would do better to have it built by a qualified landscaping contractor. This will prove more economical in the long run.

SUITABLE PLANTS

Naturally, a pool calls for water plants and the choice of the appropriate plants and vegetation often poses a major problem. If **water lilies** are to be grown, full exposure to the sun is needed — at least in the morning — and the pool itself should be at least two feet deep. Shelves should be installed underwater at either end of the pool where plants with shallower roots may be grown — such as **arrowhead, wild calla, little**

wild water lily, water crowfoot and **water caltrop.** These waterside plants add plenty of interest to a pool, and help it to fit in harmoniously with its surroundings.

The water plant section of any nurseryman's catalogue offers a choice of many varieties of the two categories of **water lilies** — the hardy and the tropical. Hardy varieties should be planted towards the end of June, and tropical varieties some three weeks later.

The actual planting is a very simple affair. All you need is an old pot, and some boxes or basins. Fill these with a mixture of eight parts of good garden loam and one part of dried cow or sheep manure, which is obtainable at any garden supply centre. To each bushel of this mixture, add a handful of 6-9-6 fertilizer.

To plant a **hardy water lily,** moisten the soil and work it well in around the roots; but leave it standing up like a cone at the spot where the stem of the plant will come through, with the tip of the stem more or less at surface level. This tip is very fragile, and care must be taken not to bruise it. Place some flat stones over the roots, and cover the surface of the soil with sand or fine stone chippings. Then submerge the container so that the neck of the plant is about one foot under water. You may have to prop the container up to ensure the correct depth.

The tropical varieties are planted in the same way, only they must not be submerged more than ten inches below the surface — and of course the water must be reasonably warm — about 70°F at the time of planting.

The **tropical water lily** is a spectacular plant: various colours are available, among them blue. The plant remains open at night-time, instead of closing as many of the **hardy water lilies** do. Judicious intermingling of the two vareties will thus not only allow you to enjoy several different colours, but will ensure a display at night-time as well as during the day.

Plants For A Town Garden

There are few places where gardening is a difficult as in the little plots in the centre of town, which are almost invariably surrounded by tall buildings. The soil is usually badly drained, and therefore constantly moist, and to make things worse it is often contaminated with the salt used to melt the snow on the streets in winter. Nevertheless, these problems can usually be solved by a judicious choice of plants, by modification of traditional gardening practices and by the introduction of new methods.

Raised flowerbeds, retained by a brick or stone wall, make for easier up-keep, and improve the appearance of a house.

TREES

The typical town garden is small, and often overshadowed by tall buildings, the shape is frequently irregular, it may be bordered by a sidewalk, and it must perfoce follow the general gradient of the street. To choose the right tree for planting in such a location is not an easy task.

Nevertheless, there are trees which can be planted successfully in such conditions, and which are even able to withstand the extra disadvantage of being splashed with salt. One such tree is the **shadbush** (amelanchier canadensis), a native species which does not grow very large. It produces very pleasant copper-green foliage in spring, and an abundance of white flowers, followed by fruit which the birds find attractive.

If salt is your major problem rather than the lack of sun, then the **Russian olive** (Elaeagnus angustifolia) is the tree for you. It seems to resist salt and other unfavourable conditions better than any other variety

Another fine tree is the **sea buckthorn** (Hippophaë rhamnoides). To obtain the full beauty of its golden fruit in autumn, you should plant this tree in groups of three or more, to increase your chances of having a male tree for pollination purposes.

The **European mountain ash** (Sorbus aucuparia) can withstand a small amount of salt but it requires plenty of sunlight if its flowers and fruit are to develop fully.

In a waterlogged and poorly drained garden, your solution might be the **white alder** (Alnus incana). It grows very quickly and has deep green foliage with brown bark.

A yellow-leaved variety exists, but you will rarely find it listed in nurserymen's catalogues.

Two other trees which don't need much sun, and can make do with poorish soil, are the **ginkgo** (Ginkgo biloba) and the **European white birch** (Betula pendula).

Coming down to bushes, suitable species include **Tartarian honeysuckle** (Lonicera tatarica), **grape hydrangea** (Hydrangea paniculata grandiflora) and **winged-bark euonymus** (Euonymus alata) or its more compact variety **Euonymus alata compacta.** Salt has no effect on **Tamarix pentandra**, a magnificent bush with fern-like leaves which produces blush-pink flowers in July and August. There is also a deeper-coloured variety, **Tamarix pentandra rubra.**

If the garden is so overshadowed that grass will not grow, try one or another of the many varieties of **creeping myrtle or periwinkle** (Vinca minor). This is a dwarf plant which spreads rapidly by means of long shoots which take root in the ground. Early in the spring, **creeping myrtle** gives pretty blooms of various colours — blue, pink, purple or white, depending on what variety you have chosen. The ordinary variety has flowers of a pale bluish lavender which appear in great profusion in May. This plant requires no pruning, other than to remove dead growth and to keep it to the desired size.

CONIFERS

Since a town garden is small, its layout should be planned in such a way as to create pleasant effects throughout the year. This may be done by the judicious use of sculptures, walls and cast-iron ornaments, and by the choice of bushes which please the eye as much by their shape as by the colour of their bark. Standing **junipers** (such as the **Pfitzer** variety) and **yews** are very suitable for town gardens, provided the soil is properly enriched. In winter-time, not only are their needles very beautiful, but their shape stands out well against the background of the snow.

If the soil is very poor, a sensible solution is to build raised beds behind a retaining wall of brick or stone, with a bottom layer of large pebbles or gravel underneath the surface soil. Be sure to leave adequate openings for drainage purposes, to prevent the beds becoming water-logged. Raised beds are easier to maintain and they enhance the appearance of their surroundings. Throughout almost all of Canada, unless beds are very large and deep, they are in general unsuitable for woody plants and herbaceous perennials which are killed off every year by the cold winter. It is therefore better to plant annual flowers or tuberous plants, or those with bulbs — such as **dahlias** and **gladioli**, which can be taken up and saved each year.

Neglected Gardens

In old, neglected gardens, it's often useless attempting to plant any-thing at all until you've improved the soil and the drainage. Very often, in such gardens, the soil has become too tightly-packed for anything to grow in it. The best way of treating this is to dig in a two-inch layer of horticultural peat, and the same depth of perlite. If you dig these in really deeply, you'll be pleasantly surprised by the results. Perlite is particularly useful in old gardens — it helps provide much-needed aeration and drainage.

ANNUAL FLOWERS

The brilliant colours of annual flowers are a real blessing for the city garden. They can be planted almost anywhere; in raised beds, or in various patio containers — troughs, pots, tubs, bowls — in short, in just about anything that will hold soil.

For very shady areas there is nothing nicer than the well-known old garden favourite, **touch-me-not** (Impatiens), which comes in all sorts of magnificent shapes and colours. Other flowers you should consider are **flowering tobacco, stock, begonia, marigold, coleus,** or **black-eyed-Susan vine,** which you can leave to hang down over the edge of its container. Also try some hanging baskets of drooping plants. In shady places, use **climbing saxifrage, spiderwort, Kenilworth ivy** (Cymbalaria muralis), **clinging ivy,** or any other creeping indoor plant.

With care and a modicum of experimentation, the cramped little town garden can be transformed into a beauty-spot. Nearly every city-dweller who has made a success of his garden will readily admit that it was a dif-ficult task, but he will go on to say that nothing is more rewarding than the sight of a lovely garden amid the greyness of the city. (It's certainly a lot better than paving the place over and painting it green!)

Artificial Lighting In Gardens

More and more people are now using artificial lighting in their gardens in summer-time. This practice is not merely the result of new concepts in architecture or landscaping, which aim at tying house and garden into one harmonious whole — though of course once evening has fallen, the lights do tend to make one inter-connected unit of both the interior and the exterior of your home.

But in addition to creating a pleasing visual effect and enhancing the appearance of your property after dark, the lighting also provides an element of security. A well-lit garden combines the functional with the aesthetic. Not only is the nocturnal beauty of your garden emphasized in pleasing fashion, but in addition you are able to spend several more hours outside on warm evenings.

In fact, sunset no longer means the end of the daily spectacle of beauty provided by your garden. With the surroundings of your house properly illuminated — particularly the garden — darkness is no longer to be regarded as a curtain rung down too soon, to terminate a delightful spectacle.

PLANNING

Before you consult your electrician, or find out about underground cables, or ask about voltages and probable consumption — and **certainly** before you go out and buy a single piece of equipment — the first thing you must do is to determine what you **want** to illuminate, and what **can** be illuminated!

Take a close look at likely spots by day, both from inside the house and from outside. Try to see your property as a coherent whole and make sure you look at it from where you'll be looking at it later on, when it's lit up at night. Don't forget that as the seasons change so do the areas of your garden where you take your relaxation. This is your opportunity to create a whole range of varicoloured floral illuminations, set against the wonderful black backdrop of the night. Make the most of it!

THE EFFECT OF COLOURS

In general white light gives excellent results when there are several colours in the garden, or when the prevailing hue is green. The bluish light of mercury-vapour lamps will intensify the beauty of your greens, whereas the yellow light of an incandescent lamp will tone down the various types of foliage and tend to deaden them.

In fact, if you want to bring out the colours of your flowers, you should light them with lamps the same colour as the flowers themselves. But there is no need to equip yourself with a complete battery of different-coloured lights — simply use ordinary lamps covered with non-flammable paper — that will do very well. Finally, to show off the general layout of your garden, set some white lamps with filters at the key points most likely to catch the eye of the beholder and retain his interest.

You can also produce a rather striking multicoloured shadow effect by using red, blue and green lamps to throw shadows onto a wall or any other flat surface.

FLOWERBEDS

Flowerbeds offer excellent possibilities for the use of artificial lighting. The flowers can be made to stand out to best advantage by beaming the light onto those that give the bed its basic design.

Use portable mushroom-shaped lamps for this purpose. They stand at ground level, and throw a large circle of light. Also, since they are portable, they may be moved to wherever fresh flowers are opening. However, it is most important that you take the greatest care to hide all these lamps. Leaving just one in full view will spoil the whole effect. Furthermore, all the electrical supply cables must be invisible, or at least well hidden among the vegetation. Lights, too, should be concealed as effectively as possible and in no circumstances should they be allowed to shine into your neighbours' gardens — far less into their windows.

THE ORNAMENTAL VALUE OF TREES

If you are lucky enough to have a tree with some ornamental value on your land, put it high on your priority-list for illumination. Make sure you light it in the most advantageous manner to suit the varying seasons — its silhouette, its bark, the whole tree in full bloom, its autumn foliage. The best way to illuminate a tall-standing tree is to set a projector at the base of the trunk, angling its beam upwards to light up the branches and the leaves. Since a tree's general shape and the way it stands are what gives it its beauty, the beams from your projectors should be aimed so that they just barely graze the trunk. Then you will find that your tree shows different shapes from different angles, with gracious lines you never even dreamed it possessed.

As new colours make their appearance in your garden, starting with, say, **golden forsythia** early in the spring, followed by various **spiraeas,** and then **lilacs** and **hawthorns**, you can illuminate them one ofter the other, using portable equipment with an assortment of lamps of the appropriate colours. This will enable you to bring out or deepen the colour of your flowers, as you wish.

WATERFALLS

Water always looks better when illuminated, whether it's still or in motion. The effect created by a small sheet of water is far more pleasing by night than by day if it is lit by skilfully placed artificial lighting. You will have no trouble in making it the focal point of your garden, whether you are strolling about outside or looking at it from inside the house. It's not hard to light up a sheet of water successfully — just put your projectors at the bottom of the pool, or hide them under the banks.

(You really **should** plan to build a little pool with a waterfall when you're laying out your garden, you will find it well worth the trouble!)

If your garden has steps and pathways in it, do not light them too directly — that ruins any possibility of giving them a distinctive look. They must be illuminated with a certain amount of subtlety — and the most effective way is to hide floodlights in the trees — they will throw fascinating shadows which keep moving to and fro over the ground and along the pathways.

STATUES

Statues and other man-made objects can also become a source of interest. If you light them from above, just their silhouettes show up after dark. You must never light them from below, however — this produces the most grotesque and unflattering results.

Use a little taste when you illuminate your garden. Highlight the features you find pleasing and conceal anything you consider undesirable. But "moderation in all things" should be the golden rule here — don't fall into the trap of trying to drive away the darkness at all costs, for you will merely destroy the artistic effect completely, and spoil the inherent charm of your garden.

A Garden For Children

It should come as no surprise to you to learn that most children like gardening as much as their parents do. Let them buy a few packets of seeds and a plant or two — they will get as much pleasure out of them as they will playing ball or splashing about in puddles.

All the same, never be never be misled into believing that your youngster is a born gardener just because he is boasting about having planted a few **sunflowers!** To a child, gardening's a game just like any other game, and his interest in it may turn out to be short-lived. Quite often, what the child really wants is not so much to do some gardening as to copy you.

Turn a small area of your garden over to your children — the results will delight you! They will enjoy gardening and it will also serve to introduce them to the beauty of nature.

It is too much to hope that children will carry out a task on a regular, sustained basis, even at the age of ten. Nevertheless, you can entrust them with the job of carting away the rubbish in a little wheelbarrow — and they will do it well. Ask them to rake under the bushes and hedges while you are busy somewhere else, and they will do their very best. If they are to be of any real assistance to you, children must have proper, well-built tools when they play "gardening". These can be bought in various sizes and weights to suit children of all age-groups.

There's no better way to encourage the young gardener than to give him a plot of his own. Help him turn the soil over and fertilize it: but you must let him choose his own seeds, and — when he's a bit older — his own plants as well. Let him make his choice of seeds from among those which are easy to grow, and which show quick results. He's bound to be delighted with **sunflowers, zinnias, kidney-beans, pumpkins** and **radishes**. Corn is another favourite, even though space may be a bit cramped.

Start by offering your child a plot three feet square, and keep adding to it as he grows older. Give him somewhere that gets plenty of sun, and has good gardening soil. Teach him how to plant in rows — and if his rows are not reasonably straight, even a child of six or seven can learn how to stretch a piece of string to make a straigt line, and then run his hoe down it to make a furrow. **Kidney-beans** or **radishes** won't take very long to sprout and your youngster will enjoy watching them grow.

As he sees his plants begin to grow, the child becomes more interested in watering them. When they are big enough, show him how to use a mulch of garden peat or leaf-mould to discourage the growth of weeds. The apprentice gardener must learn how to thin out his plants, and also how to transplant them — for he will probaly have sown them far too close together. Make sure conditions are favourable when you get him to do his transplanting, so that the operation is successful — or at least partly so. Here again, he will enjoy watering the plants he's just moved, and seeing they get the proper amount of shade.

A younger child will enjoy "gardening" in flower-pots. Give him some pots four or five inches across, and let him fill them with soil and sow some seeds in them. He'll spend hours filling them up, and emptying them, and filling them up again, sowing his seeds, and digging them up — he will have a fine old time "gardening".

If any seeds actually sprout after all this rough treatment — (**kidney-beans** will, in all probability) — the child will have had his first experience of gardening at an early age.

The methods I describe above have proved themselves of value in arousing an interest in gardening, and even though your children may not become expert gardeners, they will be of real help to you when they become teen-agers. You will be amply repaid for your patience in earlier years as you see them beginning to take a little more interest in your flowers and shrubs.

Plants For Damp Areas

Amateur gardeners with a typical, ordinary garden generally have a whole host of everyday problems confronting them — ravages caused by insects, wholesale destruction resulting from various plant diseases, what plants to choose for their garden, the actual planting and care of those plants — are only a few.

What are they to do when special problems crop up? — When ordinary flowers and ornamental plants simply refuse to grow? — When the beds are too damp, or too dry, or too sandy? — Or the slopes are too steep? — Or the soil is too clayey? Happily there are a number of attractive plants

Forget-me-not (Myosotis) is a perennial plant which does well in shady locations and in damp soils.

which do well in such conditions though you will have to use methods other than the normal ones to make thew grow in the places I've described.

Does your garden have a spot which is always damp, where water stands for a while after a fall of rain? If so, you should start by improving the soil. To do so, add organic material to it — garden peat, for example, or sand or ashes. Fill in any low spots to assist drainage, or put in weeping tile under the wet areas and let it drain off into a soak-pit.

Some plants grow really well in very damp areas. **Monkey-flower** (Mimulus) is one of the best of the annuals. Quite often it will withstand the winter and grow a second year, or even more. Get the **"Queen's Prize"** variety, and do your sowing indoors, in March.

Touch-me-not (Impatiens) does so well in the shade that it almost always seems to be planted in shady areas. However, it grows equally well in the sun and it's particularly successful in damp spots, whether in the sun or in the shade.

Toadflax (Linaria), an annual hybrid, is another plant that does well in damp areas. It produces flowers that look like **snapdragons,** but their colours are never found in the genuine **snapdragon** family.

PERENNIALS

Some perennials prefer a damp, muddy soil. **Astilbe** (Spiraea) belongs to this group). It produces extremely showy, feathery flowers — white, red, lavender and pale pink in colour — which last almost all summer long. It gives the garden a gay, fresh appearance — due, perhaps, not only to its characteristic flowers but also to the cool green of its leaves. Another plant that those who have a damp, peaty soil should bear in mind is **Kaempfer's iris,** which thrives in this sort of situation. The flowers of this Japanese **iris** are much more attractive — and considerably more noteworthy — than those of the ordinary common-or-garden **bearded iris.** They often measure as much as eight inches across, and are flat-topped, completely different from the bulbous heads of the more commonly cultivated **irises.** For **Kaempfer's iris,** the damper the soil the better — so much so, in fact, that many connoisseurs flood the area, like a rice-field, before they do their planting.

All the garden varieties of **loosestrife** (Lysimachia), such as **'Morden Gleam', 'Morden Pink', 'Croftway Pink', 'Dropmore Purple'** and **'Rose Queen',** grow well in damp areas, and they make a particularly beautiful effect when the free space between them is carpeted with **moneywort** or **creeping Jenny** (Lysimachia nummularia).

Naturally, you can discover a good deal of valuable information about plants which do well in these conditions, simply by wandering round the woods and meadows and keeping your eyes open for damp spots. It may even happen that you will decide to actually reproduce in your own garden the rare beauty of a piece of natural marshland. Once you have managed to recreate a marshy corner, complete with the luxuriant vegetation that comes from a decaying humus soil, then you can start growing **pitcherplant** (Sarracenia purpurea), with its hollow, pot-like leaves, or **sundew** (Drosera). These are two insectivorous plants you will find extremely interesting to grow.

A patch of **golden balsam** (Impatiens biflora) always catches the eye, with its shiny leaves and its stamens which unfold like springs. In the autumn, a broad bed of **cardinal flower** (Lobelia cardinalis) will amply repay you for your trouble with a dazzling display of red flowers.

Two meadow plants which love the damp and are easy to grow are **pink milkweed** (Asclepias incarnata), with its clusters of little pale crimson flowers which give Canadian meadows a rose hue in July and August and **northern buttercup** (Ranunculus septentrionalis), which produces its yellow flowers in August.

The quickest grower of all the marsh-loving plants is **marsh marigold** (Caltha palustris). Its golden yellow flowers bloom in April or early May. Nurserymen also carry a more delicate variety, a "double" marigold.

There are several shrubs that do well in damp areas — such as **black-fruited chokeberry** (Aronia melanocarpa), **cranberry bush** (Viburnum trilobum), various small **catkin williows** (Salix species), **dogwoods** (Cornus species), **sweet pepper bush** (Clethra alnifolia) and **buttonbush** (Cephelanthus occidentalis). **Catkin willows** are usually very successful — but you must choose varieties which do not grow into large trees, such as **pussy willow** (Salix discolor) and **goat willow** (Salix caprea).

Try some **Sekko willow** (Salix sachalinensis Sekko). The effects are sometimes quite extraordinary — its branches twist and twine in the most fascinating way, and sometimes look just like knotted clubs of wood. **Buttonbush** (Cephelanthus occidentalis) is an indigenous shrub with creamy white flowers about the size and shape of a golf ball. It grows well in the damp sites of Eastern Canada. The larger nurseries will probably have it in stock.

If you want to have trees in the damp area of your garden, plant **Eastern hemlock** (Tsuga canadensis), **pin oak** (Quercus palustris), **red oak**

California poppy (Eschscholtzia californica) is an annual which does well in dry soils. It is particularly recommended for sandy slopes. Planted deep, it will flower right through to the frosty weather.

(Quercus borealis) or, if you have plenty of room, **white willow** (Salix alba tristis).

For ponds, and places that are impossible or too costly to drain, you should grow special plants such as **flowering rush** (Butomus umbellatus), **yellow flag** (Iris pseudacorus) and **arrowhead** (Sagittaria latifolia). These plants will only grow in places where there is always plenty of water. Many catalogues list various types of **bulrush** in their aquatic plants section and of course these are plants particularly suitable for wet areas.

Plants For Dry Areas

Among the many problems facing every gardener are the nature of the soil, the varying adaptabilities of different plants, and the inherent disparities between different locations. But one of the greatest difficulties he must overcome is, without a shadow of doubt, the choice of suitable plants.

Those who have a very dry or sandy soil must pay particular attention to the conditions their plants will encounter at the very start — i.e., at the time of planting and during the days immediately following.

ANNUALS AND PERENNIALS

There are certain annual plants which do quite well in very dry soil, and which may even be grown in sand. Among these are **alyssum** (Alyssum), **spider-flower** (Cleome), **ice-plant** (Mesembryanthemum), **California poppy** (Eschscholtzia californica), **purslane** (Calandriania), **cockscomb** (Celosia), **African marigold** (Tagetes) and **tickseed** (Coreopsis). I should also mention that there are certain plants which grow well on dry slopes — areas which are often very difficult to deal with. These are **ice-plant** (Mesembryanthemum) and **purslane** (Calandrinia). Although most of the plants mentioned above last only for one year, they are valued highly for their lovely colours.

There are also a good number of herbaceous perennials which do well in sandy soils.

Most of them have large roots or rhizomes which serve as reservoirs in which they store the moisture they need during dry periods. Among this group, the following are worthy of mention: **day lily** (Hemerocallis), which thrives in the shade; **Oriental poppy** (Papaver orientale), which prefers well-drained sandy soils; **blanketflower** (Gaillardia) and **bearded iris** (Iris species).

Most readers will also be aware that plants with thick, fleshy leaves do well in arid, waterless conditions. Typical examples of this group are **stonecrop** (Sedum), and **houseleek** (Sempervivum). **Yucca,** the traditional plant of the Mexican and Arizona deserts, does very well in dry, sandy areas. The little **Yucca glauca** is reasonably hardy.

If the requirement is to cover areas of dry slope as quickly and as cheaply as possible, many gardeners have had good results from **reynoutria** (Polygonum cuspidatum compactum) and from **common stonecrop** (Sedum acre). Several of the **creeping junipers** are also frequently used — notably the **'Andorra', 'Bar Harbor'** and **'Waukegan'** varieties.

TREES FOR POOR SOILS

Most of the trees that do well in dry or sandy soils are quick growers, and break rather easily. I do not advise them for use on small properties, or along roads, because of their unsuitable characteristics — they are continually dropping twigs, their branches tend to break, and their bare bark is unattractive. However, if you plant them far enough away from the house, they can make quite good shade trees and their faults can be at least partially corrected by careful pruning.

Two such trees worth mentioning are **Chinese elm** (Ulmus pumila), which grows remarquably quickly, and **false acacia** (Robinia pseudoacacia), which also grows very quickly — but is to fragile that the slightest touch of frost is apt to make it lose at least one large branch.

In very poor soils I would advise you to plant **Scotch pine** (Pinus sylvestris), which is probably the best tree for such conditions. It grows quickly — about 35 feet in fifteen years — and has no particular disadvantage.

VARIOUS SHRUBS

There are quite a few good shrubs which do very well in poor soils.

For your basic planting, here are some excellent little flowering shrubs: various species of **quince** (Chaeonameles), in particular the **'Vesuvius';** **dyer's greenwood** (Genista tinctoria), a little shrub with yellow flowers; and **brooms** (Cytisus species). Try **Cytisus praecox,** an extremely beautiful variety, but you must be sure to plant it in a sheltered spot, not too far from the house and with a southern exposure.

Several of the **cotoneasters** grow well in poor, dry soils. These ornamental shrubs are noted for their attractive foliage and decorative little berries.

To ensure success when planting trees and shrubs in dry spots where the soil is poor, I advise you to dig your holes deep enough and wide enough to take the roots without cramping them. Another equally important requirement is that you enrich the soil to be used for filling in the holes. Make a mixture of one part of soil to one part of garden peat and add to this a complete fertilizer such as 12-4-8, one tablespoonful for each square foot of excavation. Water the site plentifully during the actual planting and then lay a carpet of mulch over the surface, and keep it moist until the plants have established themselves properly in their new location.

The Choice of Climbing Plants In A Garden

Climbing plants make a splendid decoration for the outside of the house.

Insufficient use is made of them in Canada, though there are few properties that would not benefit from them. They can be used simply for ornamental purposes, or to hide walls, or they can serve as a screen to camouflage some particularly unpleasant feature.

Much care is needed in choosing the appropriate climbing plant. First, establish your objective, then choose the plant that will best fulfil that objective.

There are three main types of woody climbing plants. First, those which climb by clinging to the walls with little suckers. A popular example of this type is **Boston Ivy** (Parthenocissus tricuspidata). Next, those which climb by putting out tendrils or leaf-like appendages that surround and grip whatever it is the plant is growing against. Popular examples here are **clematis** and its various cultivars. Finally, there are those which climb by entwining themselves completely around their support. An example of this type is **bittersweet** (Celastrus). Once you know which of the three climbing methods is used by your chosen vine, then you can supply the appropriate type of support.

Climbing plants which grip flat surfaces with round suckers, such as **Boston Ivy,** should never be placed against supports that require painting. They need masonry surfaces to climb on — walls of brick or concrete. They also climb well up trees. Sometimes they will produce a concentration of moisture which may contribute to the decay of your walls. This type of climbing plant is ideal for locations where no support is needed from the wall.

American ivy or **Virginia creeper** (Parthenocissus quinquefolia) climbs by gripping with its tendrils. The little shoots twine themselves round cords, wires, sticks and other similar objects of small diameter, and grip them firmly.

Plants which entwine themselves bodily around their support do so by curving round the tip of their main shoot as they grow. They cannot, however, twine themselves around tree-trunks. Some of these plants twist from right to left, others, in the opposite direction.

Let me mention three splendid climbing plants which twist from left to right. The first is **Dutchman's pipe** (Aristolochia durior), which produces very large heart-shaped leaves and little flowers that look like meerschaum pipes. This is a particularly suitable plant if you want to cover a veranda or a patio quickly. The same is true of **bittersweet** (Celastrus scandens), an indigenous plant, which displays showy fruit in autumn. (You should grow a good number of these plants together. This will assist cross-pollinaton and ensure a good growth of fruit.) The third plant in this category is **moonseed** (Menispermum canadensis).

Other climbing plants in this group which will do well in the more temperate regions such as British Columbia or the Niagara Peninsula, are **American wisteria** (Wisteria frutescens), **Chinese wisteria** (Wisteria sinensis) and **five-leaf akebia** (Akebia quinata). **Akebia,** a somewhat rare plant, is a rapid-growing climber with shiny composite leaves that last well into the winter — in fact, it is grown mainly for the effect produced by its foliage. It goes very well on a down-spout from the roof-gutters.

Among climbing plants that twist from right to left, the following are worth mentioning: **Hall's Japanese honeysuckle** (Lonicera japonica 'Halliana'), which is best suited to warmer areas; **Tellman's honeysuckle** (Lonicera Tellmanniana), with its huge orange-yellow flowers; **trumpet honeysuckle** (Lonicera sempervivens), a beautiful plant with trumpet-shaped flowers that range in colour from orange to scarlet; and the **'Dropmore Scarlet Trumpet'** variety (Lonicera brownii 'Dropmore Scarlet Trumpet'), a very showy plant particularly suitable for the Prairie provinces.

Two climbing plants that are a great success in the more temperate regions of British Columbia are **Chinese schisandra** (Schisandra sinensis), with its creamy flowers and thick green foliage, and another **wisteria** (Wisteria floribunda), which has many cultivars of various colours.

There are two kinds of climbing plant specially suited for planting against walls where there is little space for shrubs or trees. The first comprises various cultivars of **climbing euonymus** (Euonymus fortunei), which have a diversity of decorative foliages; the other is **climbing hydrangea** (Hydrangea petiolaris). These two plants cling by their tendrils and are reasonably hardy everywhere except in the Prairie provinces. However, they are perhaps best grown on the West Coast.

Among the climbing plants that use suckers the best known are **Boston ivy** and **Virginia creeper.** The latter is perhaps the less suitable of the two, though the **'Engelman'** variety does very well. These two plants adapt readily to urban conditions and grow rapidly. **Virginia creeper** is covered with large leaves which take on a remarkable colour in the autumn.

Trilliums growing in a garden.

Jackman's clematis (Clematis jackmanii) grips by tendrils which are modified leaf-stalks. It is the hardiest showy **clematis** of all and makes an excellent climbing plant for Eastern Canada. You must prune it early in the spring, before it starts to grow. It flowers on this year's fresh wood, so last year's growth should be pruned back a bit and kept within reasonable limits. There are may delicate **clematis** varieties that are suitable for temperate regions. Some of them flower on this year's wood, others on last year's. When you buy your plants, make sure you obtain the appropriate information so that you know which wood to prune.

Most woody climbing plants will almost certainly grow quickly in a soil to which compost and a complete fertilizer have been added. When you are planting close to the house, dig a deep hole and fill it in with some of this specially-prepared soil. Keep your newly-planted climbers well watered and make sure they are as close to their support as possible.

The Use Of Wild Flowers

Gardeners with insufficient time at their disposal often use wild plants to fill up their flower-garden. These plants do very well once they are properly established, even if you neglect them. All you need do every now and then is uproot any plants that are spreading too fast and have a general sort-out.

The more showy wild flowers should be planted where there is plenty of shade. These shade-lovers also solve the problem of what to plant where you have a northerly exposure. The vivid flowers from the meadows and the roadsides are ideal for sunny areas.

Every time 'wild flowers' are mentioned, thousands of people go and uproot these plants from their natural surroundings and try to replant them at random in ordinary soil. In the long run this is bound to ruin the beauty of our woodland and the vandals would get much better results if they would buy seedlings — or buy the actual seed and sow it.

If an area of woodland is about to be developed, or have a road driven through it, or if you want to take some plants from around your cottage — the following advice will help you establish them in your own garden without destroying wild flowers unnecessarily.

SEPARATE THEM FROM YOUR GARDEN PROPER

Wild flowers should be separated from the rest of the garden by shrubs. Perhaps you could make a winding path leading to their area. The ideal would be a path made of pine needles, three or four inches deep. Indigenous plants such as **bearberry** (Arctostaphylos uva-ursi) or **partridgeberry** (Mitchella repens) make excellent borders.

Most shade-loving plants need an acid soil and plenty of organic matter. The first thing you must do, then, is add plenty of peat-moss and leaf-compost to your soil.

If there is no natural shade available, and you want to grow wild flowers which must have shade, then you must provide it yourself. Plant some small trees, such as **hawthorn, alder** or **birch,** and wait for at least one year to let them get properly established. Larger trees look better but they tend to overwhelm the plants at their feet.

Use the shade of the trees, but avoid the big roots which rather exhaust the soil around them. In a wood, trees grow in deep soil which is enriched with organic matter and plants grow right up close to the trunks. In the average garden humus is rare and plant roots do not penetrate so deeply.

TRILLIUMS AND OTHER PLANTS

Trilliums are some of our more spectacular indigenous plants. They grow well in the ordinary garden, provided they have a modicum of shade. There are several species, some of them very oddly shaped. The best known is the common **trillium,** also known as **trinity flower** or **wood lily** (Trillium grandiflorum). Two other well-known species are **painted trillium** (Trillium undulatum) and **purple trillium** or **stinking Benjamin** (Trillium erectum).

53

Liverwort (Hepatica triloba) is a very interesting plant: it appears to flower underneath the snow, before the woods are even accessible after the winter. The range of colours is very wide, so be sure to pick out really handsome plants.

Be sure, too, to bed them down in plenty of peat-moss and mulch and cover them with leaf-compost or sod to prevent the flowers from shooting up.

Jack-in-the-pulpit (Arisaema triphyllum) and **wild ginger** (Asarum canadense) grow well in the shade and produce flowers in great numbers.

The main purpose of a rock garden is to grow alpine plants and other dwarf species which cannot be grown easily or to advantage in flowerbeds or herbaceous borders. Its layout should therefore be planned to reproduce as closely as possible the normal surroundings of these plants, and to give a natural and pleasing overall appearance.

They will add a touch of rare beauty to your garden. Other indigenous plants that are easy to grow are **Dutchman's breeches** (Dimentra cucullaria), both the single and the double varieties of **bloodroot** (Sanguinaria canadensis), **Canadian columbine** (Aquilegia canadensis) and **wild sweet William** (Phlox divaricata). Once these plants have taken root, there will be many others you will want to add to them.

WILD ORCHIDS

Growing **wild orchids** calls for special care. The easiest to krow are **maiden's slipper** (Cypripedium pubescens) and **royal cypripedium** (Clpripedium reginae). Prepare a special plot for them containing a mixture of peat-moss, leaf-mould and soil from their previous location. They **are** rather difficult to transplant, however, and it would perhaps be better to buy them from a nursery-garden where they have already taken root.

Do not attempt to transplant the lovely **trailing arbutus** (Epigaea repens) or **Cypripedium acaule:** neither of them will survive.

If part of your wild flower garden is fully exposed to the sun, put as many locally-growing plants there as you can. Try some of the hardy plants which grow along the side of the road, such as **yellow oxeye, Chicory, loosestrife** and **hardy asters;** Add some meadow plants too — **crocus** and various **meadow-grasses,** with some **phlox** climbing over stones.

A really damp spot is ideal for some very interesting indigenous plants such as **marsh marigold** (Caltha palustris), **pitcher-plant** (Sarracenia pur-purea), cardinal flower (Lobelia cardinalis) and several wild **orchids** — the **habenarias,** for example, and the **goodyearas.** For these, the soil not only must be marshy, but it must also contain plenty of leaf-mould or peat-moss.

A spread of moist green **fern** makes a nice little nook of freshness and tranquillity which is always very welcome. A trickle of water falling onto a rock surrounded by smaller flat stones will enhance the effect quite delightfully — especially if you have some **walking fern, maidenhair fern** or **Virginia chain-fern** around.

It will take you more than one year to plan your wild garden and bring it into being. It will grow gradually, as you bring back fresh ideas from your trips into the woods. Not merely will such a garden arouse interest in our magnificvent countryside among your visitors, it will make a unique and satisfying hobby for you.

Rock Gardens

LAYOUT

The rock garden or rockery is a diminutive alpine garden. It is well suited to cramped spaces, such as a town garden, or an odd-shaped corner of a property. The alpine garden, on the other hand, is much larger in size and is usually created on a site with natural rock features, such as an abandoned quarry.

You must not think that a rock garden consists of a pile of rocks thrown onto the site at random, with a bit of earth round each of them, and a few flowers growing haphazardly. Nor is it a collection of big lumps of slag set in cement, or round 'cannon-balls' of granite, all nicely polished and arranged in symmetrical rows on a heap of rich black earth.

There are, in fact, several types of rock garden. The three most popular forms are a rockery built up in steps on a flat surface, the 'dry wall' type — basically a wall with flowers growing out of it, and the terraced rockery — which is the most popular form, and the one we shall discuss here.

(In my opinion, flat ground is no place for a rockery, except possibly in public parks or botanical gardens where it may serve to illustrate one aspect of gardening.)

A typical layout for a rockery.

SEVERAL ADVANTAGES

Rock gardens have three main advantages. In the first place, they make it possible for you to have plants which cannot be grown under ordinary conditions. Next, a rockery enables you to transform an eyesore on your property into a beauty-spot. And finally, this type of garden lets you show off plants which would pass unnoticed in an ordinary garden.

BASIC REQUIREMENTS

The first thing to take into account when planning the layout of your rockery is that it must look natural and fit naturally into the environment — otherwise it will clash unpleasantly with its surroundings. A pile of rocks and earth tossed haphazardly onto the ground makes a very disagreeable impression — not only when you look at it, but also when you work on it — even if you have put a splendid collection of plants into it. Fortunately, professional landscape architects are playing an ever-increasing role in the layout of private properties nowadays, and such monstrosities are mercifully becoming rarer and rarer all the time.

The immediate surroundings of your rock garden play an equally important part in its success or failure. Since it is essential that your rockery should give an impression of complete naturalness, its location amidst the surrounding trees and shrubs must help create this impression. The object should be to make the casual visitor believe the rockery has been there from time immemorial as a natural feature of the landscape.

A SUITABLE SPOT

You can build a rockery almost anywhere, but one thing is certain — it will be much easier to build and much easier to keep the plants in it in good condition if you site it in a location that offers certain basic essentials.

The first thing, obviously, is to choose the site of your rockery and decide in detail where its boundaries will run. Then you need a proper plan of the site. Draw this out on paper, but bear in mind that there will inevitably be changes from the original concept as the work progresses. Now you can start assembling your material, and the final step is the actual construction itself.

Incidentally, remember that your rockery has three dimensions and you should do everything you can to avoid symmetry and uniformity to ensure that the rockery fits nicely into its surroundings.

NEED FOR DRAINAGE

Good drainage is essential in a rock garden — and when I say 'good', I do not mean a rough and ready 'more-or-less' type of drainage system — I mean a proper system, well-planned and well installed, which can deal with the excess water from a torrential downpour while the rain is still falling — not some time afterwards.

One method of ensuring adequate drainage is to instal 4-inch diameter weeping tiles under the rockery, with a foot-thick layer of gravel above them extending over the whole area of the rockery.

Although it is called a "rockery", do not forget that first and foremost it is actually a garden and "garden", of course, implies "earth". Most of the alpine and other plants which are suitable for a rock garden in the sun need good drainage coupled with a soil that holds moisture well after the surplus water has drained away. Heavy, clayey soils are no good. Nor are sandy ones.

Most people know that in their natural state alpine plants grow in "schistose" soil — i.e., soil composed of rock debris in various states of decomposition mixed with organic matter. A good soil for your rockery is somehat similar — a mixture of one part coarse sand, one part coarse gravel, one part peat and two parts screened compost.

ROCKS

A judicious choice of rocks is of prime importance, even though the rocks themselves should not be too much in evidence in the finished rockery. Use limestone rocks as much as possible above the surface of the soil — preferably well-weathered ones.

The bottom layer of rocks, which forms the 'foundation' of the rockery, should be set into the soil deeply enough to make them look as natural as possible. To this end, they should of course, be of all shapes and sizes.

Next place you "fill" around these rocks. (This could well be some of the soil from the excavation for the house, if you have had any new construction done.) Fill in as necessary with any earth removed from the rockery site during the laying-out process and then add the "rockery soil" mixture described above.

Most of the rocks should be set into the surrounding soil so that they lean slightly backwards. Thus rainwater hitting the sloping face of these rocks runs down into the soil and is retained for the deeper-growing roots. Leave about a third of each rock exposed.

As work proceeds make sure that the general architectural effect remains asymmetrical and irregular. Your rockery should not come to a point. It should finish off in a series of flat surface or ledges, at different levels.

COST OF CONSTRUCTION

It is almost impossible to give a firm, precise figure for the cost of construction of a rockery. Many factors must be taken into account — e.g., the nature of the site, whether you build the rockery yourself, or use a contractor, the sources of the materials and their distance from the site and of course the size of the rockery itself. A length of ten feet, with a front face rising on a 45° slope to a height of five feet will produce a modest little rockery of manageable proportions. The surface area of the front face will be some 70 square feet, and the volume of the whole about 125 cubic feet — say 150, to allow outward bulges here and there to keep the appearance natural and irregular. For such a rockery you will need 50 cubic feet of gravel to go over your drainage, 50 cubic feet of soil — say one good truckload (unless you already have excavated earth available on your property), some 50 rocks of varying sizes (averaging about 25-30 pounds each), and about 25 cubic feet of the special "rockery mix" I described earlier, as topsoil.

Finally, the plants themselves. You will need 50 to 60 plants of various species for a rockery of the size described above, plus a few small shrubs.

If you feel you are too busy, or not strong enough to undertake the work yourself, employ a reputable contractor. Your local Horticultural Society will give you a list of recommended names to choose from.

APPROPRIATE PLANTS

A rockery is a garden in miniature. As for any garden, you need plants chosen specially for their appearance and their colour — though with rock plants you must know how to grow them properly.

Let me say here that it is difficult, in fact almost impossible, to lay down any hard and fast rules as to where each of the various plants that can be grown in a rockery should be located. It is a question of your own taste more than anything. Obviously certain plants (especially the hardy varieties) need a lot of shade; others, a lot of sun; and others are halfway in between.

You can use plants of any size that are not out of proportion with the size of the rockery itself. I should mention here that certain plants are more easily installed during the actual construction of the rockery. Among them are **moss pink** (Phlox subulata), the tufted **rock cress** (Arabis albida), dwarf shrubs such as **cinquefoil** (Potentilla alba) and **daphne**, and dwarf conifers. These plants are mostly used to decorate little niches between the rocks. The remaining plants are placed later on, once the rockery's properly established.

To obtain the best effect from your plants it is advisable to group them according to how they grow. For example, there are the creeping plants — **gypsweed** or **drug speedwell** (Veronica officinalis), **maiden pink** (Dianthus deltoides), **wall pepper** or **yellow stonecrop** (Sedum acre), **catchfly** or **moss campion** (Silene acaulis) and **wild thyme** (Thymus serpyllum) — which form a close-knit carpet on the ground. Use them to fill up gaps on flat or inclined surfaces, or as a carpeting for your pathways.

You will need some dwarf plants such as **harebell** (Campanula rotundifolia), **alpine columbine** (Aquilegia alpina), **periwinkle phlox** (Phlox adsurgens) and **alpine aster** (Aster alpinus), which grow to a height of about twelve inches. These stiff-stemmed plants add an impression of height and are suitable for largish flat surfaces and for borders.

Tufted plants such as **alpine poppy** (Papaver alpinum), various **pinks** (Dianthus species), **juniper thrift** (Armeria juniperfolia), and various **saxifrages** (Saxifraga species) go particularly well in the higher reaches. Use them on steep slopes and in odd corners.

Drooping plants should be located at the top of steeply-sloping areas for they show themselves to best advantage hanging down the face of a rock. Some examples are **Carpathian bellflower** (Campanula carpatica), **moss pink, evergreen candytuft** (Iberis sempervirens), **alyssum** and **snow-in-summer** (Cerastium tomentosum).

THE INFLUENCE OF JAPANESE METHODS

The master gardeners of Japon have refined the art of gardening to the greatest degree possible. They have turned the simple bunch of flowers into the living symbol of a prayer, into the path towards inner meditation. We in the West are as yet only in the kindergarten stage in this search for purity and harmony through stylization.

A full study of Japanese horticulture could well take a whole lifetime. Let me just bring to your notice here one aspect of their practice which is almost unknown in the West, and which should be known much better. This is the unparallelled skill of these Oriental masters in the layout of rock gardens.

ART AND TECHNIQUE

In some rock gardens in the United States (California in particular) and in Canada (British Columbia in particular), the beneficial influence of Japanese teaching can be readily observed. Layout is deriving more and more inspiration from the abstract art and the delicate, subtle technique of the Japanese. American and Canadian landscapers are increasingly influenced by Japanese methods in their search for continuing progress and true aesthetics. There are imitative examples of Japanese gardens to be seen all along the West Coast of both countries and there are also many adaptations from the Japanese. These altter are, in my opinion, the more likely to survive.

SOURCES OF INSPIRATION The Japanese do not confine themselves to imitating Nature in their layout of rock gardens. What they look for is a source of inspiration, a synthesis of the world itself, which will allow Man to find himself and give free rein to his thoughts. Each rock is chosen with great care. It has its own personality, its own part to play in the general effect of the garden as a coherent whole. Rocks of various sizes and unusual shapes are used to serve as points of departure for the imagination. The size and shape of each individual rock has a profound symbolic meaning, as has the number of rocks and their grouping in the garden as a whole. A standing rock may symbolize a mountain, a protecting deity, or the force of masculinity; while a reclining rock may stand for a bridge, or sleep, or the delicacy of femininity.

The origin of these symbols is lost in time. Their refinement is the result of centuries of meditation by Zen Buddhist monks.

AN INCOMPARABLE GARDEN The most celebrated of all the rock gardens in Japan is without doubt the garden at Ryoanji, in Kyoto. This garden — which is several hundred years old — has influenced, in the highest possible degree, the evolution of landscaping techniques in North America. Yet the garden is simplicity itself. Fifteen rocks, arranged in five groups which resemble islands set in the midst of an apparently boundless ocean — the ocean being formed of sand carefully raked to give the impression of waves, while around the whole are set a path of stones and a wall, which represent the limits of the universe.

Ryoanji is the synthesis, the quintessence of the horticultural art of the Japanese. Thousands of tourists visit it every year. Few remain insensitive to its mystical charm, its profound symbolism, its message of peace.

EXPO '70 In 1970 Japan was the host for the most important world exhibition ever held. The choice of Osaka as the site for this world event was a happy one for plant-lovers — for this town is but a short distance from Kyoto, the horticultural centre of Japan. Foreign visitors — and especially the gardeners among them, both amateur and professional — were delighted to find outstandingly beautiful miniature gardens wherever they turned, just a few paces from their hotel or lodgings. Some of these little gardens consisted merely of a few stems of **bamboo** set upright in moss, or between rocks, skilfully arranged. Larger gardens offered a tasteful display of dwarf **pines**, and clumps of **azaleas** and hardy annuals. Some of the gardens were so beautiful that foreign tourists could scarcely believe that they were made by man. But then the visitor to Japan will find breathtaking countryside almost everywhere he goes — Matsushima Bay, for example, on the north coast of Honshu Island. The bay is studded with countless little islets crowned with centuries-old **black pines.** The effect is so stunning that even after spending the whole day in the bay, one finds it hard to believe that this fantastic view is not a mirage after all.

PRIVATE GARDENS Westerners who are lucky enough to visit gardens on private property will never forget the experience. One of the most famous collections in all Japan of dwarf or "bonsai" trees is to be found in a private garden in a suburb of Osaka. Let me state categorically that Japanese gardens — both those of the rich townsmen, and those lying behind the humble cottages of the peasants — are far more interesting (and indeed more truly representative of the real spirit of Japan) than all the modern hotels of Tokyo, or the noisy, bustling Ginza, or the super-rapid trains. Those who love nature and beauty will say 'Sayonara' with genuine regret when the time comes for them to leave Japan.

BASIC PRINCIPLES The layout of a rock garden in the Japanese style can be sumed up in two words: **Simplicity** and **Sparseness.** Conifers are used wherever possible in order to produce an effect of greenery throughout the year. Elsewhere, only the bare minimum of flowers is seen.

BALANCING SPACE AND MASS Planted areas are widely separated, so that the space between them becomes an element of the overall design no less important than the mass of the planted areas. Trees and bushes may be lopped ruthlessly to reduce their volume.

BALANCING PROPORTIONS The proportions of all the elements that go to make up the garden — rocks, foliage, flowers, trees, bushes — are maintained in strict relationship between one another, so that no matter how tiny the garden it becomes a harmonious whole in which every part is in perfect balance with all the others.

A SOURCE OF INSPIRATION Every garden must be a point of departure; it must inspire noble thoughts; it must raise up the spirit.

Western gardeners — amateurs and professionals alike — should seek inspiration from the worthy principles that underlie the Japanese rock garden. They should adhere to the basic elements displayed therein — rocks, water and foliage all brought together harmoniously in a layout of quiet, simple dignity. Blind imitation of the Japanese rock garden is not what is required. Let it, rather, act as a source of inspiration to you to seek and discover unknown and fascinating aspects of gardening.

A rockery should look as natural as possible. To achieve this, an asymmetrical and irregular architectural effect must be maintained as construction proceeds. The choice of suitable rocks is a major factor which must never be overlooked. The best rocks are well-weathered limestone. The rockery illustrated below is under construction; the first layer of foundation rocks have been set into the soil deeply enough to hold them solidly and give them a pleasing appearance.

CHAPTER 3

GROWING ANNUAL FLOWERS

A VAST CHOICE

It can never be said too often that the quickest, most practical and cheapest way of getting a lovely garden is to grow annual flowers. Of course everyone knows what annuals are — flowers which are sown, come into flower, go through their reproductive cycle and die — all in the same year.

Growing annuals is the ideal way of creating beauty around a dwelling. They are particularly valuable in the case of new houses, where they provide ornamentation for the grounds while the permanent garden is being established. Annuals allow the householder to provide himself with a beautiful flower garden at little cost. In this way, not only is the outward appearance of his house considerably improved but he also has a plentiful supply of flowers for indoor decoration.

PLANTING

There are two ways of starting annuals: grow them from seed, or buy them as plants.

Seeds are the cheaper method. The best time to sow annuals indoors is, generally speaking, some six to eight weeks before the outdoor planting season begins — i.e., about the beginning of March. The seeds are sown in small boxes or in pots. Two factors are essential for success: high quality seeds and a good vegetable compost. In addition to the compost, you could use a sterile medium, such as a mixture of coarse sand and peat-moss or vermiculite or sphagnum moss.

You must remember that young plants need nourishment to make them grow properly. Use a soluble fertilizer for this purpose. When the seedlings appear, you must also keep an eye open for the appearance of a fungal disease known as "damping-off", which will need treatment with a fungicide. Furthermore, remember that light is absolutely essential for the growth of healthy plants. As soon as the seeds have germinated, put their containers into the light. As the daylight is sometimes rather short, you may have to use artificial light — preferably from fluorescent tubes. In this way you can give your plants up to twenty hours of light every day. if necessary.

The other way to have annual flowers in your garden is to buy young plants in the early summer from a professional gardener or a nursery man. This is probably the more satisfactory method for the amateur gardener who is unlikely to have either the time, the space, or the equipment necessary to grow seeds successfully.

A List Of New Varieties

The list of new annual plants is constantly growing. As a result, the choice available to the garden-lover is almost embarrassingly large. For example, growers and nurserymen now include in their catalogues several recently created annuals which up till now were completely unknown to the Canadian public, but which have shown exceptional qualities in the testing-gardens of the trade.

'Madam Butterfly', a new type of snapdragon. It provides excellent cut flowers for floral arrangements.

Nasturtiums: dwarf 'Bijou' mixture (annual)

Dianthus or Chinese pinks: 'Bravo' (annual)

Sedum: 'Autumn Fire', 15" - 18"
(perennial)

Dicentra spectabilis or
bleeding heart, 36" (perennial)

Viburnum opulus sterilis or
European cranberry-bush (perennial)

Lupins: hybrid 'Russell', 36" - 40"
(perennial)

Hydrangea paniculata grandiflora or
peegee hydrangea (perennial)

French lilac: double flowers
(perennial)

Alyssum (annual)

Cosmos (annual)

Kochia (annual)

Morning-glory (annual)

Portulaca (annual)

Sweet pea (annual)

Garden balsam: extra-dwarf mixture, 10'' (annual)

Coleus: hybrid rainbow mixture, 12'' - 24'' (annual)

Phlox: dwarf 'Drummond Beauty', 6'' - 12'' (annual)

Some Giant Swiss Pansies

'Rhinegold'

'Raspberry-pink'

'Alpenglow'

'Ullswater'

'Beaconsfield'

'Fire Beacon'

WONDERFUL PETUNIAS

More than a hundred new **petunias** have been tested over the part few years and most of them have shown themselves to be equal to or better than existing varieties. The most noteworthy of the many-flowered "double" varieties has been the **"Empress"** series, which originated in Japan. Among the large "single" flowers, the following are high on the list: **Blue Charm, Orchid Cloud, Pink Cloud, Rose Cloud, White Frills** and **Zig Zag. Blue Fantasy** has aroused considerable interest: it has large double flowers of two colours — white and violet.

Most of these cultivars stand our climatic conditions well, and produce very colourful flowers all through the summer.

SPLENDID MARIGOLDS

Marigolds are always popular; they are easy to grow and they gleam like gold or bronze. Although their colours are limited to those two shades, they are available in every size imaginable, from tiny little single flowers which look like stars up to giant double flowers almost as large as chry-santhemums. Some of the new ones have been very favourably received. Among those are the following: **Tina,** with single flowers on stems about twelve inches high; **Bolero,** which has dwarf double flowers which are very showy — (bicoloured, gold and reddish mahogany), **Bolero** flowers very early, and reaches a height of about twelve inches; **Redcoat** is another variety with dwarf double flowers — (reddish mahogany and pale orange this time) and which is very well suited for growing in flowerbeds. **French Brocade** is another double type, of French origin. Its predominant colours are orange and reddish mahogany. Finally, there is **Moonshot** which pro-duces very large double flowers more than three inches in diameter, on stems some sixteen inches high.

PANSIES AND FLOSSFLOWERS

There are two new **pansies** that I really must mention: **Sunny Boy,** which has sulphur-yellow flowers with a splash of scarlet in the centre, and **Viola Lavender Gem,** which has show excellent results under test conditions over the past two years.

As most gardeners know, **flossflowers** (Ageratum species) are very useful plants for borders. A new and very handsome cultivar is **North Star,** which grows to a height of nine inches. It flowers copiously, with colours varying from bluish-purple to deep violet (it's the darkest of all the **floss flowers,** incidentally). It goes very well in flowerbeds.

65

COLEUSES AND FIBROUS BEGONIAS

There is nothing better than a **coleus** for planting in semi-shaded locations. These plants are well-known for their rainbow-coloured foliage.

At the Plant Research Institute, a dozen or more cultivars have been produced which grow well in full sunlight; and they have even had some remarkable results in sandy soil. **Jade Parade, Red Velvet, Salmon Lace, Sunset Glory** and **Titian Rose** keep the range and velvety sheen of their colours all through the summer, despite the rain and the hot weather.

For shady corners, let me suggest a few of the new fibrous begonia cultivars. **Lucerne, Lugano** and **Zurich** are of Swiss origin, while another, **Pink Charm,** comes from Japan. They flower abundantly all through the summer, and require a lightly-shaded location.

CUT FLOWERS

Some of the most remarkable progress made in the production of cultivars of annual flowers has been among the **snapdragon** group, where two new and very different types have been created — the **Madam Butterfly** and the **Floral Cluster** series.

The **Madam Butterfly** series has open-faced double flowers that look rather like **azaleas.** They come in a variety of colours, and do very well as cut flowers in floral arrangements. The **'Floral Cluster'** group consist of short, long-lasting plants. They flower copiously, in several distinct colours that do not vary appreciably. This abundance and uniformity make them excellent flowers both for flowerbeds and for decoration.

These newly-created annual plants are sure to be satisfactory, especially if you are looking for variety in your garden without running too many risks.

A Purchasing Guide For Annual Plants

At the beginning of summer, garden-lovers stock up with annual plants to decorate their flowerbeds, borders, flowerboxes and rockeries. However, with the vast number of plants available nowadays, some people don't really know what to choose, and just buy boxes of plants haphazardly.

Here, then, is a list which will help you choose the most suitable plants for your purpose — whether it be borders and flowerbeds, flowerboxes, rockeries, treillis or walls; and whether the areas you are dealing with are semi-shaded or dry and sunny.

BORDERS AND FLOWERBEDS

(Throughout this list, the height of each plant and the colour of its flowers are given in brackets).

Ageratum (various colours, 4 - 6")
Aster (carpet 8", medium 24", giant 30")
Sweet alyssum or shepherd's purse (white, blue, 6")
Impatiens (red, orange, pink, white, 12 - 24")
Lobelia (blue, mauve, white, 6 - 24")
Artemesia (3 - 6")

Nemesia (orange, red and similar shades, 8 - 15")
Petunia (singles, doubles, various colours — white, pink, red, etc. 12")
Portulaca (various colours)
Verbena (white, pink, red, rose, etc. 12 - 18")
Hybrid pansy (yellow, blue, purple, white, 6 - 8")
Zinnia (all colours except blue, 6" to 4')

FLOWERBOXES

Snapdragons (intermediate height, 12 - 24")
Ageratum (various colours, 4 - 6")
Dusty Miller (12")
Dusty Miller (ornamental foliage,, 18")
Climbing cobaea
Lobelia (showy varieties, 6 - 12")
Sweet alyssum (3 - 6")
Snapdragon or antirrhinum (various colours, 6 - 15")
Verbena (red, blue, mixed colours, 7 - 8")
Delphinium or larkspur (white, pink, red, purple, blue, etc. 8" to 4')

Sweet scabiosa (lavender, blue, etc. 2 - 3')
Rose mallow (5 - 6")
African marigold (dwarf 6", giant 24")
Dahlia (dwarf types, 2 - 3')
Dimorphotheca or winter Cape marigold (flowers like marigolds, lovely cream, yellow, lemon and orange tints, 12 - 18")
California poppy — a hardy plant grown as an annual in Canada (cream, pink, pale yellow and orange)
Annual phlox (white, pink, crimson, etc., 6 - 8")
Marigold or **tagetes** (short 6", tall 3'6", bronze and mahogany)
Nasturtium (yellow, orange, reddish-brown, dwarf and tall varieties)
Petunia (singles, doubles, fringed, various colours and shades)
Mignonette or **reseda ordorata** (greeny-brown, 12 - 24")
Nasturtium (yellow, orange, 12 - 24")
Verbena (white, pink, red, etc., 12-18")
Hybrid pansy (yellow, blue, purple and white, 6 - 8")
Zinnia, "Pompon" or **"Lilliput"** varieties, 18 - 24")
Heliotrope (various colours, 15 - 18")
Lantana (various colours, 12 - 15")
Dwarf pink (**'Bravo'** variety, scarlet, red, 8")
Double camellia-flowered tuberous begonia (Pendula: 8 colours, white, pink, red, etc.)

ROCKERIES

Hybrid snapdragons for rockeries various colours, 3 - 6")

Sweet alyssum (tiny flowers, 12")

Brachycome or Swan River daisy (blue, mauve or white daisy-like flowers, 12")

Dimorphotheca or rain Cape marigold (orange-gold, 8 - 10")

California poppy (bright orange, pink, etc. 9 - 12")

Toadflax or linaria bipartia (various colours, 4 - 6")

Gilia (dwarf varieties, blue, carmine, 6")

Inopsidium or Portugal diamond flower (violet, 2 - 3")

Phacelia (blue, 8 - 12")

Annual phlox, low-growing dwarf varieties, various colours, 6 - 8")

Nierembergia or blue cupflower blue, bell-shaped flowers, 6 - 8")

Portulaca (various colours)

Trailing sanvitalia (double-flowered type, 6 - 8")

Schizanthus or butterfly flower (various colours, 12 - 15")

Statice (yellow, blue, white, lavender, 12 - 24")

Thunbergia (yellow, orange, cream: climbing plants)

Few plants have a longer flowering season than petunias. No wonder they're among the most popular of all the annuals! For several years, the new hybrids have been appearing everywhere — particularly the "grandiflora" type, which is extremely suitable for flowerbeds and borders.

Verbena (various colours, dwarf varieties, 8 - 10")
Virginia stock (various colours, varieties, 12")
Bellflower (various colours, 12 - 18")
Blue stonecrop (2 - 3")

CLIMBING PLANTS

Adlumia or **mountain fringe** (white, purplish-blue)
Climbing cardinal (scarlet flowers)
Climbind cobaea
Gourd (white or yellow flowers)
Dolichos or **hyacinth-bean** (rosy-purple flowers)
Convolvulus or morning glory (various colours)
Thunbergia (yellow, cream, orange).
Annual sweet pea
Canary nasturtium (pale yellow flowers)
Hops (very decorative foliage)

SEMI-SHADY LOCATIONS

Bugloss or anchusa
Royal centaurea
Balsam
Clarkia
Delphinium or **larkspur**

Godetia
Linaria
Mignonette or **reseda odorata**
Myosotis
Nasturtium
Platycodon or **balloonflower**
Tuberous begonia

DRY, SUNNY LOCATIONS

California poppy
Coreopsis
African marigold
Winter Cape marigold
Centaurea
Annual pink
Godetia amoena or **farewell-to-spring**
Godetia grandiflora or **satinflower** (1 - 2')
Petunia
Portulaca
Sage
Sunflower

VERY DRY LOCATIONS

Petunia
Portulaca
Wallflower or **stock**
Dusty Miller

Sowing Hardy Annuals

It is not necessary to be a professional gardener or even an experienced amateur to grow hardy annuals from seeds. Even a beginner can obtain remarkable results if he takes a few essential precautions. There is nothing mysterious or particularly complicated about growing plants from seeds. Modern methods are very simple and they considerably reduce the risk of failure.

HIGH QUALITY SEED

The first condition for success is to buy good seed from a reliable dealer. Next, instead of the rich soil that was formerly used for indoor sowing, use one of the more-or-less sterile compost mixture which are free from all seeds of weeds (there are several mixtures available that give very good results). For example, try a mixture of equal parts of sand and peat-moss. The sand should be coarse and clean. The most important thing of all is to use a light mixture, porous, well-drained and without too much fertilizer in it. Mixtures without earth in them are equally satisfactory — try equal parts of peat-moss and vermiculite or ground-up sphagnum moss. However, if you use an earthless mixture you must add some soluble fertilizer every week after the seeds have sprouted.

DAMPING-OFF

The use of earthless mixtures has another advantage, in most cases you do not need to treat the seeds with a disinfectant such as "Ferbam", "Captan", or "Aramite", to guard against the fungal disease known as "damping-off". Unless you water your seeds too much and too frequently, you will probably have no need to worry about damping-off. This is the most common of all seed diseases. The pythium fungus attacks the seeds before they sprout and then another fungus, rhizoctonia, attacks the seedlings and they collapse, wither and die. Damping-off can be prevented by the use of a quick-draining seedbed and by surface-sowing the seeds to let the air circulate freely round them. Put your seeds out in the sunlight, too. A satisfactory method of watering them is also essential. The container must be sterile, whether it be a seed-box or a pot. A wise precaution is to saturate the seed-bed with a solution of "Pano-Drench". Should damping-off appear at a later stage, saturate the seed-bed again with "Pano-Drench", used in accordance with the manufacturer's instructions.

HOW TO SOW

Here is a very easy method: fill a box or tray to within three quarters of an inch from the top with a mixture of two parts garden loam, one part peat-moss, and one part sand. Add half an inch of vermiculite and level it off without compressing it. Use a piece of wood half an inch in diameter to mark out rows in the dampened vermiculite, an eighth to a quarter of an inch deep, keeping the rows two inches apart. Then drop your seeds into these shallow trenches and cover them with a layer of dry vermiculite.

The depth of the rows depends on the size of your seed — as a general rule the depth should be three times the diameter of the seed. If your seeds are very small, I would advise you to sift some peat-moss into the

Some of the equipment needed for indoor sowing: a seed-box, smoothing-board, earthenware pot, tamper, sifter and seeding labels.

rows and dampen it, then sow your seed directly onto this peat-moss and do not add any top-covering. When you have finished sowing put a piece of glass or transparent plastic over the box to keep the moisture in. Later on, as germination takes place, raise this covering gradually, to keep the box well aired. Water only when necessary, and use a mist-spray.

Instead of wooden boxes, you can use earthenware pots. In this event, fill the pot half-full with a mixture of sterilized garden soil and peat-moss, then top it up with a mixture of sand and peat-moss or sphagnum moss. When the pot is full, tamp down the contents a little to leave some space for watering, and to stop the seeds being washed from one pot to another when you water.

With earthenware pots, I would advise you to sow your seeds straight on top of the seed-bed.

I especially recommend pots made out of peat. You need not remove them before transplantation, either into the ground or into a larger pot. Plants grow better and faster in these peat pots, the peat retains moisture, and the nutritive elements in the walls of the pot stimulate growth. When the roots of the plant break through the walls, you can bury the whole pot without disturbing the plant, thus saving it the physical shock of transplantation. The pot itself disintegrates rapidly in the soil and the roots are therefore able to get well established.

DATES FOR SOWING

For most annuals, the best time for sowing is about six to eight weeks before outdoor planting starts. In general, annuals and hardy plants regarded as annuals (**petunia** and **snapdragon,** for example) may be divided into four groups, according to the length of time between sowing and flowering: —

a) Plants that need **60-70** days. Sow these in a cold frame around May 1, or sow them outdoors between May 10 and 15.

b) Plants that need **80 - 90** days. Sow these indoors, or in hotbeds, between April 15 and 20.

c) Plants that need **90 - 100** days. Sow these indoors, or in hotbeds, about April 1; or in a greenhouse about March 20.

d) Plants that need **110** days or more. Sow these only in a greenhouse, between February 20 and March 1.

Plants sown on the above-indicated dates will come into flower towards mid-July. (These rates are applicable to the Montreal area. For other regions of Canada, you would be advised to consult your local nurseryman).

Certainly, sowing straight into the ground takes less trouble, however, it does entail more risk of something happening to the seeds. In consequence, most annuals are sown indoors first and as general rule the amateur gardener would be best advised to buy plants in Groupe (c) and (d) above from a nurseryman, rather than try to grow them himself from seeds.

THE IMPORTANCE OF LIGHT

Adequate lighting is of prime importance if you are trying to grow good quality plants from seeds. Once the seed has germinated, remove the glass or plastic cover from the seed-box and put the seeds in the light. Place the box near a window that gets a lot of sun. If the natural light is insufficient or too diffused, your seedlings will turn out long and feeble. Certain types of plant need between ten and twelve hours hours of light every day, while others may require as much as twenty. The ideal solution is artificial lighting, with a bank of fluorescent tubes set about twelve inches above the plants.

TEMPERATURE

In addition to light, temperature can be an important factor in achieving success or failure. The average temperature inside most Canadian houses is usually too high for most seeds. In general, flower seeds germinate at about 65° - 70°F. A higher temperature can be tolerated if the humidity is high enough. At cooler temperatures, such as 60°F or below, germination takes place slowly and "damping-off" becomes a danger. When well-formed leaves become visible, the boxes can be placed in a somewhat cooler temperature from 50° to 60°F at night, 70° - 75°F during the day. They must be in a well-ventilated and well-lit location, free from draughts.

WATERING AND FERTILIZING

Watering must be done very carefully once the seeds have been sown in the seed-boxes or pots. The containers should be well saturated with water before sowing takes place, by placing them in a water-bath deep enough to submerge them completely so that water flows into them over the top. Keep the containers moist all the time by covering them with a sheet of glass or polythene — but make sure this cover doesn't touch the seeds themselves. This initial watering should be sufficient until the seeds germinate. If it isn't, use a mist-spray — (although irrigation from beneath is a more suitable method for fine seel, a mist-spray is simpler and quicker). Once the plants start putting down roots, they must be fertilized. The best method is to use a soluble fertilizer in accordance with the manufacturer's instruction. Light, frequent waterings with a solution of fertilizer are preferable to copious drenchings.

TRANSPLANTING

As soon as the seedlings show two proper leaves they must be re-planted. To avoid damaging the tiny plantlets, dig deep underneath them and lift several of them up together, then replant them individually. Handle them as little as possible, and don't squeeze them too hard. Replant them in the same sort of mixture you used originally as their seed-bed, but now it should be enriched by an application of a urea-based fertilizer. Replant the seedlings in small wooden boxes, at least two inches in length, breadth, and height, or use pots made from peat.

Although your seedlings must be replanted more deeply than they ware before, make sure you don't put them in too deep. Water the seed-boxes or the pots well after the transplanting. Put them in the shade for several days, then move them to a sunny and well-ventilated spot.

Finally, transplant them into the earth as soon as the temperature permits — about May 24 in the Montreal region, though other areas may differ — ask your local expert about this. If you have a cold frame, when the warmer weather comes you can strengthen your plants by putting them out into that. On warm days let more and more air into the frame. After mid-May, close the frame only on cold nights. Plants exposed gradually to the outer air are ready to be replanted in the garden around the end of May or beginning of June. It should be noted, though, that plants transplanted straight from a greenhouse are delicate and may wilt.

Transplanting should be done on a dull day, when the ground is reasonably moist. If the soil is too dry, water it. For the next few days protect the plants from the direct rays of the sun by means of paper hoods.

Finally, the distance between the plants after replanting depends on the species. For example, **sweet alyssum** plants need to be six inches away from each other, while **giant zinnias** require three times that distance.

Explanation Of
Hybrids F 1 and F 2

The symbols F 1 and F 2, relating to modern annual plants, mean very little to most amateur gardeners.

The following explanation may help you to understand the significance of these terms as well as something about the genetic strains of the annual plants to which they refer.

Formerly, it was quite common for the major seed-producing firms to spend as many as fifteen years in constantly selecting and reselecting annual strains capable of reproducing themselves faithfully by their seeds. The end-result was usually a strain that was somewhat enfeebled, but it could be placed on the market with the knowledge that for many years its descendants would invariably produce plants that were alike in type and colour.

CONTROLLED CROSS-BREEDING

Fairly recently, a new method has been introduced which produces strains that give uniform growth, appearance and flower colour from a given batch of seeds. In this method, two linked strains are selected as "parents", and they are cross-bred under strictly controlled conditions that rule out any possibility of accidental cross-breedings or self-fertilization. The seeds resulting from this original cross-breeding are known genetically as the F 1 generation — (F for 'filial'). Growers use the symbol F 1 to describe the successful varieties and strains produced by the first cross-breeding of the selected "parents". If these F 1 plants are allowed to self-pollinate, the F 2 generation is produced, and in a few rare cases this also can produce strains of superior quality. Sometimes further auto-pollination will even produce an F 3 generation, with the same facility of reproducing itself exactly by its seeds.

CHOICE SEEDS

As I implied above, seedings from the F 1 hybrids rarely produce the original characteristics of the "parents". To guarantee this, one must always go back to the original cross-breeding. Naturally this calls for a great deal of care and financial outlay — thus, guaranteed F 1 seeds are considerably more expensive than seeds produced by conventional methods. But these hybrid seeds are well worth the extra cost, because of the enhanced vigour of the plants, the copious flowering and the quantity and quality of the flowers and vegetables to be expected.

Petunias are an excellent example of this hybridization technique applied to decorative flowers, while **hybrid corn** is the classic example in the field of vegetables.

Double petunias — a perfect example of successful technique in the production of F 1 hybrids.

DOUBLE PETUNIAS

Petunias were the first F 1 hybrids to be produced for their flowers. Well before World War II, Canada was buying petunia seed from Japan that gave only double flowers. At that time there was no one in the Western world capable of isolating the necessary "parents" to produce F 1 doubles. It wasn't until after the War that Mr. F. Simonet of Edmonton, Alberta, succeeded in selecting parental strains which produced only double flowers when they were cross-bred. His work culminated in the production of all-Canadian strains of **double petunias.** Today, there are plenty of other "double" strains in the U.S. and extremely beautiful ones continue to come from Japan. All these carry the F 1 designation. Not only do all their seeds faithfully reproduce the "double" characteristic, but they all grow in exactly the same way and produce flowers of exactly the same colours or colour combinations.

I must add here that the Plant Research Institute at Ottawa has recently produced some new double varieties of the two principal classes of **petunia,** the **'Grandifloras'** and the **'Multifloras'.** Some of the better F 1

Grandifloras are **Allegro, Rhapsody, Sonata**, and the most recent creations **Melody, Princess** and **Blue Ripple**. Among the F 1 **Multifloras**, which are much more closely-related in origin, **Cardinal Riches, Cherry Tart** and **Honey Bunch** are worth mentioning. These have smaller flowers and are more compactly shaped.

SINGLE PETUNIAS

After successfully producing some splendid **double petunias**, the breeders turned their attention to the single types. There were already many inbred strains that had been featured in nursery catalogues for some time, such as **Fire Chief, Celestial Rose, Rose Morn** and **Rose of Heaven.** But they were slowly becoming less and less satisfactory, and there were few of them which could be guaranteed to produce uniform growth and colouring. **Comanche** was the first improved single-flowered hybrid produced in the two classes **Multiflora** and **Grandiflora.** The F 1 varieties of the **Grandiflora petunias** have large flowers, and their petals are very wavy-edged or fringed. Those in the **Multiflora** class have small flowers, their petals have a normal edge, and they grow in profusion on small and very compact plants.

The plants of both categories are extremely suitable for use in flower-beds which require absolute uniformity of colours.

OTHER ANNUALS

Nowadays there are F 1 hybrids among many other annual plants. Among **snapdragons** the famous **Rocket** strain was the first of many splendid F 1 creations — two outstanding examples of which are **Topper,** which is available in five distinct colours; and **Floral Carpet,** a dwarf strain also available in many different shades. Its low-growing plants very seldom exceed eight inches in height. Two other unusual F 1 **snapdragon** hybrids are **Bright Butterfly,** which has open flowers rather than the usual tubular coiled spring effect, and **Starsnap**, which has bell-shaped flowers.

Other annual plants with F 1 hybrids include the **Majestic pansy,** with large bright flowers; the **Melody fibrous begonia,** which forms a small, low-growing mass plentifully interspersed with gaudy flowers of pink and white; and the **First Lady African marigold,** a compact variety which flowers in profusion.

If you want seeds that can be guaranteed to give flowering annuals with uniform characteristics, you should try some of these carefully selected F 1 hybrids. They all have the qualities you are looking for, and in addition they have the splendid vigour of the hybrid. But let me warn you once again, don't hope for fine plants from the seeds produced by these F 1 hybrids; the F 2 generation will probably give you many sad disappointments.

Growing Pansies
From Seeds

A little packet of pansy seeds sown at the end of August will give you a lovely full flowerbed the following spring. Nothing improves the appearance of the garden at the beginning of the season as much as a show of nice healthy pansies. With some tulips and some perennials they will help make everything look much better — rockeries, borders and flowerbeds. Furthermore, pansies you grow from seed will be hardier than those you buy as plants.

A packet of pansies may seem expensive at first. Compared with the price of **zinnias** or **pinks**, it may even seem excessive, since most packets contain between 200 and 1,500 seeds, according to origin, strain or variety. But however many there are, you will get an impressive number of plants. For if you sow your seeds with a minimum of care your germination rate will be high.

This compares much more favourably with the six or eight plants of unknown quality that will cost you the same amount of money when you buy them in the spring.

AVAILABLE SPACE

The first factor you must consider when you decide to buy pansy seeds is the space available for your plants, right through from the seed-box stage (or cold frames, if you plan to use them) up to the area you will use to pot your young plants out in before you finally transplant them into the garden.

Some of you will decide that just the one packet of good seeds will do nicely. All you have to settle then is what strain or mixture you prefer.

If you have plenty of space, and want to try experimenting with the different types and varieties of pansies, you might just discover that you have found yourself a specialist hobby — and who knows? — perhaps even a source of income!

SOWING TIME

In Eastern Canada, the end of July and the month of August are the best times to sow pansy seeds in boxes or other containers. At that time, the nights are fresh and the days are still warm. (Ask a local expert for the best times in your own region.)

The actual sowing procedure is the same as that used for growing any other annual plant from seed. The seed-bed must be well-prepared, and rich in organic matter such as humus, rotted manure or compost. It is

Pansies are particularly handsome in a border and they lend a note of gaiety to your flowerbeds early in the spring.

essential to have some material with a capacity to retain moisture in the seed-bed. The seeds may be sown in rows, or broadcast, and covered with a thin layer of the "sowing soil" I described earlier on. Watering must be done very carefully. It is better to use a very fine spray in order not to wash the seeds out of the soil. Filter out some of the sunlight with a cloth or paper cover over the seed-boxes, or put them in a shady spot until germination has begun.

If you have sown your seeds carefully and taken all the necessary precautions, you will have healthy young plants by late summer, which you can then replant seven or eight inches away from each other. Replanting should be done as soon as a few leaves have made their appearance, or when the plants are obviously too crowded.

To those of you who would rather wait until the following summer to grow pansies from seeds, but would still like to have nice healthy plants early in the spring — the only advice I can give is to visit nursery gardens or professional gardeners. You can then buy healthy plants at the beginning of autumn and put them down into their gardens straight away.

PROTECTION IN WINTER

In the fairly rigorous climate of Canada, pansies need protection in winter. For young plants a cold frame is normally used. However, if you have too many plants to fit them all into a cold frame, cover them with a mulch of hay or straw, or something similar.

As soon as the ground has thawed in spring and you can start work on your flowerbeds, transplant your pansies to where you want them — where they best contribute to the appearance of your flowerbed. Faded flowers must be removed, otherwise the plants will go to seed and won't give any flowers. This simple precaution will prolong their flowering well into summer.

HARDY VARIETIES

Here is a partial list of the most popular varieties of pansies, and those best suited to Eastern Canada. (For other regional choices, consult a local expert.)

Viola tricolor: This pansy flowers very copiously and is specially suitable for growing in baskets, clumps or borders.

Pacific Hybrid: This is a new American strain of the 'Giant Swiss' type, remarkable for the size and texture of its flowers.

Steele's Jumbo Mastodon: Very large flowers of superb hues.

Felix. A large pansy with a central fringe like a moustache. There are several combinations of colours.

Steele's Butterfly Hybrid: A huge fringed pansy.

F 1 Majestic Hybrid: The flowers measure up to four inches across, and are six or seven inches high.

Limpid Crystal - **'Giant Swiss'** type. Giant pansies characterized by their early flowers, which are not 'mottled' as other pansies are.

Giant Swiss - **'Alpenglow'**, **'Rhinegold'**, whites, etc. Very large flowers, of exquisite beauty.

Jumbo (or **Mastodon**): Giant flowers, that appear earlier than the **'Giant Swiss'** types. The flowers display several new pastel tints. Flowers continuously. Suitable for forcing or for cutting.

Giant maple-leaved pansy (crossbred): Super-giant flowers, tending to blue and yellow hues. Vigorous, close-knit plants.

Hasty Crystal (crossbred): A new selection with unique colours, without the usual markings. The plants are dwarf, well-knit, uniform and noticeably round. Flowering commences early and continues until the end of summer. Mixed colours — red, scarlet, purple, orange, lilac, yellow-gold, blue, violet and white.

Mammoth Exhibition Giant: A complete assortment of all the giant pansy colours.

Renewed Popularity
Of The Geranium

Fashion influences everything — clothes, houses, furniture, food, leisure — and even plants. So it is hardly surprising that fashions in flowers go in periodic cycles, with each new change aimed at improving the decorative appearance of the garden.

In the early Fifties the **geranium** was the mainstay of the massed beds of the public parks, and could be found in most flowerbeds and flowerboxes. A few years later, as a result of the constant rise in the cost of labour and of protecting plants during the winter, the geranium began slowly disappearing from our parks and private gardens.

Today, this plant is coming back into fashion — chiefly due to the appearance of new types, with many different colours. Furthermore, the current vogue for patios, and for growing ornamental plants in containers, has considerably increased the number of locations where the geranium may suitably be grown. In addition, horticultural specialists have been making great advances in the production of healthy cuttings, which have largely solved the problems of plant diseases and the annoyance of having to take plants indoors for the winter. Thus, the geranium is once again resuming its rightful place in public parks and private gardens.

Geraniums are one of the most popular of all flowerbed species, thanks to the introduction of new varieties. These plants lend themselves to many uses in the decoration of public places, gardens and patios.

A VERY DECORATIVE PLANT

All those unacquainted with the modern shapes and colours of geraniums are strongly advised to try them out in their flowerbeds and borders during the summer. They rank among the most decorative of all plants, since they flower throughout the whole season.

The new geraniums may be obtained from most horticultural centres, nurserymen or professional gardeners.

People of good taste will like the different varieties in the **'Carefree'** group of hybrids, with flower tints ranging from crimson to white, with shades of salmon and pink between. There are also so-called "zonal" varieties, which include a superb assortment of pink and red flowers. Another splendid group of hybrids is **'First Lady'**, in which the most noteworthy varieties are unquestionably **Mamie,** with its superb rose-red flowers; and **Jacqueline,** which has bright red flowers. The **'Irene'** group must not be overlooked either: this has fifteen or so varieties, all extremely beautiful.

You must not think that the wide availability of choices presents a problem when it comes to buying your geranium plants. On the contrary, it's usually quite easy to make a choice at the horticultural centre or the nursery, for most of their cuttings carry at least one flower, which gives you a good idea of what each plant looks like.

AN UNDEMANDING PLANT

The geranium is one of the least demanding of all plants. If you are growing the old varieties, bear in mind that they seem to prefer a location protected against the midday sun, or somewhere that offers partial shade almost all through the day.

While it is quite true that plants of the old varieties flower well in full sunlight, the opposite is true of their foliage, which turns yellow and loses its fresh appearance. In actual fact the flowers themselves will not attain their full size if placed in direct sunlight.

The new varieties have been specifically selected for growing in full sunlight. However, they need good rich soil which is well-drained. Thus, if you have a clayey soil, you have to improve the texture of the soil, and the drainage, by working in some garden peat or perlite in order to get plenty of flowers and a good deep colour to the foliage of these plants.

The geranium can be grown alone, or with other kinds of plant, in flowerbeds or borders. Grown by itself in large masses, it produces an arresting effect, and the addition of some annual flowers will enhance its bright colours. For example, a flowerbed of pink-flowered geraniums set off by a border of pale blue **ageratum** makes a very pleasing combination. A basket of red geraniums bordered with deep blue **lobelia** is equally attractive.

FOR THE PATIO

A patio is not really complete without some showy geraniums — especially in tubs or decorative containers, or in geometric masses at the level of the patio itself. All the same, you should not have too many geraniums in the borders of your patio. You would do better to plant them against a background of grey or green — they show up better that way. One excellent method of providing them with this background is to plant rapid-growing leafy annuals behind them, such as **castor-bean** or **goosefoot**.

Geraniums need very little looking after. You must water them frequently all through the summer and remove any withered flowers. If they grow too high or too profuse, it is advisable to cut them back and let them branch out anew down at the base.

SUCCESSFUL WINTERING

Some people will doubtless wish to winter their geranium plants with a view to growing them again the following year. I would suggest that they take cuttings of fresh shoots in September, before the frost, and plant them in sand. To keep them growing through the winter, you must expose them to the light at a window, and divide them in March ready to be planted in the garden in the coming summer.

The successful wintering of geraniums calls for certain precautions to prevent them from becoming sickly. The plants must be carefully watched for signs of diseases such as mildew or rot. If these appear, the fungicide "Captan" should be applied. Success depends on foresight, patience and continual observation, but even if the outcome is failure, it is some consolation to know that next May, for a modest outlay, one can buy fine, vigorous replacements at the nurseries or the horticultural centres.

Some Biennials
To Sow In June

Although, strictly speaking, this chapter is devoted to annual plants, it may not be out of place to say a few words about biennials. The terms "biennial plants" or "biennial growth" are used to describe plants which to a greater or a lesser degree require exposure to the winter cold to enable them to flower later on. This special effect which gives the plant its ability to flower is known as "vernalization". In consequence, these biennials should be planted in the autumn — or even earlier in the summer, and it is not until the following year that they come into flower.

Further, their growth should be watched, to ensure that they don't produce flowers in the autumn or an abundance of delicate leaves which would be unable to withstand the rigours ot winter.

BIENNIALS AND PERENNIALS

Biennials grow vigorously during their first year, then they flower in their second year, after which they die. Certain herbaceous perennials such as **pansies** are treated as biennials because they flower the year after they have been sown. Although they do not die after flowering, these plants almost invariably present such a wretched appearance the following year that they have to be rooted out.

METHOD OF SOWING

The best way to sow biennials is to sow the seeds in the shade, in little rows about six inches apart. A soon as the seedlings appear, let them have progressively more light. To achieve this, gradually remove the straw matting you are using to protect them from the rays of the sun. Begin by doing this for a short while at the beginning and end of each day, then increase the periods until the young plants are shaded only during the sunniest hours of the day. After a few days of this, you can remove the matting completely.

As soon as the plants are large enough to be handled easily, transplant them into a cold frame or a seed-bed.

Although most of the biennial plants are hardy and can be grown entirely outside, you should understand that certain of them need the protection of a cold frame in winter, while others can make do with a thin covering of straw.

POPULAR PLANTS

Given that each species of biennial demands its own special type of care, here is a partial list of the most popular ones:

Sweet William (Dianthus barbatus), most of the better varieties of which are biennials. Sow them in good loam in June or July and transplant them in August or September. The best way to sow them is to put the seeds in rows twelve inches apart and to leave nine inches between the rows when you replant.

During the past few years a fair amount of work has been done on different varieties of **sweet William,** notably at the Plant Research Institute, where experimentation goes on continuously. The following varieties grown there are specially noteworthy — 'Pheasant Eye', which produces brilliant scarlet flowers, emphasized by a clearly-marked demarcation line of pure white; 'Scarlet Beauty', which produces short, compact plants, covered with flowers all of the same reddish-scarlet hue; 'Harlequin', a very vigorous plant with flowers that are white and two tones of pink; and 'Indian Carpet', a strain not quite so tall, (no higher than six inches), and which is compact and very handsome and produces flowers that vary from white through pink to deep red.

Mullein (the garden variety, not the weed). This is an extremely attractive biennial for semi-shaded locations. The plant grows between eighteen inches and three feet high, and bears white, lavender or purple flowers. Sow the seeds in a seed-bed, and leave a foot between the seedlings on transplanting.

Digitalis This family of biennials attains a height of three to five feet. They are magnificent plants, with tall spikes trimmed with hanging bells. The **Sherley** and the **gloxinaeflora** strains are quite superb. They do very well in shady and semi-shady locations, where they reseed themselves very easily.

You can begin growing them by sowing the seeds in June, twelve inches apart, in seed-boxes or seed-beds. Keep them in a semi-shady location. In the autumn, cover them with branches to protect them against intermittent frosts and thaws.

Canterbury Bells (Campanula medium). This is a very handsome and decorative biennial. The most popular in the 'cup-and-saucer' type which grows about two and a half feet tall. It should be noted that none of the **campanulas** can really withstand the rigours of an Eastern Canadian winter properly, and need some form of protection during the cold season. If covered with a thin mulch, however, they will last until spring easily enough. For your own region, consult a local nurseryman.

Hollyhock. Although some varieties flower during the first year, these are really biennial plants. They reseed themselves easily, but it is preferable to buy new seed if you wish to preserve your choesn strain. Space your seeds a foot away from each other in a seed-bed.

More than luck is needed to produce fine peony plants. Certain precautions are essential, and must be carried out if you are to obtain healthy plants with a splendid crop of flowers.

CHAPTER 4

HERBACEOUS PERENNIALS

THEIR MANY ADVANTAGES

Among the group of herbaceous perennials are the plants with roots which live from one year to the next, and those in which the leafy stem dies each autmun but grows again the following spring. Also included in this group are plants like **pinks** (Dianthus species) and **moss pink** (Phlox subulata), which have persistent leaves that do not die in winter. Plants like **candy tuft** (Iberis) and **alyssum** (Alyssum) are also classed as perennials, though because of their woody stems they would more correctly be included among the shrubs. However, they are regarded as herbaceous perennials because of the way they are normally used in a garden, as a result of their growth and behaviour.

PREPARING THE GROUND

Autumn is the time to prepare the ground for borders or flowerbeds intended for perennials. The ideal place to grow these flowers is down one side of a lawn with bushes or conifers along the far end. Lay the border or flowerbed out so that it gets plenty of sun, and the necessary protection against high winds and heavy rains.

Work the soil over thoroughly, whether it is a bed or a border. Give it the same sort of treatment you would give a kitchen garden.

PLANTING

Most perennials are planted in the spring. However, **iris** and **peony** give better results if they are planted in August or at the beginning of September. Certain other plants can wait until even later in the season.

Some plants require more surface area for successful growth than others. Therefore, plants with a vigorous growth, such as **peonies,** require some 2½ to 3 feet between each plant, while smaller plants like **pinks, coreopsis,** and the like, only need one foot.

There are four different ways of planting perennials, and you must use the correct way for each particular plant:

a)..Long-rooted plants ,such as the **althaeas** and the **gypsophilas,** should be planted deep, with the root running straight downwards and the bud of the flower just below the level of the soil.

b) Plants like **peonies** should be planted with the points of the buds just below the soil, and with never more than two inches of earth covering the main root. When **peonies** fail to flower it is often because they have been planted too deep.

c) The **iris** should be planted with the root set flat beneath the soil.

d) Plants in which the leaves start sprouting from the crown should be set with the crown level with the surface of the soil. **Digitalis** and **coreopsis** are among this group.

When planting has been completed, the soil should be firmly packed around the plant. Later in the autumn, when the ground is frozen, the more delicate plants should be protected with a mulch of straw, hay, dead leaves, strawy manure or garden moss. The object of this mulch — which should not be removed until the following spring, when all danger of frost has passed — is not only to protect the plants but also to ensure that alternating frost and thaws do not force the plants up out of the ground. However, the best protection against winter damage is a good thick layer of snow. If the snow is likely to be swept off by the wind, then you should place some branches of spruce or other brushwood over the flowerbed to keep the snow in place.

LONG-LIVED PLANTS

Without fear of contradiction, the most valued flowers in the garden are the herbaceous perennials, which produce a fine crop of flowers year after year despite the rigours of the winter. Their popularity also stems from their ornamental value, especially among the new cultivars which the plant researchers have produced by selection and other methods. Modern perennials offer the gardener a vast assortment of shapes and colours. Nevertheless, long-lasting perennials are not too numerous, and some of them do not even manage to produce flowers each year.

The first, the most noticeable and the most appealing of all the perennials is undoubtedly the **herbaceous peony,** which can be used in many different ways. This plant has the advantage that it flowers in the same spot for an almost unlimited period, producing a fine crop of flowers every year. However, you must divide it every five or six years if it is to continue producing large flowers — even though plants left completely untouched for ten years or more will continue to produce flowers of quite reasonable size.

PEONIES

Peony plants should be divided at the end of August or the beginning of September. The tubers should be set in the soil so that the crown lies about two inches deep. If your peonies are not producing any flowers the reason may be that the tubers have been set too deep in the soil.

DAY LILIES

Day lilies (Hemerocallis species) are equally well known for their longevity. They will outlast most of the other plants around them, whether they are planted in the sun or in the shade. The flowers grow in clusters on long straight stems, they last only a day, but buds follow each other in close succession and continue to open every day, so that the clusters give the impression of flowering over a long period.

Day lilies may be planted at any time in spring, summer or autumn — in fact, at any time when the soil is not frozen. They propagate themselves by reseeding, but the hybrids are reproduced by root-division.

OTHER EXCELLENT PLANTS

PLANTAIN LILIES or **FUNKIAS** (Hosta species) are plants that go very well in shady flowerbeds. They are also suitable for planting under small trees like **crab apples,** which have roots that do not take too much out of the soil. Plant them in the spring, when the shoots are beginning to break through the soil. **Plantain lilies** prefer a rich, deep and very moist soil.

RUDBECKIAS are showy plants, quite easy to grow. They reproduce by reseeding or by root-splitting. These plants put out suckers which will need cutting back.

FALSE DITTANY (Dictamus fraxinella) has reddish-purple or white flowers. This is another very hardy plant and is extremely long-lived. It is a somewhat slow grower, but does well in any location.

Among other long-lasting perennials which require little attention — in some cases none at all — we must not overlook the **sneezeweeds** (Helenium species). The autumn-flowering species of these perennials are very useful as background decoration for your flowerbeds. The flowers are spherical discs with drooping ray-like florets. **'Gypsy'** is a particularly pleasing variety, with red and yellow flowers.

PHYSOSTEGIA (False Dragonhead) is very useful for flowerbeds, because of its late flowering. It grows easily, forming tubular flowers on long stems, which are splendid in bouquets.

PURPLE LOOSESTRIFE (Lythrum salicaria 'Morden Pink') is another longlasting perenninal plant. It has light, lacy flowers.

These autumn-flowering heleniums of the 'Gypsy' variety make a very good background for a flowerbed.

A Purchasing Guide For Perennial Plants

A flowerbed of perennials is, without doubt, one of the more important contributory factors in a beautiful garden. If you have laid it out properly, it will be full of flowers from early in the spring to the end of autumn. To get the best out of it, it is most important that you choose the best site you can from the ground at your disposal.

Generally, a bed of perennials should be sited along the side of the garden, to act as a border. Once you have settled the location of the bed, your next task is to choose your plants, bearing in mind the size of the various perennials, when they come into flower, and what colours their flowers will be.

THE SIZE OF THE PLANTS IS IMPORTANT

Usually the tallest plants are placed at the back, the middle-sized ones in the centre, and the dwarf varieties in front. But there is no strict rule about it. If you want to obtain some special effect, it is perfectly permissible to put some tall plants in the centre of the bed and some middle-sized ones in the front. Remember, however, that no matter how carefully you may have laid out a flowerbed, you will have to make some corrections to it every year. This is absolutely normal! In order not to forget to make the necessary alterations when you next do your planting, you must take note of the changes you will have to make while the plants are still in bloom. Do not forget to mark the appropriate places in the flowerbed — push in a seedling label, or a small stick marked with the name of the plant you intend to put there.

Herbaceous perennials provide the basic essentials among your rockery plants. Use them to form tufts and clumps. They are also very suitable as dwarf plants, and as 'droopers' and 'climbers'.

Among the many herbaceous perennials, delphiniums or larkspurs are real star performers. Their tall spikes covered with lavender, blue or white flowers brighten the garden, and are also extremely useful in floral decorations.

The various species and varieties of perennials suitable for flowerbeds and rockeries offer you a very wide choice. Whatever the conditions, whatever your needs, you will find something to fill the bill.

Amateur gardeners who have never tried growing perennials from seeds can buy boxes of plants from nurseries and gardening centres. Here is a list of plants for various purposes: in each case, the height of the plant, the colour of its flowers, and its flowering season are given in brackets.

EARLY FLOWERING

Golden tuft (Aurinia saxatilis), (12"; yellow; May-June).

Columbine (hybrids with long spurs) (2 - 3'; various colours; June-July).

Wall rock-cress (6 - 8"; white; May)

Aubretia (4 - 6"; purple, lavender, or rose; May).

Carpathian bellflower (6 - 18"; blue, violet, white; June-September).

Snow-in-summer (6"; white; June).

Perennial coreopsis (1½ - 3'; yellow-gold; June-October).

Delphinium or larkspur (2 - 7'; blue; July).

Bachelor's button (3 - 6"; various shades of pink and white; June-July).

Blanketflower (1 - 3½'; part yellow, part reddish-mahogany; June-October).

Pyrethrum (1 - 2'; red, pink; July).

Sweet William (1 - 2'; red, pink; July)

Violet (4 - 6"; various colours; May-September).

MIDSUMMER FLOWERING

Achillea (4" to 2½'; white, yellow, red; May-September).

Perennial coreopsis (1½ - 3'; yellow-gold; June-October).

Caucasion scabiosa (2 - 3'; white, blue, mauve; July-September).

Oxeye daisy (1 - 2½'; white; May-June).

Perennial poppy (6" to 2½'; red; May-September).

Hollyhock (9'; white, rose, scarlet; July).

BORDERS AND FLOWERBEDS

Bachelor's button (3 - 6"; shades of pink and white; June-July).

Coral-bells (1½ - 2½'; coral; June-August).

Violas or horned violet (5 - 6"; several varieties, white, yellow, blue, violet; May-October).

FOR ROCKERIES

Golden tuft (12 - 15"; yellow; June-August).

Columbine (18" to 3'; various colours; June-August).

Rock-cress (6 - 12"; pink; May-June)

Aubretia (4" to 2'; several varieties, blue, violet, white; June-September, according to variety).

Bachelor's button (3 - 6"; shades of pink and white; July).

Carpathian bellflower (6 - 18"; several varieties, blue, violet, white; June-September).

Snow-in-summer (6"; white; June).

Baby's breath (Gypsophila paniculata) (6"; pinky-white; June-July).

Coral-bells (1½ - 2½'; coral; June-August).

Iceland poppy (18"; yellow, orange, pink, red; May-September).

Alpine poppy (6"; white, yellow, pink; May-July).

Yellow flax (1"; yellow; July-August)

Myosotis (6 - 12"; rose; May-June).

Balloonflower (2 - 3'; blue, white; July-August).

Primula (various species) (6 - 12"; various colours; May-July).

Violet (4 - 6"; various colours; May-September).

Evening primrose (4 - 6"; yellow; April-May).

Bugleweed (6 - 10"; blue; May-June).

Rock soapwort (9'; pink; July).

Clavenn yarrow (8"; white; May-June).

Yellowtuft alyssum (Alyssum argenteum) - (12 - 15"; decorative silvery foliage, yellow leaves; June-August).

Glacier worwood (Artemisia glacialis) - (4"; finely-cut silvery foliage; August-September).

Dwarf pink (alpine, glacier and short-stemmed varieties) - (6"; various colours; June-August, according to variety).

Maiden pink (6 - 12"; pink; June-August).

Evergreen candytuft (12"; deep green foliage; June).

Moss pink (Phlox subulata) - (several varieties, 4 - 6"; white, pink, blue, etc; May).

Saxifrage (Saxifragia decipiens) - (6"; white, pink, red; May).

Stonecrop (several varieties, 6 - 18"; attractive foliage; June - October, according to variety).

Houseleek (several varieties, 2 - 6"; attractive foliage; July).

Wild thyme or serpolet (several varieties, 2 - 6"; attractive foliage; white, red; June - August, according to variety).

Creeping veronica (1 -2"; pale blue; July).

Violet boltonia (dwarf; August - September)

Arctic chrysanthemum (6 - 8"; pinky-white; October).

Common thrift (foliage resembling grass, pink flower clusters; July - August).

Wide-leafed sea-lavender (3"; lavender blue; July-October).

Gentian (Gentiana septemfida) - (9"; blue; August)

Saxifrage (varieties suitable for rockeries - e.g., aizoom, bursar, ivyleaf, mossy, etc).

Plantain lily or funkia (Hosta species) - (18 - 24"; lilac, white; August-September).

SEMI-SHADED LOCATIONS

Bachelor's button (3 - 6"; various shades of pink and white; July).

Herb-bennet (Geum) - (18 - 24"; red, scarlet; July-September).

Perennial lupin (1 - 4'; pale blue, deep blue, pink, etc; June-July).

Myosotis (6 - 12"; blue, rose; May-June).

Balloonflower (2 - 3'; blue, white; July-August).

Monkshood (Aconitum) - (3 - 6'; blue, white; August-October, according to variety).

Anemone (4" to 3'; various colours; May-October, according to variety).

Astilbe (3-4'; creamy white, deep pinkish-violet; July).

Bellflower (4" to 4'; blue, white, etc. July-September according to variety).

Bugbane (Cimicifuga) - (2 - 8"; shades of cream; July-October, according to variety).

Tube clematis (Clematis heracleaefolia 'Davidiana') - (2 - 4'; pale blue; throughout September, according to variety).

Digitalis (3 - 5'; creamy yellow, rose, purple; June-August).

Leopard's-bane (Doronicum) - (1½ - 3'; various colours; June-August).

Geranium (3 - 20"; purplish, purplish-blue, purplish-pink, pale pink; May-August).

Day-lily (1½ - 4'; yellowy-orange, tawny orange; June-August).

Plantain lily or funkia (Hosta species) - (8 - 30"; white, blue; June-July).

Giant St-John's-wort (6'; yellowy-gold; June-September).

Wild blue phlox (12"; white, blue, lavender; May-June).

Primula (several varieties, 6" to 2'; pink, mauve, white, etc; May-July, according to variety).

Globeflower (several varieties, 6" to 2'; bright yellow; May-August).

Myrtle (creeping plant; blue; June).

Geneva bugle (Ajuga genevensis) - (5 - 12"; blue; May-June).

Perennial columbine (2 - 2½; various colours; June).

Aster (several varieties, 1 - 4'; white, lavender, blue; August-October, according to variety).

Lily-of-the-valley (6"; white; May-June).

Bleeding heart (Dicentra) - (1 - 2½'; pink; May - September).

Bishop's hat (Epimedium) - (8"; red, violet, white; May-June).

Cardinal-flower (2 - 3'; red; August).

Virginia bluebells (1 - 2'; blue; May).

Bee-balm (Monarda didyma) - (3 - 4'; crimson, pink, scarlet, mauve; July-September).

Solomon's seal (Polygonatum) - (2 - 4'; white; May-June).

Meadow-rue (1 - 5'; white, mauve, yellow; June - July).

FOR DRY, SUNNY LOCATIONS

Sneezewort (Achillea ptarmica) - (4 - 6"; white; June - September).

Golden marguerite (2'; yellow; June-September).

Columbine (1½ - 3'; various colours; June-August).

Sweet William (1 - 2'; red, pink; July).

Blanketflower (1 - 3½'; yellow and reddish-brown; June-October).

Baby's breath (Gypsophila) - (2½ - 3½'; clustered flowers; July-August).

Sunflower (Helianthus) - (4 - 8'; yellow; August - October).

Tall bearded perennial iris (yellow, violet, pink, etc; June).

Bouncing Bet (Saponaria officinalis)- (3'; mauve, rosy, white; July - October).

Stonecrop (6 - 18'; orange, pink; June - August).

Golden tuft (Aurinia saxatilis) - (1'; pale primrose; May).

Blue wild indigo (4'; deep blue; July).

Carpathian belleflower (6 - 18"; blue, violet, white; June-September).

Oxeye daisy (1 - 2'; white; June).

Coreopsis (grandiflora, lanceolata) - 1½ - 2½'; golden yellow; June-October).

Maiden pink (6 - 12"; pink; June-August).

Cottage pink (several varieties, 8 - 12"; white, pink; June-August).

Yellow digitalis (3'; creamy yellow; July-August).

Common shooting-star (1-2'; peculiar flowers; June).

Russian globe-thistle (3-4'; blue flowers, dry well; July-September).

Gaillardia (several varieties, 1 - 3½'; large flowers, pink, reddish-brown; June-October).

Flax (1'; pale blue; June-September).

Maltese Cross (Lychnis chalcedonica) - (2 - 3'; bright scarlet; July-August).

Rose campion (Lychnis coronaria) - (1'; crimson; July - August).

Round-leaved mallow (6'; red; July).

Wild bergamot (Monarda fistulosa) - (3'; mauve; July-August).

Sundrops (Oenothera species) - (several varieties, 1'; yellow, white, pink; June - September).

Ozark sundrops (Oenothera missouriensis) - (1'; yellow; July-September).

Prickly pear (8"; yellow; June).

Poppy (several varieties, 6" to 2'; golden yellow; May-September).

White-flowered penstemon (6 - 10"; white; July-August).

Eggleaf penstemon (2-5'; lavender; June).

Hoode's phlox (2 - 3"; white; May - July).

Moss pink (Phlox subulata) - (4 -6"; white, pink, etc; May).

Garden phlox (Phlox paniculata) - (various heights; white, red, etc; flowering season depends on variety).

Thyme or serpolet (several varieties, 2 - 8"; pale pink, red; June-August).

FOR VERY DRY LOCATIONS

Fernleaf yarrow (5'; yellow; June-September).

Bugloss (2 - 5'; various shades of blue; June-September).

Alpine arabis (6-8"; white; May).

Snow-in-summer (6"; white; June).

Oenothera perennis (1-2'; yellow; June-July).

Stonecrop (6 - 18"; orange, yellow, blue; June-August).

Houseleek (Supervivum) - (6- 12"; leaves in rosettes with centre surmounted by flower cluster; July).

Stokes' aster or blue aster (1½'; lavender blue; July-September).

Perennials In Combination
With Other Plants

It often happens that amateur gardeners become bored with growing flowerbeds of herbaceous perennials. They find the beds tend to look somewhat monotonous, especially at certain periods of the year when there are no showy flowers to be seen. Even though it is nearly always possible to have plants in bloom all through the summer, it's inevitable that at some time or another part of a flowerbed will be bare or covered with dead stalks. As a general rule, gardeners tend to group their perennials in large clumps, without taking into account the length of their flowering periods, or even how certain species are going to look growing (and blooming) next to each other.

A MIXED FLOWERBED

One of the most popular ways of using your perennials is to put them into what has come to be known as a 'mixed' flowerbed. As the term implies, this consists of a flowerbed planted not only with herbaceous perennials, but also with annuals and biennials, not to mention bulbs — and even bushes and small trees.

A good way to break the monotony of a bed of herbaceous perennials is to combine these plants with bulbs and annuals.

IN THE SUN OR IN THE SHADE?

Although a flowerbed generally does better in the sun, it is possible to find plants which can stand almost any amount of shade. The main thing to watch out for when putting in a flowerbed is to locate it as far as possible from large healthy trees, for their roots rapidly exhaust the reserve of nutritive elements that any new bed must have.

A flowerbed in which herbaceous perennials predominate needs an appropriate background if it is to took its best. The best way to do this is to plant a slow-growing hedge, such as **white cedar** (Chamaecyparis thyoides), which has persistent leaves, or **alpine currant** (Ribes alpinum), which has deciduous leaves. Alternatively, you might build a fence, which could give you an attractive background if properly planned. (Remember, however, that a fence must have sufficient openings in to let the air circulate freely).

Here's how to plan a mixed bed. Begin by drawing your bed on a sheet of paper, and mark off areas for six groups of nice showy plants. Then fill up the free spaces with plants which best meet the needs of the changing seasons, and give you the colour-combinations you would like to see in each section of the flowerbed.

Your six basic perennials should be: **iris, peony, day lily, larkspur, perennial phlox** and **perennial aster.** Whatever the size of your flowerbed, it must contain a good number of these six basic plants.

If you intend to be away during the summer, plan to plant **iris** and peony bulbs during the spring, and put in **phlox** and **aster** in the autumn — or you could use a lot of outdoor **chrysanthemums** instead. On the other hand, if you want a gay, showy flowerbed all through the summer,

Among the hardy phloxes, the 'John Ball' variety is noted for its lengthy flowering period.

then you must certainly plant some big **larkspur** and **day lily,** as well as some annuals, with their lovely colouring. You will need some annuals anyway, to fill up the gaps that will start showing when the spring-flowering plants have finished. Remember, too, that several herbaceous perennials are very popular in flowerbeds because of their lovely foliage. Three very attractive ones among this group are **satiny wormwood** (the 'Silver Mound' variety), **plume-poppy** (Bocconia) and **fragrant plantain lily** (Hosta plantaginea).

IMPORTANT LITTLE DETAILS

It is very important that you give proper consideration to the height and growing-habits of the plants you wish to use in your flowerbeds so that the tall plants don't hide the shorter ones. The tall plants — from three to five feet high — should obviously go at the back; the medium ones — two to three feet high — in the middle; and the small ones — less than two feet high — go in the front.

To break the monotony of a wide flowerbed, plant some large, showy perrenials at intervals, somewhere near the centre. This will serve to interrupt the somewhat repetitious uniformity of the bed.

For a small garden, where the bed must of necessity be relatively narrow, it is better not to use tall plants like **rudbeckia, sunflower** or **perennial aster** — all of which can grow at least five feet high. Instead, choose smaller plants which do not grow higher than, say, three feet.

HOW TO EXTEND THE FLOWERING SEASON

One of the major problems facing amateur gardeners — especially those whose garden isn't very spacious — is how to put together an assortment of plants that will give flowers throughout the season.

In reality the problem is not all that difficult to solve. If your garden is small, all you need to is restrict your planting to perennials that have a long flowering period.

BULBS

Here is a list of plants grown from bulbs, which have a long flowering period and are decorative without being too demanding:

At the top of the list comes **Siberian squill** (Scilla siberica), which stays in bloom for more than three weeks. As soon as its stems are out of the ground, it starts producing little fowers of a brilliant blue, which open slowly. To ensure flowers in the spring, it must be planted in the autumn.

The **golden narcissus** (daffodil) is another bulb which has a long flowering season, starting in April. Either the **large-cupped** or the **small-cupped narcissus** is also very successful. Try the **'Louis de Coligny'**, **'Duke of Windsor'** and **'Insurpassable'** varieties.

The **'Mrs. Moon'** variety of **Bethlehem-sage** (Pulmonaria saccharata) flowers from the beginning of April to the end of May. Besides its lovely flowers of tender pink and gentian blue, this plant has most unusual foliage, all covered with white spots.

The **'Bountiful'** variety of **bleeding heart** (Dicentra) thrives in full sunlight, and blooms from May until the end of August. In shady locations, the **'Sweetheart'** variety of **Pacific bleeding heart** (Dicentra formosa) will give iridescent white blooms from May to September.

The **'moss pink'** variety of **Phlox subulata** flowers in May, while the **'autumn pink'** variety gives a second flowering in November.

The **bearded iris** needs little attention and adds much beauty to the garden in the month of June. Elsewhere, a few clumps of **day lily** dotted along the borders can give pretty flowers from May to August. To achieve this, choose different varieties — such as **'Earliana'**, an early bloomer;

'Frances Fay, for mid-season flowers and **'Mabel Fuller'**, which blooms up until the end of August.

For the period from June to early August, the **'Double Beauty'** variety of **Oregon fleabane** (Erigeron speciosus) will be particularly appreciated for its big blue flowers. In addition, **cottage pink** (Dianthus plumarius) and its hybrids, **blanketflower** (Gaillardi) and **coral-bells** (Heuchera), flower abundantly from June up to August — and even September — without requiring much attention.

Other plants that will decorate your garden from July to September with pretty pink, blue and white blooms (depending on the varieties you choose) are **balloonflower** and **veronica.**

Several varieties of **perennial aster** bloom from August to the end of September, and they have the advantage of being able to withstand the early frosts.

Amateur gardeners who want to keep flowers blooming in their gardens as long as possible should use **garden chrysanthemums** which will provide a rich array of colour in the flowerbers until late in the autumn. These plants are hardier than any other garden flower, and they will last even longer if you take the precaution of protecting them against the first autumn frosts by covering them with a light mulch.

All the plants mentioned above are quite easy to grow, and their flowering period will be that much longer if you take the trouble to remove dead flowers as and when they wither.

AVOID INVADING PLANTS

There are certain gifts which, like the Trojan Horse, aren't really gifts at all, and which should be refused, in order to avoid a load of trouble. Without a shadow of doubt this category includes roots or cuttings of herbaceous perennials surplus to the amateur gardener's requirements, and which he offers to his friends, relatives and neighbours.

If anybody offers you a 'gift' of this nature, accept it politely in order not to offend the giver, but be very careful indeed what you do with it. Remember that the perennials which are being given away so generously are usually plants with extremely vigorous growth. They need continuous dividing, since they spread so rapidly. If planted haphazardly, they are more than likely to reduce your garden to a shambles.

For obvious reasons, few nurserymen grow or sell invading plants of this nature — though several kinds of them will be found in seed catalogues. Amateur gardeners must avoid the costly error of ordering any of these. Generally speaking, all garden-lovers are familiar with two perennial plants to be avoided for characteristics similar to those of the most unwelcome weeds.

These are **Chinese lantern** or **strawberry ground-cherry** (Physalis alkekengi) and **goatweed** or **bishop's-weed** (Aegopodium podagraria). **Chinese lantern** produces particularly bright red fruit, framed in a sort of lantern made of bracts — so that it really **does** look like its name. It's obviously a very decorative plant, and it has the advantage of lasting through the winter, if its fruits are properly dried. Nevertheless, anyone who proposes to plant it would be well advised to start by choosing a corner of his property where the plant won't invade the rest of his garden — or his neighbour's — for the roots spread very widely.

Goatweed is without doubt one of the most detestable of plants. The variety usually grown is the one with silver edges — a most showy plant, with its mottled leaves. But despite its attractive appearance, it is an extremely persistent invader. It can be used to advantage as a ground cover where other plants won't grow — on a dry, sandy slope, for example; or on either side of a path which is kept well swept of snow in winter. However, it is imperative to control its expansion by removing all flowers as soon as they form. Although goatweed does not flower abundantly, it can become a source of serious inconvenience if you let it go to seed.

BEWARE OF BELLFLOWERS

The **garden bellflowers** (Campanula species) are lovely plants, tall and graceful However, there are some varieties that will take your garden over completely if you are unfortunate enough to have them move in on you.

The most harmful of the bellflowers are the **clustered bellflower** (Campanula glomerata) and the **creeping bellflower** or **false rampion** (Campanula rapunculoides). The **clustered bellflower** has tufts of a dozen flowers at the end of its stems, while the **creeping bellflower** is a plant with deep blue flowers and heart-shaped leaves. Both varieties are very aggressive, and will invade every nook and cranny of your garden.

Be extremely careful if anyone offers you small plants growing near proper, easily-identifiable examples of well-known species. Almost invariably, they are 'poor relations' of the original plants and by this time are really little better than weeds. This is particularly true in the case of **sunflower** and **perennial heliopsis.**

According to the experts at the Plant Research Institute at Ottawa, the most sensible course is to buy cultivars with known names. They are smaller and more bushy, they bear showier flowers and they don't spread — while those little shoots that spring up at the foot of the existing plant in your friend's garden don't have the same characteristics as the mother-plant, and quite often should really be classed as weeds.

NEGLECTED PLANTS

It often happens that a neglected plant, even if it comes from one of the best-quality new cultivars, will degenerate into an unattractive thicket of infertile stems which spread like weeds. This happens with plants like **bergamot** (Monarda officinalis). However, they can be extremely attractive if you take the trouble to divide them every three or four years and bed them out in a new site with well-prepared soil.

Obedient plants (Physostegia species) are also of this type. Some of them have been given names, and do quite well in the garden, but if you hope to keep them within limits you must divide them every year and put them into a rich, moist soil.

A PLANT TO REFUSE

There is one plant above all others from which you must never, ever accept any roots or cuttings — and that is **Japanese fleece-flower** (Polygonum cuspidatum). This Japanese plant has stems that look like bamboo, and grows to a height of six to eight feet. It bears large, graceful, oval leaves and white flowers that look something like a puff of dust. Although it grows rapidly, and has some impressive qualities, it is one of the worst of the invading plants, and once it has taken hold of a piece of ground it is very difficult to root out. The only place it is really suitable for is a damp, gloomy city garden — for it is the only plant which can hold out in a place like that. Above all, you must keep it isolated in its own beds.

In this same group we must include **Sakhalin knotweed** (Polygonum sachalinense), an even larger species, which produces reddish stems that look like bamboo and are ten to twelve feet tall. This plant has large leaves and greenish white flowers.

FOR A WILD GARDEN

In the case of a wild garden where no ordinary plant can grow, there are two perennials you might try, which are more like weeds. One is **comfrey** (Symphytum officinale) and the other is **valerian** (Valeriana officinalis). Each of them grows to a height of about five feet.

Comfrey carries tufts of tubular flowers, pink and pale blue in colour, while **valerian** has little white fragrant flowers in big loose clusters.

CARPETING PLANTS

You must be particularly careful about plants which are sold as ground coverings. In fact, quite a number of them have definite invading propensities. Their capacity for spreading, which enables them to provide vegetation in places which would otherwise remain bare, is hardly likely to be popular in a flowerbed. The most important of these creeping plants is **creeping Jennie** or **moneywort** (Lysimachia nummularia), which produces yellow flowers and fine green foliage on its creeping shoots.

There is also **low Japanese fleece-flower** (Polygonum cuspidatum compactum), a dwarf form of **Japanese fleece-flower,** which spreads fairly quickly by means of its underground roots. Another one is **ground ivy,** a very hardy creeping plant. The several varieties of **ground ivy** are very useful when a drooping plant is needed, say, for a window-box; but it should never be planted among other perennials.

If you want to avoid trouble and worry and steer clear of problems for which the experts are still trying to find solutions, you will make it a rule never to include any of these invading plants when you place your orders for perennials with your nurseryman!

Even though creeping Jennie is useful for providing vegetation in places which would remain bare without it, it is still an invading plant. Therefore, you should keep it out of your flowerbeds.

CHAPTER 5

TREES

Watering

During the extreme heat of summer all trees and bushes need water. Watering is especially necessary in the case of new plantings, when shrubs or trees have been affected by disease, and finally, where the roots lie on the surface, as is the case with the **dogwoods** and the **azaleas.** In some cases it can literally be a matter of life or death.

TRANSPLANTING ALONE IS NOT ENOUGH

When a tree or a bush has been transplanted and has begun to grow again, many amateur gardeners believe that this particular woody palnt is now properly settled into its new location, and all they have to do from now on is watch it grow. This is by no means the case — quite the contrary! A good many of these transplants are not finally settled in for a couple of years — in some cases, as many as six. So it is frequently a matter of vital necessity to give them plenty of water, until their roots have **really** 'taken' in the soil — and I repeat, this can take from two to six years.

I should also mention here that trees or bushes transplanted without a ball of their original earth will take more time to re-establish their root-system than those which had a good lump of earth left clinging to their roots.

Furthermore, older, larger transplants will take longer to settle in than younger and smaller ones.

Until they are really at home, these transplanted trees and bushes need a lot of watering during the dry days of summer. As a general rule, you should water them once a week during the hot weather — even if there has been some heavy rain during the previous ten days.

PLANTS WELL ROOTED-IN

Trees and bushes which are well-established do not require so much attention — except those suffering from some wound or disease. Under normal conditions, these long-established plants are able to draw sufficient water from the subsoil. However, if there are periods of prolonged drought during the summer, even these plants will benefit from watering. This is particularly true when the roots lie on or close to the surface.

WATER THOROUGHLY

One of the best ways of watering well-established trees and bushes is to use a lawn sprinkler with an oscillating head. To get the soil properly damp requires a watering that supplies the equivalent of two inches of rain. During the prolonged dry spells of summer, watering on this scale should be repeated every two or three weeks. A good way to make sure that your trees and bushes are getting the right amount of water is to place one or two coffee-can lids on the ground near the sprinkler. The water from these lids will of course overflow before the trees have received the two inches of water they require. If this overflow remains on the surface of the soil and does not sink in, then the ground is already well soaked, and in this case I would advise giving the trees only half the amount of water that day, and the remaining half the following day.

When you water, don't be satisfied with a light surface watering. One good deep watering every now and then is far more beneficial than a light watering every day. In fact, the water that falls on the surface of the ground works its way downwards only very slowly. A superficial watering every day, that sinks about an inch into the soil, is of little or no value to woody plants or lawns. These roots generally go deeper than that, and thus lie in a layer of soil that remains dry unless it gets a good **deep** watering.

DO NOT WASTE WATER

As I indicated above, there is no point in pouring water onto the soil faster than the soil can absorb it. Not only does the excess water run to waste, but there is also the risk of its eroding the soil as it does so. You must bear in mind that water sinks fairly slowly into the heavier, clayey soils — which are also slow to drain. They need more water at each watering, but they should be watered less frequently than the lighter sandy soils. On the other hand, water sinks rapidly into the light soils which don't have much capacity for retention, so they need watering more frequently than heavy soils.

I repeat the general rules I gave above — the equivalent of two inches of rain is required for a proper watering — and in the long dry spells of summer watering should be repeated every two or three weeks.

Watering a newly-planted tree is made very much easier by building a little rampart of earth three or four inches high all around the trunk. The circle should be as wide as the hole in which the tree was planted.

The resulting 'saucer' should hold enough water to keep the soil properly damp around the roots of the tree. Fill it up every seven to ten days, depending on whether the soil is light or heavy.

A root-irrigator allows you to give your trees and bushes the water they need — and exactly where they need it, too — directly on the roots. All you have to do is attach the hose to the irrigator, push the irrigator down into the ground to root-level and turn on the tap.

WATERING FOLIAGE

Frequent watering of the leaves of your shrubs and trees — especially the conifers — cuts down the loss of water from transpiration, and also washes away accumulated soot and any mites there may be on the leaves. The best time to water foliage is in the morning, or late in the afternoon.

There is one precaution to be observed when watering. Do not **over**-water, and keep in mind that for normal development plant roots need air as well as moisture. Too much water can, in fact, be just as damaging to a plant as too little. Regular and prolonged waterings are probably neither necessary nor desirable — (except, of course, during abnormally dry periods). However, if the soil is well drained, you should not really have to worry about too much water.

(Despite what I've just said about over-watering, I'm going to stress here that the watering of newly-transplanted trees and shrubs **must** be continued during the second year after transplanting, though at less frequent intervals).

USE OF MULCH

In most cases of transplanted trees and shrubs — especially conifers — it is desirable to spread mulch on the surface of the ground around the plants, and keep it there for a full year after transplanting — sometimes even longer than that. The mulch can consist of peat-moss, pine bark, wheat husks, sphagnum moss or similar kinds of material.

A layer two to four inches thick covering the whole root-area is useful from more than one point of view. It retains the humidity of the soil by reducing evaporation from the surface, it discourages weak growths and it prevents hardening of the surface of the soil. Preventing the formation of a crust on the soil surface allows water to penetrate more easily, and also facilitates the aeration of the soil. A mulch also helps to maintain an even soil-temperature, which encourages good root development.

However, remember that this mulch should not be spread immediately after transplanting (which should be done early in spring). It is better to wait until the soil has warmed up a bit. If you put a thick mulch down too early in the spring, it is likely to keep the ground cold for two weeks later than normal — or even more, and this will slow down the growth of new roots.

One final remark on this subject. Most conifers prefer a cool soil during the really hot summer months. A nice thick mulch, spread late in spring or at the beginning of summer, will help them achieve normal growth.

Why Trees Should Be Fertilized And How To Do It

You may wonder why it is necessary to fertilize trees planted by the roadside, in parks and on private properties, when the trees in the forest seem to get on very well without the aid of any fertilizer at all

To understand the necessity of fertilizing trees planted outside their normal habitat — the forest — you must realize that the concrete and the asphalt covering our streets and sidewalks deny our trees their normal access to the moisture and fertilizing elements that are essential to their healthy growth.

Furthermore, trees grown by man are subject to stresses far greater than trees grown naturally. In addition, the soil of the forest is covered by a layer of organic debris which grows thicker from one year to the next. This mulch not only retards the evaporation of moisture from the soil, but also helps to improve the fertility and texture of the soil.

FERTILIZING IS NECESSARY

Trees should be fertilized at least once a year. The best times to do it are either the autumn or the spring. Flowering trees and fruit trees may be given an additional dose of fertilizer after the flowers or the fruit have appeared.

A well-organized programme is based on annual fertilizing, which is even more necessary if the soil is poor in fertilizing elements. In fact, it is rare to find a private property with soil that needs no fertilizing. Another thing to bear in mind is that fertilizing trees can often be a formidable task, especially if you have several large trees on your land. If you **do** have large trees to fertilize, let me advise you to plan the work with some care — for it takes several hours to fertilize a big tree properly. Accordingly, many people prefer to get a tree specialist in to do their big trees for them.

AFTER PLANTING

Arborists advise against the fertilizing of trees at the time they are planted. They say that newly-planted trees should be allowed to grow for at least one season to get used to their new surroundings before they are treated with chemical fertilizers.

However, small trees growing close to a lawn will probably receive a sufficient dose of nutritive elements — provided, of course, that the lawn is regularly fertilized.

FERTILIZER FOR DECIDUOUS TREES

There are several methods of applying fertilizer to deciduous trees. Here are four of the more common ones:

1. Drilling holes in the root-zone with an iron rod or an auger.

2. Spreading a granular fertilizer on the surface of the ground beneath the tree just before rain.

3. Injecting a liquid fertilizer into the root-zone.

4. Watering the leaves with a liquid fertilizer.

The most popular method, and also the most practical, is the first one mentioned above.

These holes should be some eighteen inches to two feet away from each other. Make them a foot deep, and put them in concentric circles around the trunk of the tree. However, if you use this method, there is one precaution to be observed. Do not dig any holes within two feet of the trunk. This will avoid the risk of wounding the principal roots, or the base of the trunk itself.

In deciding where to put the holes, remember that, in theory, the roots of the tree grow outward from the trunk the same distance as the extreme

The most popular, and also the most practical method of applying fertilizer to fully-grown deciduous trees consists of drilling holes into the ground with an auger or an iron bar, and then putting fertilizer into each of the holes.

tips of the lower branches. This limit, known as the 'drip line', is illustrated in the sketch. However, in many species the smaller roots or rootlets extend well beyond this line, so the outermost circle of feed-holes should lie approximately one-and-a-half times the distance between the trunk and the 'drip line'.

The amount of fertilizer you should use is calculated according to the diameter of the treetrunk, measured 4½ feet above the ground. Thus, for each inch of trunk-diameter, use two pounds of complete fertilizer such as 5-10-5 or 6-9-6, or use one pound of 12-4-8.

How much fertilizer to put into each hole is worked out by dividing the total amount of fertilizer by the number of holes. In this way, the whole root system of the tree is uniformly fertilized.

You may use an organic or semi-organic fertilizer on your trees, if you prefer, but make sure you follow the instructions closely as to the quantity to be used — too much can burn the root-endings.

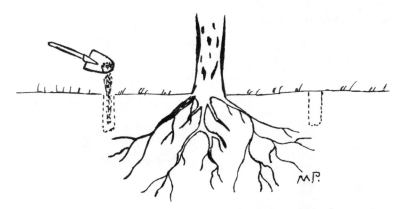

Fertilizing a big tree in the autumn, with a complete chemical fertilizer, provides a constant supply of nutritive elements for the rootlets.

Finally, give the area a thorough watering. When the water has penetrated properly into the soil, fill up each hole with surface earth. Remember that plants cannot absorb fertilizer in the solid state. Once the fertilizer has been dissolved, however, the roots absorb it readily. This is why a thorough watering is an absolute necessary if you have used a granular fertilizer in your feed-holes.

There are several other factors you should bear in mind, whatever method of fertilizing you may have chosen. First, if your trees are fairly close together, their roots will very often be intertwined. In this case, you can cut down on the amount of fertilizer you use. Next, do not fertilize a heavy soil when it's saturated with water. If you are boring holes into a lawn, make sure that your chemical fertilizer is below the layer in which the grass-roots are located.

Remember, too, that fertilizers are always more effective when the soil is damp, because the dampness helps to cary the nutritive elements to the network of rootlets in the soil.

Use a garden fork to work some strawy manure into the soil above the root-zone of a small tree. This will improve the texture of the soil and increase the proportion of humus in it.

WHEN TO FERTILIZE

Fertilizing trees with deciduous leaves can be done from April onward. At that time the roots are growing very quickly, and the soil is dry enough to be worked properly. If for any reason you cannot do your fertilizing between mid-April and mid-June, then do it between mid-August and mid-September, in which case you should use a special fertilizer, 3-6-12 MgBo, allowing one pound of fertilizer per inch of trunk-diameter. As you probably know, root-growth is very vigorous all during the autumn until the ground freezes, which means that the nutritive elements are easily absorbed.

Please note that fertilizing trees between mid-June and mid-August is definitely **not** advisable. Fertilizing in mid-summer can retard growth, with the result that tender new shoots will be unable to withstand the low temperatures of the following winter. Experience has shon that summer fertilizing is one of the most frequent causes of damage sustained by trees during winter.

Growing Trees And Bushes
From Cuttings

Most amateur gardeners know — because they have already tried it themselves — how easy it is to propagate willows and poplars by means of cuttings. All that is necessary is to cut off the end of a branch in the autumn and push it into the ground. In the spring it will have rooted. This is basically the same method as that used by nurserymen, botanical gardens and plant research centres to propagate several woody plants — though naturally rather more stringent horticultural rules are applied by these experts.

A TECHNIQUE THAT EVERYONE CAN USE

From autumn onwards you can propagate several of your woody plants with no other materials than some sand, some sawdust, some sphagnum moss and a wooden box. However, to guarantee success you must use only fully ripened cuttings — i.e., cuttings that have gone woody right up to their ends.

To propagate your woody plants, take some fully ripened cuttings from this year's growth. Use a pruning-knife or a sharp pair of secateurs for the job.

Cut them in November or December, after the leaves have fallen. It is essential that the cuttings be taken from the current year's growth — that is, the shoots at the foot of the bush in the case of most shrubs.

To tell the difference between this year's shoots and older ones, compare the colours of the shoots. The current year's growth looks pale, and has only a few sprigs on it. A specific example will be helpful: if you have any **spiraea** plants, compare them with some of your other shrubs and you will see that, unlike the others, spiraea's new growth is carried on the older shoots, which are a deep brown in colour and had flowers on them the previous summer.

Here is a list of trees and shrubs which can be propagated by means of fully ripened cuttings: **privet, spiraea, forsythia, willow, bushy honeysuckle, poplar, alpine currant, tamarisk, dogwood, elder** and **syringa**.

The following climbing plants can be propagated in the same way, and should be added to the list: **climbing hydrangea, Virginia creeper,** ordinary **vines, Boston ivy** and **climbing bitter-sweet**.

HOW TO GO ABOUT IT

Preparing the cuttings is a very straightforward operation. First of all, take a pruning-knife or a sharp pair of secateurs, and cut some slips from the new growth, six to ten inches long, and each with two or three nodes or joints. Make your cuts about one inch below a node, and as far as possible from the end node on the shoot. Then arrange the cuttings in bundles, making sure that the lower ends of the cuttings are all at the same level.

The next step varies according to the species of your cuttings. For **poplar, willow, alpine currant,** and **elder**, all you need do is plant the cuttings outside.

At the spot you have chosen as the winter resting-place for your cuttings mix some sand with the earth. Then bury your bundles of cuttings, standing upright, with only the end nodes showing above the surface. When the ground freezes, cover the bundles with leaves to avoid any damage when the soil heaves in the spring.

For cuttings of other species of shrub, the procedure is a bit more complicated. Essentially, it involves burying the bundles of cuttings in a large wooden box filled with sawdust, sand and sphagnum moss, or a mixture of sand and ground peat-moss. There is one precaution you must take — put the bundles of cuttings into the box leaning at a slight angle, but, as before, only the upper tips of the cuttings must show. When that is done, give the box a thorough watering then put it into the cellar, or the garage, or anywhere where the temperature will range between 60° and 65°F during the winter.

Let the cuttings stay there from four to six weeks, to give the cuts at the bases of the shoots an opportunity to start healing. Then move the box to a cooler place that will be around 50°F during the winter. A cellar or a cold-larder for fruit and vegetables makes a very suitable spot in which to store these cuttings.

ACTION NEXT SPRING

Early next spring, as soon as the ground becomes workable, plant your cuttings in a deep, narrow trench — once again, letting only the end node of each cutting appear above the soil.

Here are a few hints:

Begin by stretching a string between two pegs to give a straight line along the ground. Next, form a trench parallel to this line by driving the blade of your spade down into the soil and working it to and fro to form a V. Repeat the operation until you have a V-shaped trench. Insert the cuttings individually along the trench, two or three inches apart, spaced evenly. Then push the sides of the V back inwards, to hold the cuttings firmly in the ground. Finally, tamp the earth well and give it a thorough watering, to ensure that the cuttings are in proper contact with the soil.

If your cuttings are going into a wet, heavy, clayey soil, dig a larger square-sided trench, cover the bottom with an inch of sand, and rest the lower ends of your cuttings on this sand. Here, too, you must water the soil well, to ensure proper contact with the cuttings.

Keep the cuttings well watered during the summer, and they will then be ready for transplanting into a seed-bed. The following year, you can transplant them to their final locations.

Pruning
Ornamental Trees

Most woody plants, ornamental trees, fruit trees and shrubs with excessive growth can be pruned at the end of the autumn and during the winter. The autumn is also the appropriate time for a light trimming of shrubs with persistent flowers or decorative fruits which need thinning out. But before you launch your attack against these plants with saw or secateurs, it is essential for you to realize that you must not prune haphazardly. Except for dead or decaying branches, which must be removed without a moment's hesitation, no branch should be cut away without some good reason. In addition, when you are thinning out the smaller branches on threes and shrubs, you should always cut sparingly, and above a bud on the outside of the branch.

When the structure of a fully-grown tree contains two 'main leaders', or major stems, the one that grows sideways and throws the tree out of balance must be removed (except in the case of trees with outspread branches, such as apple trees).

YOUNG TREES

Most ornamental trees and fruit trees are already beginning to develop when you buy them from the nursery. The first, thing that must be done with these trees after they have been planted in the spring, is to give them an initial pruning.

First, choose the branches which will form the main shape or "structure" of the tree. All you should cut from them is the tender tips at the very end of the branches, to discourage withering. Then remove all, or nearly all, the other branches. This initial pruning will encourage vigorous growth of both branches and roots.

These illustrations show how smaller branches should be pruned. (1) Hold the secatur so the cutting-blade cuts upwards, to avoid leaving the bark of the branch attached to the trunk. (2) Pruning with a pair of tree-shears. Here too the cut is made upwards. (3) When removing a branch with the pruning-saw, first make a saw-cut below the branch, then work from the top downwards.

The second pruning is carried out late in the winter or very early in the spring, when the tree is in a dormant state. The main purpose of this pruning is to remove unwanted branches.

This second pruning is when you really begin shaping the "structure" of the tree, so that it will grow compact and strong, able to carry its branches well and resist violent winds. As part of this pruning you should remove the terminal buds from the branches you are leaving on the tree. Though you must be careful not to make the tree look too tall and slim, you must ensure that the leader has no rival (the leader is the primary or terminal shoot of the tree). Thus you must do away with weak forks, which always develop when two leaders spring from the same trunk, or when a strong lateral branch turns upwards and grows parallel with the leader. If you leave two leaders on the tree, they will eventually split apart, at the point where they join. To avoid this, you must allow only one leader to develop.

During the third and fourth years after planting, the supremacy of the leader becomes firmly established, and you can then turn your attention to the final structure of the tree. Major branches should be encouraged to put out secondary and tertiary branches, though the major branch itself should be prevented from growing too long.

In pruning shade trees, your aims should be to develop a strong structure which will enable the tree to withstand high winds, and to shape young trees the way you wish to see them grow — short and bushy, perhaps, or tall and slender — perhaps even conical. It is also important to stop branches growing too close to each other, or one above the other. Naturally, you must remove any damaged branches as well as any that are growing downwards, or are becoming a nuisance to people passing by.

A point worth remembering is that branches never change their height. If you start a branch off three feet above the ground, it will never become any higher or any lower — it will always be three feet above the ground. It is therefore very important that you make your mind up as soon as possible how high you wish your branches to be, and remember that once acted on your decision cannot be altered!

PRUNING LARGE TREES

When the structure of a fully-grown tree includes two leaders, and the tree is so large that it would be too difficult or too risky to remove one of these leaders, I would advise you to couple them together — either by means of a steel cable, or by a thick iron bar threaded at either end and running through holes drilled in the two trunks.

Also, if you have two branches crossing each other, the less important of the two should be removed. If a branch is growing more quickly than the others it must be cut back to let the tree retain the shape planned for it.

When removing a branch (especially a large one) you must prevent it from tearing bark off the trunk as it falls — as is shown happening in the left-hand sketch. The correct procedure is illustrated at the right. (1) A preventative saw-cut is first made on the underside of the branch. (2) Rather than remove the whole branch at once, it is preferable to leave a fairly long stump. (3) Another preventative saw-cut is made on the underside of the stump, up against the trunk itself. (4) Finally, the stump is severed from the trunk by cutting from above.

Any tough shoots growing upwards from the major branches in the centre of the tree should be taken off at the roots.

Be very careful when cutting large branches, whether you are removing them from a major branch, or from the trunk itself.

First, make a saw-cut underneath the branch, a few inches away from the trunk. Then saw the branch off, two or three inches on the far side of your first cut, sawing from above downwards; this will leave a stump, which you then cut off flush with the trunk, using the same process — first making a saw-cut underneath the stump (to prevent the bark being torn away all down the trunk as the stump falls), and then sawing from above downwards.

Finally, you should cover all the major raw surfaces with special coating, such as Braco or Mastic Pelton. (If you have only a few branches to deal with, you could cover the raw surfaces with polythene instead — but you must do it that same day.)

Birch and **maple** trees must always be pruned before March 1st.

How To Prune
Fruit Trees

TWO METHODS

There are two methods of pruning fruit trees. The first is the one used in commercial orchards, while the other is the one recommended for gardens in which the main role of the trees is decorative. In both cases, there are two objects in the pruning: first, to develop a solid structure with well-spaced branches and to produce a tree of moderate height to facilitate the picking of the crop; and second, to remove excess growth. By thinning out the centre of the tree, proper pruning allows the air to circulate more freely, and also makes it easier to deal with parasites.

TREES IN COMMERCIAL ORCHARDS

Trees grown specifically with a view to the sale of their fruit — i.e., in commercial orchards, are pruned to give a squat, dumpy shape. The branches are deliberately kept low, which makes it easier to prune and water them, and also to collect the crop. In commercial orchards, the appearance of the trees is definitely of secondary importance.

WHERE APPEARANCE IS THE MAJOR CONSIDERATION

On the other hand, amateur gardeners who have one or two fruit trees on their land want the trees to have a pleasing appearance — for them, the production of fruit is of far less importance. Understandably, trees grown in these circumstances are pruned in such a way as to produce a structure sufficiently high off the ground to let people walk underneath the lower branches in comfort. Very often, good fruit-bearing branches and healthy young shoots with buds on them are sacrificed to obtain a tree with a nice clean unobstructed central area.

PRUNING AND PRODUCTION

I must emphasize that **apple** trees give a much higher yield when new growth is cut back to one or two bud-bearing shoots, for this encourages the formation of fruit spurs (which are very short little fruit-bearing branches). This method produces solid trees, with branches that are less prone to break under the weight of the fruit.

The branches of **peach, apple** and **plum** trees tend to grow sideways — hence the necessity to start the branches of these trees somewhat higher up the trunk than with other species. In contrast, the branches of **pear, cherry** and certain varieties of **plum** trees grow upwards at a fairly sharp angle.

The pruning of fully-grown fruit trees — that is, those actually bearing fruit — must be done when they are in the dormant stage. When pruning trees in their third or fourth year after planting, you should remove branches that are rubbing against each other, or casting shade on other branches. You should also remove useless shoots and suckers, as well as all dead and damaged wood. This is also the time to do a little thinning out to improve the quality of the fruit.

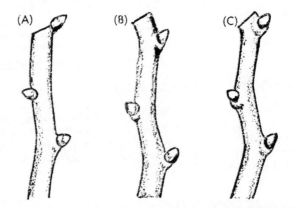

How to prune a branch or a stem: Sketches (A) and (B) illustrate faulty pruning. In (A), the cut has been made too close to the bud, this stem will wither back as far as the next bud. In (B), too long a stump has been left above the bud. Sketch (C) shows the correct method of pruning. Note that the cut has not left a long stump, nor is it too close to the bud. Furthermore, the cut has been made at an angle, to facilitate the shedding of superfluous moisture.

OLD FRUIT TREES

Combined with the application of a fertilizer with a high nitrogen content, pruning carried out at the end of the winter or early in the spring can give a new lease on life to long-neglected fruit trees.

For **apple** and **plum** trees, remove all diseased or damaged branches the first year, together with useless suckers and all branches growing vertically, or too close to each other. This pruning work will normally get some new growth under way and this will let you discover which are the vigorous branches worth keeping and which are the tired old branches which should be got rid of during the following winter. If the tree is too tall, cut a few branches right back each year, both to reshape the tree and to get it down to a reasonable height, which will make it easier to prune and water, and to pick the fruit.

THE PRUNING RULE

Since no two trees grow alike or have exactly the same structure, pruning is a matter of judgement more than anything else. Let your rule be **not** to follow the old-fashioned method, which consisted of giving the tree one very drastic pruning (which usually resulted in the loss of future crops, if not in the death of the tree itself). The modern method spreads the pruning over two years, as we have seen above.

The Technique
Of Espalier Planting

The technique of 'bidimensional' planting, or growing trees and shrubs against a flat surface, is coming back into fashion. The text-book term for the process is "espalier". As a noun, it means a trellis or frame on which trees or shrubs are trained to grow flat, or a plant so trained; as a verb, it means to train on an espalier. Thus a tree or plant flattened against the wall, with its branches trained into special shapes, is described as an espalier, or as having been espaliered. European arborists have grown fruit trees this way for centuries, because of lack of space in their old walled gardens. Skilful pruning enabled them to keep the flowers flat against the warm, sunny walls, and also to grow fruit trees too delicate for the open ground, such as **peach, grape, nectarine** and **pear:** a small garden could thus produce much more fruit.

The espaliers were started in open ground and then transplanted against the garden walls or trellises in the greenhouses. In the commonest form of espaliering, the branches were trained in parallel horizontal rows, either single or double, with right-angled bends to make squares or rectangles. Another popular choice was a palm-shaped fan.

Today, the term "espalier" refers to all forms of trees or shrubs grown 'bidimensionally'. Besides fruit trees, several ornamental species make good espaliers, and are used to replace hedges or enclosures, or to decorate a wall.

CHOICE OF TREE

For espalier work, first erect a wire mesh frame, or a trellis. Then choose a young tree with one single vertical stem. Cut this back to wherever there are three buds that will grow, one straight up and one to each side, about twelve inches above the ground. Train the lateral spurs slightly upwards during the first year, then bring them back to the horizontal. These form the bottom branches of your espalier.

Early in the first autumn, cut back the central vertical shoot — again, wherever you can find three buds about twelve inches above the previous branches from the spring pruning.

TIMING

Reapeat the operation every spring. Each pair of lateral branches will thus be one year older than the pair above. With fruit trees, do not try to train more than one pair of branches per year.

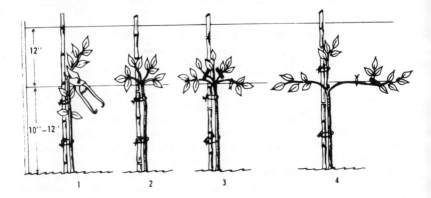

1   2   3   4

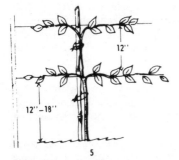

5

To grow an espalier, cut the stem back as shown, and let new buds grow. Choose three suitable buds and remove the rest. The growing shoots form the first layer. Start the second layer with three more buds on the central stem, about 10-12 inches higher up.

Apple trees for espaliering should be grafted on dwarf-producing stock. The sketches above illustrate the general process.

For a fan-shaped espalier, start with a year-old grafted tree with a healthy stem. Cut the stem back to just above the graft, in order to stimulate the growth of new shoots which will form the 'ribs' of the fan, making sure these ribs are symmetrical. The beginner should try to obtain enough shoots right from the start, in the first year. The art of making additional shoots grow in later years, by specialized pruning of the main branches, is only acquired after long experience.

You can buy fruit trees already espaliered, which need nothing more than normal routine pruning. This pruning should be carried out at the end of autumn or in early spring, just as for fruit trees in an orchard.

As soon as the leaves have fallen, remove most of the secondary branches growing from your main horizontal branches. Those you leave should be spaced five or six inches apart, and you must cut them back so that only some three or four fruit-buds are left on each.

The central vertical stem should have some of its buds trimmed off, unless it has grown very strongly; in that case, it should be cut back by about a third.

Espaliered fruit trees should also be pruned in July each year. Cut back lateral shoots to within five or six leaves from their base, and then nip off all secondary growths from these laterals.

Among ornamental shrubs which are easy to espalier are **flowering quince, cotoneaster, forsythia, magnolia, pyracanth, tamarisk, yew** and **viburnum.** They produce a pleasing effect in gardens which would normally be too small for flowering shrubs.

For these shrubs, the espaliering process is the same as for fruit trees, though there are certain specific requirements to be met. For example, you must never prune the spring-flowering species at the end of the winter, or just before they flower in the spring.

Why Conifers
Shed Their Needles

Some amateur gardeners are worried to find their conifers shedding their needles in the spring and during the summer. Here are some explanatory notes provided by the specialists in the laboratory at the Laurentian Research Centre for the Quebec region, which will explain the cause of this apparent anomaly.

Conifers only retain young needles — those up to two to three years old. The one exception is the **fir-tree,** which sometimes keeps its needles as long as seven years. Contrary to what most people believe, the old needles do not necessarily all fall in the autumn. The loss of needles (which is somewhat similar to the fall of leaves from a deciduous tree) varies according to the species — **pine, fir, spruce** and **thuya** (usually incorrectly described as "cedar"). The phenomenon is a perfectly normal one, and is particularly evident in the cases of **white pine** and **thuya.**

The tips of conifer needles may get "winterburn" — turn yellow or become discoloured as a result of the freezing of the shoots — which means that the shoots wither and die late in the spring.

Another cause of needles dropping from conifers has to do with cold. During the cold season conifers are unable to draw enough moisture from the frozen ground to compensate for the evaporation caused by their exposure to the wind and the sun.

To avoid the inconvenience of this loss of needles in the spring, it is essential to water the soil around your trees and shrubs very thoroughly, if the autumn is dry, and to keep it up until the frosts arrive. Further, if the trees or shrubs are not too large, it is a good idea to wrap them up — in a layer of burlap, for example — to protect them from the wind and the sun during the winter.

Bushes used as specimens of their kind are necessarily isolated. They must therefore present an elegant appearance, stand gracefully, and display attractive characteristics, whether these be flowers, foliage or fruit. This American arbovitae (Thuja occidentalis), of the "pyramid" variety (fastigiata), has a pleasing appearance which helps to bring out the details of the bed as a whole.

120

CHAPTER 6

SHRUBS

Choosing Your Plants

Your choice of plants depends entirely on your own taste, and on your knowledge. Once the layout of your garden has been finally decided, you are ready to make a properly-considered choice of shrubs, straight from the lists in the nurserymen's catalogues.

SIZE IS IMPORTANT

Whether you are considering deciduous or persistent plants, you must never fail to take their size into account. For any given location, there is always some shrub that is just the perfect size for that location. A wise choice at the start may very well prevent the later destruction of a shrub that has grown too large for its surroundings.

Good hardy shrubs with deciduous leaves, which go very well at the corners of a house or as 'eye-catchers', include the following: **ninebark** (Physocarpus), **mock orange** or **syringa** (Philadelphus virvinalis 'Virginal'), **beauty bush** (Kolkwitzia amabilis), **smoke tree** (Cotinus coggygria), **bottle-brush buckeye** (Aesculus parviflora) and **Tartarian honeysuckle** (Lonicera tatarica).

For smaller plants to go underneath windows, for example, try some of these: **'Anthony Waterer' spiraea** (Spiraea bumalda 'Anthony Waterer'), **'Somerset' Burkwood daphne** (Daphne burkwoodii 'Somerset'), **Farrer's small-leaved cinquefoil** (Potentilla parvifolia 'Farreri'), **'Annabelle' smooth hydrangea** (Hydrangea arborescens 'Annabelle') and some of the **brooms,** such as **Bean's 'Golden Carpet' broom** (Cytisus beanii 'Golden Carpet'), **spike broom** (Cytisus nigricans) and **purple broom** (Cytisus purpureus) which do well in sandy locations.

DIFFERENT SHAPES

Plants are available in several different shapes. For example, among the small trees with persistent leaves both column and globe shapes are available. For a classic garden you could use **'Skyrocket' eastern red cedar** (Juniperus virginiana 'Skyrocket'), a small pyramidal variety with grey-green foliage, or **pyramidal American arborvitae** (Thuja occidentalis fastigiata). Alternatively, you could try **globe arborvitae** (Thuja occidentalis globosa), or some of the **spreading** or the **creeping junipers.**

Don't overlook the deciduous shrubs, and the effect their bare stalks will make in winter. For example, the **winged-bark euenymus** or **corkbush** has very handsome branches which make a charming picture in the winter.

TEXTURE

Another point to be considered when choosing shrubs is the "texture" of their foliage. Skillful use of the difference in shape between one leaf and another will add weight and character to the overall effect, resulting in a pleasing and imaginative layout. For example, all the **viburnums** have large leaves that look like leather, while the **spiraea** have delicate little leaves. Certain shrubs, such as the **magnolias** and the **rhododendrons,** produce very heavy and somewhat jagged leaves.

One normally thinks of flowers and fruit as the things that bring colour to a garden, but foliage and bark also have important roles to play. **Lilac** is usually chosen for the colour of its flowers, but there is a **golden syringa** where the beautifuly greeny-gold leaves are the attraction. **Purple-leaf sand cherry** (Prunus cistena) and **blue spruce** are predominantly important for the colour of their foliage.

Dogwoods and **shrubby willows** are grown for the colour of their bark, while **European cranberry bush, snowberry** and **crab apple** are grown for the colour of their fruit. Colour must be used discreetly, to blend in with other values in the overall scheme. The strong colouring and heavy texture of **blue spruce** can dominate the whole garden and overshadow some of the characteristics of other trees. The same holds true for other species such as **purple birch** (Betula verrucosa 'Purpurea'), **purpleleaf sand cherry** (Prunus cistena) and sometimes **Russian olive.**

Obviously, the best places for your pleasant-smelling shrubs are near the patio or the paths. **Syringa** (Philadelphus, **'Elinor' lilac** (Syringa prestoniae 'Elinor'), **fragrant viburnum** (Viburnum carlesii) and common **lavender** are all pleasant-smelling shrubs and they should be planted to bring out this particular characteristic to best advantage.

GROUPING SHRUBS

One you have chosen your shrubs, you must decide how you are going to group them to create a pleasing, restful view. Begin by making a set plan and following it, but you will almost certainly want to make a few changes here and there every year, to achieve a better balance.

Shrubs around the borders of your property should be of different heights, to avoid a monotonous effect. Also, you would be well advised to mix both persistent and deciduous types together. This produces a better effect in winter. Using different shrubs with differing "textures" gives some interesting results.

How To Have Some Shrubs
In Flower All Through The Season

Even in the colder parts of Canada, it is quite possible to grow very attractive shrubs which will give blooms right through the season, from March to November.

MARCH

The first shrub to flower in March, while it is still very cold, is the **willow,** with its catkins — though I should warn you that the ordinary variety, which grows in marshy locations, only produces very small catkins. If you decide to plant willow, choose **goat willow** (Salix caprea), a plant that originally came from Europe. It goes very well in a shrubbery and produces the best catkins of all, very early in the spring.

February daphne, as **Daphne mezereum** is popularly known, is a sturdy tree-shrub that flowers very early when the weather is mild in March. It is often covered with flowers even though there is still snow on the ground. The common white variety, **Daphne mezereum alba**, with its lavender flowers, is preferable to the others. It seems to blend better with the **crocuses, grape hyacinths** and **squills** which are often in flower at the same time.

APRIL AND MAY

In April, **forsythia** takes over — it always produces a plentiful crop of flowers. Then there is **Nanking cherry** (Prunus tomentosa), a very handsome shrub with an interesting crop of flowers. There is also **dwarf Russian almond** (Prunus tenella alba), with its flowers that look like big almonds. Towards the end of the month, **saucer magnolia** (Magnolia soulangeana) starts blooming, with a crop of very beautiful pink tulip-shaped flowers.

In May, so many shrubs come into flower that it is difficult to make a choice. Among the numerous species, **dwarf flowering almond** (Prunus glandulosa) deserves special mention, with its small red cherry fruit, together with its larger relative **Prunus triloba,** which produces double flowers, white or pink. In mid-May, the best shrub is **Judd's viburnum.** This very handsome plant produces numerous bunches of scented white flowers tinged with pink.

A very popular flower for the end of May and the beginning of June is **Van Houtte's spiraea,** sometimes known as **bridal wreath.**

However, the experts recommend that you should choose **Lemoine deutzia** instead. This is a more compact shrub, which bears large white flowers. All the same, it cannot be denied that **Van Houtte's spiraea,** when properly pruned, presents a magnificent spectacle with its flower-laden branches drooping down to the ground.

May and June are also the months for **lilac**. No garden can be said to be complete without some **lilac** in it. One of the Preston hybrids named 'Elinor' is an excellent variety. It flowers somewhat later in June than the others and produces very sweet-smelling pink flowers.

JUNE AND JULY

June is the month for **syringa** (mock orange). I can recommend two very elegant, compact varieties which will not invade your garden — **'White Lady'** and **'White Bouquet'.** Kolkwitzia, which blooms at the same time, is a favourite among many gardeners because of its bell-shaped pink blossoms.

Curiously, shrubby trees which flower in July are somewhat rare. There are three popular ones, however, **spike broom** (Cytisus nigricans), **bush clover** (Lespedeza bicolor) and **buttonbush** (Cephelanthus occidentalis).

Spike broom is yellow, and grows to a height of four feet. Each of its stems ends in a bunch of deep yellow flowers. **Bush clover** has stems eight feet long, which carry graceful bouquets of bluish flowers that look like peas. **Buttonbush**, which is also found growing wild, is covered with spherical flowers about an inch in diameter, which look someting like pincushions. It is also noteworthy for its shiny bright green foliage.

Smoke tree (Cotinus coggygria) has a remarkable grey "smoke" of hairs among the seeds. It flowers in July and August, and sometimes lasts until the end of September. One particular variety, the **'Royal Red',** has rich purple foliage and a delicate pink "smoke".

AUGUST AND SEPTEMBER

The **'Hills of Snow' hydrangea** is in its prime during the month of August, although it will have begun flowering in July. It produces huge tufts of snowy-white flowers and big heart-shaped leaves.

However, the best and most graceful of all the shrubby trees that come into flower in August, and remain in bloom during nearly the whole of September, is **'Summer Glow' five-stamen tamarisk** (Tamarix pentandra 'Summer Glow'). This shrub has soft pale-pink frond-like flowers which rise up out of a pale misty-green foliage.

In September, **peegee hydrangea** (Hydrangea paniculata grandiflora) changes from white to deep pink, and then to green.

124

OCTOBER AND NOVEMBER

The flowering season for shrubby trees comes to an end with the handsome **witch hazel** (Hamamelis virginiana), which is covered with a delicate lace of yellow flowers all through October and right up to the hard frosts of November.

This shrub is in flower even while its leaves are beginning to fall.

Except for **broom,** you can easily obtain all the shrubs mentioned above from your nurseryman. Planted in a shrubbery or around your house they add a touch of beauty to your property from spring right through to autumn.

Dwarf Shrubs
For Family Gardens

The two important problems facing the amateur gardener are how to make a wise choice of dwarf woody shrubs suitable for his property, and then how to succeed in keeping them alive.

Since the persistent varieties of conifer need a considerable amount of attention, and since they do not actually offer a great deal of choice when you are looking for shade-trees, we will not consider them any further here.

Instead, I shall confine myself to an examination of ornamental shrubs which can grow strongly near the house. The remarks which follow are applicable mainly to Eastern Canada, you should therefore discuss conditions in your own area with a local expert.

IN SHADY LOCATIONS

We shall begin by considering shrubs suitable for shady locations. Assuming that the shrubs will get plenty of light, but little sun, except for a short time early in the morning and late in the afternoon, we are therefore considering a location on the north side of the house, then, or in the shade of a large tree — which we'll suppose is far enough away not to cause us any problems with its roots.

The woody plants which would be best in conditions such as these are shrubs with broad persistent leaves: **Canby's paxistima** (Paxistima canbyi), a low-growing plant with deep green leaves that makes a handsome bush, round and firm, standing from 12 to 18 inches tall; **holly mahonia** (Mahonia aquifolium), so called because its leaves resemble those of **holly** — (they will probably turn brown at the end of winter, but the shrub produces lovely shiny green foliage in the spring, with an abundant crop of yellow flowers followed by blue berries); **Japanese spurge** (Pachysandria terminalis), which produces a pleasant-looking green carpet eight to ten inches thick; and finally, **periwinkle** or **creeping myrtle** (Vinca minor), a low-growing plant with blue flowers and persistent foliage which spreads like **spurge** and helps to blend the shrubbery into the general layout plan of the garden.

Other shrubs suitable for a shady spot are **February daphne** (Daphne mezereum), which has pale pink or white flowers, grows about three feet high, and will bloom very early in spring, even while there are still patches of snow on the ground; **wintercreeper** (Euonymus fortunei) and its cultivars, which are determined creepers and will spread even underground, beneath the beds. **Cutleaf stephanandra** (Stephanandra incisa) is a shrub which does well in shady spots, but it is difficult to buy. It is a compact shrub, about three feet high and the same distance across with deep green leaves and white flowers. For their striking berries, you might try **European cranberry** (Viburnum opulus 'Compactum') or the **'Skogholm'** variety of **bearberry cotoneaster** (Cotoneaster dammeri 'Skogholm'), neither of which grows more than three feet high. Remember to order the compact type of cultivars, and not the ordinary sort which will start overflowing the area allotted to them in their very first year.

FOR SANDY SOILS

Among shrubs suited to very clean sandy soils that get plenty of sun

Double-flowered dyer's greenweed is a handsome bush which attains a height of eighteen inches. It does well in completely clean sandy soil that gets plenty of sun.

are the following: **dwarf lead-plant** (Amorpha nana), **orange pea-tree** (Caragana aurantiaca) and **globe pea-tree** (Caragana globosa), **Bean's 'Golden Carpet' broom** (Cytisus beani 'Golden Carpet'), which grows no higher than twelve inches, and **spike broom** (Cytisus nigricans) which grows four feet high. These are all excellent plants for dry spots. The double variety of **dyer's greenweed** (Genista tinctoria 'Plena') is a handsome, well-shaped bush which grows about eighteen inches tall and three feet wide. It, too, is suitable for dry, sunny locations.

FOR SUNNY LOCATIONS

The choice of shrubs suitable for sunny locations and fertile soils is very much larger.

Among the **spiraeas** there are many dwarf shrubs extremely well-suited for planting close to the walls of buildings and beneath windows, or as "eye-catchers" in places where height has to be limited. The **'Anthony Waterer' spiraea**, which produces pink flowers from June to September, is a dwarf shrub some three feet high which needs little care other than the removal of dead flowers to permit further blooming. A compact dwarf form of **'Garland' spiraea** can now be obtained from nurserymen under the name of **Spiraea arguta 'Graciosa'**. Like **'Big Nippon' spiraea** (Spiraea nipponica), it is worth planting for its big clumps of white flowers.

Goldendrop cinquefoil (Potentilla parvifolia 'Farreri'), also sold under the name of **Farrer's small-leaved cinquefoil,** is another very popular dwarf bush. It grows no higher than two feet, and becomes covered with flowers of varying depths of yellow at the beginning of June, and then blooms a second time towards the end of September. This shrub is easy to grow, and will do well in any soil. It will flower even if you prune it into the shape of a sphere.

Everyone loves **syringa** — though most people find it a little too tall for their liking. The **'Snowflake'** and **'Virginal'** varieties can easily reach a height of ten feet. You should try **'Frosty Morn'**, a semi-double variety which never grows more than three feet high, and **'Silver Showers'**, a compact, dense variety which only grows to a height of two feet, and produces an abundance of large, single, saucer-shaped white flowers.

For a dwarf bush that will produce a pleasant effect in winter, choose **dwarf red osier dogwood** (Cornus stolonifera 'Nana'). It has red stems which will stand out beautifully against the snow.

Dwarf Lemoine deutzia (Deutzia lemoinei 'Compacta') is compact and hardy, and produces a vast number of flowers. It grows about three feet high, and spreads to about the same diameter. It produces an abundance of pearly white flowers and does very well in Eastern Canada.

Dwarf flowering almond (Prunus glandulosa) in both its forms, the pink and the white, never fails to please with its showy double flowers set on the stem in such a way as to give a sort of "bottle-brush" effect. It seldom grows higher than four feet, even in the most favourable of soils, and it comes into flower at the same time as the **tulips.**

Finally, I must mention **golden dwarf syringa** (Philadelphus coronarius 'Aureus'), with its golden leaves and spherical shape, **dwarf eastern ninebark** (Physocarpus opulifolium 'Nanus'), **dwarf fragrant viburnum** (Viburnum carlesi 'Compactum'), the **'Bristol Ruby'** and **'Eva Rathke'** varieties of **bush honeysuckle,** and the lovely **Indian currant** (Symphoricarpus orbiculatus) with its salmon-red berries, which grows to a height of four feet whether planted in the sun or in the shade.

Pruning Shrubs

Older shrubs often lose their pleasing appearance over the years and must then be pruned to restore them to a proper shape. Some of them have a tendency to become scrawny and 'moth-eaten' and these, too, will need putting back into shape. This is done by cutting back the overlong stems, down to buds which are pointing towards the interior of the plant, thus altering the direction of the shrub's future growth. You must also give the shrub a rather more drastic pruning than usual, so that the new shoots will start growing as low down on the bush as possible.

On the other hand, if the stems of a shrub are too close together, the corrective procedure is quite different. In this case you must cut branches here and there, to open the plant up and give it a more graceful look. This time, cut your stems back down to buds which are pointing outwards.

Different methods of pruning bushes — on the left, an over-compact hibiscus. In the centre, a sprawling quince-tree. On the right, a whortleberry bush which should have a bushier top.

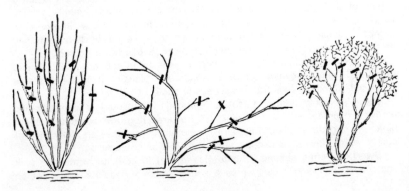

Every time you prune a shrub the first thing to do is to remove any dead, diseased, or over-long shoots — in fact, all those which are showing little or no sign of new growth. Next, prune out any shoots which are crowding the others, or crossing other shoots, or hindering the growth of those you want to keep.

REJUVENATING OLD SHRUBS

Old shrubs which have been neglected for several years can be given a new lease on life by cutting about a third of the old stems down to ground level early in the spring. Then give them a dose of a well-balanced fertilizer — 6-9-6, for example — followed by a thorough watering. Repeat this treatment in succeeding years until all the old shoots have been removed.

Shrubs which lend themselves well to this treatment are **spiraea, syringa (mock orange), deutzia, bush honeysuckle, lilac, barberry** and common **honeysuckle.**

This pruning should be done in spring — at the end of March or the beginning of April, before the year's growth gets under way.

The dotted hawthorn is noteworthy for its horizontal branches, its glossy foliage — particularly attractive in the autumn — and for the beauty of its flowers and fruit.

But whether you have grown your plants from seed, or bought them from a nurseryman already grown, the time comes when you have to transplant them into the ground. Here are two useful and important tips which should help to make the operation a success; first, choose a day when there is not much sun, and second, bed your young plants out in damp soil.

FRUIT-BEARING SHRUBS

The procedure for fruit-bearing shrubs is more-or-less the same as that for shrubs which flower periodically throughout the year — remove some of the old stems every now and then, and give them a light pruning to encourage the growth of new shoots.

SPRING-FLOWERING SHRUBS

Shrubs which flower in the spring or early summer — such as **spiraea** and **forsythia** — should be pruned after they've flowered. On the other hand, **hydrangea** and **orange-eye butterfly bush** (Buddleia davidii), and other similar late-flowering shrubs should be pruned either in November, or in March or April. Since their flowers are borne on the current year's growth, the object of the pruning is to encourage the growth of new shoots. **Shrubby hydrangeas** can be thinned out a little by removing old shoots and cutting back about a third of the remainder.

CHAPTER 7

HEDGES

Appropriate Maintenance Measures

When one talks about hedges, the discussion usually centres around the choice of suitable plants and the best methods of getting them properly established. But the subsequent maintenance of the hedge is equally important.

PRUNING AT THE TIME OF PLANTING

New hedges planted in the spring need an initial pruning sometime during the next two months. Hedges with deciduous leaves should be cut back to a height of two or three inches above the starting-level of the previous year's growth. This encourages the growth of new shoots, and produces a thicker hedge in consequence. The real pruning and shaping of a hedge with deciduous foliage — **privet**, for example, or **alpine currant, Chinese elm,** etc. — won't start until the second year.

SECOND YEAR PRUNING

At the beginning of the second year, before any greenery appears, prune all the plants to the same height, and trim and dress the sides. Prune the plants in such a way as to leave the base broader than the tip. A second pruning is recommended at the end of June, when the first flush of the year's growth is over. Some plants with extra-rapid growth such as **Amur privet** may need a third pruning towards the end of the summer.

LATER MEASURES

After the second year, hedges with deciduous leaves should be pruned towards the end of June, and thereafter as often as may be necessary.

However, you should avoid pruning during the autumn (September or the beginning of October), for this encourages the formation of young shoots which are likely to be damaged by frost. Late pruning, in November or December, when the plants are dormant — i.e., no longer growing, may be carried out if the hedge was not pruned during the summer, or if it is in obvious need of rejuvenation.

Mugho pine plants are always very bushy. This handsome hedge has obviously had every attention called for — trimming, fertilizing, watering and spraying against insect pests.

CONIFERS

Hedges of conifers such as **pine, spruce, juniper, thuya** and **fir** need treating in quite a diffrent manner. With these species, it is particularly important to choose plants which are really bushy at the base, for it is difficult, if not impossible, to get branches to grow close to the trunk in the case of most of the conifers.

After planting, trim all the plants to the same height. While they are growing to the size you want them to be, prune them only once a year. The best time for this is in June, when the growth process is slowing down. Then cut back half the new growth — which is easily recognized; the shoots are more tender, and their colour is a clearer green.

For hedges of **thuya, yew** or **juniper** pruning can be carried out early in the spring, before new growth starts. Here, you should shorten the previous year's growth by one half.

When the hedge has grown to the desired size, all new growth must be clipped.

THE EVER-USEFUL PINES

Excellent hedges may be obtained by using some of the **pine** species — **white pine, red pine, Scotch pine** or **Austrian pine.** All the same, they will need very careful pruning in every case. You must wait until new growth is standing upright before you cut it back to half its length. Furthermore, you must leave more sprigs on the lower branches — your objective being to develop a good-looking hedge, well-shaped and broadening out at the base. Repeat the same process every year, until the hedge reaches its proper height. From then one, cut back the new shoots every year to within about an inch of their base. This will make the hedge a little broader year by year.

Another point to remember is that in regions where snow is plentiful, hedges should always be trimmed so that they are wider at the bottom than at the top. This exposes them better to the light, which helps to give them a healthy appearance. Furthermore, the top of the hedge should be trimmed to a ridge shape, or rounded off. This helps to get rid of snow or ice in winter.

FERTILIZING IS NECESSARY

Like all other shrubs, hedges need fertilizing every two years, to ensure that they produce vigorous new shoots. I would advise the use of a good complete chemical fertilizer — suitable formulas are 6-9-6 or 10-6-4 — in the proportion of two to four pounds of fertilizer for each twenty-five feet of hedge. At the same time, apply some well-rotted compost or ground peat-moss.

Hedges of **thuya, yew** and **juniper** are better served by a nitrate fertilizer. Urea-form is very suitable for this type of hedge. Apply it late in autumn.

Fertilizing is not the only care hedges require however. Hedges need watering during dry periods. Also, if your hedges have been neglected for a few years, they will have grown too tall and too wide and no longer fulfil their original purpose — to provide an attractive, utilitarian screen. In fact, they may be quite ugly! To return them to their original state of beauty, you will need to carry out some renovation work every now and then.

How to Prune Hedges

To preserve the shape of an older hedge and to control its growth, it is essential to prune it every year. Do not, however, wait for the hedge to attain its desired height before you start pruning it. If you do, the top will go all bushy and the sides will be thin and skimpy.

RENOVATION PRUNING

It is very difficult, if not actually impossible, to renovate a hedge of coniferous shrubs which has been neglected. All the same, it is true that **yew** and some other coniferous shrubs will often put out new shoots from old wood, if they are treated correctly. However, most of the time the best thing to do with an old overgrown hedge is to take it out and plant a new one.

WHEN TO PRUNE

The right time for pruning hedges varies with the location and the season. The most practical answer is to prune when the hedge has almost come to the end of its annual growth-period. In eastern Canada, that means towards the end of June or the beginning of July for hedges consisting of deciduous bushes such as **Japanese barberry** (Berberis thunbergii), **pea-tree, cotoneaster, hawthorn, privet, honeysuckle, syringa** (Philadelphus), **currant** (Ribes), **Chinese elm** or **wayfaring tree** (Viburnum lantana.

Most hedges pruned in July will have grown enough to need a second pruning during the first week in September.

Conifers

The pruning of conifers **(spruce, Canadian hemlock, pine** and **yew)** is carried out towards mid-July, preferably when the weather is overcast, so as to avoid "burning" of the tips as much as possible. It sometimes happens that people prune their conifer hedges very early in the spring, because they forgot to do it during the preceding autumn. This practice is not advisable, since evergreens should not be clipped before they have begun their annual growth — there is a risk that the pruned branches will dry out and wither.

It is sufficient to cut new growth back halfway. It is easy to recognize the new shoots — they are more tender, and a clearer green in colour.

It must be noted that **thuya** (often incorrectly described as 'celar') must **not** be pruned until until early in September — which is when its active growth-period begins.

Let me repeat here that the **pine** species will give some very fine hedges. You should try one of the following: **white pine, Scotch pine, Austrian pine** or **red pine.** However, as I said above, you must take the greatest care when you prune them. First of all, the new shoots must be standing properly erect before you start work, and you must only cut them back halfway. Next, remember to leave more sprouts on the lower branches than on the upper ones. This will give you a well-formed and good-looking hedge, broader at the base than at the top. Carry on this way each succeeding year, until the hedge has grown as high as you want it. After that, cut the new growth right down to an inch from the bottom in your annual pruning. Keep this up, and your hedge will grow a little broader each year.

THE BEST METHOD

Correct pruning of shrubs with deciduous leaves consists of removing the oldest branches each year, right down to ground level. This encourages the constant production of new growth. However, don't shorten the remaining stems — for that will give you a hedge that is too thin and scrawny at the bottom, and looks like a corn broom at the top. As a general rule, the best time for pruning is immediately after flowering and the reason for this is that the major portion of the plant's annual growth takes place after the flowering period. The shrubs in the hedge gain from the removal of the old stems, since their vitality then becomes directed solely into future growth.

This type of pruning keeps shrubby hedges young, that is, green and leafy all the way down to the bottom.

WATCH THE SHAPE

The shape developed by pruning has a cultural and aesthetic value of its own. A hedge should be trimmed, as I pointed out earlier, so that the sides slope inwards, leaving the hedge broader at the bottom than at the top. That lets the light get at the underside of the leaves, which helps to keep them in a healthy condition. Some people think — quite wrongly — that the proper shape for a hedge is squared-off, with a flat top. A hedge so shaped is far more likely to give way under the weight of snow or ice. Further, this shape considerably decreases the amount of light available to the lower branches. In fact, when the sides are perpendicular, the lower foliage is no longer able to play its proper part, and may well wither and die.

So it is extremely important — especially in the case of high hedges such as **honeysuckle** or **pea-tree** — to prune a hedge so that it is broader at the bottom than at the top.

To get a ridged or rounded top to a hedge, those whose experience in this sort of work is limited should stretch two cords along the hedge, one on either side, each at the height from where they want to start the ridging or rounding effect. These cords will help them trim the top symmetrically, and thus produce the desired neat and graceful shape.

Trimming a hedge is not done solely to improve its appearance. The main object of the operation is to facilitate the growth of the individual shrubs that make up the hedge. To give a hedge the shape best fitted to our Canadian climatic conditions, it must be trimmed with the sides sloping inwards, so that it is broader at the base than at the top. Then light will be able to reach the underside of the foliage, which keeps it in good condition. Also, if the top is rounded or comes to a point, the hedge is much less likely to suffer damage from the weight of snow or ice upon it.

CHAPTER 8

GROWING ROSES

COUNTLESS USES

Rose bushes are a real godsend to those who have just bought a new property and want to make the garden look presentable as quickly as possible in order to improve the appearance of their home. New properties generally look a bit bare during the first year and this cannot really be corrected simply by putting in a lawn — you will need plants which will produce lots of foliage and richly-coloured flowers. However, I must emphasize that while newly-planted trees and shrubs will show only a modest amount of foliage during their first season, rose bushes will give satisfactory results almost immediately. No sooner have you planted them than they seem covered with a mass of handsome leaves and magnificent flowers of rich and varied colours.

Once properly settled in, a rose bush will increase in size and beauty during the summer and well into the autumn.

Nothing is prettier than a few roses planted around a new and still somewhat bleak-looking patio, or alongside a drive or a pathway. The roses seem to blend with the rest of the garden most effectively and tastefully. And even later on, when the permanent shrubs and trees are beginning to produce their full decorative effect, you will find that rose bushes will always prove themselves most useful, in many different ways.

The delicate grace of these flowers, whether they are grown as bushes or on a tree, allows them to be used in all sorts of situations. They will improve the general appearance of the garden, wherever the need arises. In particular, they are especially valuable around entrances, patios and flights of steps. Roses are not very large flowers, and the average rose bush grows to a height of from three to four feet. The bushes bloom all through the summer. You should try some **hybrid tea rose** trees, for a start. I suggest the highly-esteemed **'First Prize'** variety, which has unusually large and handsome flowers.

As with all other plants during the growing season, don't forget to remove dead flowers to make way for fresh blooms.

HYBRID TEA ROSES

Remember, however, that **hybrid tea roses** that have been planted more than a year sometimes produce suckers that come from the wild stock they were grafted onto originally. You will recognize these suckers easily from their leaves, which are smaller than normal, and of a lighter green. To get

137

Every gardener who wants rapid results from the very first year, and is looking for an abundance of beautiful leaves and magnificent flowers of rich and varied colours, plants roses on his property.

rid of them, dig down to where they spring from the main roots, and cut them off as close to their parent stem as possible. It is essential not to overlook this operation, for these suckers will become very sturdy and can easily wipe out your hybrid tea rose bush completely, leaving nothing but a useless shrub.

FLORIBUNDA ROSES

Floribunda roses were introduced into North America for the first time at the New York World Exhibition in 1939. They are now the most popular roses on this continent, for they are hardier than the hybrid teas, and produce far more flowers. Floribunda flowers grow in enormous clusters of many different shapes and sizes, and appear in almost every colour known to rose-growers. The clusters contain from 30-40 roses each — either semi-doubles, or (like the hybrid teas) a mixture of double flowers and single flowers together.

All the floribundas need in order to produce flowers in abundance is a good, well-drained garden soil and plenty of sun. You might like to try some of the following new varieties, which are all well-recommended: **'Eutin'** (double flowers in red clusters), **'Iceberg'** (sweet-smelling white double flowers), **'All Gold'** (a handsome golden yellow), **'Gene Boerner'** (a tender pink), and **'Pinocchio'** (big deep-red double flowers).

138

Free-form hedges are becoming more and more popular nowadays and the general preference is to use flowering shrubs. Rose bushes are widely used in this role, with considerable success.

ROSE BUSHES FOR HEDGES

Fashions change in hedges, as they do in almost everything else. Very often nowadays the classic well-trimmed hedge, with its formal and more or less immutable lines, has given way to freer shapes. People spend more time outdoors during the summer season then they ever did before, and they expect to see beauty combined with utility in their surroundings. **Grandiflora rose** bushes (which are very sturdy and grow to a good height), and the **floribunda** bushes too, are extremely suitable for creating the modern style of hedge, which is both functional and very decorative at the same time.

The grandifloras produce tall bushes which go very well in high hedges, or in the formation of screens. The floribundas, with their shorter, denser bushes, are the perfect answer for the lower type of hedge, where they will make an unforgettable display.

Roses For Landscape Gardens

Only a few years ago, rose bushes were never planted anywhere but in a formal rose garden with a rigidly geometrical layout. Nearly all amateur gardeners subscribed to this practice, which created the desired classic effect, with rectangular flowerbeds laid out symmetrically to enclose a central sun-dial or bird-bath.

Today, that has all been changed by the appearance of the new cultivars, which grow in great bunches like the **hybrid teas** and lend themselves very readily to the less formal style of modern decorative landscaping.

The hybrid tea rose has always had a delightfully classical cachet of its own. On the other hand, the **polyanthas,** which are descended from the hybrid teas (and are far more widely distributed), cannot possibly be grouped among the truly classic roses. Yet the crossing of the polyantha with the hybrid tea has given us the floribunda rose, so named for its bountiful crop of flowers. Some of these cultivars retain the delicate shape of the tea rose, with the added vitality of the polyantha. The new hybrid teas of today flower over a longer period, and are very suitable for use in landscape gardens.

PLANTING

Nowadays, when we need a long-lasting decorative effect from a combination of flowers and their colours, we have a choice between the tea rose, the grandiflora and the floribunda. The new breeding methods have opened the door to a whole world of new ideas on the layout of the modern garden.

There is literally no other plant that offers flowers so varied or so long-lasting as the rose. You can plant it anywhere in the garden where a touch of colour is needed. Let it stand out against a background of bright green foliage, or a wall, or a dark-coloured screen. All that roses ask is at least half a day of sunshine, and no competition from trees or large bushes over water and the nutritive elements in the soil.

Around the edges of the garden you could plant hybrid teas, long-stemmed grandifloras, or the shorter floribundas which will provide colour and greenery at the same time. To give an effect of depth, plant hybrid teas as a backdrop for the floribundas.

SOME EXCELLENT VARIETIES

Just imagine the splendid multicoloured effect produced against an old yellowed wall by **'Granada'** or **'American Heritage'!** These are two wonderful double-tinted varieties; the first is mixed red and yellow, the second is ivory shot with scarlet or vermilion. They would mix very well with some bunches of pure white — **'Saratoga'**, perhaps, a floribunda type; or **'Pascali'**, a new and very clean-cut hybrid tea. If you're looking for something along those lines but a little less modern, try the enormous **'Christian Dior'**, or **'Mr. Lincoln'**, which are both a vivid red, combined with that old favorite **'Ivory Fashion'**, which is creamy-white.

Wherever the garden needs a touch of colour, roses provide the perfect answer.

To break the monotonous succession of persistent-leaved plants all around the building, add a dash of colour with some roses, either in a bed of their own, or dotted here and there among the shrubs. Two cultivars are obvious choices here — **'Spartan'**, a floribunda type with salmon-pink flowers, and **'Masquerade'** which has multicoloured flowers. Some gardeners only use roses in landscaped beds at the front of the house, choosing colours which go well with the surroundings either in harmony or in contrast.

A GOOD WORKING FLOWER

Roses also go very well along pathways or drives, or near the patio. What could be more pleasing to the eye than a border of floribundas along the drive leading to the garage? Roses can also be planted in a belt around the patio, which they will turn into a pleasant, colourful, resting-place. Plant some of them in tubs and place them on the patio itself — but be sure to bury the tubs in October, to avoid frost. And if snow is plentiful in your area, your roses will need proper protection — so pile earth up around the roots, and put a plank shelter over them.

141

Even though roses have a strong personality of their own, they fit in very well with almost all species of annuals and perennials. In borders a most distinctive effect can be obtained by planting vivid red roses, such as the new **'President Lincoln'**, with golden-yellow pansies or deep blue lobelias. Another nice contrast can be obtained by combining white or cream bunches of floribundas with blue or purple violets, or perhaps the new **'Apricot Nectar'** variety, with some lavender pansies such as **'Delft'**.

SHRUB ROSES

Shrub roses may be planted almost anywhere, in any sort of soil. Some of them grow in sandy soil, most of them do quite well in clayey soil, and some of them like damp conditions. This group of rose bushes produces flowers of varied colours: whites, yellows, every shade of pink, reds and purples — and there are some particoloured varieties, too.

The best kinds for the garden are the strong growers which have been especially bred to withstand rigorous climates — such as we have in Eastern Canada. Among these, possibly the best of the hardy types, in my opinion, is the **Altai Scotch rose** (Rosa spinosissima 'Altaica'), which stands the cold extraordinarily well. It has lovely big white flowers, while the fruit is black. The Altai Scotch is a well-formed compact shrub, which grows to a height of five feet.

The **redleaf rose** (Rosa rubrifolia) is noteworthy for its hardiness, its reddish foliage, and its purple fruit which appears in the autumn. Its flowers are rather small. Other excellent varieties are **'Stanwell Perpetual'**, which produces fragrant salmon-pink double flowers all through the summer; **'Betty Bland'**, a bush five to six feet high which gives an abundance of pink double flowers; **'Spring Gold'**, with its big yellow flowers; and

Planting rose bushes properly requires no experience or skill. All you have to do is follow these instructions carefully.
You must choose good healthy plants, and plant them in a well-prepared and well-drained bed, somewhere where there is plenty of sun. The recommended method is as follows: (1) Dig a hole 12 to 15 inches deep where you want to put the plant. The diameter of this hole should be about the same as its depth.

To help spread the roots out properly, build a cone of earth 4 or 5 inches high in the centre of the hole. Be sure to tamp it well in order to prevent its crumbling. Then put the bush on top of this cone and spread its roots out evenly all round. (2) Tamp earth firmly round the roots, making sure no pockets of air are left. Fill the hole three-quarters full, treading the earth down hard. (3) Pour plenty of water in — enough to fill the hole. This ensures that the earth is in close contact all round the roots and is more effective than merely stamping it down with your feet. (4) When the water has soaked in, fill up the rest of the hole with earth, and water again. (5) Build up a mound of earth round each bush, some 8 to 10 inches high — this will prevent the bush from drying out. As buds begin to appear, remove some of the mound accordingly. At the end of 7 to 10 days, it should be all gone.

All-America Rose Selections

many others. The **'Agnes'** variety, which was bred at the Experimental Farm at Ottawa must not be overlooked. This hardy and vigorous rose bush grows to a height of six feet, and has a magnificent crop of coppery-yellow flowers which cannot fail to catch the eye.

Those who are thinking of planting shrub roses in borders, or in an informal hedge, should choose the **'Pink Grootendorst'** variety. This is a bushy shrub, some six feet high, which produces little pink double flowers, or particoloured red and white ones.

In the autumn — preferably at the end of October or the beginning of November — you should cut back all shrub roses bearing attractive fruit, and those with remontant flowering, by about one quarter of their height. This will prevent stems being broken by the winter winds, and will stimulate the growth of short stems. These stems, which grow on the older stems, will bear the major part of the following year's flowers.

Because of their height, grandiflora rose bushes make excellent screens. They grow especially well in the temperate regions of Ontario and Quebec. They enable you to create intimate little corners with restful colouring — something not always possible with other shrubs. Among the grandifloras recommended for this role are **'Pink Parfait'**, **'Queen Elizabeth'**, **'Scarlet Knight'**, **'Carousel'** and **'Buccaneer'**.

SUCCESS NEEDS MORE THAN LUCK

There is nothing more interesting to the gardener than growing roses. With a minimum of care, these plants can be a source of satisfaction to the most inexperienced gardener. Rose bushes lend a touch of beauty to a property, an air of distinction — an aesthetic "something" not offered by other plants. All through the summer, not only do they provide superb and fragrant flowers, but their foliage is also very decorative.

Some people manage to get magnificent roses without any apparent efforts, while others must use exceptional skill to produce successful results. On the other hand, some people never have anything but disappointments, no matter how much effort they put into their rose gardens.

THE BASIC PRINCIPLE

I believe success lies within the reach of everyone who has a little knowledge of the physical make-up of the rose bush. The most important requirement for successful rose growing is to keep as much foliage as possible on the plants during the active growing season. As a matter of fact, it has been shown that almost 95% of the solid content of a rose bush — that is, all the elements that go to make up the plant, except water — is in the leaves. Furthermore, it is within the leaves that the nutritive elements required by the plant are created, by the process of photosynthesis.

Air and water are the principal "prime elements" used by the leaves to create the substances necessary for the growth of the plant. In the presence of sunlight these elements are transformed into carbohydrates, which are the basic material of the solid content of the plant. Small quantities of minerals or other nutritive materials are necessary if the leaves are to successfully carry out their allotted task of providing food for the plant.

AN ABUNDANCE OF FLOWERS

The number of flowers a plant will produce depends on the quantity of its leaves, where the nutritive elements are created. The production of sufficient nourishment for the growth of the plant in spring, and the creation of a reserve to let it get through the winter, depend entirely on the leaves.

Cryptogamic diseases, attacks by insects, and every other factor adversely affecting the health of a plant and the number of its leaves — all these diminish its capability of producing nutritive elements, and hence its flowering capacity.

Here are some measures which will help you to achieve success with your rose growing:
• Choose hardy varieties.
• Buy plants which are resistant to disease — unless you are prepared to water them regularly, or run the risk of failure.
• Plant the bushes with care.
• Water them whenever they need it and fertilize them sensibly, using a well-balanced chemical fertilizer.
• Give them a moderate pruning, after cutting out all dead stems.
• Spray or dust them whenever necessary against insects or diseas.

A CHOICE TO CONSIDER

Rather than plant one or two specimens of several different kinds of rose bush, you might find it better to choose fewer varieties and have three or four plants of each. This makes the arrangement of your garden somewhat simpler, and also makes it easier for you to prepare bouquets of cut flowers — for you will have more flowers of each colour to work with. You will find that a bouquet of all red or all pink roses, for example, is much more attractive than a bouquet made up of flowers of various colours.

PLENTY OF SUN

Sun is of prime importance in rose growing. The plants grow well in full sunlight, but they can also be grown in places where they only get four hours' direct sunshine. However, in these latter cases they will produce less nutritive matter, and will be more susceptible to various diseases.

Rose bushes also need a friable, well-drained soil and their roots must not be cramped. The roots of rose bushes require a certain amount of oxygen in the soil. Anything that adversely affects the normal aeration of the soil can hinder root-growth. If the circulation of air is impeded over a long enough period of time, rose bushes will become enfeebled, and may even die.

A WELL-AERATED SOIL

There are some things which interfere with the normal aeration of the soil:
- Planting too deeply.
- Inadequate drainage, which allows the water to lie in the soil.
- Use of too much manure, peat-moss, or other hydrophilic material which prevents the water from draining away from around the roots of the plant.
- Watering too frequently.
- Packing and hardening of the soil over the course of the year.
- Neglecting to remove the hillocks of earth bulit up around the plants to protect them during the winter, in the spring.

Growing roses in a heavy, clayey soil does present some difficulties. Normally, holes dug in this type of soil are refilled with a mixture of garden loam and organic matter, which means that the holes then "capture" water quicker than the surrounding clayey soil. Thus, every time it rains the holes fill with water. If this excess water becomes a problem, you may have to install drains to take it away. Another method of solving the drainage problem is to grow your rose bushes in raised beds.

KNOWING HOW AND WHEN TO FERTILIZE

Some amateur gardeners fuss over their rose bushes too much. For example, they use too much fertilizer on them, in the hope that this will make them produce a real bumper crop of flowers. Admittedly, it is difficult to lay down hard-and-fast rules on how to fertilize rose bushes. In fact, a formula which gives excellent results in some cases may be a complete failure in others. It is better to go at it very cautiously, and risk not giving the plant enough fertilizer, than to overdo things and give it too much.

It is equally important not to use fertilizer too late in the season — say after August 1st. If you do, you can bring on the formation of new shoots which will not have time to ripen — that is, harden — before the cold weather comes.

One final word of warning — too strong a dose of fertilizer applied all at one time can burn the roots.

WEEDING AND TRIMMING

Sometimes the roots of rose bushes lie very near the surface. Weeding, cultivating, and other routine gardening work carried out to get rid of weeds, break up the soil around the bushes, or for any other reason, may well damage the roots — so proceed with caution when you do this work.

When pruning rose bushes in the spring, the main objective is to get rid of dead or diseased wood. You should also cut out any stems that are rubbing against each other. Any pruning beyond that risks reducing the quantity of flowers the bush will produce at the start of the flowering season.

A light pruning tends to make the plants look a bit scrawny at the beginning of the season, with little foliage at the base. However, this type of pruning encourages stronger growth and more flowers in the upper portion of the bushes.

If your rose bushes were attacked by black spot during the previous season, they must be thoroughly pruned back to about eighteen inches from the ground. This cuts down the chances of any infestation being carried into the current year on the upper stems and shoots.

OTHER PRECAUTIONS

During the sweltering hot days of summer, you should water your rose bushes very thoroughly every seven to ten days. It is better to water the soil rather than to spray the water all over the plant. Remember, however, that watering rose bushes late in the afternoon or during the evening increases the risk of their getting black spot disease.

A mulch one or two inches thick, of pine needles, wheat husks, pine bark, or other similar material, will help preserve the humidity of the soil and keep down weeds.

If your rose bushes are attacked by aphids or aracids (mites), you must protect them with an appropriate insecticide. If they are infected with black spot, or white powdery mildew, then you must use a fungicide.

How To Keep Your Roses Flowering Longer

Although June is traditionally the month for roses throughout most of Canada, the peak of the rose season actually comes during the first two weeks of July. Of course flowering is not limited to that short period of the summer — quite the contrary. All you need do is give your rose bushes the necessary attention during summer, and they will go on producing flowers in abundance well into the autumn.

You must already know that generally speaking hybrid tea roses and the multifloras are chosen for their long flowering ability. Give them the proper attention at the right moment, and they will go on flowering for a long time.

AN EASY TASK

Do not think that the maintenance of rose bushes through the summer is a difficult task that will take up all your time. If you develop a regular programme, it can become quite an easy and agreeable task. On the other hand, I must emphasize that the duration of the flowering period depends to a very large extent on the health and vigour of your plants. These two essential requirements are met quite simply by watering, mulching, trimming and pruning. Application of fertilizer and presticides also helps prolong the period the roses remain in bloom.

OFF TO A GOOD START

One precaution which will help a great deal to get your rose bushes of to a good start is to use a complete chemical fertilizer, either when you plant the bushes or at the start of the season (between May 15 and June 15). The formula 6-9-6 will do very well — this contains a systematic insecticide, a herbicide and some trace elements. Besides supplying the plant with the necessary nutritive elements, this fertilizer repels the sucking insects, through the interior of the plant itself, as well as controlling all the soil insects — and this for a period of six weeks or more. It also prevents the growth of weeds in the area treated for a period of two months. You may repeat the treatment in the middle of the season — around July 15. This will deal successfully with insect pests and weeds.

INSECTS AND DISEASES

Generally speaking, the dusting-on of powered pesticides which contain a fungicide and two insecticides, will prevent mildew and black spot on the foliage and will also destroy insects such as aphids, beetles and caterpillars.

Weekly dustings with efficient fungicides such as 'Captan', or insecticides such as 'Malathion' or 'Spectracide', will put a stop to attacks by microscopic funguses and to the ravages of insects. Be sure, however, to dust **both** sides of the leaves with the fungicide.

If you wish to keep your rose bushes in good shape and prolong their flowering-period, it's essential that you give them plenty of nourishment during the summer. If you fertilized them at the beginning of June, do it again sometime in July. This time, give each plant a cupful of a complete chemical fertilizer — use the 6-9-6 formula, in which 75% of the nitrogen

The rose reigns supreme as queen of all the flowers. The amateur gardener must take certain precautions, and give his rose bushes a minimum of care, if he wishes to see them enhance the beauty of his property. The most important requirement for successful rose growing is to keep as much foliage as possible on the plants during the active growing season. It is also necessary to combat insects and diseases, control weeds, use sufficient fertilizer, keep a mulch round the roots of the plants, and remember to water them.

content is in the form of a combination of urea and formaldehyde which releases the nitrogen slowly, over a long period of time. Spread the fertilizer around each plant, work it into the soil with a rake, and then water thoroughly.

You should not fertilize after mid-August, in order to give the soft, tender new growth time to ripen properly before the winter. However, you may fertilize your plants between October 15th and 30th if you use 'Hibernal' fertilizer — 3-6-12 Mg Bo — which will protect the rose bushes during the winter months.

NEED FOR WATERING

Water is an absolute necessity for rose bushes, especially during the long dry periods of mid-summer. When the soil gets dry, wet it with a thorough watering that gets the water down a good six inches under the surface. As with other plants, a short surface watering is **not** advisable — it does more harm than good. If the water does not get down deep enough into the soil, the result is that the roots come up towards the surface, and will dry out and die shortly afterwards.

A mulch spread over the ground around your rose bushes will help them through the difficult periods of blazing summer heat. Besides preserving the humidity of the soil, this mulch avoids the necessity for weeding and cultivating. It also lowers the temperature of the ground, and stimulates the growth of the plants.

Another important piece of advice to help you to grow roses success-fully is to wet the leaves as little as possible. A good idea is to use a hose perforated at regular intervals along its length, and lay it on the ground between the bushes. Alternatively, you could use a perforated metal pipe, or a canvas irrigator, both of which will allow the water to trickle slowly between the plants. If you decide to plant new clumps of rose bushes, or to lay out a formal rose garden, you should consider installing an underground supply-pipe ending in a vertical length coming up to ground level in the centre of the area, with a perforated polyethy-lene hose leading off from the vertical piece.

MULCHING

Mulching is an excellent method of preserving humidity. Putting mulch down reduces evaporation during the summer months, allows the soil to

The healthier and more vigorous your rose bushes are, the longer and more abundantly will they flower. The health and the vigour of your plants depend largely on certain indispensable attentions, such as watering, mulching, trimming and pruning, and the application of pesticides and fertilizers.

stay fresh and hinders the growth of weeds. The best practice is to cover the soil of your flower-beds with a layer of mulch some two to three inches thick.

To form a mulch, use buckwheat hulls, cocoa shells, chopped bark, ground corncobs or rotted leaves. However, in my opinion peat-moss is the best of all, for not only only does it insulate the soil, it also improves it if it is worked well into the soil at the end of the season. Always moisten the mulch thoroughly before applying it — otherwise it will merely draw water out of the soil and stop any available moisture reaching the plants.

There is one other thing which must be done before spreading a mulch. Apply a nitrogen-rich fertilizer, 12-4-8, for example, around the plants. This complete fertilizer helps break down the mulch into its constituent elements. If you do not use a fertilizer, then the bacteria that start the mulch decaying will inevitably use up all the available nitrogen and even draw it out of the soil. If that happens, then the lack of nitrogen turns the leaves yellow, and the flowers are smaller and less numerous.

Here is another bit of advice that will save you some trouble — don't take too long a stalk when cutting roses from your bushes. It is a known fact that every unnecessary reduction of the stems or the foliage tends to destroy the equilibrium which exists between the growth of the root-system of a plant and the part that stands above the surface of the ground. As we have seen, the more leaves left on a rose bush, the more nutritive matter it will have available (because of the process of photosynthesis) — resulting in better growth and more abundant flowers. This precaution is important even in the case of older plants and is even more important in the case of young rose bushes, which need to be as strong as possible to survive our rigorous Canadian winters.

How To Prune Rose Bushes

One of the more annoying features of most of the advice generally given on the subject of pruning rose bushes is that it never seems to take into account the fact that differences in soil and climate are of vital importance in deciding when to prune, and how thoroughly.

Rose bushes, particularly teas and hybrid teas grown in the south and along the Pacific coast, will grow to three times the height of those grown in Eastern Canada. Plants grown under favourable conditions, sheltered from the wind and in a good rich soil, or fertilized by spraying the foliage, will produce twice as much greenery during the season as the same varieties grown in the same general area, but in a middling soil somewhat exposed to the wind. Furthermore, plants which enjoy advantageous conditions produce their greenery earlier, and retain it longer.

THE OBJECT OF PRUNING

You must take the strength of a plant into consideration when the time comes to prune it. The object of pruning is to encourage healthy, vigorous new growth, capable of bearing the greatest possible number of lovely flowers. The branches of most rose bushes do not last very long. They harden after two or three years, and their foliage grows smaller, as do their stems and their flowers. These branches should then be pruned. Also, the extent of the pruning depends on the natural vigour of the particular variety; the stronger a given variety, the less pruning it needs.

Remember that a really drastic pruning causes a new growth of long, rich stems with larger, but fewer, flowers.

Before its spring pruning, this hybrid tea rose is just a clump of tangled stems.

After a moderate pruning, the bush has taken on a new shape.

VARIOUS TYPES OF PRUNING

Expert opinion on how to prune rose bushes **(hybrid teas, floribundas, grandifloras, teas)** is hopelessly divided. Some recommend high pruning, some say medium, others claim low is the best, while yet others recommend no pruning at all, or the barest minimum at most. Although there is no exact text-book definition of the various terms, let us say that "high pruning" means pruning the stems to a height of 2½ - 4 feet; "medium" or "moderate", to a height of 12 - 18 inches; and "low", a thorough pruning down to a height of 6 - 12 inches.

Another method sometimes used to differentiate between the various types of pruning consists of counting the number of terminal and lateral buds from where the new shoots start. From some points of view, this method gives us a more precise and practical answer — for the normal height of the different varieties of rose bush is by no means a set figure. Further, the length of the branches is not necessarily the same in every specimen of a given variety — it will vary according to the differences in the climate, the soil and the general conditions under which the plant is growing.

In general, it can be said that a vigorous plant that has come through the winter well, with its stems intact and measuring three feet or more, will benefit from a high pruning which leaves fifteen to twenty buds on each stem.

A moderate or medium pruning will leave six to eight buds, a low or thorough pruning leaves only two or three buds on each stem.

The least complicated description, (but also the least precise) is to consider that high pruning removes about one third of the shoot; moderate pruning, about one half; and low pruning, at least two thirds.

When you prune your rose bushes, make sure that whatever instrument you use is properly sharpened, and make your cut just above a bud. Pruning is really an extremely simple operation, but what a sorry spectable so many rose bushes present after they've just been pruned — stems hacked off crudely, with strips of bark hanging down — each of them an open invitation for all sorts of diseases to attack the plant!

(1) A rose bush in spring, with new shoots beginning to appear. Now is the time to prune it.

(2) High pruning: only about one third of the stem has been removed.

(3) Moderate pruning: about half of the stem has been removed.

SPRING PRUNING

The spring pruning is the most important one of all. On stems that are to be retained, all cuts should be made just above a bud that points to the outside of the bush, with about ¼ inch of stem left above the bud. The object of pruning just above outward-pointing buds is to produce an open, spreading bush, in which the rays of the sun can penetrate everywhere, and around which the air can circular freely.

THE RIGHT TIME TO PRUNE

The right time to prune depends on whether the rose bush bears its flowers on the branches that grew the previous season or on the current season's growth. In the former case, pruning should be carried out just before flowering starts; in the latter case, it should be done early in the spring.

PRUNING TO SUIT THE TYPE OF BUSH

Here are a few pointers on pruning the various categories of rose bush:

Shrubby rose bushes — In most of these bushes the branches are more permanent than those of the other categories. The majority of them are hardy, and stand up well to the rigours of the Canadian winter. New growth springs from the terminal and lateral buds on the previous year's branches. Thus, pruning of these bushes consists merely of cutting out all dead wood and old branches. Immediately after flowering, these branches are cut back as close to the ground as possible.

Remontant hybrid rose bushes — These 'repeat bloomers' all require almost the same treatment at the start of spring. In the first place, you must remove all dead, damaged or sickly stems. Then cut back close to ground level all stems that are hindering each other's growth, and those which are more than two years old. These latter are generally cut down to a height of twelve to eighteen inches above the ground, just above an outward-pointing bud.

Hybrid teas, pernetianas, and floribundas — These are pruned at the beginning of spring — and much more thoroughly than **remontant hybrids.** It is sufficient to leave only three or four healthy stems from the previous year, and these should be cut back to within a few inches of the soil.

Miniature roses — Other than the removal of dead wood, these bushes need little pruning. Simply trim back any overlong branches, to retain the desired symmetrical shape.

Tea roses — These bushes need little pruning: all that is necessary is to remove dead wood and old branches.

Climbing roses — Since they flower on the current year's growth, pruning is limited to removing dead wood and thinning out the older branches. Lateral shoots should also be cut back.

Winter Protection For Rose Bushes

Winter protection for your rose bushes ranks with pruning as one of the most important factors in successful rose growing. It is difficult to set out rigid overall rules for the protection of rose bushes during winter, there are too many variable factors. For example, resistance to cold is not the same for each variety. You must also take into account what method of fertilizing was used, the temperature in the autumn, and the general climatic conditions of the region.

On the other hand, although the cold is obviously a significant cause of damage and destruction during the winter, it even more essential to combat the effects of alternate freezing and thawing, and of the wind.

The precautions you must take to protect your rose bushes during the winter season must depend largely on the particular conditions that cause whatever damages are suffered by the plants during the course of the winter, and on the nature of these damages.

SHRUBBY ROSES

For those lovers of roses who have neither the time nor the patience to lavish attention on rose bushes such as hybrid teas and multifloras, there are some very fine rose bushes that require very little attention, and no particular care. These are the **hybrid shrubby rose** bushes (either in tree form, or on normal stems), which produce a plentiful crop of delicately-perfumed flowers in very beautiful colours. However, they do not have that air of distinction which characterizes the hybrid teas, nor do they flower as long as the multifloras.

On the other hand, though shrubby roses are definitely different from other rose bushes in that they only require the minimum of care, they nevertheless fit in very well with their neighbours in clumps of mixed shrubs or in informally planted beds. Several of them bear attractive fruit together with their flowers, and all of them have very decorative foliage which can be very useful wherever you need a contrast in texture.

Every rose is botanically classified as a shrub, and some of the oldest types of all are found among the shrubby roses — the moss rose, for example, and the Damask rose. In addition, there are some modern hybrids which have been improved, and are now hardy enough for our climate. The floral effect they produce is no less attractive than that of any other type of rose.

The pruning of shrubby roses at the start of the growing season presents no difficulties. It is necessary only to cut out a few old stems.

WINTER CARE

The most effective way of helping shrubby roses survive the winter without too much damage is to grow them in solid containers made of galvanized steel mesh, which can be taken out of the ground in the autumn and stored in a cold, damp cellar or in a deep trench. Gardeners who grow srubbuy roses directly in the ground, without containers, very often dig them up in the autumn and lay them on their sides in a trench dug specially for the purpose.

Another method which has been used with some success in very cold climates is to give the longest stems a moderate pruning, and then put a sheet of "pliofilm" over the top of each rose bush and tie it tightly around the stems at the base of the bush to form an inverted sack. Then a sort of wigwan is built over each bush in its "pliofilm" cover. This is made out of conifer branches long enough to be tied tightly together at the top, above the bush.

This process does not call for a great deal of effort in the autumn; and when spring comes, it only takes a few minutes to "unwrap" your rose bushes.

Professional gardeners and rose-growers all agree that there are no hard-and-fast criteria governing winter protection for your rose bushes, which are applicable under all conditions. Amateur gardeners who grow a lot of roses usually manage to find the means and methods best suited to their own particular needs by observation and experiment.

VARIOUS KINDS OF DAMAGE

The kinds of damage that can befall rose bushes vary according to the type of bush. Thus, hybrid teas and multifloras are very delicate, while hybrid rugosas are very hardy.

Pernetiana rose bushes — a variety formed by cross-breeding the **Chinese rose** and other hybrids — have given us a wide range of new tints, and better flowering performance. They resist winter conditions less effectively than other varieties.

The new varieties of today and of tomorrow, with their magnificent flowers, bring with them new problems of growth — a reduced resistance to insects and diseases and, in several of the varieties, less vigour in their growth.

However, you can grow modern rose bushes successfully, and produce superb flowers, if you restrict your choice as far as possible to those varieties which not only give an abundance of richly-coloured flowers, but also can resist the winter well.

Most winter damage is caused by very low temperatures which destroy plant tissue. Different sections of the plant, particularly those towards the top, may be killed at once, while others may be severely affected, although the damage may not become apparent until the growth-season of the following year.

Remember that the "hardiness" of a plant, or its "resistance to winter", is a combination of its capacity to withstand low temperatures and its ability to recover its strength rapidly if it has been damaged.

157

SOME ESSENTIAL PRECAUTIONS

The first steps to prepare your plants to get through the difficult winter months without trouble should be taken during the growth-season. Green shoots, which have a lot of water in them, are to be avoided. Late fertilizing — especially with fertilizers rich in nitrogen — tends to make your plants produce new wood, instead of letting their metabolism slow down in the normal way and thus allow the shoots already produced to ripen and grow hard. For this reason, in Eastern Canada, the final application of fertilizer for the year should be applied no later than the end of July. Ask your local expert for the appropriate date in your own region.

The amount of water you should give your rose bushes at the end of the season will vary according to the temperature at the time. As a general rule, the less you water them the better although you must keep the soil damp enough to avoid any possibility of plants suffering damage from over-dryness. A mulch on the surface of the soil is unnecessary, except in very dry conditions.

The end-of-season flowers, growing as they do on plants which have been supplied with the minimum of water, will not be as large as those on well-watered plants. But they will be just as beautiful, and will last even longer after they have been cut.

WEAK GROWTH

Certain varieties of rose grow more slowly than others. This is a hereditary characteristic which cannot be changed. However, slow growth is by no means the same as weak growth, which is caused by inadequate fertilizing, or by damage resulting from a blow, with its resulting loss of foliage. A rose bush weakened in this way is in poor shape indeed to face the rigours of the coming winter.

LATE PRUNING

Late pruning is another possible cause of winter damage. If this pruning is followed by a period of mild weather, the result may very well be the appearance of new, soft shoots which will be unable to survive the frosts later on. On the other hand, if the weather turns cold after the pruning, then the cuts will not heal as rapidly as they should, and these weak points will constitute so many potential sources of danger for the plants during the coming winter.

However, if very tall stems have appeared on the plant during the closing days of summer, the danger is that they will act as whips in the winter winds and damage other shoots, or even loosen the plant's roots as they thrash to and fro. Obviously, these over-long stems must be cut back. In this case, you are merely choosing the lesser of two evils. The sooner this pruning is done the better — even if you destroy some good late growth in the process. The cuts made during the pruning should be covered with a protective coating such as 'Braco'.

Wherever the temperature drops below 15°F during winter, you must provide winter protection for your rose bushes. There is a simple and effective method of protecting them: —

First comes **pruning**, which must be done at the end of October or the beginning of November, after the first few frosts, but before the ground has frozen hard. Cut back all the branches on your hybrid teas, floribundas and grandifloras, to a height of eighteen inches. Not only will this pruning prevent your rose bushes from being slaughtered by the winds and ice of winter, it will also make it much easier for you to carry out the various tasks that have to be done if your plants are to be properly protected against the winter. Shrubby roses should be cut back to one quarter of their height, to prevent the stems being broken by the winter winds, and also to encourage the growth of short stems, which grow on the older ones, and will provide the major portion of the following year's flowers.

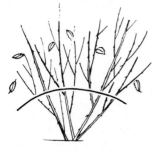

PRUNING — After the first two or three frosts, but before the soil has become deeply frozen, cut back all the branches of your rose bushes — hybrid teas, floribundas and grandifloras — to a height of eighteen inches. Besides preventing the plants from being slaughtered by wind and ice, this pruning makes it easier to carry out the various jobs necessary to protect them from the winter.

Next comes **watering** and the process is as follows: remove all dead branches, leaves and debris, and then use your rake carefully around the base of each plant. Water all the bushes, as well as the soil beneath them, using a mixture of insecticide and fungicide, to inhibit the presence of both insects and diseases.

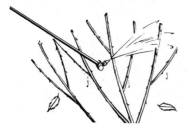

WATERING — Remove all dead branches, leaves and other debris, then rake carefully around each plant. Water each of the bushes, as well as the ground, with a mixture of insecticide and fungicide, in order to keep insects and diseases away from the plants and from the ground below.

The third step to take for the protection of your rose bushes is **banking-up.** As soon as the cold begins to affect the leaves of the bushes in the autumn — either at the end of October or the beginning of November — you must cover up your plants to protect them from the winter.

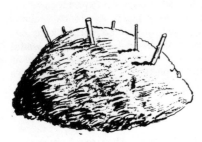

BANKING-UP — Build a mound of earth one foot high round each rose bush, so that no more than six inches of the stems remain exposed to the air. The object of banking-up is to protect the bushes against sudden changes of temperature, and to protect the stems from damage caused by wind and ice. Finally, when the ground is frozen hard, cover the mounds with conifer branches, hay or straw. Protect the earth from erosion during the course of winter.

The best protection is a covering of earth, so heap up the soil around each plant to form a mound about twelve inches high which will cover the bush almost completely.

A mulch of peat-moss, dead leaves, conifer branches, ground-up corn cobs, etc., may be laid on top of the mounds when the soil is frozen to a depth of at least one inch. This protective layer will stop the snow melting too quickly under the heat of the spring sun, which could cause a premature thaw.

Well-rotted compost, coarser in texture than the soil itself, makes an excellent material for banking-up. It is less dense than the soil, and when you remove the mounds in the spring, it can be worked into the soil of the bed, thus adding humus to the earth and increasing its fertility.

If they are to work properly, the banked-up mounds must stay frozen, otherwise the buds at the base of the plants may produce a premature growth which is liable to be killed off by a late frost after the mounds have been cleared away in the spring.

In the very cold areas of Canada, where the depth of the snow is uncertain, and may prove insufficient to provide adequate insulation, some amateur gardeners who grow **hybrid tea roses** prefer to dig up their rose bushes every autumn and bury them in a trench some eighteen inches deep.

Although this method definitely affords better protection to your rose bushes, it is much more time consuming and should be carried out exactly as follows:

160

'The Doctor'

'McGredy's Sunset'

'Virgo'

'Ena Harkness'

'Margaret Rose'

'Madame René Coty'

'Crimson Glory'

'Thanksgiving'

'Queen Elizabeth'

Tuberous begonias with double flowers

'Miss Canada' rose bush

'Golden Heart'

'Potgieter'

Some Varieties of Dahlia

'Lavender Perfection

'Pride of Holland'

'Pioneer'

'Chamoisroschen'

'Yellow Show'

'Magnificat'

'Darcy Sainsbury'

'Pink Giant'

'Red and White'

'Stalze Von Berlin'

Four varieties of 'Darwin' tulip

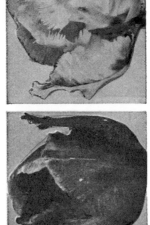
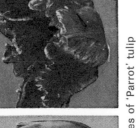
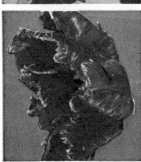

Four varieties of 'Parrot' tulip

Four varieties of narcissus

'Muscari'   'Galanthus'   'Chionodoxa'   'Ranunculus'

Four varieties of hyacinth

'Golden
Chalice'

'Mid-Century'

'Fiesta'

'Bellingham'

'Heart's Desire'

Some Varieties of Lily

'Jillian Wallace'

'Olympic'

'Aurelian'

Cannas: dwarf 'Pfitzer'

'Felin Crousse' Peony

'Festiva Maxima' Peony

'M. Jules Elie' Peony

Gloxinia: 'Emperor Frederick'

The plants are placed in serried rows at the bottom of the trench, each lying at an angle of 45°, with the roots lower than the stems. Then the plants are covered with a layer of earth or sand, twelve to eighteen inches thick and, finally, a layer of dead leaves is placed on top.

CLIMBING ROSES

With both shrubby roses and climbing roses, the closer the variety is to the tea rose, the more protection it needs. Thus, the larger the flowers, the smaller the plant's capacity to withstand the rigours of winter. The degree of protection you give a climbing rose will determine how well the plant gets through the cold season. If it is in a spot well shelterd from north and west winds, the risk of loss or damage is considerably reduced.

In eastern Canada, climbing roses are protected by unfastening them from their support and stretching them out horizontally along the ground. They are fixed in that position with lengths of wire mesh screen or with forked sticks, and then covered with earth or mulch. The surface of the earth is protected with waterproof building paper, the edges must be held down with planks or stones, for the covering must not be left open to the air. This protection must be provided before the cold weather finally sets in.

Sometimes, climbing roses are trained up trellises hinged about a foot above the ground. With this system, the plant does not need to be unfastened from the treillis and can easily be stretched out on the ground in the autumn.

Rose bushes covered with magnificent flowers of rich and varied hues add a touch of incomparable beauty to any property.

When there is not enough rainfall, artificial watering allows you to supply plants with the water which is essential for their normal growth. Among the various types of apparatus available for the purpose are pressure sprinklers branching off from a water-line. Sprinklers of the oscillating type are adequate for watering fairly small areas. They are especially useful for lawns and for a kitchen garden.

CHAPTER 9

WATERING YOUR PLANTS

Using Water Sensibly

Low water-pressure in the interior system of our garden plants is somewhat similar to low blood-pressure in human beings. When a person has low blood-pressure, he has it treated as soon as possible. Similarly, when an amateur gardener discovers that his plants are withering as a result of insufficient water-pressure within their system — whether it be the lawn, the trees, the shrubs, the perennials or the annuals — he must correct the situation without delay, otherwise he will suffer losses that may well be irreparable. It is well-known that lack of water in plants causes more plant deaths than all other causes combined. Statistics compiled by serious observers prove beyond all doubt that plant losses caused by storms, insects, diseases, wounds received during transplanting, transplanting itself or handling, amount to no more than one quarter of the total.

WHERE DOES THE WATER GO IN THE GROUND?

Some of you will no doubt be wondering what happens to the water poured out over the garden and the lawn, either in the form of rain or as deliberate watering. Briefly, this water serves several purposes, and although some of it does trickle away across the surface of the ground, nearly all of it sinks down into the soil.

The soil retains a certain amount of this water and incorporates it into its nutritive elements, but most of what has filtered down from the surface is ultimately released into the atmosphere again by evaporation through the leaves of plants. The plant absorbs water from the soil by capillary action through its roots.

Part of the water in the plant is lost by evaporation above the surface; another part remains in the plant and builds up the hydrostatic pressure inside the plant until it is greater than the pressure in the surrounding soil; then water passes from the plant back into the soil, for further use. Remember that water in the soil is never static — its quantity varies constantly, and it is continually welling up and sinking back again into the subsoil. Therefore, whenever there is insufficient water within reach of a thirsty plant's roots to let it "drink" by capillary action, the plant will wither. It then becomes essential to water the plant, otherwise, it will quickly die.

AMOUNT OF WATER NEEDED BY PLANTS

Most garden plants need an inch of rain every week during the hottest parts of the summer. That, of course, is the ideal — which is very seldom attained. Many garden-lovers, especially those living in the city, have lost new plants, and even plants long established in their gardens, as a result of municipal bylaws regulating the use of the public water-supply. During a long dry period, many a town dweller all too often sees his favourite plants withering and dying through lack of water. In just a few days, the results of weeks and even years of toil and care can disappear completely. Not only does this almost always result in financial loss — sometimes quite considerable — but even more regrettable, the appearance of the property must inevitably suffer.

INCREASING THE STRENGTH OF YOUR PLANTS

Fortunately, several methods exist of maintaining and even increasing the strength of your plants during water shortages.

First of all, there are certain organic and other materials which can be added to the soil to increase its capacity to retain moisture. For example, there are literally millions of sponge-like reservoirs in commercial humus and in the humus you can make yourself from autumn leaves, peat-moss, farm manure and compost. These various materials add fresh nutritive elements and bacteria to the soil. However, their role is not limited to that alone. They can also collect and hold more than their own weight of water, either from rainfall or from your watering of the garden.

The moisture captured by this organic material is released very sparingly by the action of wind and sun and the tiny rootlets of your plants have no difficulty in sucking up the water they need.

In addition, certain inorganic materials such as vermiculite and perlite will also retain moisture in the soil.

The organic additives referred to above play an important role as mulch, on the surface of the soil. But they are even more useful to the plant when mixed in with the soil, provided this is done deeply enough to get them down to the level of the plant's root-spread.

Most professional gardeners and nurserymen use these materials below and around the roots of new plants at the time of planting. In addition, well-established woody plants, trees and shrubs will profit from the application of materials of this nature, both organic and inorganic.

For woody plants, it is necessary only to dig some holes two to three feet deep in the ground near the roots using an auger, an iron bar or a length of piping. Fill these holes with one of the moisture-retaining materials, and tamp it down firmly. From then on, whenever it rains, water will soak into these "fillings" for several hours and this will provide the plants with a deep, efficient reservoir holding enough water to see them through the next few days. Furthermore, fertilizers in either solid or liquid form can also be added to these "fillings" of humus, to keep the plant's roots properly nourished.

RESISTANCE TO DRYNESS

Mulches spread on the surface of the ground will resist the drying effects of hot sun and strong winds.

For a mulch for plants around the walls of the house, buckwheat hulls, peat-moss, or sphagnum moss are the ones most frequently used, because of their appearance and their cleanness. Flowerbeds, borders and even kitchen gardens may also be improved by these particular mulching materials. You can also use lawn clippings, old hay, straw or strips of black plastic as mulches. Even weeds can be put to good use and become a mulching material, helping to preserve moisture around more worthy plants.

Lawns will resist the dryness of summer better if the grass clippings are left lying on the lawn after the first mowing in the spring. It will also help if, later on on the summer, you adjust the blades of the mower to leave the grass at least two inches long.

A MISTAKE TO AVOID

Like fertilizers, rich desserts and penicillin, mulches are excellent in small quantities. Used too freely, they can cause serious trouble. As a general rule, a layer of peat-moss 1 to 1½ inches thick is plenty around woody plants; and if you are using buckwheat hulls, even less will do. Most of the long-stemmed annuals, hardy perennials and summer-flowering bulbs need no more than an inch-thick layer of mulch. However, tomatoes and other thirsty vegetables need a mulch four to six inches thick. Here, you must bear in mind that thick layers of grass clippings and freshly-cut weeds will get warm and start fermenting within a week or two. If you must use these materials, I would therefore advise you to add them gradually in thin layers throughout the season, rather than pile them up all at once in a thick layer around the plants.

USE WATER SPARINGLY

Amateur gardeners must make sure to get the maximum possible value out of a scanty water-supply. First of all, do your watering at night, when there is no sun or wind to cause any waste of water by evaporation. To avoid watering the foliage of rose bushes, phlox, delphiniums, or chrysanthemums — (thus avoiding the risk of causing diseases in these plants) — use perforated plastic hose for watering, and make sure the perforations are turned down towards the ground, so that the water will not touch the leaves. Alternatively, you can use canvas irrigators. These are made of porous cloth which allows the water to trickle out slowly and uniformly onto the surface of the soil.

If the soil is so dry that the water stays on the surface or just trickles away, instead of sinking in, I advise you to drill some holes into it about three feet deep, using an auger — the object being to get the water soaking deep down into the soil.

The specialists at the Plant Research Institute at Ottawa have suggested that watering should be carried out in the following order:

a) Hedges of thuya — (commonly described as 'cedar hedges');
b) Trees with persistent leaves, and plants which form the "backbone" of the garden;
c) Tomatoes;
d) Dahlias;
e) Deciduous shrubs;
f) Perennial plants and vegetables;
g) Annual plants and lawns.

When can one stop watering? According to these experts, you should water until the cool weather at the end of September. Plants with persistent leaves should continue to receive water until the start of the hard frosts, towards the end of November.

BANKING-UP YOUR PLANTS

Banking-up ornamental plants is almost always harmful. During dry periods, this practice can be fatal to plants if it pushes the small supply of available water away from the plants themselves. What you should do is the exact opposite — dig little basins or trenchs round the plants. This will help channel all the available water down to the roots.

WATER-SUPPLY — A PROBLEM FOR EVERYONE

Water is becoming more and more precious in our modern urban and suburban areas. As populations grow ever larger, pollution of our lakes and rivers is continually on the increase. Thus, the water-supply problem has become a matter of serious concern to every garden-lover. It is of the utmost importance that both individually and collectively we do everything we can to support the efforts being made to conserve and improve our existing water-resources.

This is a matter of civic duty, of common-sense — and perhaps even of our survival.

Watering The Garden
In July And August

Around mid-July it often happens that many gardeners find themselves short of water. Among all the ornamental plants, only the petunia seems unaffected by the situation. Despite the dry conditions, it is possible to avoid damage to your plants and keep your garden in good shape, provided that you take the necessary care and carry out the necessary horticultural measures. You need only visit one of the large public gardens, such as the Botanical Garden of any large city or the Plant Research Institute at Ottawa. Alternatively, you may know an amateur gardener who always manages to keep his garden green. Ask him how he does it. You will soon see that both perennials and annuals can be made to grow just as strongly in July as in June.

ORGANIC MATTER FIRST

Of course, adequate watering and the use of an appropriate fertilizer have contributed to the successful outcome. But these essential precautions would not have been of too much use if the soil had not been given a good supply of humus in the form of organic matter. This humus retains moisture, picks up the nutritive elements from the soil and prevents leaching of the soil.

In my opinion the cheapest source of organic material, the most easily available, and one which can be kept going on a permanent, regular basis is a compost heap on your own land. This should be started early in the fall, around the beginning of September. As your basic material, you may use dead leaves, peat-moss or vegetable scraps, and the addition of a complete chemical fertilizer will speed up the decomposition process. A compost heap is an economical, practical and effective method of producing the means to make a considerable improvement in the quality of your garden soil.

DRYNESS

However, you must not think that just because your soil is rich in humus your plants can do without water when the dry periods of July and August come along. Quite the contrary — watering is just as necessary as ever. But that is not all. What is important is to know when and what to water. Obviously, if you have a dry period that lasts two weeks without a good long heavy shower of rain, then most of your plants are bound to feel the lack of water.

Furthermore, you should understand that for plants, the soil is nothing but a sponge — a reservoir from which they can draw water in which the minerals necessary for their growth have already been dissolved. The presence of these minerals explains how it is that one can described a plant that dies from lack of water as having died of "hunger", not of "thirst".

To understand how essential it is to provide your plants with water, all you need do is recall what an important part water plays in their physical make-up. Lawns are 75 - 80% water; fresh vegetables, 90%; fruit and lettuce, 95%.

How much water does a growing plant require? As a general rule, flowering plants and vegetables need an inch of water each week — which is approximately two pints of water per square foot of garden.

Questions about watering and irrigation cannot really be answered without a good look at the soil. The texture of the soil will tell you exactly how to go about providing the right quantity of water — neither too little nor too much. Thus, soils that are sandy, gravelly, light or poor in vegetable matter will retain very little water — they act more or less like sieves. For them, short and frequent waterings are indicated. On the other hand, if you have a "heavy" soil to deal with — clay or loam — then you must remember that this type of soil is almost impervious to water. Such a soil needs watering slowly, for a fairly long time, but you must regulate the flow so that pools of water do not form, for this would be harmful to your plants.

PLANNING YOUR WATERING PROGRAMME

In dry periods, the first thing you must do is to decide which plants will benefit most from being watered. Then draw up a regular programme and stick to it. Begin by watering your trees and shrubs which form the "backbone" of your garden. Besides their aesthetic value, these are often very costly and difficult to replace. Break up the soil around each woody plant, then lower the soil level around the trunk by scraping earth away from the trunk for some distance until you have formed a raised circular rampart around the plant. Fill in the resulting saucer-shaped depression with mulch — (e.g., peat-moss), then pour water into it until you have produced a sort of swamp. This water will then trickle slowly down to the roots of the plant.

Some amateur gardeners use a root-irrigator. This instrument delivers water directly to the roots of trees and shrubs, thus supplying these plants with the moisture they require. Simply connect the irrigator to the garden hose and push the metal spike down into the ground. It can also be used with liquid fertilizer, which is then delivered directly to the roots.

Three final points: Avoid watering under a hot sun if at all possible. The foliage of conifers may be watered lightly — but only in the shade. About 20 minutes in the same spot constitutes an average watering.

WATERING DEVICES

The finest lawns are the ones that get the most regular and the longest waterings. But you must choose the proper spraying device to get the full benefit from your watering.

There are a whole range of apparatus for delivering water uniformly over an area. First, the traditional rotating device which throws water out in a circle from two revolving nozzles mounted on a tripod base. These are always very popular. The new models have double jets which can be adjusted to give different watering patterns, as required.

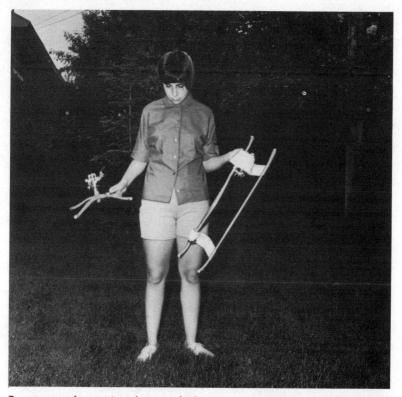

Two types of watering device which are very popular with amateur gardeners. On the left of the picture is a pulsing spray, which can be adjusted to cover either a small area or a wide circle. On the right is an oscillating spray, a versatile piece of apparatus which will solve most of your lawn-watering problems.

Next, the pulsing sprays, which also rotate, but in a jerky fashion. They are very adaptable, and can be set to cover just a small area, or a circle thirty feet in diameter.

Oscillating sprays are the latest type. They are easy to use, and produce many diffrent effects. Some models are equipped with a regulator which can be set to shut the water off automatically and thus prevent any waste. This feature is particularly useful in dry periods when the water-supply is at its lowest.

CHAPTER 10

GROWING PLANTS IN CONTAINERS

A FLEXIBLE FORM OF GARDENING

Growing plants in containers out of doors is becoming more and more popular nowadays. It is a very flexible form of gardening, and can be used with all sorts of different plants. It also allows the amateur gardener to try many different experiments with his plants. For example, he can quite easily grow indoor plants outside, anywhere on his property — in a flowerbed, say, or on the patio; or he can do just the opposite — take plants from out of doors and grow them inside the house.

The practice of this particular form of ornamental horticulture allows one to have plants which could not be grown in any other fashion. It is also an excellent way to experiment with the growing of any one particular plant, or with a whole group of them.

MANY ADVANTAGES

One of the advantages of growing plants in containers is that it is relatively easy to take care of a potted plant in the garden. You have only to decide on a location — sheltered from the wind, of course; but in the shade? or in the sun? After that, it just a matter of watering and fertilizing. If you have to move it away for some reason or other, its removal does not leave a gap in a flowerbed, or elsewhere on the property.

Growing plants in containers has many other advantages. It is the one sure way to highlight certain plants, and get the best out of them more easily. It is also the most suitable method of ensuring that throughout the season you have the full value of whatever flower is looking most beautiful at that particular moment.

A WIDE CHOICE

Over the past few years the use of flowerboxes has become fairly widespread in Canada. In the course of the last decade, several different types of planter have come into fashion — hanging baskets, tubs and so on. The main reason for this is, of course, the growing popularity of patios. These containers lend themselves very readily to decorative arrangements and landscaping schemes to beautify the garden. The choice of container depends on where you want to grow your plant or plants, and on the special requirements, if any, of those plants. A good container must be able to stand up to waterings, and to the periods of dryness between waterings. The conditions of dampness and dryness will often cause a container to not. A good container must also be able to retain moisture long enough to satisfy the water requirements of the plant or plants, while at the same time allowing surplus water to drain away. Small chocks under wooden containers, and a tripod or a stand for clay pots, will facilitate drainage and increase the circulation of air. This, in turn, will help to prevent mildew developing in certain kinds of wood.

FOR ALL TASTES

The various types of container are fairly easily obtained from any gardening centre or nursery. Even some department stores carry a stock. You will find a whole range of them of every conceivable shape and size. Prices vary according to the different types, which range from earthenware planters to white pine flowerboxes to fine ceramic pots.

It is interesting to see how the use of asbestos-cement tubs, for example, has grown in the most remarkable way — especially since 1965. This is doubtless due to the fact that they last well, and always retain their original good looks.

But there is no denying that the good old-fashioned tub-shaped planters, in red pine or in cedar, are still one of the most popular types of all. You can make good use of them anywhere. They are used to decorate patios and their surroundings, both on private properties and in commercial or industrial buildings. Most of the large municipalities in Canada use them — and very successfully, too — to improve the appearance of their municipal buildings, their parks and their main roads.

Although a wide choice of planters is available on the open market, some people — amateur handymen in particular — prefer to make their own. The easiest type to make, and also the most popular, is without any doubt the ordinary rectangular flowerbox made of **pine** or **cedar.** But whatever sort you choose, whether you buy it or make it yourself, the container must above all be suitable for the kind of plants you will be planting in it.

SOME FACTORS FOR SUCCESS

Among the factors leading to success in your attempts to grow flowers in containers, the most important are: the soil, watering, drainage and fertilizing.

The first thing plants need, if they are to grow in a restricted area such as a planter, is a porous soil rich in nutritive elements, and one which drains easily.

Plants grown in containers need more water than those grown in, say, a flowerbed. In addition, the water must not be allowed to stand and grow stagnant — hence the need for a porous soil that drains easily.

These plants need a regular and plentiful supply of nutritive elements during the growth-season. The frequent waterings needed must inevitably result in some leaching-out of these nutritive elements. One excellent way of ensuring that your plants receive the fertilizing elements they need is to give them a dose of soluble fertilizer, formula 20-20-20, every two weeks throughout the summer. This particular fertilizer is completely soluble and fertilizes the plants through their roots and their foliage.

THE IMPORTANCE OF LOCATION

The location of containers is of prime importance, since plants grown in this way are exposed to every change in temperature, against which the walls of the container offer scant protection. Thus these plants are more likely to be affected by extremes of temperature than are those grown in the garden in the normal way.

LESS WORK

It is true that most plants grown in containers need watering and fertilizing more frequently. Nevertheless, this particular method can save the amateur gardener a considerable amount of time.

Among their other advantages, planters allow the gardeners to produce flowers earlier in the season — almost immediately after the ground thaws in the spring, when the ground is still too wet to work outside.

Another feature of planters is that you can cut down the time and energy spent on watering quite considerably, simply by gathering the containers together in one place.

Flowerboxes

Pliny the Elder, the Roman historian of the 1st. Century B.C., remarks somewhere in his writings that "these imitations of the window-gardens of Rome reflect the general trend of activity throughout the nation". This is very probably the first reference to flowerboxes in recorded history. Even at that time, the citizens of Rome felt the need to remind themselves of the beauty and the charm of their countryside by using plants to adorn the exteriors of their houses. Today, Europeans still make use of flowerboxes in great numbers, which never fail to add to the picturesque charm of the public places in their towns, villages and hamlets. This is always a source of happy inspiration to the North American tourist.

Following the example of the Europeans, we Canadians are beginning to show considerable interest in flowerboxes, which are such a handsome form of decoration for the outside of our homes and our properties, and are also an excellent means of expressing our sense of civic pride. One of the most attractive aspects of this method of growing ornamental plants is that it offers us the opportunity to contribute to the beautification of the town in which we live.

THE HARMONY OF COLOURS

The aesthetic value of a flowerbox, and the contribution it makes to the external beauty of a home, do not depend solely on your choice of plants. Even more important is the colour of those plants, which must harmonize with the colour of the house itself. Actually, this is not really very difficult to achieve — all you need do is put together an assortment of flowers or foliage from different varieties of one chosen species — though you can, or course, use several different species if you prefer. Either way enables you to create very pleasing colour effects.

The best time to choose your plants is at the beginning of spring, for the gardening centres and the nurseries and seed catalogues are all full of plants at that time.

SOME FACTORS LEADING TO SUCCESS

Although the choice of suitable plants to ensure colour harmony calls for a certain aesthetic sense, there are other basic requirements which are also essential for success in this area of horticulture. The type of planter used, its maintenance and the soil mix with which you fill it — these are factors which must not be overlooked.

As a general rule, wooden flowerboxes are the most satisfactory, provided that you use a suitable wood, and that the box is made with care.

Red pine and cypress are better than all other kinds of wood, because they don't rot easily, and will last for several years. Cedar is also very good, and white pine is quite satisfactory, as well. It is important to use planks of the right thickness: $7/8$ - $1\frac{1}{4}$ inches is the usual. The width of the box should be 9 - 10 inches, and the depth about 8 inches. The length will depend on where the box is to go. One other point to remember: it is better to use screws rather than nails and don't forget to reinforce the corners of the box with angle-iron brackets.

Metal boxes are not really satisfactory — especially those made from thin sheet steel. This material is an excellent conductor of heat, so that if boxes of this type are put in a sunny location the soil warms up to such a degree that the plants can't grow normally. The soil dries out very rapidly, and watering becomes a problem.

DRAINING FLOWERBOXES

It is absolutely necessary to allow water to drain out of a flowerbox properly. To make sure this happens in a wooden box, drill holes ½ an inch in diameter every 6 inches along the bottom. These holes should be covered with a 2-inch layer of coarse gravel (from ½ to ¾ inch in diameter), or with shards of broken earthenware pots, to prevent the possibility of the soil eventually blocking up the drainage holes. The layer of gravel or broken shards not only allows any surplus water to circulate freely, but also retains some of this water, which the roots will need. Above this layer, you should place a little straw, or peat-moss, or really damp sphagnum moss; or you could use some half-rotted leaves. Soak a piece of burlap in water and spread it over the top to keep the soil from getting mixed into the layer of drainage material.

A SUITABLE SOIL

Even the best plants and the most handsome box are not enough to make a successful flowerbox. You will have no success at all unless you have a suitable soil.

Because of the restricted space available to the plants, the soil needs to be particularly rich in nutritive elements. The best choice is a good friable garden soil, rich in organic matter. Never use a heavy, clayey soil in flowerboxes. A clayey soil will become too packed, and during heavy rainfalls the water can't drain away properly and the plants are therefore deprived of oxygen because the soil is too waterlogged to let them "breathe".

To make a clayey soil a bit lighter, work in a little sand and peat-moss. This makes the texture of the soil a bit less dense, and it won't have such a tendency to pack together.

A good mixture consists of one part garden soil, one part peat moss, and one part coarse sand (building sand, for making mortar). However, if the soil already has some sand in it, change the mix to two parts of soil to one of peat-moss and one of sand.

You should note that tuberous begonias and fuchsias have certain special requirements — an acid humus, for example.

NECESSARY CARE

Plants grown in flowerboxes need little attention — simply fertilizing, weeding, the removal of dead flowers to make room for fresh blooms and watering. Watering is the most important factor leading to success with plants in flowerboxes. The first watering takes place immediately after you have done your planting. Thereafter, throughout the growth season, water them every time the sun begins to dry them out — but make sure not to saturate them. Remember, too, that you should never water under a hot sun. The best time to water is in the evening, unless the nights are beginning to get too cold.

A mulch of damp peat-moss is also strongly recommended. This stops excessive evaporation. Another measure that will help keep the plants in good shape is to water the foliage several times a week, using a mist-spray.

HOW TO FERTILIZE

The addition of nutritive matter is absolutely indispensable. To make sure your plants get the elements they need, add a commercial fertilizer for flowering plants at the time you plant them. Suggested formulas are 6-9-6 or 5-10-15, and you should use a tablespoonful per square foot of the surface area of the box.

Every two weeks during the summer, apply a soluble fertilizer in liquid form. Use formula 20-20-20. A soil that has been properly enriched like this will give you a plentiful crop of healthy plants that will flower right through the season.

PLANTING

When the container is ready, with the drainage material properly in place (the shards or gravel, sphagnum moss, etc.), the next step is to fill your flowerbox to within two inches of the top with the proper soil mix. Then comes the planting — and here, of course, you must take into account the size of the flowerbox. Ordinarily, plants are spaced about 8 inches apart — though sometimes this distance is reduced to 6 inches. For example, plants which tend to spread out a bit, such as petunias and geraniums, need a minimum spacing of 8 inches. On the other hand, lobelias and white alyssum need only 6 inches between plants.

Across the width of the flowerbox, you could plant three rows of plants in a box 10 inches wide. But if you have more than one row you must think about the height of the plants.

The tallest ones (12 - 15 inches high) must go at the back, the middle row could be composed of plants 8 - 12 inches high, while the drooping or trailing plants go in the front — some of the cascading petunias known as "balcony petunias", perhaps, or the creeping lobelias, which will help to hide the front of the flowerbox.

Of course you must plan an arrangement of flowers and plants in your flowerboxes which will harmonize with the colour of your house. If your house has a plain white exterior, the perfect flowers to make it stand out nicely are ageratum and lobelia, with their bright blue flowers; or you could use the yellow-orange flowers of dwarf French marigold set off by white alyssum in the foreground.

Red brick walls are admittedly something of a problem. In fact, there are not very many colours that blend in well with them. You will probably get the best results from white flowers, or those with pastel shades, or from plants with a good thick growth of foliage.

USE THE PLANT CATALOGUES

In order to produce the sort of floral effect we have been discussing, you must choose your flowers very carefully. Before you visit the nursery or the gardening supply shop, take a look through your plant catalogues. These will give you full details of the colours and heights of the various annuals, and thus help you to pick out a selection that you know will go well together.

When arranging plants in a flowerbox, you must take their height into consideration. Naturally, you should put the tallest ones at the back, the medium-tall ones in the middle and the drooping or trailing plants in the front — plants such as "waterfall" petunias or creeping lobelias, which will help to camouflage the front face of the flowerbox.

MARIGOLDS

AGERATUM

Here are some groupings suggested by the experts at the Plant Research institue: at the rear, as the "backstop" of the group, some salmon-pink geraniums; in the middle, some silvery-grey lavender-cotton (Santolina chamae-cyparissus); and in the front, some drooping plants — deep blue balcony petunias, say. Another pleasing grouping would be to have white geraniums at the back, scarlet annual phlox in the middle and the same deep blue balcony petunias in the front.

Another very interesting mixture (again, from back to front) would be orange French marigolds, blue ageratum, large periwinkle (**'Variegata'** variety) and blue lobelia. Yet another fine colour-combination would be produced by **'Blue Magic'** or **'Capri'** petunias, **'Harmony'** French marigolds, blue balcony petunias.

There is one precaution which you should take immediately after putting the plants in the flowerbox — and that is to cover the surface of the soil with peat-moss to a depth of about ½ an inch. This thin layer will prevent the sun from overheating the soil while the plants are still too small for their foliage to provide any shade for the box, the avoiding unnecessary evaporation of water.

SELECTION

For early flowering, I would recommend pansies, violets, English daisies (Bellis perennis 'Montrosa'), golden-tuft (Aurinia saxatilis 'Compacta'), and wild blue phlox (Phlox divaricata), as well as spring-flowering bulbs such as Spanish squill (Scilla hispanica), grape hyacinth, narcissis, jonquil and the "botanical" tulips.

178

SINGLE PETUNIAS   COLEUS

Follow these spring plants with petunias, geranium, begonia, fuchsia and other summer-flowering annuals. Later, a few pots of meadow saffron and some of the other autumn crocuses will add interest and a touch of colour. Finish the season off with chrysanthemums, which will bloom in October.

Incidentally, amateur gardeners who have cold frames or a greenhouse can plant a succession of different flowers all through the summer, and thus keep their window-boxes looking colourful and attractive at very little cost.

PLANTS FOR SHADY LOCATIONS

There are some plants which are very suitable for flowerboxes in partially-shaded locations, or on the north side of the house. Patience plants, those superb perennials which can be used as annuals for the purpose of decorating window-boxes, are now available in various colours — (pink, lavender, mauve and purple), and they flower abundantly over several months. Hybrid begonias also produce a plentiful crop of flowers. They have fibrous roots and are very strong and hardy plants. Multiflora begonias, with tuberous roots, are remarkable for the beauty of their foliage and the splendour of their flowers and are excellent plants for semi-shaded locations. They will remain in flower until the frosts. Nor should you overlook the creeping plants and the vines. Some of the more prominent among them are the large periwinkle (Vinca major variegata), the magnificent creeping geranium and the many varieties of ivy.

Certain new dwarf cultivars of balsam do very well in window boxes, giving flowers in abundance. You could also try some nasturtiums. Some plants are chosen primarily for their foliage; coleus, for example, or the deep purple perilla (Perilla frutescens crispa), with its crisp crinkled foliage that reminds one of the background of some gaily-coloured carpet.

PLANTS FOR SUNNY LOCATIONS

For boxes located on the sunny side of the house, I would recommend succulent plants such as cactus, aloe, creeping ceropigia and little pickles (Othonna crassifolia) — but do not forget the different varieties of geranium and ageratum, the various species of petunia (particularly the new hybrids which give a beautiful crop of flowers all season long), and lantana, which stands up to the heat very well. Incidentally, lantana is available in several colours, including pink, lavender, gold, yellow and red.

Other plants for your flowerbox that do well in the sun are dwarf annual phlox, lobelia and alyssum.

Some amateur gardeners finish off their flowerboxes rather neatly with a light treillis at each end of the box, up which they train plants such as cupand-saucer vine (Cobaea scandens), convolvulus and clockvine (Thunbergia alata).

A MINIATURE KITCHEN GARDEN

Not only do flowering plants, or those with decorative foliage, grow well in flowerbxes, but vegetables and herbs may also be grown success-fully. Anyone who likes fresh vegetables, but does not have a kitchen garden, can make good use of a flowerbox to grow tomatoes, dwarf string beans, chives, Swiss chard, parsley and kidney beans.

Growing Bulbs
In Pots

Flowering bulbs grown in containers — pots, tubs, bowls, boxes, etc. and presenting a magnificent display of colour during the earliest spring days soon make you forget the dull, dreary days of winter.

To make sure of this happy result, you must plant your bulbs in their containers in the autumn, before the frosts arrive. The most popular containers — and also the most practical — are earthenware pots 8 - 12 inches in diameter. They can hold up to a dozen tulips, or about six hyacinths or jonquils.

SUITABLE SOIL

Spring-flowering bulbs will grow in most kinds of soil. Any good mould is fine for them, provided that it is properly drained. In the case of a heavy, clayey soil, the texture must be improved by the addition of coarse sand, garden moss or rotted leaves.

POTTING

When potting plants or bulbs, the first thing you must do is arrange proper drainage for the pot. Put some broken earthenware shards or some gravel over the drainage hole in the bottom of the pot. As with the window boxes, this will make it easier for any excess water to run off, and will avoid the possibility of the hole becoming blocked by soil. Then fill the pot three quarters full.

Next push the bulbs firmly down into the soil. In the case of tulips, be careful to set the bulbs pointing towards the wall of the pot. Press the soil around and between the bulgs until only the tips are left showing above the surface.

Water each pot thoroughly several times until the outside of the pot begins to sweat.

A TRENCH FOR THE POTS

Dig a trench in the garden, at the back of a flowerbed, say, or in some well-drained spot well away from all garden traffic, and bury your pots in it.

I would advise you to spread a layer of leaves below your pots, and a similar layer above. This precaution will prevent the soil from clinging too tightly to the pots and make it much easier to remove them in the spring. You should also drive in stakes to mark the positions of pots. If you think the squirrels may dig down and damage your bulbs, put some chicken-wire down over the pots and then cover it with a little earth to hold it in place.

AFTER THE SPRING THAW

To hasten flowering in the spring, take your pots out of the trench after the soil has thawed out and put them somewhere sheltered from the prevailing wind, but open to the south or to the west. You can leave the bulbs to flower in their pots — they will flower more or less at the same time as bulbs planted in the open soil. It is extremely important not to neglect regular and thorough watering.

As soon as the shoots start breaking through, put the pots into your flowerboxes or other large containers. Or, set them out on a balcony overlooking a footpath, or on the patio.

FOR THOSE WHO DO NOT HAVE A GARDEN

Some people must live in lodgings, or are otherwise deprived of the privilege of having a bit of land they can call their own. If they would like to have some boxes of spring flowers on their balcony, or some window-boxes, they can always ask a friend or a relative to keep their pots

Containers filled with spring-flowering bulbs and placed at key spots on your property will produce a magnificent colour effect to mark the start of the growing-season. These containers are easy to move about, and can thus be used to provide all sorts of different floral arrangements.

(Photo: Malak)

buried for them during the winter. Another way of getting round this problem is to buy spring flowers, already potted, from a nursery in the spring.

It is, of course, perfectly possible to remove the bulbs from their pots and transplant them into a flowerbox, a tub, or any other sort of planter. But it is much better to put the bulbs wherever you want them without removing them from the pots.

Bulb-growing experts insist on the necessity of always buying top-quality bulbs if you are to grow them in pots. They will flower more readily, and will give larger flowers.

One last point; if the bulbs you have chosen for growing in pots give flowers that are suitable for laying out in concentrated blocks, then you should plant them as close as possible to each other — without touching, of course. This enables you to take full advantage of them later on, should you wish to incorporate them into a block.

Hanging Baskets

Nearly everyone has dreamed at some time or another of improving the look of his garage, or his balcony, or the light-standards in his garden, or some covered passage-way, by using hanging baskets with long garlands of flowers cascading over the edges.

This is an easy dream to make come true — for there are very many flowers that are suitable for this sort of arrangement, whether it is to be in the sun or in the shade. There are three factors that determine the success of this sort of floral decoration: properly-constructed baskets, a wise choice of plants, and the appropriate care for these plants.

A METAL LATTICE-WORK

The first thing to consider is the basket itself. You can find this type of container easily enough at any nursery or garden supply store. Almost all of them stock a complete range of baskets of all shapes and sizes, in both wire mesh and moulded plastic. Or you could make your own easily enough, using a piece of metal trellis or some 12-gauge wire. It important to put something solid at the bottom of a basket, so as to stop the water draining away. Also, the inside of the basket must be lined, to stop the soil escaping. Both these purposes can be served by lining the basket with a sheet of polyethylene.

The best way is to take some thick sphagnum moss and mould it into the shape of a bird's nest, to fit the bottom of your basket. If you are using polyethylene to conserve moisture and prevent leakage, build it right inside the walls of the moss "bird's nest".

Now you must prepare the soil. The best mix would be two parts of

PLANTING

Planting can be carried out as soon as the outside temperature is warm enough. Once you have lined the bottom of your basket with a "bird's nest" of spaghum moss plus polyethylene, and filled it with earth, you can arrange your chosen plants on this bed so that the tops of the plants hang down over the sides of the basket. Then fill the basket up with more earth, to within an inch of the top.

Immediately after planting, put the basket in the cellar or some other shady spot, to give the plants a chance to "take" properly.

WATERING AND FERTILIZING

Watering is important in the summer especially since the soil in a basket dries out very rapidly. If the basket is located in a position where dripping would be distracting, don't water it until the end of the day.

Every two or three weeks, give it a dose of 20-20-20 fertilizer in solution — 2 teaspoonfuls or fertilizer per gallon of water.

PLANTS FOR THE SHADE

There are many plants which do well in shady locations. Strawberry saxifrage, Wandering Jew (Tradescantia fluminensis), ruins of Rome (Cymbalaria), achimenes, philodendron, hanging tuberous begonia, columnea, garden balsam, climbing cobaea, Chilean gloryflower (Eccremocarpus scaber), clockvine (Thunbergia alata), climbing ivy, moneywort and ivy-leaved geranium (Pelargonium peltatum) are all excellent species for shady areas.

PLANTS FOR THE SUN

Most of the trailling plants do very well in the sun. Of special mention are Italian bellflower (Campanula isophylla), the "Sapphire" variety of edging lobelia, variegated ground-ivy (Nepeta hederacea variegata), balcony petunias (both the "avalanche" and the "cascading" types), nasturtium, lantana, the "Bijou" variety of dwarf sweet pea, the "Royal Ensign" variety of morning glory, German ivy (Senecio mikanioides), trailing sanvitalia, Canary nasturtium (Tropaeolum peregrinium), and succulent trailing plants such as little pickles (Othonna crassifolia) and burro's tail or Morgan's stonecrop (Sedum morganianum). Some of these plants may be brought indoors for the winter if you want to keep them to use again next year.

The quickest growers among the above are nasturtium, dwarf sweet pea, morning glory, gloryflower and sanvitalia. You can sow them directly into the basket at the beginning of May.

184

Columnea is an excellent plant to grow in a hanging basket set in a shady spot.

good garden soil to one of sand and one of peat-moss. For each bushel of this mixture, work in a soupspoonful of a commercial fertilizer such as 6-9-6.

Hanging baskets are not necessarily reserved solely for growing trailing plants. Almost any sort of plant may be grown successfuly in hanging baskets

If you do something different each year, and change from one type of plant to another, growing flowers in baskets can become a really interesting hobby.

Tulips are "democratic" flowers. They bring pleasure to everybody, from the flower-girl to the princess in her palace. They are excellent for planting in large masses, to welcome the spring in a blaze of beauty.   (Photo: Malak)

CHAPTER 11

FLOWERING BULBS
Summer-Flowering
Tender Bulbs

HOW TO GROW THEM

In February and March, amateur gardeners go about enthusiasticly from nursery to nursery, and spend many happy hours pouring over seed catalogues planning and choosing their summer-flowering and autumn-flowering bulbs — (the word is used here to include bulbs proper, corms, tubers and rhizomes).

When we talk about growing "tender" bulbs, we mean those kinds of bulb which all come into flower during the summer or the early autumn, and are then removed from the ground at the end of autumn and put into shelter. This category includes **tuberous begonias, dahlias, gladioli, caladiums, cannas, acidantheras, achimenes, lily-of-the-Nile** (Agapanthus africanus), the **'De Caen'** and **'St Brigid'** varieties of **poppy anemone, summer hyacinth** (Galtonia candicans), **Inca lily** (Alstoemeria pelegrina), **cypella herbertii, eucomis, crinum, amaryllis, calla lilies** (Zantedeschia species), **montbretia** (Crocosmia crocosmaeflora), **glory-lilies** (Gloriosa species), **rosette oxalis, ranunculus, Mexican shell-flower** (Tigridia), **tuberoses** (Polianthes), and **zephyr flowers** (Zephyranthes species).

Although the **lily** species are summer-flowering bulbs — (and are in fact the only ones that can withstand the rigours of the Canadian winter without having to be lifted), we will not deal with them here, since most of them are planted during the autumn.

There is nothing to equal flowering bulbs for imparting lovely rich colours to the garden from early in spring till late in autumn. There are so many different types and varieties of plants that may be grown from bulbs that it is difficult to describe them all. There are, however, several books available on the subject, so I will not elaborate here. As mentioned earlier, there are three other categories of bulbs — corms, tubers and rhizomes — which are all planted and cared for in the same manner.

The requirements for growing flowering bulbs are dealt with in the following paragraphs.

SOIL

As a general rule, bulbs grow well in most garden soils, provided that they are well-drained. It does not make much difference whether the soil is light and sandy, or heavy and clayey. However, as with most plants, bulbs prefer a good garden loam, either neutral, or slightly alkaline. However, if the soil is poor, you should enrich it with plenty of humus underneath the bulbs.

DRAINAGE

Bulbs do well if their roots receive plenty of moisture. All the same, it must be clearly understood that it is quite useless to try to grow this type of plant in a watery morass. So, if your land is badly drained, the first thing you must do is put that right. If you have a reasonably well-drained clayey soil, the experts advise spreading a layer of sand at the bottom of your furrows before planting the bulbs.

A fine specimen of regal lily. Lily bulbs should be planted in September or October, before the first frosts of winter.

FERTILIZING

The bulb-growing experts all agree that it is very difficult to decide which are the best fertilizers for bulbs.

In soils which are reasonably well provided with nitrogen, phosphorus and potassium, most of the hardy spring-flowering bulbs — **tulips, crocuses, hyacinths, snowdrops,** etc. — do not respond to treatment with a chemical fertilizer. This is readily understandable, since the dormant bulbs have already received an adequate supply of nutritive elements for the future plants.

Nevertheless, experiments in fertilizing carried out on hardy bulbs at the Central Experimental Farm at Ottawa seemed to show that if a fertilizer rich in phosphorus and potassium is introduced into the ground immediately before planting — three pounds of 6-9-6, say, or 5-10-15, per 100 square feet — it will contribute to the formation of better bulbs the following year.

The experiments also showed that this autumn fertilizing could be advantageously completed by using one pound of ammonium sulphate per 100 square feet as a top-dressing early in the following spring.

WATERING

Watering before and during flowering is a great help to all plants, of course. Bulbs should be watered regularly in the same manner. Incidentally, you should note that hardy bulbs — **tulip, narcissus, squill, chionodoxa,** etc — usually do better in regions that have a long, cool spring.

LIGHT

Most bulbs prefer full daylight, provided they get plenty of water. However, full daylight is not necessary right through the season, and intermittent shade is certainly not harmful to the young plants.

INSECTS AND DISEASES

Like other plants, bulbs are subject to attacks by insects, fungal diseases and viruses. It is thus essential to carry out adequate defense measures.

On this subject, you should remember that it is almost impossible to grow **gladioli** without dusting them with an anti-thrips insecticide: or **tuberous begonias** without dusting them with a fungicide against mildew.

For successful bulb-growing, the following general precautions are essential:

a) cleanliness of the bulbs themselves

b) disinfecting of the boxes, containers, pots, etc., with a fungicide that is harmless to plants, such as Ceresan

c) bulbs that have been kept in a cellar during the winter must be sprinkled with an insecticide combined with a fungicide

d) In fact, for best results, all plants should be dusted with a combined insecticide-fungicide.

Gladioli

Tender bulbs which flower during the summer or autumn should be planted the moment the danger of frost is past — i.e., between 15 May and 1 June, when the ground is no longer frozen and the soil can be worked easily.

Even though you can plant these summer-flowering bulbs straigt in the open, after the frosts, you should also know that most of them can be put to sprout in the house or in a hotbed. This "pre-growth" allows you to enjoy a much earlier flowering than if the bulbs are simply planted straight in the ground without being allowed to sprout beforehand.

The **gladiolus** takes pride of place among summer-flowering bulbs. Few flowers can offer such a wide range of colour and at the same time lend themselves so well to the creation of magnificent bouquets and floral arrangements.

HIGH-QUALITY CORMS

The first, and basic, requirement for success in the growing of gladioli is to buy top-quality corms (bulbs). You must therefore use a trustworthy supplier who markets the different varieties by name and also clearly indicates the size of the bulb.

Gladioli like plenty of sun. However, they grow better if they get a bit of shade towards the middle of the day, and at the end of the afternoon. Avoid planting them in places exposed to the wind. This spoils the beauty of the flower.

WELL-PREPARED SOIL

Gladioli do not require a rich soil, but to get heavily-laden spikes with well-formed flowers you must enrich the soil, either with compost or with an organic fertilizer and peat-moss. The soil should be well loosened first, turned over to a depth of about 10 inches, and improved with a complete fertilizer.

Plant your gladioli as soon as all danger of frost is past, and while the soil is still very dry and may therefore be worked easily. The corms are then put into the ground, 3 to 5 inches deep and 6 inches away from each other. If the soil is slightly sandy, plant them a little deeper.

Gladioli are perhaps the top-ranking summer-flowering bulbs. They should be planted as soon as all danger of frost is past, and the soil has dried out properly after the thaw. The four varieties illustrated above were chosen as the best in 1971 by the 'All-America' selection committee. These prize-winning varieties are 'Cascade', 'Anniversary', 'Orange Chiffon' and 'Little Tiger'.

I would recommend that you leave a large gap between corms if the soil is very rich, or if you want really heavily-laden and well-formed spikes. Planting can be done at any time during the month of June, depending on which way the soil is exposed. Corms for late planting should be kept in a cool place damp enough for them not to dry out before they're planted.

Little offsets which sprouted from the 'mother' corm, and were dug up with it the previous autumn, can be planted in rows quite close to each other, from 1½ to 3 inches deep. They will grow bigger during the summer, and some of them will flower the following year.

Although gladioli can be grown without any particular difficulty, the soil should be loose and free from weeds. The most important time in the plant's development is when the shoot is sprouting and the new offset is forming in the soil.

FERTILIZING

Make sure your gladioli have a surplus of nutritive elements (preferably in liquid form), and enough moisture. This latter requirement can be met by covering the soil with compost which is already decomposing, or with peat-moss. This will also discourage the growth of weeds. It also a good idea to supply high-stemmed varieties with a wooden stake to support them — especially if they are exposed to the wind.

Gladioli corms can be gathered in either after a really sharp frost, or before the onset of frosty weather. The most important thing is to let them have as long a growing-season as possible prior to digging them up in the autumn before the ground freezes. If you have only a few bulbs, you can wait till mid-October before lifting them, but if there are a fair number of them, it is better to start a little earlier.

After the first sharp frost — or better, before — when the foliage has begun turning brown, dig up your gladioli row by row, and pick out the corms carefully. Cut the stems off close to the corms. Spread the corms out to dry, and store them in a well-ventilated place sheltered from the frost.

WATCH OUT FOR THRIPS

Thrips can cause considerable damage to gladiolus flowers, so there are certain precautions you must take when you lift and store your gladioli. Before you begin lifting them, have some boxes, labels and insecticide handy. Each variety should be separated and put into its own labelled box.

As soon as a box is filled, sprinkle the corms with insecticide, to prevent the thrips settling on the corms and laying their eggs on them. Let the corms dry in a warm, well-ventilated place. When the offsets — the new bulbs — have separated from the old ones, the time has come to begin cleaning up. Take each corm out of the box and strip their old covering off them. Remove all the dried-out bits from the old corms — but make sure to leave **some** covering on them.

If you want to increase the number of your corms for next year's planting, keep all the young offsets that were sticking to the old bulbs. Do not forget to dust the corms with an anti-thrips insecticide when you have cleaned them. Put the clean bulbs in boxes stacked one on top of the other, with pieces of wood between them to separate them and allow for ventilation. Alternatively, you can store your corms in paper cones left open at the top, or in boxes provided with little air-holes. For winter storage, choose a spot where the temperature varies between 40 and 50°F.

Dahlias

Dhalias are one of the most frequently-grown flowers of all. They owe their popularity to their dazzling colours, their majestic height and the vast number of their varieties. The smaller kinds are only about ten inches high, but some of the decorative varieties grow four or more feet tall.

Let the bulbs sprout beforehand in a well-lit place, so that they're already showing vigorous shoots when you come to plant them outside — which should not be done before mid-May.

For the very tall-stemmed varieties — which, incidentally, should not be planted too close together — you must build a sort of treillis-work out of wooden stakes which will support them as they grow. Loosen up the ground well, and put a little compost and complete fertilizer in each of the holes you make for the bulbs before planting.

PLANTING AND MULCHING

You should note that a fertilizer too rich in nitrogen will encourage the growth of the foliage at the expense of the flowers. Plant the bulbs at various depths, depending on their size, but make quite sure that the soil covers the bulb properly up to the beginning of the stem. It is absolutely essential that the ground around each plant is always damp enough, and make sure, too, that it is kept loose by working the soil around each plant regularly.

To help conserve moisture and hinder the growth of weeds, cover the soil with mulch or peat-moss.

Tuberous Begonias

Few plants are as popular as **tuberous begonias.** This is undoubtedly due to the fact that few plants give as much pleasure by their diversity of colour, shape and texture. They are easily grown, from tubers stored in the cellar over the winter, and, unlike so many other species, it is not necessary to worry about protecting them against frost.

Growing tuberous begonias is always exciting — not only for the seasoned gardener, who with a little extra care can produce some really marvellous blooms; or for the real connoisseur, who is constantly enthralled by the new types created every year — but also for the amateur with no previous experience.

The great variety of shapes puts one in mind of many other flowers — the **camellia**, the **rose**, the **single dahlia**, the **pink**, and even the **narcissus**. Others have speckled edges, and perhaps even crumpled or wavy petals.

There are also many different types — **hanging begonias** for baskets, single-flowered types ornamented with roughened patches, and multifloral types.

BUYING TUBERS

In January and February you will find a good choice of tubers in the seed catalogues and at the local nurseries.

Plant your tubers at the beginning of March, in boxes containing damp peat-moss, taking good care not to cover them completely. Make sure there is no excess water in the hollows where you place the tubers. Water here could make the stems rot. Keep them at a temperature of 50°F for 5 to 7 days, then at a temperature of 65 to 75°F for two or three weeks. As soon as the first leaves appear, any tubers you plan to put in your flowerbeds should be potted in earthnware pots 4 or 5 inches across, or in 4-inch 'Fertil' pots. Those you plan to grow in pots should go into shallow half-pots 6 to 8 inches across.

A SUITABLE MOULD

The ideal bedding-material for tubers that have started growing is a mould consisting of one part peat-moss to one part sand leaf-mould, or one third peat-moss to two thirds mould — which incidentally is the ideal mix for **African violets** (Saintpaulia). Water moderately, increasing the amount as the plant grows larger. Keep at a temperature of 50 to 60°F. Since light is important, put your containers in a window, where the plants will receive some filtered sunlight. Alternatively, you could well use artificial light from fluorescent tubes. You should note that too much heat and lack of light will result in a tall, fragile plant, which risks being damaged by rain or wind once it has been transplanted to the garden.

TRANSPLANTING

Once the danger of frost is past — say towards the end of May or the beginning of June — plant your begonias in the flowerbed you have prepared for them, or in a flowerstand.

They can be planted in a shady or semi-shady spot. Set them in the ground with the first leaves facing you, otherwise many of the flowers will be facing the wrong way. The collar (the spot where the stem grows out of the tuber) shouldn't be more than one inch deep in the ground. Also set in some stakes, to protect the plants.

DRAINAGE AND THE SOIL

It is important to remember that drainage is the essential factor in the growing of begonias, either in flowerbeds or in flowerstands. The level of the bed should be as high as, or just a little higher than, the

One of the most important factors for success in growing tuberous begonias is to set the tuber head downwards in a box filled with ground peat-moss. The object of the upside-down position is to avoid the rot which is often caused by an accumulation of damp in the flattened or hollow area at the top of the tuber.

surrounding ground. The ideal soil is loose but consistent, and contains sufficient nutritive elements for normal plant-growth. However, you can improve an ordinary garden soil and make it suitable for growing begonias. For example, if you have only heavy clay, or a badly-drained soil, add some leaf-mould, sand and peat-moss or any other organic material — (although in my opinion fresh straw is better than manure).

Tuberous begonias are strongly recommended for planting in shady or semi-shady locations where a diversity of colour, shape and texture is required.

On the other hand, if your soil is sandy you should add leaf-mould, peat-moss or garden compost.

WATERING AND FERTILIZING

Before transplating, wet the soil really deeply. At the bottom of each hole put a soupspoonful of a complete fertilizer for indoor plants, or a similar amount of fish-meal. Cover this fertilizer lightly with soil before putting the bulb into the hole. Incidentally, the soil must not be banked up round the stem, for that would considerably reduce the efficacy of rainfalls or watering. After transplanting, water the flowerbed deeply, without actually drenching the soil. Later on, throughout the season, water whenever the surface of the soil is dry. As the plants grow, you should water them more frequently. At the end of August, gradually cut down ont the watering.

If you want a longer flowering-period, with bigger and more beautiful flowers, water your begonias every two weeks with a soluble fertilizer.

PROTECTION AGAINST INSECTS

Tuberous begonias are not exempt from attack by most of the harmful insects. It is therefore advisable to dust them with a polyvalent pesticide not merely to ward off the ravages of insects, but also to help put a stop to diseases. The major enemy of the begonia is begonia mildew (oidium), which infests it in summer and in autumn. Regular dustings with Karathane is claimed to be the most effective method of defence against this disease.

LARGE FLOWERS

To obtain large flowers on the ordinary upright types of begonia, you should only keep one shoot on each tuber, and remove all the others as soon as they appear.

In varieties with drooping stems that have been grown from tubers, keep all the shoots, but pinch them off when they're about four or five inches long. In this way you will stimulate lateral growth and the production of new shoots. However, you should make sure to pinch off lateral buds before you pot the plant. Remember that during the first year you should not do this to plants with drooping stems that have been grown from seedlings — otherwise they won't have enough time to produce their flowers, and it also interferes with the formation of tubers.

AUTUMN STORAGE

When the leaves have been hit by the first frosts, cut the stems about three inches from the ground and pull the tubers out — leaving as much earth on them as possible. Keep these docked plants at a temperature of 45 to 50°F, just as they came out of the ground, and leave them to dry out completely — (this will take about two months). Then clean the tubers up, removing all the earth and any withered roots.

Store the cleaned tubers at a temperature of 50 to 60°F in completely dry peat-moss, sand, or fermiculite, until it is time to start the cycle all over again — about the beginning of the following March.

Another method consists of pulling the tubers up, cleaning and washing them immediately and then letting them dry for a few days before storing them as described above. For plants grown in pots, you may simply place the pots on their sides and store them in a cool, dry place (50 to 60°F), without watering; and then start again the following March, as previously described.

Growing Peonies

When they are in full bloom, **peonies** dominate the garden with their delicate grace and charm. If the varieties have been well chosen, they give flowers for more than a month. One important advantage is that **peony** plants keep their looks all through the growing-season. Furthermore, in the autumn — even without flowers — several varieties are very decorative by virtue of the colour of their leaves.

PLANTING

The autumn is the time to plant peonies. Nursery-gardeners who specialize in these plants send out tubers during the month of August. In Eastern Canada, planting and transplanting start early in September, and continue until the soil is frozen. It is preferable to get them into the ground as early as possible, in order to let them start growing while the soil is still warm.

Since peony plants are meant to last several years, it is very important to choose the right places to plant them in your garden. It is equally important to provide them with a rich, deep soil and good drainage, and to leave a space of four to five feet between plants. At the same time, you must take into account the possibility of clashes with other plants in five or ten year's time. Will the spot you have chosen be invaded by the riots of neighbouring trees, shrubs, or hedges? Again, will these peony plants find themselves overshadowed by any rapid-growing plants nearby?

Although peonies can stand a bit of shade, they prefer to be in full sunlight during the afternoon. Remember, too, that these plants come in clumps, with large strong roots, and they demand a great deal of nutritive material and moisture from the soil. If they are obliged to compete with other plants, they will become weak, and will not produce any flowers.

A GOOD MOULD

The soil best suited to peonies is a good garden mould, slightly clayey. However, if you prepare a small pile of good earth for each plant, and water frequently, you can grow peonies in sandy soil. Besides, the surface soil in flowerbeds and borders is rarely rich enough and deep enough to keep a clump of peonies in full vigour. Because of this, when you have chosen where you want to plant your next peony root (and make sure it's at least three feet away from the edge of the bed), you should work and fertilize the soil for about two feet all around the plants.

It is better to leave your peonies in the same spot for several years without disturbing them — which is why you must prepare the soil properly before you plant them.

Begin by digging a hole two feet deep. At the bottom put some surface soil, enriched with humus and half a pound of a fertilizer of low nitrogen content. Plant your peony, then fill up the hole with good surface soil. Before you plant, you should water the soil thoroughly, to consolidate it. Set the roots so that the uppermost "eye" is not more than two inches below the surface of the soil. Water each plant thoroughly. Put a mulch around new plants for the first winter.

DIVIDING THE CLUMPS

Clumps which are growing well should not be disturbed unless it is absolutely necessary. If you must move a plant, do not divide it unless it was planted three or more years ago. Do your dividing at the beginning of autumn. Cut off all the foliage carefully, then dig up the cump. Wash off the earth clinging to the roots and let them dry in the shade for a few hours, to make them less fragile.

If you do not take this precaution, you will find it difficult to divide the plant without breaking the roots.

Cut the root into pieces, so that each piece has at least three "eyes" on it, but not more than eight. Prune large roots down to 6-inch size, and preferably 4-inch. If possible, plant the divided roots somewhere where peonies have not been grown before. Quite often, the new plants won't flower the first year, and they may be rather stunted. But after three years, most varieties will give flowers in abundance. Always cut flowers as soon as they begin to fade — but remove as little of the stem as possible. Each spring, sprinkle a handful of nitrogen-poor fertilizer around each plant. Weed regularly, but be careful of the plant roots when you hoe. If the summer is dry, water frequently and thoroughly, to ensure a good crop of flowers the following year.

Never apply fertilizer or put mulch around the plants during the summer.

PLANTS WITHOUT FLOWERS

It sometimes happens that peony plants don't bear any flowers. This can be due to one of several reasons. First of all, the plant may be too young. Peonies rarely bloom during their first year; and several varieties may take even three or four years before they produce flowers. Next, peonies that are moved every year or every two years will not give good results. Failure to bloom may also result when you replant an old plant without dividing it. Incidentally, I believe that failure to bloom is far too often attributed to planting too deeply. Most amateur gardeners, even the beginners, know that peonies should be planted near the surface of the soil. Even if a plant has been set in a bit too deep, it will correct the error in time, by forming new "eyes" at the proper level.

All the same, a plant cannot correct a poor choice of site — perhaps too shady, or too close to hardy plants. Furthermore, peonies cannot take a prolonged excess of water near their roots, nor an over-acid soil. Failure to bloom often results from cutting flowers with too long a stem. Leaves are essential to any plant and the plant suffers from their absence. Since peonies are unable to replace foliage lost during the current year, it is essential to cut your flowers with as short a stem as possible, and never to remove more than a half or two thirds of the flowers on a plant. If growth is feeble due to a lack of nutritive elements, there won't be any flowers either. Use commercial fertilizers poor in nitrogen, such as 4-12-10. If there is too much nitrogen, the plants may be growing quite vigorously — but they will not blossom. Temperature also plays an important role in the flowering of peonies.

ADVERSE FACTORS

A dry spell or a sudden heat-wave can have adverse effects. Hot, sticky weather can hinder buds from developing normally, and flowers from blooming.

There are other factors that can affect flowering besides weather conditions. Of these, mildew is perhaps the least disquieting, since the effects of this fungus are easily identified. Very often, young shoots grow at soil level when they emerge early in spring. Buds and flowers can be damaged at any stage of their development. Gardeners are all too familiar with the little black buds which have stopped growing. Sometimes buds are deformed, and do not open up properly, or the petals of a flower which has bloomed look all blotched and spotted. The foliage may also be infected, but the effects are less obvious to the gardener whose main concern is with his flowers.

THE CONTROL OF MILDEW

The control of mildew begins with cleanliness — i.e., you must remove all infected buds and burn them. In the autumn, before the frosts arrive, trim down the stems of each plant to just below the level of the soil. When the new growth appears in the following spring, spray it with fermate, and repeat two or three times at two-day intervals. Mildew is often spread by ants, which are attracted by the sticky buds of the peonies. It is advisable, therefore, to do away with these insects by scattering chlordane at the base of each plant. However, except for spreading mildew, ants are not really harmful to your peonies.

INSECT PESTS

Thrips can infest both buds and open flowers. Their presence stops the buds from opening, and turns the flower petals brown. Lindane is an excellent insecticide to put an end to these little pests. Sometimes Japanese beetles from the rose bushes will gnaw the petals of your peonies. They can be suppressed with lindane and chlordane.

Sometimes the plants are attacked by tiny little worms called nematodes, which make their way into the smaller roots, where they cause irregular swellings. Plants infested in this way are generally stunted, slow to grow and pale green in colour. However, before blaming nematodes for the sickly appearance of your plants, make sure there is no other cause. If the plants **are** infested with nematodes, get rid of them without delay — and do not plant any more peonies in that location. Sometimes moles will cause havoc with your plants. In this case, you would be well advised to sprinkle your flowerbeds and the neighbouring areas of lawn with chlordane, which will destroy the insects on which the moles are feeding.

Growing Lilies

PLANTING

The months of September and October are the time for planting lilies. Lily bulbs, unlike the bulbs of **tulips** and **hyacinths,** do not enter a dormant state. Although no growth is evident before the spring, the bulb is fully alive in the soil, from which it draws the nutritive elements it needs to get through the winter. The bulbs of **hardy** lilies can be transplanted easily enough if you take the necessary precautions to protect them and ensure their growth. They should not be left exposed to the sun, or allowed to dry, nor should they be roughly handled in the shops and stores — if they are, their vigour will be affected. The best time to plant them is the autumn, as soon as they are available at the nurseries and garden supply stores. I would advise you to prepare the soil beforehand, and to make sure it is well drained.

HOW TO SUCCEED IN GROWING LILIES

There are two essential conditions that must be fulfilled if you want to succeed in growing lilies — a good garden soil, slightly sandy, but rich in humus, and good drainage. If the soil is too heavy, add some sand and some humus — (peat-moss, compost, etc) — and mix it in well. Soils that are too sandy can be improved by adding humus.

The polyethylene or other plastic bags which are used nowadays for the packaging of bulbs allow them to be handled and transported in first-class condition. However, these bags should not remain closed for more than two weeks.

These bulbs need air, and cannot live in a hermetically-sealed bag.

DEPTH OF PLANTING

How deep should you plant your lily bulbs? One simple and effective method consists of planting them twice as deep as their own height. Thus, a bulb two inches high should have four inches of soil above it. However, this method does not apply in the case of Madona lilies, which should not have more than two inches of soil cover.

If you are only planting a few bulbs, dig a hole one foot deep and big enough to take them all. Mix a handful of chemical fertilizer — 6-9-6 or 5-10-15 — into the soil at the bottom of the hole, then add a bed of peat-moss a few inches thick — just enough to bring the bulbs up to the requisite level. Then pack the earth well down on top of them.

Mark the location of each bulb with a weatherproof plastic marker — for lily stems are fragile in the early days of the growing-season, and it is only too easy to damage them when you are cleaning up your flower-beds and borders.

OTHER PRECAUTIONS

On the subject of mulches to protect the bulbs against the cold, I would advise you to spread a layer of granulated peat-moss about two inches thick. You should wet this thoroughly beforehand, to stop it drying out and being carried away by the wind. When it freezes, this peat-moss gives adequate protection to the bulbs while they are in the process of putting down their roots. Lay your peat-moss as soon as the ground is frozen, before the snow covers up the clumps of flowers and the flower-beds and borders.

ATTENTION DURING THE SUMMER

During the summer, it is important to keep your lily plants well watered. One good watering a week, or even two weeks, is preferable to short daily watering. One indispensable precaution, if you want to have fine plants you must provide stakes or some other form of support for those tall plants which may be partially in the shade.

As to the use of fertilizers, the organic kind is essential. Enrich your soil with well-rotted manure if you can get it — though you must be careful not to let it come into contact with the bulbs themselves. Dehydrated chicken-droppings are also very good for the soil. However, no matter how much organic fertilizer you use, do not forget to apply a complete chemical fertilizer such as 5-10-15 Mg (nitrogen, phosphoric acid, potassium and magnesium), both before the flowering-period and immediately after.

The magnesium and the phosphate give volume and colour to the flowers, and help the bulbs to regenerate, so that they put out numerous little bulbs. Many gardeners also apply bone-meal freely to their **lily** clusters, to provide the necessary elements.

A mulch of peat-moss helps to preserve moisture and keep the roots near the base of the stems fresh. It also a good method of keeping weeds down.

INSECTS AND DISEASES

Few insects or diseases attack the lily. For this reason, many amateur gardeners never put any insecticide or fungicides on their plants. Howevere, both the plant louse and the bulb mite need to be kept under control — the first, because it carries the mosaic virus from infected lilies to healthy ones; and the second, because of the extensive damage it can cause to lily bulbs. A solution of malathion eliminates plant lice, mites and other harmful insects.

Two specific diseases affect lilies: mosaic and botrytis. Mosaic, the worst thing that can befall a lily, is caused by a virus. Infected plants look stunted, and their stems and leaves are misshapen and twisted. Botrytis is a serious fungal infection which produces yellowish blotches on the leaves and sometimes on the stems and buds.

GROWING LILIES IN CONTAINERS

Besides the Bengal lily, other varieties of bulb do better when they are planted in containers — big pots, bowls, basins, etc and set on a patio. When winter comes, these containers may be easily moved down to the cellar where the plants can be kept intact. This is a method particularly suited to the **glory lily** (Gloriosa), which is one of the most interesting flowers of all. The glory lily is a climbing plant, which clings by tendrils at the ends of its leaves. Its flowers have wavy petals in delicate tints of red and gold.

At the end of May, dig your pots into the soil, in a part of the garden which receives full sunlight. Take care to water them about once a week during dry periods. Bring the pots back inside for the winter, without removing the plants, and repeat the process the following spring.

PRINCIPAL VARIETIES

During the last two decades in particular, plant breeders have made great strides in the creation of new varieties of lily by means of hybridization. Of the better-known and most frequently-grown species **Japanese goldband lily; Canada lily** (canadens); **Madonna** (or **St. Joseph) lily** candidum), **Dahurian lily** (dauricum). **David lily** (davidii), **Hanson lily** (hansonii), **Henry lily** (a lovely yellow) (henryi); **tiger lily** (tigrinum), and the **Martagon lily** (martagon). Other beautiful lilies are the **'Golden Clarion'** hybrids of the regal type, the yellow trumpet lilies, the **'Olympic'** hybrids of the regal type with large white drooping flowers and the regal lily, with very fragrant flowers faintly tinged with pink on the reverse side of the petals.

Other Summer-Flowering Bulbs

Growing **gladioli, dahlias** and **tuberous begonias** has been very popular for many years, but there are other bulbs which are equally popular. Here are one or two that deserve our attention.

CANNAS

Cannas, or **American reeds,** should be started off indoors between February 20 and March 15. Be very careful to use only rhizomes that are entirely free from rot. Outside, cannas need a sunny location. They prefer a soil enriched with well-rotted manure, or with a mixture of peat-moss and a complete chemical fertilizer. These plants are susceptible to frost. In eastern Canada the best period for transplanting them into outside beds is between May 25 early June, although you will realize that the former date will vary according to the temperature at the time.

USE OF FERTILIZERS

During the summer, to stimulate growth and ensure plenty of flowers, it is advisable to apply a liquid fertilizer — 20-20-20 — every ten days. In hot weather cannas need regular, thorough watering, especially during dry spells.

It's a good idea to loosen the soil frequently, both to keep it well aerated, and to control the growth of weeds. I would also advise removing each floral spike as soon as its flowers begin to fade. This will ensure an abundance of flowers.

PULLING UP AND STORING FOR THE WINTER

After the first frost has hit the foliage, cut the stems down to within about three inches of the ground. Leave the plants like this for a few days, to allow any surplus water accumulated in the rhizomes to evaporate. Dig up the clusters on a sunny day, preferably in the morning. These clusters should be left on the ground for three or four hours, to get rid of any surplus moisture prior to storing for the winter. However, you should keep a little earth around the rhizomes. Put the clusters in the cellar before October 15, to avoid damage from the autumn frosts. To stop the rhizomes from drying out while they are stored, you should cover them with peat-moss or some lightly-dampened sand. The temparture of the place where they are stored must stay above freezing-point — between 40° and 50°F, if possible.

ACIDANTHERAS

These plants are a graceful variety of the **iris** family. They have one single stem, which carries five or six butterfly-shaped flowers with brown spots at the heart of the corolla. The flowers open one after the other over a period of about two weeks. Their leaves resemble those of the gladiolus. **Acidentheras** go very well with **galtonias, montbretias,** and **tigridias** in a mixed cluster of summer-flowering bulbs. These plants need a rich, loose, slightly sandy soil. They do not need full sunlight.

Grow them as you would gladioli. Dig the rhizomes up in the autumn and dry them; then store them the same way as you store gladioli corms.

ACHIMENES

These plants are usually grown in the shade, in pots or in boxes, from little rhizomes that look like caterpillars. **Achimenes** stay in a dormant state from the end of the summer until March or April. During this period the rhizomes should be kept in dry sand, in pots or containers, at a temperature between 45° and 50°F.

Achimenes are planted in pots during May, and transplanted outside early in June, at the same time as tuberous begonias.

POPPY ANEMONES

The 'De Caen' and 'St. Brigid' varieties of these charming exotic flowers have extraordinarily rich colouring, and are surprisingly large. Happily, they are quite easy to grow.

The bulbs should be planted in spring, 2½ inches deep and 3 inches apart.

ROSETTE OXALIS

This beautiful little flowering bulb can be grown just as easily indoors as outdoors. It is highly valued for its delicate foliage and its little pink or white flowers on long. stems. It makes an excellent border for a bed of flowers, or as a winter decoration in a window that gets plenty of sun.

It flowers almost indefinitely. If you are growing it outside, it should be planted fairly shallow, in sandy soil enriched with organic matter. This plant always prefers a sunny location.

RANUNCULUSES

Ranunculuses or **garden buttercups** require the same treatment as **anemones.** These plants produce clusters of flowers like tiny balloons on long stems, in red, yellow, orange, scarlet and other hues. Mixed with anemones, or planted in clusters in the garden, they make a charming effect, thanks to their variety of colours. They also make very pretty bouquets.

TIGRIDIAS

Tigridias or **tiger-flowers** are some of the most original of flowering bulbs. Although the flower only lasts one day, a bed of tiger-flowers presents an enchanting spectacle, due to the richness of the blooms. Tigridias offer a wide choice of colours, including white, yellow, orange and flame-red. The flowers bloom easily if you take care to thin out the other stems that carry buds.

Grow your tigridias as you would gladioli. Remember, however, that they are less susceptible to frost. Nevertheless, they should not be stored the same way gladioli are stored, although that's often recommended —

Anemones are charming exotic flowers which are very easy to grow.

too often, in fact. It is much better to dry the bulbs thoroughly in a well-ventilated room, at a temperature of from 70° to 75°F. Clean them, then store them in vermiculite in a cool cellar at 50° to 60°F. Do not divide the bulbs after drying, rather leave them in clusters.

AGAPANTHUS

Agapanthus or **lily-of-the-Nile** is usually grown in big pots as ornamentation for the patio or other similar location. The plants should be left in their containers and stored in a cool cellar for the winter. They should be watered two or three times during the course of the winter.

ALSTROEMERIA

Alstroemeria or **Inca lily** should be planted two inches deep in the soil. The tubers produce handsome flowers that resemble lilies, with lively colours ruuning from yellow to pale pink. In the autmun, treat them the same way as cannas — i.e., dig them up, then store them for the winter in a cool cellar.

CALLA LILIES

Calla lilies include the white-flowered **common calla** (Zantedeschia aethiopica), **pink calla** (Zantedeschia rehmannii, or the **'Superba'** variety thereof), and **golden calla** (Zantedeschia elliottiana). They prefer a rich soil, and grow better when planted somewhere where there is some shade during the hottest hours of the day. Calla lilies should be grown outdoors, and do best of all in pots. They are ideal plants for using in planters around a garden pool.

They should be stored for the winter in sphagnum moss, lightly moistened. The tubers should not be allowed to dry out completely. Water them in January, and again in March.

GLORIOSA OR GLORY-LILY

In the autumn, dig up the roots (which look like fingers) and store them in dry sand or in spaghnum moss at a temperature between 50° and 60°F.

ZEPHYRANTHES

Treat these in the same way as gladioli. Pot them at the beginning of spring, then transplant them in June.

CALADIUM

This is an exceptionally useful plant if you want to put some colour into a shady corner. During the winter, the bulbs should be stored in the same fashion as begonia tubers.

CYPELLA

Treat the bulbs of **Herbert's cypella** in the same way as gladioli corms.

CRINUM

Crinum bulbs should be dealt with in the same manner as agapanthus bulbs. If they become too crowded, re-pot them early in the spring.

ISMENE

If you want beautful, white flowers which resemble narcissuses, in your garden, then you should grow Peruvian daffodil or **ismene** (Hymenocallis calathina). Many varieties exist, and the big trumpet-like flowers with delicate fringes are pleasantly perfumed. Some of the hybrids bear yellow flowers. These are very interesting flowers to grow — not only for their beauty, but also because they flower scarcely a week after they have been planted. Plant them after June 1st, when the soil has warmed up properly. However, you can also pot them in May, keep them indoors until they have blossomed, and then plant them in the garden in the summer.

Lift your **ismenes** in the autumn and store the bulbs in dry sand, vermiculite or peat-moss at a temperature of about 60°F.

TUBEROSES

The **tuberose** (Polianthes tuberosa) is so strongly perfumed that it is a good idea to plant it in a remote part of your garden! These plants require a long growing-season in warm soil. The soil must be well-prepared and the plants must lie in a protected location. The large spikes with their white flowers reach a height of around three feet. The bulbs are stored in vermiculite over the winter.

Ismene or hymenocallis is the perfect answer for the amateur gardener who would like to see a lightly perfumed plant in his garden with large, delicate flowers. It often blooms within a week after being planted.

Spring-Flowering Bulbs

HOW AUTUMN PREPARES FOR SPRING

Spring and autumn are two seasons that are poles apart in the cycle of growth, yet they have several characteristics in common. In both cases, Nature is more than generous with her lavish display of rich colours. After the long winter months, the greenery of spring appears as if by magic to make us forget the cold and the snow. Then, in the autumn, the various tones of green are replaced by the warm tints of the leaves as they change gradually to deep brown or vivid red.

But what really knits these two seasons close together most of all is the fact that autumn prepares the way for spring. The beauty of the garden, its first flowers, the growing array of colours, everything that goes to make up the charm of spring would be missing were it not for the preparations made the previous autumn. And we must remember that 'spring flowers', obviously come from spring-flowering bulbs such as **tulips, hyacinths, narcissuses, crocuses** and so on.

Autumn is the best season of all for gardening. The temperature is generally comfortable up to, say, mid-November, and rainfall is regular. The period from the end of September to the closing days of October is the ideal time for planting spring-flowering bulbs.

To avoid being disappointed the following spring by bulbs which do not seem to have produced flowers, you should not leave your planting until late in October. If you wait too long, the bulbs cannot get their roots down until the spring — whereas they ought to be well ahead with this before the soil is completely frozen in the autumn.

Although the colours from his spring-flowering bulbs make the garden look like fairyland in spring, what really interests the amateur gardener is the ease with which he was able to prepare his spring garden during the previous autumn.

Few ornamental plants are as easy to grow as bulbs. They are at home almost anywhere — out in the sun, or in the shade. All they need for satisfactory growth is a loose, slightly sandy garden soil, well drained and enriched with organic matter.

CHOOSE HIGH-QUALITY BULBS

The choice of bulbs is a very wide one. However, to ensure that you get the flowers you hope for, it essential that you buy good-quality bulbs. Consult the catalogues produced by the reputable seed houses. You should choose only large bulbs, and stick to the varieties which are known to be suitable for your region.

When the time comes to decide where you want the display of blooms the following spring, pick the locations and the colours to suit your own

In the spring, a bed of tulips will take pride of place in the garden for the beauty of its flowers, with their many different colours, and will help us forget the rigours of the winter.

taste. Look on yourself as an artist creating a wonderful picture. For example, besides the usual flowerbeds and borders, why not have some bulbs under the bushes at the front of the house? This is a sure way of breaking the monotony of green everywhere you look next spring.

ENSURING A GOOD CROP OF FLOWERS

Flowers grown from bulbs are so graceful that they can decorate the garden all by themselves at the beginning of the season. They produce an atmosphere of beauty and fresness wherever they are grown. The best possible effect may be achieved by planting different kinds together. You will find that you are copying Nature by doing this, since you very rarely see just one flower, all on its own, in a natural setting. Plant bulbs around the entrance to your house — and they will perfume the air for you next spring. To work in a bit more contrast, add a row of **narcissus,** for example. Even little forgotten corners can be pleasantly transformed, thanks to the smaller bulbs such as **grape hyacinth, chionodoxa, squill** and so on.

The spacing between bulbs is an important point and should be planned before you begin to plant. **Tulips** need a 4-inch gap between them, while for **narcissuses** and **hyacinths** the minimum distance is at least six inches.

Crocuses are the most popular of the small-flowered bulbs. They lend themselves admirably to planting in all sorts of different places — lawns, flowerbeds, rockeries and so on. Their wide range of colours enables one to make some fascinating flowerbed compositions.

On the other hand, you can set **crocus** bulbs as close as two inches away from each other — this gives a better effect, whereas **snowdrops** and **monkshoods** need four inches of space between them.

How deep the bulbs should be planted varies with the species. Thus, **tulips** and **hyacinths** should be set deep enough to allow about 1½ times their own height of earth above them — about four or five inches for large bulbs while **crocuses** need about three inches on average. For **snowdrops** and **monkshoods,** the right depth is about three or four inches.

Children love the feel of fresh daffodils. Double varieties such as the 'Copeland' — shown below — are splendid as cut flowers for interior decoration. *(Photo: Malak)*

THE PROPER TIME FOR PLANTING

Most amateur gardeners are anxious for autumn to arrive — for autumn is the proper time to plant spring-flowering bulbs. They get a very real satisfaction out of setting each bulb carefully into the warm, moist soil, where it will put its roots down and then lie dormant through the long winter months. With a little imagination, these plant-lovers can almost see the results of their autumn toil already, and enjoy the rich colours of the plants in full bloom, as they will be in the spring.

In October, the air is cool and dry, the sun's rays paint the countryside a golden yellow, and the leaves on the trees begin to take on warmer hues. This is the perfect month to prepare the garden for the coming spring — to plant your bulbs — **tulips, narcissuses, hyacinths, crocuses** and so on.

To achieve success when planting bulbs, you must remember that they need time to form their roots before the frost has got deep into the ground. Nor must you forget that spring-flowering plants are at home in any sort of garden, and in almost any sort of situation. Furthermore, unlike many plants, bulbs may be put in shady spots.

EXAMINE BULBS CAREFULLY

Before you plant your bulbs, you must look them over carefully, to make sure they are all in good condition. In the case of the true bulbs **(narcissus, lily** and **tulip)**, the scales or layers should be tightly closed. With rhizomes, corms and tubers **(calla, crocus** and **dahlia)**, the skin should be firm and fleshy.

Good quality bulbs are rather heavy. It is not at all rare to find bulbs of the same species which are the same size but quite different in weight. Almost invariably the poorer-quality ones are lighter.

For **hyacinths, tulips** and others, the skin should be smooth and shiny, and free from deep cuts and scratches — particularly on the flat part at the bottom. If the bulb shows any traces of cuts or diseases, it will probably rot or fall to pieces after planting. Always buy your bulbs from a house with a well-established reputation. Furthermore, if you do not plant them straight away, it is essential to keep them in a cool, well-ventilated place. Remember, too, that squirrels and mice love nibbling at bulbs — (the only exception being **narcissus** bulbs).

PLANT FROM MID-AUGUST ONWARDS

While it is perfectly true that October is the ideal month to put your bulbs into the ground, the planting-period starts in mid-August, and lasts until the ground has frozen too hard to dig.

I recommend that you plant **crocuses, hyacinths, trumpet narcissuses** and **small-cupped narcissuses** at the end of September or the beginning

When the time comes to rake the leaves, it is also time to plant tulip bulbs. When spring arrives, the tulips will stage their multi-coloured pageant to enliven the fresh green colouring of the new season's foliage.

of October. These bulbs need time to put down plenty of roots before the cold weather arrives. **Tulips** are hardier, and can stand being planted right up until the ground has frozen.

BEWARE OF OVER-LATE PLANTING

Many amateur gardeners are disappointed to find, when the spring comes along, that their bulbs are not flowering at all, or very sparsely. Yet it is easy enough to prevent this sad outcome. Very often the failure is due to the bulbs having been planted too late in October. This has resulted in the bulbs having waited until spring before getting their roots down — which they should have been allowed to do the previous autumn, before the ground froze.

THE BEST SOIL

Spring-flowering bulbs do not require a rich soil. Quite simply, what they need is a loose, porous soil which is well-drained. If the soil is clayey, you must mix in some sand and garden moss or garden compost, to a depth of 15 to 18 inches — well below the usual depth at which bulbs are planted.

Thorough preparation of the soil is indispensable if you want to grow bulbs successfully. Turn the ground over to a depth of 1½ - 2 feet, in order to bring the subsoil up to the top, Next, break the soil up and level it with a rake. Bulbs require a loose crumbly soil, and you must remember to enrich the soil with well-rotted manure, or with bone-meal (2-11-0). Alternatively, you could use a complete commercial fertilizer (6-9-6 or 5-10-15) in the proportion of five pounds per 100 square feet of surface. If you remember to take this precaution at the time of planting, you will have made a good start toward preserving the vigour of your bulbs.

DEPTH OF PLANTING

Big bulbs such as tulips and hyacinths are planted five or six inches deep Small bulbs such as **crocuses, chionodoxas** and **squills** should go four inches deep, while **grape hyacinths** and **snowdrop** (Galanthu) need only three inches of earth above them. **Narcissus** bulbs should be planted nine inches deep.

PROTECTION IN WINTER

As soon as the earth is frozen, but before the snow comes and covers it, the bulbs in your beds and borders should be covered with a layer of ground peat-moss about two inches thick The peat-moss must be thoroughly dampened, to prevent its drying out and being carried off by the wind. This damp peat-moss will freeze, and thus form an excellent protection for the bulbs while they are putting down their roots. One large bag — (usually 100 to 115 pounds) — will cover an area of 120 square feet (10 ft. x 12 ft.) to a depth of two inches, or 240 square feet (12 ft. x 20 ft.) to a depth of one inch.

WATERING IS ESSENTIAL DURING PLANTING

It is absolutely essential to water your bulbs immediately after planting. Also if there is a long dry period later on, they will need watering then. This is very important in order to let their roots develop normally. If the roots do not develop normally, the flowers will be poor and sparse.

Many people will be asking themselves whether it is necessary to protect their bulbs against the cold in winter. This will largely depend on local conditions, of course, and you should seek the advice of an expert in your own region. In Eastern Canada, where the winters are fairly severe, bulbs are usually covered with a protective layer of peat-moss, straw or pine branches. However, this mulch should **not** be put down until the soil is actually frozen — otherwise mice and other rodents may well take refuge inside it for the winter.

PLANNING YOUR LAYOUT AND FLOWERING PATTERN

When you buy the bulbs for your garden, choose both large and small bulbs, early-flowering bulbs and late-flowering bulbs. Thus, your garden will present an ever-changing pattern, which will begin with **snodrops** and

The sketch shows the depths at which various bulbs should be planted. From the left — crocus, grape hyacinth, hyacinth, daffodils and various tulips (hybrid fosteriana; triumph; parrot; Darwin).

end with **tulips** — not to mention the different kinds of **lily** which will be in flower from the beginning of the summer until late in autumn.

THE FIRST FLOWERS

The first bulbs to give us flowers are irresistibly delightful. There is always something special about 'the first flowers of spring'.

Winter aconite (Eranthis hyemalis), with its lovely yellow cups, starts the season off. These are soon followed by **snowdrops** and **crocuses**. The ideal arrangement for these little bulbs is to have them in groups or colonies where they can adapt themselves and multiply freely. Set at the foot of early-flowering trees or shrubs such as **witch-hazel** (Hamamelis) or **honeysuckle** (Lonicera), nothing looks better than a carpet of **snowdrops, crocuses, squills, Dutch hyacinths, narcissuses** or **early tulips**.

Finding suitable spots for these bulbs calls for a certain amount of planning. Some kinds of **narcissus** and **tulip** go better in rockeries, where they find themselves next to **rock-cress** (Arabis), **alyssum, aubretia, sandwort** (Arenaria), **primula**, and other early-flowering rock garden plants.

In flowerbeds and borders, the later-flowering varieties of **narcissus** and **tulip** will combine harmoniously with **dicentra, leopard's-bane** (Doronicum), **phlox, pansy**, the hardy **candytuft** (Iberis), early **iris, Virginia hyacinth** and **myosotis**.

MAGNIFICENT GROUP EFFECTS

A single tulip is a thing of beauty, but a group of them certainly catches the eye more readily! Hundreds of flowers massed in a bed make a most stirring sight in springtime.

Slopes might have been designed specially for the purpose of planting bulbs **en mass**. In fact, if you stand on the opposite slope, you can see the whole display at one glance. Remember that when you are planning to put flowerbeds in on level ground, they should be laid out in such a way that you can see them properly from the windows of the house.

Note that tulips are particularly suitable for planning **en masse**. Using different flowerbeds will let you keep gay colours in your garden longer, from the early varieties (including the wild or 'botanical' species) to the later-flowering tulips such as Darwin, parrot, etc.

Alternatively, you could plant them in bunches of a dozen or so flowers, scattered here and there.

Also, when planting small bulbs, put them in places where it will be easy to see them — such as alongside a path, near a window or near a garden door.

Hyacinths are famous for their colours and their fragrance and they should always be planted where these two qualities are going to be well in evidence. So use them along a pathway, close to an entrance or near the patio.

GROUPING YOUR BULBS

If you want to obtain the best possible effect from your bulbs, the most important thing to do when planting is to set them in groups of a dozen or so. Try to avoid putting them in long neat rows like a regiment of soldiers on parade.

Nearly all bulbs are suitable for one or another of the many forms of mass planting. This includes even little bulbs such as **glory-of-the-snow** (Chionodoxa Luciliae), **crocus** and **Armenian grape hyacinth** (Muscari) armeniacum), which flower while the ground is still covered with patches of snow, and thus herald the arrival of spring. These pretty little plants are very hardy, and multiply easily. They are eminently suitable for planting **en masse,** and they make little waterfalls of colour between the other plants.

Daffodils should be planted in such a way as to bring out the full beauty of their trumpets.

HOW TO SUCCEED WITH MASS PLANTING

Successful mass planting of bulbs depends on two factors: (1) all the flowers coming into bloom at the same time, and (2) all the flowers being the same height.

For flowering to take place at the same time, you must ensure that the flowerbed contains only one single variety of bulb — or at least only one single species.

It is also preferable to have different beds for early-flowering, semi-early, and late-flowering varieties, rather than to have them all mixed together in the same spot. As I suggested above, the best mass plantings are done with flowers of one single variety.

On the other hand, if you are planning to plant different kinds of bulbs in the same spot — a flowerbed, say, or a border — the first thing you have to do is make certain that all these bulbs are going to come into flower at the same time. You can create some very beautiful group effects by mixing **narcissuses, grape hyacinths** and **botanical tulips** with **Siberian squills** or **hyacinths,** as well as **double early tulips.**

When you plant the same variety or type of bulb with the object of having them all flower at the same time, it is essential to have the bulbs either all in the shade, or all in the sun — otherwise part of them will flower before the rest. Remember, too, that bulbs grown in a semi-shaded location will flower a little later than those planted in full sunlight. This is a point you must bear in mind when preparing your flowerbed.

DEPTH OF PLANTING AFFECTS HEIGHT

If you have used the same variety or type of bulb in your massed planting, then the height to which they grow will depend very largely on how deeply the bulbs were planted. The best way to get a uniform planting is to dig out the whole flower-bed to a depth suitable for the bulbs you want to grow in it, plant them all at the same time, and then cover them with good garden soil. Large bulbs, such as **tulips, narcissuses** and **hyacinths,** are planted about six inches deep, while small bulbs like **crocuses, grape hyacinths** and **chionodoxas** need a depth of about three inches.

The Great Value Of Hyacinths

Connoisseurs of beautiful flowers love the **hyacinth** for its exquisite perfume, its many colours, and its graceful shape. The origin of the hyacinth is lost in the mists of time, and its story has given rise to numerous legends. It even has a genuine place in history, for together with the tulip it enjoyed a considerable vogue in Holland during the 1630s, and became quite famous.

The ancestor of the common or Dutch hyacinth, as we know it today, was a flower which grew wild on the shores of the Mediterranean. It was imported into Holland about 1570 and has undergone many transformations over the ensuing 400 years.

ITS MANY USES

The hyacinth is a member of the lily family, the Liliaceae. It has a delicate, elegant flower set on a fairly tough stem. The bell-like cluster of little corollas is most attractive. The hyacinth can be grown in several different forms in the garden, both large and small. It looks just as well in formal, symmetrical arrangements as it does in random groups of five or six. It can be planted almost anywhere — in front of conifer trees, near the front door, along a border of hardy flowers, against a screen or a stone wall.

ITS VARIED COLOURS

Thanks to the work of hybridizing specialists in Holland, hyacinths come in all sorts of colours nowadays. Besides the traditional blue, there are red, pink, yellow, white, and various shades of oranges. When you choose your bulbs, you can take your pick of varieties of many vivid colours, as well as pastel shades.

Hyacinths go very well alongside other spring flowers such as **tulips, narcissuses** and **crocuses.** The red, blue or purple hyacinths will look very attractive beside yellow or white narcissuses. White or blue hyacinths make an attractive display alongside pink or red **azaleas.** It is always a good idea to plant narcissuses next to the varieties of tulip with large corollas. You could also put some under your trees and between your bushes.

Gardeners also find that hyacinths do very well in mixed flowerbeds with pansies, violets and lily-of-the-valley. Choose two or three colours and plant them beside your other favourite flowers.

EASILY GROWN

Hyacinths make a magnificent sight, no matter where you plant them in the garden and they are quite easy to grow. Plant them in September or October, six inches deep in a well-drained soil, with six inches spacing between each pair. A mulch two inches thick will protect your hyacinths against the sharp frosts of winter. The short-stemmed varieties are perhaps better for growing outdoors — they are not so easily damaged by the wind as the long-stemmed kind, which are ideal for indoor forcing.

Remember to include some hyacinths next autumn in your order for spring-flowering bulbs — then you will be able to enjoy their delicate perfume when spring comes round.

Hyacinths are easy to grow. Planted in September or October, in well-drained soil, they make a magnificent spectacle in any garden.

(Photo: Malak)

Narcissuses - Splendid Hardy Bulbs

More than ever before, lovers of flowering bulbs are including **narcissuses** in their autumn planting programme. In any garden, narcissuses represent a permanent investment with an ever-increasing value as each flowering-season comes along.

Narcissuses bulbs may be left permanently in the same spot, or they can be lifted after their foliage has dried out. Most amateur gardeners plant annuals between or on top of their narcissuses, and don't disturb the bulbs until they need dividing. Even after being divided, the bulb can be replanted immediately at the same spot, or it can be stored for planting at the end of September or the beginning of October.

UNDEMANDING PLANTS

There are few hardy bulbs that are so easy to grow. Any reasonably fertile soil suits them. They prefer sunny or semi-shady locations. However, the biggest crop of flowers is obtained when the bulbs are put in humid but well-drained spots where they can be planted in natural-looking clusters — under trees and bushes, for example. They are equally suited for use alongside pathways. In a large flowerbed, clusters of 15 to 20 bulbs make a very pleasant effect. In a small flowerbed, cut the cluster down to five or six. On a country property where there is plenty of room, you can set great clumps of narcissuses underneath the trees or in the fields; they'll make a lovely view in springtime.

Narcissuses make a lovely impression near pools and streams. There are dwarf varieties too, and these are ideal for rockeries.

METHOD OF PLANTING

Space the bulbs six to eight inches apart, and set them in about six inches deep. A thin layer of sand, or of non-fertilized earth makes an excellent bed for them to rest on, but you should take the precaution of mixing in a handful of bone-meal for each square foot of soil beneath the bulbs. Then replace the surface soil above and around them. When the surface of the ground is frozen, spread a mulch of ground peat-moss, leaves, hay, straw or any other suitable organic material you have handy. Remove this mulch gradually during March, or when the first stems make their appearance.

The great variety of shapes and colours makes the appearance of narcissuses in spring an unforgettable event. Although yellow-gold narcissuses — the traditional 'daffodils' — are always the favourites, the fairyland of colours such as white, yellow, orange, scarlet and tender pink produce a gay note which is very welcome in this period of the year that follows hard on the heels of winter.

USE THEM WITH OTHER PLANTS

The flowers of the narcissus contrast very pleasantly with their own foliage, but they look even more beautiful if they're mixed in with other plants.

A background of deep green **yews, firs, junipers,** or other conifers will make the flowers stand out. **Azaleas** and **rhododendrons** both go very well with **decorative hawthorns, plum trees, white birch trees, quinces, forsythis** and early-flowering **thunberg spiraeas.**

In borders, narcissuses can be grouped to excellent effect with low-growing plants such as **Drummond's phlox, cress** and **Dutch hyacinths.** Here's a very popular threesome that you will find well worth trying: **trumpet narcissuses, early tulips** and **Dutch hyacinths.** Late-flowering varieites of narcissus can be used with **bleeding heart** (Dicentra) or **wild sweet William** (Phlox divaricata). If you have sufficient space, why not create a little bulb garden? You could lift your bulbs from your beds and borders after they've flowered, and plant them in the 'bulb garden' to rest. Then lift them after their foliage has faded, dry them and store in a cool, well-ventilated place until the month of August. The clustered bulbs are then divided and cleaned. The large bulbs are replanted in the flowerbeds, while the little bulbs are planted in rows until they grow big enodgh to bear flowers — which takes about a year.

THE ROLE OF THE VARIETIES

Each variety of narcissus has a particular role to play. The big yellow and white trumpet varieties, and the bicoloured ones also, stand out beautifully when set in group of six to a dozen in flower-borders.

The same goes for **Narcissus incomparabilis** and **Barr's small-cupped narcissus.** For planting in borders, or to show some rustic charm alongside a fence, try some **tazetta narcissuses,** which flower in clusters instead of singly.

CHOICE OF VARIETIES

When you are choosing your narcissus varieties, colour and date of flowering are two factors you must take into account. In order to keep the flowering-period as long as possible, choose some of each variety — early-flowering, mid-season, and late-flowering. All the following varieties are easy to obtain, and between them they will give a splendid range of colours: **trumpet narcissus,** with a long stem and a big trumpet; **Narcissus incomparabilis,** which looks very like the **trumpet** variety. except that the cup of **incomparabilis** is a bit shorter, and should correctly be described as a corona; **Barr's short-cupped narcissus,** with its vivid colouring; **poet's narciussus,** with a perianth that is nearly always white with a red or orange corona — its flower is fragrant and its bulb is large and multifloral; **tazetta narcissus,** with multifloral stem, which looks very like **poet's narcissus,** except that the stems carry three flowers or more — here, too, the bulb is large and multifloral.

Forcing Hardy Bulbs

One of the best ways of prolonging the gardening season is to force your bulbs — which means making the plants come into flower in a much shorter time than usual. Thanks to a simple technique, you can make your hardy spring-flowering bulbs bloom inside your house during the gloomy winter months. Picture windows are the ideal location for the containers — pots, boxes or large dishes — since they will receive the maximum of natural daylight during the short winter days, and their display of flowers in bloom will be seen to best advantage, both inside the house and outside.

THE BEST TIME

To obtain the desired result — i.e., several weeks of flowering — you must obviously do a certain amount of planning. You should also note that the month of October is the best time to start forcing your bulbs.

Before describing the recommended method, I should also point out that most spring-flowering bulbs differ from perennial plants (which last a long time), since a bulb is a complete flowering plant in miniature, with its stems, its petals and its leaves all ready to surge upwards as soon as conditions are favourable. Furthermore, each bulb contains the nourishment which it needs during the time it is getting ready to come into flower.

WHICH BULBS TO USE

Several spring-flowering bulbs are suitable for forcing indoors during the winter. The most popular are **tulips, hyacinths** and **narcissuses** — though it is equally easy to force the smaller bulbs such as **crocuses, grape hyacinths** (Muscari), **squills, snowdrops** and **fritillaries.** It is also possible, with a moderate degree of forcing, to make **Dutch iris** and **lily-of-the-valley** come into flower indoors in winter.

Although nearly every **kind** of spring-flowering bulb can be successfully forced, you must realize that not every **variety** is capable of being brought to flower indoors during the winter months.

One of the most important factors in growing fine plants is to choose top-quality bulbs. On this point, let me advise you to consult with your nursery-gardener or with one of the specialists at your local gardening centre. These experts will show you bulbs which have been specially selected for winter forcing.

Thus, **hyacinth** bulbs are pre-refrigerated with a view to being forced, while **tulips** and **narcissuses** are specially chosen to a uniform size, to produce a uniform flowering, with the largest flowers possible. Such bulbs should be large, firm and healthy. The largest are usually the best. To avoid being disappointed, never buy bulbs at sales or 'bargains', and deal only with establishments with good reputations.

SUITABLE CONTAINERS

You can use a wide range of containers of all shapes and sizes to force your bulbs — from wooden boxes to plastic pots. However, the best results are usually obtained with ordinary clay pots or bowls. The essential thing is for the container to have a hole in the bottom for drainage purposes.

Furthermore, the container should be at least twice as tall as the bulb, in order to let the roots develop properly.

It is a good idea to choose containers suited to the type of bulb you want to plant in them. You may grow narcissuses and tulips together in pots six inches across, which can hold three narcissus and five or six tulip bulbs. For hyacinths, use 5-inch pots for planting one single bulb, and 6-inch pots for three bulbs.

You can use containers six to eight inches in diameter to hold several smaller bulbs but each bulb must have an inch of clear space all round.

Also, it is essential always to put the same variety of the same kind of bulb all in the same container — otherwise you may get uneven flowering taking place at different times.

THE BEST SOIL

A porous, easily crumbled soil is the most suitable for potting purposes, since it lets the roots develop easily and facilities drainage. If, on the other hand, your soil can be easily compressed into a compact ball, you must improve it with some sand, peat-moss or vermiculite.

These last two materials can also well be used to improve the soil mixes which are available commercially. Avoid using soil which has already been used for growing bulbs, or soil which has had fresh manure added to it.

Also add a little charcoal to the soil in order to stop it from going acid. A good potting loam contains 50% garden soil, 25% sand and 25% dry peat-moss, plus two ounces of complete chemical fertilizer (4-12-10) per bushel of the mixture.

It is also quite possible to force your bulbs in any medium capable of supporting the plants and retaining their nourishment — for, as we saw earlier, the bulbs already contain all the nourishment they require during the time they are forming their flowers. Such a 'soil substitute' could be formed by mixing equal parts of vermiculite, garden moss and sand.

HOW TO POT YOUR BULBS

First of all, put some pieces of broken earthenware or some little pebbles over the drainage hole (or holes) in the bottom of your containers to stop the drainage hole becoming blocked, and prevent the earth from leaking out.

Cover these shards or pebbles with a layer of sphagnum moss. Then add your soil mix, using enough to ensure that when the bulbs have been planted and the soil well tamped down, the tops of the bulbs will lie half an inch below the rim of the pot.

Then fill each pot about half full, and put the bulbs as close to each other as possible — but remember to leave the requisite spacing between them.

After that, the bulbs are pressed gently down into the soil. Never **force** them in — you could damage them that way. Try to get as many bulbs as possible into each container, so as to get the best effect when they come into flower. This is particularly applicable to the smaller bulbs — **crocuses, grape hyacinths,** etc.

Once you have placed your bulbs, fill up the spaces between them with earth: then tamp everything down firmly.

Finish off with a generous watering. The best way of providing the right amount of water for bulbs planted in a clay pot is to stand the pot in water halfway up its sides, and let it soak until the surface of the soil becomes damp.

THE EFFECT OF COLD ON ROOT-GROWING

All spring-flowering bulbs need some cold for the development of a healthy root system. As a general rule, these bulbs need at least twelve weeks of cold. Most **tulips** and **narcissuses** need a cold spell of about fourteen weeks, while certain varieties require as much as 15 or 16 weeks before their roots are properly developed. This 'cold treatment' can be carried out by placing the containers outside, in a trench or a rooting-bed, or they can be kept inside, in a cold spot.

BULBS INDOORS

The easiest and best way of letting your bulbs put down their roots is to put them under cover in a dark, cold location. This could be a cellar, a garage or a shed near the house.

The temperature should be between 40° and 50°F. Temperatures below 40°F draw the root-growing process out abnormally, while temperatures above 50°F hinder the growth of roots.

If you have somewhere cool and shady where you can keep your bulbs at the proper temperature for root-growing, put all your containers there for at least six weeks, to get the root-growing process under way. Then, for about the next three weeks, expose them to a temperature of 50°F, with enough light to stimulate the growth of the stems and leaves. Then water the bulbs. When the leaves have grown about four inches, and the bud of the flower can be seen, raise the temperature to 60°F and increase the amount of daylight. After two days, expose the plants to full sunlight and a surrounding temperature of 75° to 80°F.

BULBS OUTDOORS

If you do not have anywhere cool and shady indoors with a temperature of 40° to 50°F, then the best thing to do is to dig a trench outside.

First of all, choose a suitable location in the garden — well-drained, and reasonably close to the house.

Dig a trench a foot deep, and wide enough to take your pots. Cover the bottom with a 3-inch layer of pebbles, to provide drainage. Set your pots on this drainage layer, fill up all the spaces, and cover everything with a 1-to 2-foot thickness of dry peat-moss or vermiculite. Dead leaves may also be used, but if your **do** use them, take care not to spread them thicker than about four inches — anything more than that will cause them to start generating heat spontaneously, and the bulbs will open up prematurely.

If you have any spare pots, put them upside down on top of the pots or containers in which your bulbs are planted then cover over the top of them. This will save you having to clean off the fill material when you take the pots out of the trench.

Put six inches of earth over the top of everything, then give the trench — or, rather, the solid ridge it has now become — a good watering.

As soon as the ground is frozen hard, cover the trench with a mulch of leaves, straw or peat-moss. This mulch will keep the temperature stable inside the trench, and will prevent any damage from frost.

If you are worried about rodents such as mice, squirrels or fieldmice, lay a wire-mesh cover over the top, and cover that with leaves, straw or peat-moss. My personal preference is for leaves, since they easier to clear away once the frost has set in properly.

You could also put your pots in a cold bed, one beside the other, and bury them up to the top of the lip.

THE ROOT-GROWING PROCESS

After ten or twelve weeks, according to the type of bulb, the roots will have developed far enough to fill the pots, and the leaves will be starting to show; now is the time to take the pots out of their cold bed. Then leave them for at least two days in a dark place where the temperature is constant between 40° and 50°F. (Before you do this, remember to stand the pots for a while in a flat pan of water. After three days, when the leaves have grown a bit more, put the pots somewhere warmer (about 50°F) without too much light.

At this stage, it is of the utmost importance to water the plants. When the leaves have grown about four inches high and the flower bud is visible, raise the surrounding temperature to 60°F, and let the plants have more sunlight. This new transitory period lasts two days, then it is time to expose the plants to more sunlight, and to let them have more heat — normal room temperature, say, at least 72°F. Keep your pots protected from the direct rays of the sun and away from artificial heat sources such as radiators and hot-air vents. I should mention here that **narcissuses** and the smaller bulbs prefer a somewhat lower temperature — 60° to 65°F.

HYACINTHS ARE EASILY FORCED

Among all the spring-flowering bulbs that can be grown in pots, **hyacinths** are the easiest to force. In gardening centres you can even buy special plastic containers for the purpose. You fill the container with water, up to the base of the bulb — and that is all., Set the container, with the bulb inside, in a cool dark place such as a cellar or a cupboard, until the roots are well developed and the flower-stem has emerged and is about four inches high. Then put the container in the light. Make sure that the level of the water is always just above the base of the bulb.

Many amateur gardeners find, to their disappointment, that the flowers on their hyacinth plants are lost in the foliage, and they wonder vainly how they may avoid this problem.

There is a very simple procedure which speeds up the growth of the floral stems and produces flowers that rise above the foliage. You need only make some paper cones twelve inches tall and four inches across the mouth and stand them point upwards on top of your 6-inch pots. For smaller pots, use empty pots of the same size.

THE NARCISSUS IS THE IDEAL BULB

The **tazetta narcissus** is the ideal bulb for those with little gardening experience who want to try their hand at forcing. Success is almost certain if you start forcing at the end of September or in mid-October, for this particular bulb needs to be planted earlier than the others. The procedure

The easiest and most advisable way to plant bulbs for forcing is to pot them, and put them under cover in a cold, dark place — a trench, or a forcing-bed, or in some cold spot indoors.

used in this case is different from that called for with other bulbs, for this narcissus cannot stand excessive cold. Set the bulbs into their pots so that three-quarters of the bulb is sticking up out of the soil mix. Put the pots into a dark corner of the basement, or in any other suitable place, that is, one which is cool and dark — in order to let the roots develop before the leaves start showing. After two or three weeks, when the leaves start poking through, water the plants and then set the pots in front of a sunny window and keep the surrounding temperature between 60° and 70°F.

Digging Up And Storing Spring-Flowering Bulbs

Most spring-flowering bulbs, such as **tulips** and **narcissuses,** have to be dug up and replanted when they have grown so big they are beginning to be cramped for space.

The proper time to do this depends on the type of bulb. Narcissuses, for example, can stay in the same place for five or ten years without having to be disturbed: while tulips start getting cramped after only a couple of years. If you want good flowers from them, you must divide their bulbs without delay and replant them.

Spring-flowering bulbs must be lifted from the ground, because they multiply so rapidly that the soil around them soon becomes exhausted and needs refertilizing. Sometimes, too, the amateur gardener will choose to dig up his bulbs in order to use the space for growing annual plants.

DAFFODILS

Commercial growers of **daffodils** dig their plants up every year, in order to obtain sound little bulbs for multiplication purposes. The amateur gardener need only lift **his** bulbs when they get too crowed. If they are allowed to be crowded they will produce fewer and smaller flowers.

Daffodils are not usually dug up until the stems are dead. They will have begun to droop and turn brown by then, though they still remain firmly attached to the bulbs. At this stage, the leaves won't break away easily from the bulbs, either, so that you can use them as a handle by which to pull the bulbs up out of the soil. If the leaves have died, however, you cannot do this, and will have to dig the bulbs up out of the ground. In most soils a flat-pronged fork is the best tool for the job; but you must take great care not to cut the bulbs or spear them.

Once bulbs from sandy soils have been cleaned off and dried, they need little further drying before being put into storage. On the other hand, if they have come out of a heavy soil, or from a shady location, you must dry them properly. Actually, you do not need to put them into storage at all. It is often better to replant bulbs a little while after you have dug them up.

The beds you plan to put them into may not be ready for them — or they may be already occupied by beautiful annual plants which are still in flower. In this case, you will, of course, store the bulbs.

The two principal requirements for storing bulbs are a reasonably low temperature and good ventilation. A shed, a storehouse or a garage are usually ideal locations, provided they are well-ventilated.

When the bulbs are quite dry, you must clean them off and size them. The large ones should be transplanted wherever you want the best show of flowers, and the little ones into a seed bed until they have grown sufficiently to be planted somewhere permanently. You can replant them as soon as the ground is ready to receive them — which means any time up until the end of September, in most parts of Canada.

TULIPS

To ensure that they will do well next year, **tulips** should be dug up once their stems have gone completely brown. After lifting them, treat them the same way as you do **daffodils** — i.e., keep them in a shed, or a cool, well-ventilated garage. Later, during the summer, remove their outside skin, which will come off easily, together with the old roots. Then grade them according to size.

When it is absolutely necessary to lift **tulips** from a flowerbed immediately or shortly after they have flowered, while the leaves are still green, you must do this very carefully if you want them to flower again next year.

The easiest way to lift **tulips** is to treat them as you would treat annual or perennial plants that must be transplanted — keep the soil intact around the roots, and then replant them in a seed bed. Later, when the leaves have turned brown, you dig them up again, and divide them in the normal way. However carefully you carry out this task, it may happen that the bulbs do not produce flowers that are up to the usual standard the next season, but everything should be more or less back to normal in the second year.

GRAPE HYACINTHS

Grape hyacinths soon become very cramped, but they may be left in that condition for several years. However, if you want to increase your holding, you must lift them and divide them.

Almost everywhere in Canada, **snowdrops, squills, winter aconite** and **chionodoxas** will last a lifetime without becoming overcrowded. But if you ever want to divide them or transplant them, you should do it after the leaves have turned brown, and you should transplant them straight into their new position rather then let the bulbs dry out first.

CHAPTER 12

THE LAWN

The Early Tasks
Of Spring

Early maintenance work on your lawn in spring is very important, for the effects will be evident throughout the summer in the general appearance of the garden and the ease of its upkeep.

As soon as the soil has dried out sufficiently, first of all clear all rubbish off the scene. Use a metal rake to collect all the dead leaves and other debris. Next, rake the lawn thoroughly with a flexible rake, to remove all dry, dead grass.

After that, you should aerate the soil — either with a specal aerator, or with a lawn roller fitted with aeration spikes. This lets the lawn absorb fertilizer and water more easily.

USE OF FERTILIZER

The next thing to do is to fertilize the lawn with a complete chemical fertilizer — 12-4-8, for example — using two pounds per 100 square feet of surface.

The formula 12-4-8 is particularly well suited to 'greedy' grasses, such as **'Merion' bluegrass.** Your lawn will go green very quickly, and thanks to the special minerals in this ferilizer, the grass will keep its handsome colour and stand up well to dry conditions.

Bald patches in the lawn, where the grass has disappeared as a result of ice, frost, fungal diseases or insects, must be dealt with without delay. First, remove all dead grass, then work the soil with a spade, then sow grass seed or lay some sod. It is perhaps pertinent to remark here that a few brown patches or brownish areas on the lawn are probably not due to any crptogamic diseas — they are likely to have been caused by dogs, a mulch of grass cuttings, excessive composting, an accumulation of peatmoss, dead leaves, or planks or other similar objects that kill the grass if they have been left in the same place too long.

Brown stains can also be caused by week-killers, fungicides, fertilizer applied to wet grass, an overdose of fetrilizer, insecticides, oil or gasoline. In addition, certain larvae — such as those of the Japanese beetle or the june bug — are reponsible for some brown stains.

Then again, if the lawn is too sparse, or doesn't have enough good green grass in it, you should add some seed — one pound of a top-quality grass mix per 1,000 square feet of suface. If the lawn happens to have less than 30% of its surface covered with decent grass, and the rest is either bare or covered with weeds — then you should lay the whole thing over again.

RELAYING

The process of relaying a lawn, either partially or completely, means destroying all existing grass and weeds in order to bring a completely new lawn into being. The easiest way of doing this is to use either of the weed-killers 'Weedrite' or 'Gramoxone', which will do the job in only 24 hours. After that you can lay a new lawn, either by sowing seed or by covering the ground with strips of turf.

If you have any areas covered with moss — which is usually caused by poor soil, inadequate drainage, or too much shade — scatter some fertilizer on the affected area and improve the drainage, if necessary. You could also use one of the commercial products such as 'Moss Killer'.

TAKE CARE WHEN ROLLING

You must roll the lawn in spring if the ground has heaved from frost, and also to replace any grass that was uprooted during the winter. You can also use the roller to press your grass seed properly down into the soil. However, you must avoid rolling areas that are too damp, or using too heavy a roller, which will merely harden the soil. Incidentally, you should bear in mind that rolling a heavy soil can do more harm than good. Never use a roller to try to improve the level of the ground.

KILLING WEEDS

At the end of the spring, when the weeds have gone yellow and the temperature outdoors is up in the 60°F range, apply a composite fertilizer with a weed-killer in it, to destroy creeping and broad-leaved weeds. A typical application would be two pounds of a weed-killing fertilizer, formula 12 - 4 - 8, per 100 square feet.

If your weed problem is mainly **crab-grass** (Digitaria), you should use instead two pounds of special anti-crab-grass fertilizer, formule 6-9-6, per 100 square feet of surface. This treatment will also stop the growth of **foxtail** (Setaria) and **cockspur** (Echinochloa).

Before the start of the gardening season proper, you should also remember that grass needs a plentiful supply of water for its normal growth, and to preserve its lovely green colour. You should have a suitable sprinkler, large enough to cover the entire area of your lawn. If you have one already, make sure it's working properly.

GETTING THE MOWER READY

The first thing to do when getting the lawn-mower ready in the spring is to remove all dust and dirt which may have accumulated on the frame of the mower or on its motor. Free the rotating parts and the blade or blades from all bits of grass and leaves. Next, you should clean and replace the oil filter on the carburator. Take the spark-plug out and

Before you begin your gardening work for the year, it is a good idea to check your equipment. The lawn-mower is probably the most frequently used piece of machinery and it deserves special attention. Read the instruction-book first, and then give it a thorough overhaul, checking the spark-plug, carburetor, filters, blades and so on.

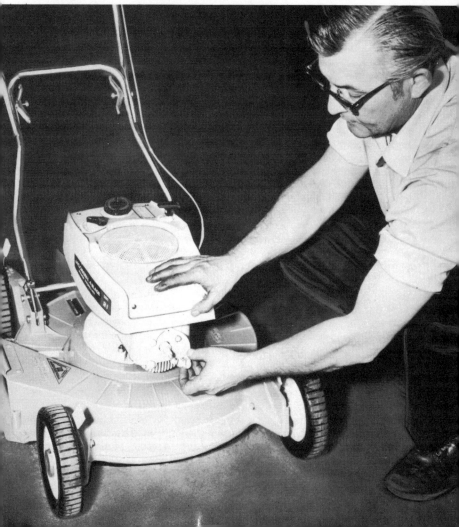

clean it — or put a new one in, if necessary. Make sure that the gap between the electrodes is the same as that recommended by the manufacturer. Also clean the fins of the cylinder-head with the help of a steel-wire brush. Empty out the gas-tank and fill it up with fresh gas and change the oil in the sump. If it is a two-stroke motor, fill the tank with the appropriate mixture of gas and oil. Then adjust the cutting system — whether it is a single blade or more. Make sure the blades are properly sharp. A dull cutting-edge crushes the ends of the blades of grass, and may cause discoloration of the lawn. Finally, tighten up all nuts and bolts, to avoid damage from vibration, and oil the mower at the points recommended by the manufacturer.

Caring For Your Lawn
In Summer

It cannot be stressed too often — a handsome lawn is the display-cabinet for the treasures of your garden. Even though it may be somewhat easier to grow a lawn than it is to grow other plants — herbaceous, annual or perennial, not to mention woody plants — all the same a lawn worthy of the name calls for a certain amount of effort on your part. Do not think that once you have sown seed or laid sod, all your problems are over and you can just sit back and admire the result of your labours. Even if you have used top-quality grass-seed mixed as recommended by horticultural specialists with the proper proportions of **Kentucky bluegrass, bent grass, tescue,** and **rye-grass;** or if you've put down the most expensive turf, that is only the **start,** even though it's a **good** start.

HOW TO KEEP YOUR LAWN IN GOOD CONDITION

You must understand that a well-kept lawn requires that the grass be kept cut all the time to a uniform height, and that it be thick and well-packed. Despite the crowded conditions, every little blade of grass must be kept in good health by strong fertilizing, sufficient watering and rigorous control of insects. As opposed to grass that grows wild in the fields and along the sides of roads and open spaces, a lawn has to withstand conditions which would cause the grass to deteriorate noticeably if the necessary care and attention were suspended for a few weeks. The **sine qua non** for keeping your lawn in a condition of which you can be proud is constant care. It must be stressed that dwarf plants such as lawn grasses have no reserves of nutritive elements — nor do they have roots deep enough to allow them to withstand prolonged dry spells or serious diseases.

AN ELEMENT OF BEAUTY

Although a really decorative lawn calls for a lot of attention, it is worth every bit of your time and trouble — for it is the essential basic element of a lovely property. With the methods, products and equipment that modern technology makes available to the amateur gardener, it is relatively easy to have a lawn you can really be proud of. Everything necessary for success is there, right under your very hand. All you have to do is make use of it! There are precision seed-spreaders for sowing fertilizers and soil improvers, there are sprinklers, automatic clippers, weed-killers and fungicides — to mention only a few of these modern aids.

When the first warm days of spring come along, garden-lovers can scarcely contain their enthusiasm. They are always impatient to get busy on their land, to care for their plants — and especially for their lawn. But when summer comes, many of them find their enthusiasm waning considerably — if not completely — as they hear the call of the sea or of the mountains, or perhaps the pleasures of golf or fishing attract them — in any case they put off the care of their lawns until the autumn or even the following spring. If the grass grows too high, it gets a rough going-over with the mower every now and then. Inevitably, this sort of negligence during the summer months brings problems in its wake that often prove very difficult to solve, because above all else a beautiful lawn demands appropriate and sufficient care during the summer season.

Several factors influence the appearance of a lawn. The most important factor is the quantity of water it receives, either from Nature or at your hands.

Then there is the degree of compaction of the surface of the soil; drainage; the frequency of mowing and the height of the cut; the level of fertility of the soil; and, finally, weeds, insects and diseases.

A MINIMUM OF WORK

Under normal conditions, it should be possible to create a good lawn and manage to keep it going in most regions of Canada. But this means using guaranteed grass-seed, or top-quality strips of turf, it means preparing the ground properly and it means faithfully applying the appropriate maintenance measures.

If you give your lawn the necessary attention in the spring — such as raking, rolling, fertilizing, liming and sowing fresh seed when necessary, maintenance tasks during the summer will be reduced to the minimum, and will consist mainly of mowing, watering, fertilizing, and possibly having to deal with **crab-grass.**

Most lawn problems can be solved with an appropriate mowing and an application of a nitrogen-rich fertilizer, for these two measures encourage a vigorous growth of grass while inhibiting the growth of weeds and clover.

WEEDS

In addition, it may be necessary to use a weed-killer to get rid of undesirable growth once and for all. You must remember that the use of such chemical products will be that much more effective if you have been giving your lawn the proper attention. The best defence against infestation by weeds is healthy, well-fertilized grass.

It seems as if weed seeds are always present — either they are already in the lawn itself, or they get blown in from outside. The best way to fight them is to spread some complete chemical fertilizer over your lawn early in spring. The formula to use is 6 - 9 - 6 with some pre-emergent control additives in it — chlordane and certain arsenates, which are particularly effective against **crab-grass.** Besides killing off the weeds, this fertilizer will do your grass good.

If your weeds (including **crab-grass)** have already come up when you spread this fertilizer with its pre-emergent control additives, then you should apply a weed-killer directly onto the leaves of these harmful plants.

WEED-KILLERS

It is essential to attack weeds at the right moment. Thus, the action of the hormones in weed-killers is most effective when the weeds are growing fastest — either in spring or in early summer. For broad-leaved weeds, such as **dandelions** and **plantains,** use a selective weed-killer - 2,4-D amine. For weeds which are resistant to 2,4-D, such as **chickweed, clover,** and several other species, apply some 'Brushkill 64' or the equivalent in September or October, to make sure of dealing with these weeds effectively before the frosts set in. To control **crab-grass** when it appears in June, and August, use a product such as 'Crab-Grass Killer'.

INSECTS AND DISEASES

Even though you keep your lawn well watered and properly fertilized, it can still be attacked by diseases. Happily, there are a number of excellent fungicides for lawns on the market, which enable you to check these diseases.

For example, 'Merfusan' is a mercury-based product which may be used in spring, summer and autumn to prevent and treat infections in your lawn. Then 'Acti-Dione RZ' is an antibiotic fungicide which is very effecttive in controlling nearly all lawn diseases, including **Kentucky bluegrass** leaf spot and **'Merion' bluegrass** rust. Insects are usually less harmful to lawns than diseases are. However, when they are in the soil, they can cause widespread damage. Treating the soil with chlordane or dieldrin is a wise precaution to take, whether insects have caused any damage or not. These insecticides control insects such as ants, white grubs and wireworms.

CARE NEEDED WHEN MOWING

A lovely lawn can easily be destroyed in a single season by means of bad mowings — for these will enfeeble the root-systems of the grass plants and make it impossible for them to recover their full vigour.

THE ROLE PLAYED BY THE BLADES OF GRASS

Of course grass plants, like any other living organism, need nourishment by using elements they draw from the soil and from the air. As the grass grows taller, the base of the blade finds itself more and more shaded, and begins to go white. This part of the blade lacks chlorophyll, and cannot manufacture the vital nutritive elements. If you remove too much of the blade every time you mow, it follows that you are also removing too much chlorophyll — and the result is that the grass plant is deprived of nourishment.

If that only happens once, the grass will not die, but it will be weakened, and its roots in particular will be affected. On the other hand, if it happens several times in the same season, the effect is disastrous.

MOW THE LAWN FREQUENTLY

This loss of chlorophyll is exactly what hapens when you let the grass grow too long before cutting it. The best procedure is to mow the lawn frequently, so that no more than a third of each blade of grass is removed at each mowing. How often you should mow depends on how quickly the grass grows. A lawn consisting mainly of **Kentucky bluegrass** needs moing twice as frequently in spring as in summer or autumn.

If your grass is not cut often enough and grows very long in consequence, do not cut it all off in one mowing. Regulate the height of the cut so as to take off just a little, making sure there is enough left to provide the necessary chlorophyll. Repeat this process, removing just a little at a time, until you've got the height back to normal.

THE HEIGHT OF THE CUT IN AUTUMN

Regular and systematic mowing during the summer is an operation you must not neglect. The height of the cut depends on several factors — such as what kinds of grass there are in your particular lawn mix, the climatic conditions, and what the lawn is used for — (games, sitting out, etc). For example, **'Merion' bluegrass** (which is an improved variety of **Kentucky bluegrass)** can be cut much shorter than **Kentucky bluegrass** itself.

A thick, well-fertilized grass can usually be cut more often than a thin, sparse grass that lacks fertilizing elements. Regular low mowing encourages the lateral growth of the grass and makes the lawn compact — and thereby easier to maintain — as well as helping to control broad-leaved weeds.

Most of the grasses used in ordinary lawn mixes grow better when they are cut to a height of 1½ to 2 inches. A lawn cut to 1½ inches is less subject to diseases, winter damage and suffocating under its own weight than one cut to 2½ inches. Mowing of the lawn should start jn spring and go on till autumn, as long as the grass continues to grow.

The length to be removed at each mowing should never be more than 1½ inches. Thus the lawn may have to be cut twice a week in spring-time and only once a week later on during the summer.

Furthermore, recent experiments have shown that too low a cut — that is, one that leaves the grass too short — has a definite harmful effect on the growth of the grass roots.

It is wrong to think that leaving the grass long in autumn is a good thing. Such a practice brings serious trouble in its wake. The blades of grass are pressed together under their own weight, or as a result of heavy rain, or under the snow, and this creates a situation very conducive to snow-mould. If mowing is carried out at regular intervals, before the grass can get too long, the clippings should be left on the lawn, since they are rapidly absorbed into it, and they enrich the grass as they decompose. Above all, it is important not to let the grass grow three or four inches long, and then cut it back to 1½ or two inches all at once.

To cut the grass properly, it is of prime importance that the blades of your mower are really sharp. Blunt blades crush the blades of grass rather than cut them — which exposes the grass to fungal diseases. It is also worth noting that rotary mowers — (such as the one shown on p. 235) — do a much better job than the one that have a rotating cylinder made up of several spiral blades.

THE NEED FOR FERTILIZING

Even if a fine lawn was given an adequate dose of fertilizer when it was laid, it must still be fertilized regularly thereafter. Nitrogen is the chief fertilizing element needed by grass, since it helps both the growth and the colour of the blades.

Even for the best of lawns life is so precarious — especially when the grass clippings are raked up and not left in place — that a complete chemical fertilizer containing phosphorus and potassium, as well as nitrogen, is recommended for most applications. As a general rule, a good mix consists of two or three parts of nitrogen to one of phosphorus and one of potassium — such as 12 - 4 - 8, for example — with small quantities of sulphur and calcium and some trace elements. If your grass is to grow regularly and present a handsome appearance, it is essential that these nutritive elements should be present throughout the entire growing season.

Mowing the lawn is an operation which should be carried out with some care, if you want to have a handsome-looking lawn. A mowing properly carried out strengthens the root-system of the grass, and makes it grow more strongly. You should set the blades to give a cut 1½ to 2 inches high. This is the best and surest way to improve your lawn.

If you use completely soluble fertilizers, you must apply them more frequently than you would a granular fertilizer, for the soluble fertilizers will have been absorbed, washed away or filtered right down into the soil before the summer has even started.

NUTRITIVE ELEMENTS

Grass plants easily absorb the three main nutritive elements: nitrogen, phosphorus and potassium. Lawn fertilizers always contain these three, in varying proportions. The essential element in any lawn fertilizer is nitrogen, as we have seen.

Phosphorus and potassium are needed for the development of the rhizomes and for a strong network of roots. Even if generous quantities of organic matter such as manure, compost and peat-moss have been used in preparing the site and laying the lawn, it is still necessary to fertilize. In fact, spring thaws and subsequent waterings involve losses of the fertilizing elements, and these must be replaced at regular intervals. I would advise using a complete commercial fertilizer — i.e., one that contains the three elements nitrogen, phosphorus and potassium: two formulas commonly used are 6-9-6 and 12-4-8. Fertilizer should be applied at the beginning of spring and again in mid-summer. Lawns grown from 'greedy' grasses such as **'Merion' or 'Flyking'** should also be fertilized again between August 15 and September 15, with two pounds of 12-4-8 per 100 square feet. The fertilizer can either be applied with a special spreader which allows an exact measurement of the quantity required — from twenty thirty four pounds per 100 square feet of surface, according to the formula of the fertilizer being used; or it can be scattered in handfuls and then dissolved into the soil by watering.

There are some long-acting organic fertilizers which do not burn the grass, and enrich the soil with precious bacteria that form rumus. The usual formula of these fertilizers is 5-5-0. Then there are some chemical fertilizers such as 6-9-6 and 12-4-8 in which the nitrogen come from urea formaldehyde, which releases nitrogen slowly over a long period. These fertilizers also contain calcium, sulphur, magnesium, zinc and iron, to improve the vigour and the colour of the grass.

As noted earlier, two treatments should be sufficient — the first at the beginning of spring and the second in the middle of summer, using two to three pounds per 100 square feet each time (depending on the formula of the fertilizer).

WATERING

To keep your lawn beautifully green and attractive all the time, you must water it all summer. It needs watering every time inspection of the soil shows it to be dry to a depth of more than half an inch, or if the grass is starting to take on a bluish tint, which shows it is beginning to wilt. Let me advise you to water often enough, and in sufficient quantity each time, to make sure that the deeper layers of the soil never get completely dried out. On the other hand, you should never water the soil to the point where it is completely soaked all the time. Also, when watering a lawn, you must never forget that different soils have different structures.

Thus, light, sandy soils call for light but frequent waterings; while heavy, clayey soils need less frequent, slower and longer watering.

Certain areas of the same lawn may very well need extra watering and fertilizing.

An obvious example of this category is any area lying beneath a tree: here, the strong, woody roots of the tree are competing with the grass for the available water and essential nutritive elemens. **Maples,** for example, have roots very near the surface and these tend to dry out the grass and rob it of its nourishment. In cases like this, you must double the amount of fertilizer, and water more frequently and more fully. If one inch of water per week is needed for open areas of a lawn during dry weather, then two or three inches per week will be needed for areas beneath trees.

A QUESTION OF JUDGMENT

Waterings must be carried out with judgment. In the first place, you should ensure that your grass plants have deep roots, so that they retain water as long as possible. The humidity of the soil is a factor of prime importance in the upkeep of a beautiful green lawn. When the temperature and the state of the soil show that the lawn lacks moisture, you must water it until the siil is thoroughly damp down to a depth of three or four inches below the surface. Watering like this helps the grass plants to extend their roots deeply. If you want to know when to water your lawn, dig a narrow hole — with an auger, for example — three or four inches deep into the soil. If the soil is dry near the surface, you should water it until it is moist to a depth of three or four inches.

Water the lawn until the water begins tricking over the surface, then stop watering for a moment or two, and then begin again. Go on doing this until the soil is damp to the full depth required.

A few hours devoted to the care of your grass during summer will give you a magnificent lawn that will form a background of rich green velvet for your flowers and home.

The Truth About Mowing
And Fertilizing

The upkeep of lawns is one of the favourite subjects of gardening experts who write in countless magazines and newspapers. Unfortunately, some of the articles are not too clear, and sometimes they are even completely and utterly incorrect! House-owners who are anxious to improve their lawns, but who know little or nothing about the subject, are all too easily impressed by these fallacious articles. Here are a few popular errors about mowing and fertilizing, together with the true facts about these matters:—

FIVE ERRORS ABOUT MOWING

1. Cutting the grass short means you needn't mow the lawn so often.
2. Raking up the grass clippings damages the lawn.
3. Close cuts in spring encourage the grass to spread.
4. Cutting the grass short stops weeds coming to seed, and thus reduces the problems they pose.
5. Letting the grass grow long to face the winter helps it to survive.

FIVE TRUTHS ABOUT MOWING

1. Grass that has been cut too short grows less than grass cut to the proper height (1½ to 2 inches), but it still needs cutting just as often. It's the untidy look of shaggy grass that dictates when it's time to mow. Experiments carried out several years ago showed that grass cut to a height of ¾ of an inch needs cutting just as often as grass cut to two inches.

2. A thinly-sown lawn which has not been suitably fertilized can benefit from the clippings being left where they lie. On the other hand, a thickish and well-fertilized lawn always looks better, and is generally in a better condition, if the cuttings are raked up — though this does not mean to say it impossible to have a handsome lawn without removing the clippings. Often, the improved appearance is not worth the trouble it takes to rake up the clippings.

3. The shorter you cut your grass, the more you reduce its vigour. There is no doubt that the vigour of the grass depends entirely on the area of the blades that is exposed to the sun.

4. Some weeds cannot survive short cuts, but others do, quite easily — even if they are cut lower than the average mowing height. **Crab-grass,** and many other weeds will produce seeds even if they're cut back to 3/16 or 1/4 of an inch. Also, experiments have shown that **Kentucky bluegrass** cut to a height of one inch produces twenty times more seed than if you cut it to 1/4 of an inch.

5. Winter rarely kills off perennial lawn grasses such as **bluegrass,** the **fescues,** or the other 'cool-weather' types. However, if the grass is too long when winter sets in, it is more subject to diseases such as snow-mould. The proper practice is to go on cutting the grass until it stops growing in the autumn.

FIVE ERRORS ABOUT FERTILIZERS

1. Chemical fertilizers are harmful to grass.
2. Chemical fertilizers should never be applied in warm weather.
3. A fertilizer provides all the nourishment needed by the lawn.
4. Every time you fertilize your lawn, you should use a complete fertilizer.
5. You shouldn't use acid-forming fertilizers on lawns.

FIVE TRUTHS ABOUT FERTILIZERS

1. You can produce a fine lawn by using solely a chemical or inorganic fertilizer; or an entirely organic fertilizer; or a fertilizer in the form of urea; or a mixture of all these types — provided only that you use them properly.

2. Heavy applications of fertilizer should always be made in the spring but light applications made in the summer are sometimes very useful. Summer applications of nitrogen improve the colour of the grass and prevent **'Merion' bluegrass** rust. However, the summer is not really the best time to fertilize thinly-sown lawns which have **crab-grass** and other summer weeds in them.

3. As for other plants, the basic nourishment of the grasses is carbohydrate, produced by the process of photosynthesis — the action of the

sun on the green colouring matter in the individual blades. What fertilizers provide, with the help of the soil and its constituent elements, is the minerals required for the formation of more complex compounds, and for numerous biological processes.

4. The soil can retain large quantites of phosphorus and potassium. If it has built up a good stock of these elements it may well be that nitrogen is the only fertilizing element required for several years. Nitrogen is exhausted rapidly, and must be replaced as required.

5. Most of the products used to provide lawns with nitrogen are acid-forming. The exceptions are sodium nitrate and calcium cyanamide, which are rarely used. The commonest chemical fertilizers (which use ammonium nitrate) and natural organic products containing urea (either pure or in other forms) generally have much the same effect on the acidity of the soil. Any acidity caused by nitrogen-rich fertilizers can easily be neutralized with lime.

How To Water Your Lawn Properly

To keep your lawn a lovely uniform shade of green throughout the summer calls for a programme of watering tailored to fit the requirements of the grass. Although it is not a very arduous task, using modern equipment, there can be no doubt that watering is still an absolutely essential factor for successful gardening.

In most soils, the grass roots go down two feet and more — unless they are hampered by lack of humidity or by the compactness of the soil. The roots will not penetrate a dry soil, or one that is so badly drained that lack of oxygen hinders the normal growth of the plants.

RAIN

In most regions of Canada, there is enough rainfall for the grass to grow, but this rainfall is not equally distributed throughout the year.

During heavy storms, almost all the water runs off without benefiting the plants; while during hot, dry spells there is not enough rain to provide all the water needed. In consequence, you must resort to artificial watering.

WHEN SHOULD ONE WATER ?

Water your lawn before the grass begins to show that it is necessary. The first sign is loss of elasticity. For example, your footprint remains visible in the grass after you have moved on. If you fail to water immediately, the grass will begin to turn brown.

The best time for watering is in the early evening, when the air temperature is beginning to drop. That cools the grass and the soil down a bit, and helps produce more dew. If the grass is being dried out by too much warm, dry weather, then you must water it in the middle of the day to lower its temperature. The blades of grass will soon return to their normal condition then.

If there are trees and bushes competing with the lawn for the available water, then obviously some extra ration will have to be supplied. A **Norwegian maple** can evaporate as much as 150 gallons of water a day — which is equivalent to the loss of three pints of water per square foot of ground. Thus, lawns which lie beneath big trees may need up to a gallon of water per square foot per day during really hot weather.

THE RATE OF WATERING

Never water faster than the absorption capacity of the ground will permit. If water starts trickling over the surface of the ground before soil is saturated to the proper depth, then that water is being lost almost as fast as you are pouring it on. It is likely to cause erosion, too, or to leach out the fertilizing elements. This is the sort of situation you see very frequently on slopes, such as embankments.

Water slowly, until the soil is dampened right down to the very bottom level of the root-system — (i.e., from 8 to 12 inches). Then wait until that water has been used up before you carry out another watering.

Another method of watering consists of supplying only half the necessary water, then repeating the operation a few hours later. This method keeps the root-system in excellent shape, and very active.

TYPE OF SOIL

Do not forget that the composition of the soil determines the quantity of water required. A heavy, clayey soil can be saturated quite easily, but the water soaks into it slowly. On the other hand, a sandy soil will absorb water almost as fast as you choose to pour it. So it is important to know what sort of soil you have. You must also know its water-absorption capacity — which indicates how long you must wait before you can apply more water without causing it to trickle over the surface of the soil. Each type of soil also has its own water-**retention** capacity. The larger the soil-particles, the less time water is retained. Thus, a block of sandy soil ten feet square by two feet deep can only hold 120 gallons of water; whereas a block of clayey soil of the same size can retain 320 gallons.

This means that a lawn laid on a sandy soil should be watered more frequently than one on a clayey soil.

246

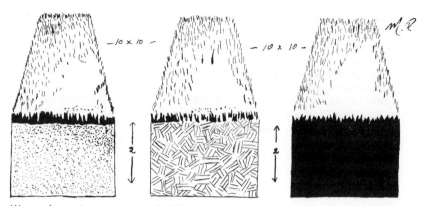

Water-absorption capacity of different types of soil. On the left, sandy soil — 60 gallons; in the centre, vegetable soil — 90 gallons; on the right, clayey soil — 160 gallons.

AERATION OF THE SOIL

Heavy soils often need surface aeration, to let the air circulate and to form pockets in which the water can be absorbed. Various sizes of aerator are available, from the cheap little devices you strap onto the bottom of your boots to a large apparatus four feet in diameter, which does an excellent job in almost no time at all.

AMOUNT OF WATER

Several methods can be used to measure the amount of water delivered to the lawn. The simplest is to stand a series of empty tin cans at strategic spots over the area. Since these cans have parallel vertical sides, the amount of water they collect gives you a reasonably accurate picture of the amount of water the lawn receives in a given time.

SPRINKLERS

There are many different sprinkler systems to choose from. A good sprinkler should produce a fine vapour, thus avoiding trickling water and the formation of puddles. Some of the stationary sprinklers spread their water in a circular pattern, while others cover a square area. Oscillating sprinklers are becoming more and more popular. Moving sprinkers cover a large area uniformly. Some models can travel as much as 30 to 40 feet in an hour, watering automatically as they go. For watering in flowerbeds and between shrubs, some people use canvas irrigators or lengths of pierced water-pipe.

More and more large properties are being equipped with automatic underground sprinkling systems — which consist essentially of a network of pipes buried under the soil, with jets set at surface level at regular intervals covering the entire area. Most of these systems also include a regulator, which shuts the water off automatically.

Although most of the water used for watering contains various chemical products — chlorine, alum and others — rain will wash away the more toxic chemical compounds. You can use your local water-supply without fear of damage from chemical products, unless there is something very obviously wrong that calls for a proper laboratory analysis.

Weeds

The most embarrassing lawn weeds are perennial plants such as the **dandelion.** These plants start growing almost at ground level, and produce their seeds very near the surface of the soil. They will remain from one year to the next, despite repeated mowings of the lawn. Other perennial plants such as **yarrow,** with flower-bearing stems that usually grow a foot high or more, can survive several mowings and cling tenaciously to your lawn in the form of low patches of vegetation that do not flower.

ANNUAL WEEDS

There are several annual weeds that generally show up in new lawns but most of them disappear after they have been mowed a few times. However, mowing will not succeed in getting rid of certain weeds with leaves and flowers that hug the ground — like **chickweed, black medic, annual veronica** and **crab-grass.**

Although the weeds that cause problems in your lawn are relatively few in number, they are well-adapted to growing in these particular surroundings, and it is therefore extremely difficult to get rid of them.

SELECTIVE WEED-KILLERS

The discovery of the selective weed-killer 2,4-D offered the first effective method of dealing with several broad-leaved weeds such as the **dandelion** and the **plantain,** without damaging the surrounding grasses.

More recently, other selective weed-killers have been developed which allow lawn-owners to keep their grass free of most broad-leaved weeds, and of several weeds from the grass family.

Here are two points about using these chemical products:
- Only apply the quantity of weed-killer recommended on the label of the container.

- Use a pressure-spray with a capacity of several gallons. This is the most effective method, and the most economical in use.

However, proper management of the grass is still the most effective means of suppressing weeds in your lawn. Use of a weed-killer can ensure the destruction of weeds which are already growing in the lawn, but a new invasion of a similar nature can only be prevented by the presence of a dense and strongly-growing crop of grass.

The Effect Of Salt
On Your Lawn

The use of salt during the winter often causes damage to lawns, but it is an easy and effective way of ridding the streets and driveways of snow and ice.

Canadian researchers have studied the effect of salt on various species of lawn grass. The results they obtained reveal that sensitivity to salt varies considerably from one species to another. One series of experiments led to the conclusion that house-owners could ward off much of the damage by giving their lawns a really deep soaking in spring, to wash out the salt deposited on them throughout the winter.

SCIENTIFIC EXPERIMENTS

During some experiments carried out under greenhouse condtions, 14 separate cultures of grass, representing seven different lawn species, were watered twice a week with solutions of road-salt — first with a 2% solution, then with a 4% solution. All the cultures proved reasonably capable of withstanding the weaker of the two solutions; but they showed clear differences in their reactions to the 4% solution. The most sensitive were common **bent grass,** which is often planted in damp ground; and **red fescue,** a species particularly suitable for planting in the shade and in sandy soils with little fertility. By contrast, **tall fescue,** a tough, clumpy plant endowed with a network of vigorous fibrous roots, proved extremely tolerant. 'Norlea' perennial **rye-grass,** currently used as a temporary cover while the permanent lawn grasses are being installed, was the most tolerant of the 14 cultures under test.

Kentucky bluegrass, the main lawn grass grown in Canada, proved superior to both **bent grass** and **red fescue,** but inferior to **all fescue** and 'Norlea'.

After the salt treatments, all the cultures were rinsed by immersion in water ,and were then allowed a period of recuperation.

At the end of 35 days, all the salt-resistant grasses had recovered their usual vigour, and their blade-growth equalled that of grasses which had not been treated. This recovery suggests that the harmful effects of salt on lawns can be lessened by soaking the lawn thoroughly in the spring.

Renewing A Lawn

THE IDEAL TIME

In the climatic region of Eastern Canada the temperature is ideal for grass-growing during the period after the extreme heat of summer and before the cold of winter. During this time, rainfall is usually adequate and regular. In this region, then, the end of August and the beginning of September represent the perfect time for sowing a new lawn or renewing an existing one, either by seeding or by sodding.

If you are dreaming of a lovely deep-green lawn, don't waste any time! Find out from your local experts which is the best time for your own particular region; and get to work without delay!

When it is necessary to renew a lawn as quickly as possible, the usual method is to use strips of turf. However, seeding is a less costly method — and it also gives grass which is much more uniform, and freer from weeds into the bargain.

The days during the last two weeks of August are the most favourable for sowing lawns. In fact, the warm temperatures of the seed-bed at that time ensure rapid sprouting, while the soil is still dry enough to be easily worked.

At this time of year, weeds grow much less vigorously, so you need no longer fear the constant appearance of harmful intruders. Furthermore, the shortened period of sunlight and the cool air of the night provide conditions which are simply ideal for grass-growing.

A NEW LAWN

To lay a handsome new lawn, the first thing you must do is prepare the seed-bed properly. Remove all stones and rubbish from the soil, and leave the surface clean. Next, if there is any vegetable soil on the surface, move it away to the edges of the area. Grade the ground so that it slopes away from your house, not towards it. If possible, avoid forming any terraces and then fill in any depressions or holes. After that, loosen up the subsoil to a depth of five or six inches. Then level the surface and add at least four inches of good arable soil — which should be fertilized by mixing in a complete chemical fertilizer, using thirty pounds of 6-9-6, or twenty pounds of 12-4-8, or fiften pounds of 24-12-6 per 100 square feet.

ORGANIC MATTER

If the surface earth is not rich enough in humus, you must add organic matter, mixing it well into the soil. This could be manure, compost, horticultural peat-moss, or rotted leaves, and it should be added at the same time as you apply the chemical fertilizer. Like most amateur gardeners, you will probably find it difficult to obtain well-rotted farm manure and you won't have any compost or rotted leaves — so you will use peat-moss as most people do. The correct quantity of this material is two bales per 1,000 square feet of surface area. Happily, it's an excellent substitute, which supplies the necessary organic matter as well as a certain quantity of nitrogen as it decomposes.

After you have loosened the soil, rake over the top of the seed-bed to remove all humps and dips and to break the top-soil up into pieces not exceeding ¼ to ½ an inch in diameter. This gives you the best possible surface for sowing your grass-seed. In addition, you should know that surfaces formed of small pieces of earth of this size help to prevent the seed being washed away during heavy rains. Another advantage is that particules this small will not harden when they dry out.

GOOD-QUALITY SEED

The quality of your lawn depends on the quality of the seed you use at the start.

I cannot possibly stress too strongly how important it is to use top-quality seed of guaranteed composition, when you come to sow your lawn. You **must** avoid buying haphazardly, and saddling yourself with just any old mixture, merely because it sounded such a bargain. I advise you to go to a nursery-gardener or a horticultural centre of well-established reputation. The best grass mixes for Eastern Canada are those which contain at least 70% of first-class permanent grasses — namely **Kentucky bluegrass** and **creeping red fescue** in more or less equal proportions. The remaining 25% to 30% should be made up of quick-growing grasses — **white bent grass, creeping bent grass, fine bent grass** and **rye-grass.** These protect the **Kentucky bluegrass** and the **creeping red fescue** by preventing weeds from getting the upper hand.

'MERION' BLUEGRASS

I should mention here that the **'Merion'** variety of **bluegrass** is becoming more and more popular, since it gives a good thick lawn which is a rich green in colour, and which resists weeds and bad weather well, provided that it receives the appropriate attention (watering and fertilizing in particular.

The amount of seed you should use is 4½ pounds per 1,000 square feet — (an area of 20 x 50 feet), or one pound per 200 square feet — (an area of 10 x 20 feet).

Alternatively, you could use another mixture recommended by the Institute of Plant Research as a result of their experiments on lawns. For a lawn which has been reasonably well prepared and irrigated, they suggest a mix containing 80% **'Merion' bluegrass** and 20% **'Norlea' rye-grass,** sown to a density of three pounds per 1,000 square feet. Another mixture recommended, under the same conditions, consists of 60% **'Merion'** and **Kentucky bluegrass,** 30% **creeping red fescue** and 10% **rye-grass.**

In damp, shady locations, use **Kentucky bluegrass** and **common bluegrass,** mixed with stoloniferous **bent grass.** In dry, shady soils, sow a mixture containing 60% **creeping red fescue,** 25% **Kentucky bluegrass** and 15% **Canada bluegrass.**

HOW TO SOW YOUR GRASS SEED

The best way to sow grass seed is to use a mechanical sower, or a fertilizer and grass seed spreader. If you do not own such a machine, you can rent one from your nursery-gardener or seed-merchant, or at a horticultural centre.

Sow the seed in both directions — up and down, and across. Then rake lightly, to work the seed properly down into the soil, and finish off with a light rolling.

Keep the seed-bed damp, but not saturated with water, until the grass has taken properly. To ensure that your seed does not wash away, moisten the soil frequently with a fine spray of water, rather than giving it a heavy watering every now and then.

Growing a lawn on a steep slope or on a terrace presents certain difficulties. Use mulches made out of chopped straw, one to two inches thick. You could also use a material loose enough to let the rain and the sunlight through, while still preventing drying-out or erosion of the seeds. Typical examples of this material are screened sphagnum moss, layers of netting and wood chips. Some people use peat-moss to cover their terraces. However, it is not generally necessary to put down mulch or lay turf on flat surfaces so long as they are kept suitably watered when there is insufficient rainfall.

FIRST MOWING NEEDS CARE

Normally, the seed will take two weeks to sprout. If the temperature stays warm, you will need to mow the new grass, but not before it is two inches high. Adjust the blades of your mower to a cutting height of 1½ inches. This first cut is a delicate business which calls for care — for it is very easy to tear the young grass out of the ground before its roots have taken hold properly.

The best results are obtained with the spiral-bladed 'rolling cylinder' type of mower — but the blades must be properly sharpened. If you must use a rotary mower, you should make sure it does not leave lumps of clippings in its wake — these could stifle the new growth during the winter.

After the grass-seed has been sown evenly, using a spreader, the soil should be raked lightly with a grass-rake, to cover the seed.

RENOVATION OF AN OLD LAWN

You can easily make a new lawn out of the one you have now, provided it contains at least 50% grass.

By a programme of weed-removal, cleaning, aeration, fertilizing and reseeding, your old lawn can be transformed into a superb carpet of green. Use selective weed-killers to remove the weeds. For the control of broad-leaved weeds (e.g., **dandelions** and **plantains**) the recommended selective weed-killer is 2,4-D amine, which is soluble in water. It is effective, and easy to use — (though ground ivy and several of the grass species of weed are resistant to it). To destroy not only **dandelion** and **plantains,** but **clover** as well — (provided that there's no **chickweed** present) — use 'Brushkill 64', 'Killex' or 'Super Compitox'. These products should be applied in September and October, to deal with the weed effectively before the frosts set in.

If your weed problem is **crab-grass,** you can control it once it comes up by the application of an anti-crab-grass liquid such as 'Crab-Grass Killer'. But it is better to eliminate it with a pre-emergent weed-killer which destroys weeds seeds as soon as they sprout. One application of this sort of product stops weeds from growing throughout the season. This type of weed-killer is recommended not only for control of crab-grass, but also for the destruction of **foxtail, chickweed, goosefoot, knotweed, lady's thumb** and so on. Another excellent way of ridding your lawn of that dreadful scourge crab-grass is to spread 'Lawn Doctor' early in spring. This is a 'fertilizer-cum-insecticide-cum-weed-killer', of formula 6-9-6, which deals effectively with crab-grass, other weeds and insects — while nourishing the grass at the same time. You could also apply 'Evergreen', very early in spring or late in the autumn. This is another 6-9-6 anti-crab-grass fertilizer, which contains Tuperson to stop crab-grass from germinating. It has the same effect on **foxtail** and **cockspur.**

CLEANING AND AERATION

After you have removed the weeds with the aid of a weed-killer, mow the grass shorter than usual to expose the surface of the soil as much as possible. I suggest you should then aerate the lawn before you fertilize or do any seeding. The best instrument for this kind of work is the aerator, which serves both to till the soil and to aerate it in one simple operation. It is just as easy to use as a lawn-mower and it can make your lawn look as beautiful as a well-kept green on a golf-course. The blades produce tiny little invisible cuts which allow air and moisture to circulate freely found the roots. Incidentally, a strong healthy lawn stifles **couch-grass** and many other weeds.

For small areas, or on a lawn which is in fairly good condition, use a 'Gardevator' — a very useful tool for loosening up the soil before you sow your grass-seed. This device consists of sixteen steel wheels, each with eight spikes on it, all mounted at the end of a 4-foot handle. It is very easily managed, and it is rather inexpensive to buy.

If you already possess a roller with flanged rims, you should buy some aeration bars. It only takes a few minutes to fix these onto the roller. Once they are in place, all you need do is roll the lawn — which will then absorb fertilizer and water more easily.

When the ground has been well aerated, use a rake to remove old grass clippings and dead grass. You could also bet rid of this rubbish with a lawn-sweeper. A rotary mower fitted with a collecting-bag is equally suitable for the purpose.

FERTILIZING AND RESEEDING

It is essential to fertilize the grass which is left in the lawn after the aeration and cleaning process. Fertilizer gives old plants a much-needed renewal of vigour, and helps seeds get firmly established. Apply a complete chemical fertilizer with a spreader: use three pounds of 6-9-6 fertilizer per 100 square feet, or alternatively two pounds of 12-4-8 for the same area.

Use one of the seeds (or combination thereof) mentioned earlier for new lawns. Sow this grass seed just as you would for a new lawn, but use only half the amounts given previously for new lawns.

Water the seeded areas, and keep them moist until the new blades of grass appear. It is important that the sprinkler should throw fine, light jets of water which will not pack the soil or scatter the seed. Though the first watering should saturate the soil, subsequent ones should be light — although frequent; they should be continued until the seed sprouts.

If it is not necessary to renew the whole of an old lawn, but merely to repair a few bald spots, all you need do is scratch the surface with a metal rake, sow grass seed and then water it thoroughly.

Of all small fruit, strawberries are the most popular — and deservedly so. Recommended varieties of strawberry, planted in good soil that faces south, will give high yields provided that you follow the approved methods of planting, mulching and picking.

Broccoli:
F-1 hybrid
'Green
Comet'

Cucumber:
hybrid
'Beauty',
for forcing

Brussels sprouts: 'Jade Cross'

Chinese cabbage: hybird
'Wong Bok'

Romaine lettuce

Cabbage: F-1 hybrid
early 'Stonehead'

Lettuce: 'Butter Crunch'

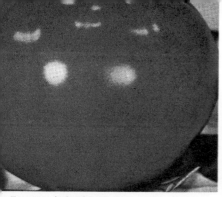

Tomato: hybrid pink 'Pinkie Gem'

Peppers: hybrid 'Bountiful'

Radishes: 'Cavalrondo'

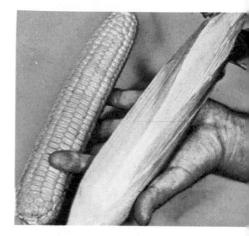

Indian corn: 'Earliking'

Carrots: 'Kuroda', long 'Chantenay' variety

Radishes: 'French Lunch'

Tomatoes: hybrid red 'Small Fry' in the basket. The smaller hybrid pink on the vines are 'Mini Pink', which are recommended for salads.

CHAPTER 13

THE KITCHEN-GARDEN
How To Make A Success Of
Your Kitchen-Garden

A kitchen-garden is not only a source of nourishing and savoury fresh vegetables, it is also an integral part of your properly which you must not overlook when you plan your general layout.

To make a success of growing vegetables you need certain basic essentials — among them, fertile soil, top-quality seeds, the proper tools and a sunny exposure near the house. It is also useful to have some knowledge of modern gardening methods.

THE SOIL

The best soil for growing vegetables is a good, deep garden loam containing sand, clay and organic matter, all in reasonable proportions. Gravelly or clayey loams are equally suitable. Furthermore, the deeper the "arable bed" or surface soil, the better the crops will be.

White onions

Celery

FERTILIZING

When it is available, well-rotted manure makes an ideal additive. Besides providing nutritive elements, manure improves the physical condition of the soil. Failing manure, you can use compost made from decomposed vegetable matter such as hay, straw, peat, weeds, grass clippings, leaves, or any other refuse that is free of diseases — even household garbage

String beans

will do. Since manure and compost do not supply the soil with either the quantity or the quality of nutritive elements it needs, you will have to fall back on commercial fertilizers. There are many chemical fertilizers on the market, and all sorts of formulas are available. The choice of fertilizer, and how much to use, will vary according to the fertility of the soil, the quantity of organic matter (manure, compost, etc) that has been added to it, and the nutritive requirements of the vegetables being grown. Thus, sandy or clayey loam with no manure in it would need about three pounds of commercial fertilizer, formula 5-10-15, per 100 square feet; while a soil treated with manure would call for 6-9-6 fertilizer, and a reduced amount would be sufficient if the quantity of added manure had been considerable.

TOOLS

For a small kitchen-garden, there is no need to buy a complicated and costly set of tools. All you need is a few simple items — a spade, fork, hoe, rake, trowel, hand cultivator and a cord for marking out straight edges.

Good quality seed is essential. Compared with the value of the resulting vegetables, the cost of such seed is almost negligible. To prepare the soil properly for the seed, you must dig it or till it in the autumn or the spring, as soon as the ground is dry enoug. Before tilling or digging, you should spread some rotted manure or some compost over the surface. If the soil already has a fair amount of organic matter in it, fifty pounds of manure per 100 square feet of surface will be enough. On the other hand, if the soil is poor, then you should add 100 pounds, or even more, of manure or compost per 100 square feet.

You can make your soil even more fertile by adding a chemical fertilizer to it. Suggested formulas are 5-10-15 for light or sandy soils — use three pounds per 100 square feet; or 6-9-6 for heavier soils, using two pounds per 100 square feet.

Finally, you should loosen up the soil to a depth of eight to ten inches, and then mix in the manure and/or the fertilizer as thoroughly as possible.

PREPARE A PLAN

Lay your kitchen-garden out in such a way that the taller vegetables — such as **Indian corn, tomatoes** on stakes, and string beans — are in the northern portion of the plot, where they won't overshadow the smaller plants beneath them. In order to avoid water trickling away and thus causing erosion, I suggest you set the rows of plants to run horizontally across the slope. Also, to make cultivating easier, put the **asparagus, rhubarb,** and other perennial vegetables at the side of your garden. As a general rule, a square or almost square garden is easier to manage than a long, narrow one. If possible, rotate your crops so that the same vegetables are not planted on the same piece of land year after year. It

Evergreen' lettuce

Hybrid 'stonehead' cabbage

Cauliflower

Brussels sprouts

Hybrid broccoli

is especially important to alternate certain items, such as **cabbages** and **turnips,** to avoid depleting the soil.

However, **onions** and most long-stemmed plants can be grown in the same soil year after year.

SOWING THE SEED

Over-generous sowing is to be avoided. It merely results in a waste of seed and extra work in thinning-out. You would be well advised to dig a level, flat-bottomed trench for the seed. This ensures even sprouting thoughout.

Big seeds — **peas** and **string beans,** for example — are put into the soil one by one. Small seeds, such as **carrots** and **lettuce,** can be sown most conveniently by using the envelope as a 'seeder', and tapping the seeds out of a hole made in one corner.

CULTIVATING AND WEEDING

Start cultivating as soon as the seedlings break through the soil, or as soon as the young plants have been transplanted from their containers into the open soil of the kitchen-garden. It is of paramount importance to destroy weeds while they are still small, before they have had time to steal the nutritive elements and the water intended for your plants.

Weeding the garden in full sunlight allows you to destroy the weeds completely, but you should pull the bigger weeds only when the soil is damp, otherwise the roots of the vegetables may dry out. Also, certain plants such as **cabbages** and **string beans** should not be cultivated during rainy weather, for then you run the risk of spreading diseases.

TRANSPLANTING

Plant out as soon as the first true leaves have formed. Space the plants out in boxes with two to five inches between them, according to

Small garden turnips

White beets or Swiss chard

262

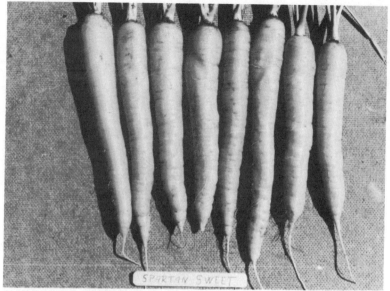

Cooking carrots

Beetroot

their variety, or transplant them into flower-pots, little fruit baskets or paper pots. Transfer them to the open ground before the roots have completely filled the inside of the container, to avoid stunting their growth.

If you use the little 'Jiffy Pots', there is not much danger of the roots being overcrowded. These pots are made entirely of peat and wood fibre, and contain small amounts of nitrogen, phosphorus and potassium. You can plant out young plants in these pots, and then put them into the ground still in the pots — for the roots will penetrate the walls of the pots easily enough.

'Red Globe' radishes

Early hybrid turnips

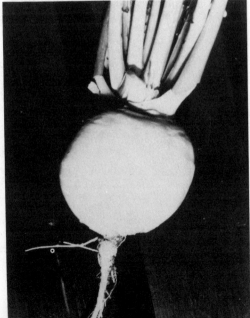

A few days before you transplant them into the open ground, start gradually exposing your plants to outdoor conditions. Water them thoroughly several hours before you transplant them. Transplant them during overcast weather, or in the evening, making sure that the soil is damp at the time. Choose stocky, healthy plants with a well-developed root-system. **Cabbages** should have leaves four to six inches long, and **tomato** plants should be at least eight to ten inches tall.

To transplant plants from fruit-baskets, cut the baskets down the four corners and lift the plants out, keeping the lump of earth intact. To free plants from pots, hold the pot upside down and tap its rim against a hard surface. In the case of boxes, cut the earth inside into squares around the plants, going right down to the bottom of the box. Dig holes the

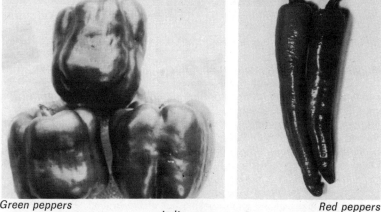

Green peppers

Indian corn

Red peppers

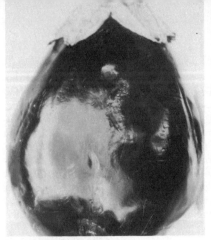

'Hybrid Beauty' eggplant

Rough-skinned 'Hubbard' squash

correct distance apart, large enough to take the plants, and set the plants into the holes without disturbing the earth around their roots. Then fill the holes up with earth and press it down firmly round the plants.

In very dry soil, water the plants once, to get the soil really moist so that it can be packed in properly around the plants. As soon as the soil has dried out a little, cover the surface with a thin layer of dry earth. If the plants you are transplanting do not have earth around their roots, set a plank on edge or drive a shingle down into the soil in front of each plant to act as a wind-break. If you place it to the south of plant, this protective shield will also provide the plant with shade. Press the soil firmly round each plant — but take care not to crush the stem.

Plant young **tomatoes** taller than ten inches in a fairly shallow trench, leaving six inches of the stem sticking out of the ground. Pour water over the base of each plant so that the moist soil comes into contact with the roots. This stimulates their growth.

Gherkin cucumbers

'Butternut' squash

Pumpkin

As soon as the plants have taken root properly, heap some more earth round them, taking care not to damage the stem at ground level. It is difficult to transplant **Indian corn, string beans** and long-stemmed plants. The most convenient course is to put them into pots, and to make sure

Watermelon

Muskmelon

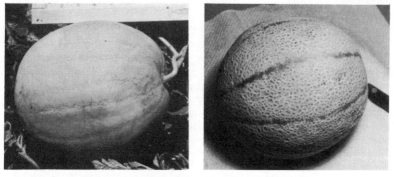

Strawberries

that you do not disturb the clumps of earth around their roots when you transplant them. **Cantaloupes, cucumbers,** and other plants which are difficult to transplant in the usual fashion can be successfully planted out in 'Jiffy Pots'.

Preparing The Kitchen-Garden In The Autumn

Amateur gardeners who already have a kitchen-garden, or intend to start one in the following spring, should prepare the ground in the autumn, before the soil is too deeply frozen.

Any work done on improving the soil in the autumn has a considerable effect on the next year's crops. Before the season is too far advanced, you should till or dig the ground you intend to devote to vegetables, in preparation for the planting you will be doing the following spring.

MANY ADVANTAGES

Many advantages accrue from tilling or digging the soil, and loosening it up. Besides burying weeds and incorporating humus into the soil, this sort of work improves the drainage, gets air into the soil and brings new soil to the surface to be broken up by exposure to the cold.

Though it is generally understood that light soils can be worked as satisfactorily in the spring as in the autumn, I should point out that it is preferable to incorporate organic matter into these soils in the autumn. This is especially true if you are dealing with a fairly large quantity of matter which is not too well decomposed, and will need as much time as possible to do so.

There are many small garden tractors available. They come in various models, with power-units of several different sizes. They offer an almost limitless variety of uses with their many accessories — rotary plough, mower, scraper blade, rotary cultivator, rotary scythe, snow scraper, snow blade and so on. The tractor shown above is pulling a small tip-truck, which can be completely emptied without uncoupling it.

Many gardeners wonder whether it is really possible to improve thin, poor soils which are not bedded directly onto rock, merely by tilling them. In my opinion it is very easy to improve them — and the procedure is very simple. All that is necessary is to add a layer of subsoil one or two inches thick every year. After a few years you will have a deep, rich soil — especially if you take care to add some organic matter every year.

ROTARY SPADES

Owners of large properties, or those who want to get on with things as quickly as possible without much physical effort, often make use of mechanical tilling devices — especially rotary spades or rotary cultivators. Some models can till a strip twenty-four inches wide.

However, the vast majority of amateur gardeners still use the good old hand spade, so I think it would be appropriate if we examined the best way of using this tool.

First of all, let me draw your attention to the fact that digging — while a healthy and invigorating form of exercise — does require a fair amount of muscular exertion, especially on the part of those whose daily life is sedentary, and whose bodies are not accustomed to this kind of work. It is best to take things fairly slowly — at least at the beginning.

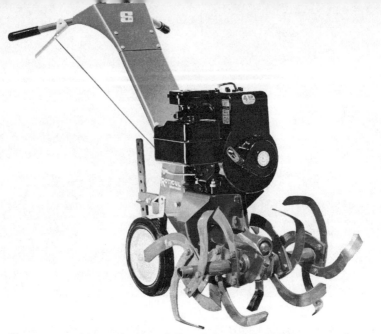

The rotary cultivator is one of the most useful machines a gardener can have. Perfectly balanced, and designed for easy handling, this machine is driven by a powerful air-cooled motor. It is fitted with self-sharpening steel teeth that will not jam.

Using a square-ended spade (which, incidentally, digs deeper than the curved round-ended shovel) dig a trench across one end of the area, as wide and as deep as the blade of the spade. Move the soil from this

Gardening tools — spade and fork

trench in a wheel-barrow and place it along the far edge of the area you are going to dig. After that, spread a layer of organic matter — compost, rotted leaves or manure — along the bottom of the trench, and start digging further trenches across the area, one after the other.

Each of these trenches is dug by driving the spade almost vertically into the ground ,six or seven inches back from the edge of the previous trench, and as deep as possible. Then pull the handle back towards you, lift the spade, and turn it over to deposit the earth in the previous trench, on top of the layer of organic matter you have already put there. Note that you must turn the spade over every time, so that the **underside** of each spadeful of earth is exposed on top. When you have dug the trench all the way across, spread a layer of organic matter along the bottom, as you did for the first trench, before you start digging the next one. Carry on in this way till you reach the other end of the patch. where you placed the soil which you moved from the very first trench with the wheel-barrow. This earth will be used to fill in the final trench, after you have spread the usual layer of organic matter in it.

Gardening tools — hoe and adjustable five-tined cultivator

HEAVY SOILS

I must emphasize that it is particularly necessary to work heavy soils in the autumn. Furthermore, the good effects of your autumn spade-work are more evident in clayey soil than they are anywhere else. This trenching procelure leaves the surface of the soil very rough and the lumps of earth are fully exposed to the effect of frost, which helps to break them down. When spring comes, they crumble away, leaving the surface loose and friable, so that all that is necessary is to rake it over before you do your sowing. I should add here that the application of lime, after you have done your digging, encourages the crumbling of the lumps of earth and loosens up the soil. Lime also has the advantage that it frees the nutritive elements locked into the tightly-packed soil particles, and makes them available to the roots of the plants. The advantage of leaving the surface of the ground in ridges after your trenching is in increasing the effect of frost on the soil. This way, the ground will drain off rapidly in spring, and will be ready to be worked on several weeks before sowing-time.

One last word. If the soil in your garden is light and sandy, do not spread any chemical fertilizers in the autumn. Then you will not run the risk of having your fertilizer washed away before the spring.

A Herb Garden

Some edible herbs are so ornamental that they are often grown in flower-gardens. On the other hand, some look so unimpressive that one prefers to plant them in out-of-the-way spots where visitors are not likely to notice them. However, if you bring them all together to form a herb garden, you can creat such an effect of old-world charm that every plant seems to be playing its part in making the garden an attractive part of your property.

GOOD SOIL

Many herbs have the reputation of growing well in the poorest of soils. All the same, the soil best suited to every variety of herb is a well-drained, average-quality garden soil. Nearly all herbs demand full sunshine, and most of them stand up well to very dry soil conditions.

LOCATION

The herb garden should be as near the kitchen as possible. This is much more convenient for the cook, who can easily run out and pick a few leaves while her pots are simmering on the stove. Somewhere sheltered from the wind has obvious advantages for a herb garden doubles as a 'scent garden', and its delightful aromas last longer in an enclosed space. If the garden must be located a little way from the house, it should be possible to reach it along a stone pathway, so that you can keep your shoes dry and free from mud when you visit it.

YOUR FAVOURITE HERBS

Though there are several ways of making a herb garden look very pleasant, you can of course content yourself with planting your choice of herbs among your other plants. Thus, little flower-beds in each corner of a sunny patio can easily be organized, and you can grow your favourite herbs in them. You could reserve one corner for **mint,** grow **chives** in another or **parsley** and have **carawway** or **fennel** or **dill** in a third.

If you adopt this sort of plan, you will probably find yourself with more herbs to grow than you have places to grow them in, and you will be forced to open up other little patches of ground to accommodate all the different species you want to grow.

The old way of growing herbs — and to me, still the most fascinating of all — was in a 'knot garden' — so called because of its supposed resemblance to a length of rope with knots spaced along it. The herbs were set all in a row and then trimmed all to the same height, so that they look like a length of hedge, all carefully clipped. Many different designs and colours were worked into the layout, with hedges winding in and out and crossing each other in accordance with a pre-set pattern. Herbs such as **lavender, thyme, mint, rue** and **wormwood** are ideal for this purpose, together with a few low-cut hedge plants such as **box** and **germander.**

Another interesting idea is to use an old cartwheel laid flat on the ground. This makes an interesting centre-piece for a herb garden.

Parsley

Dill

Thyme

273

Peppermint

Green mint

Sage

Choose a nice sunny spot and use a good sandy soil that has been well prepared. Plant **thyme** as a border all round the wheel, and put different herbs between the spokes. **Chives, sage, parsley, mint, tarragon, basil** and **chervil** are some of the plants you can use inside the wheel. If you still have room to spare, sow some **marjoram** and **winter savory.**

If you just want to grow herbs for ordinary utilitarian purposes, you can sow them in rectangular beds four feet wide with pathways running between them.

274

ANNUAL HERBS

You can divide herbs into groups, and make it easier to grow them by adopting standard methods. Aromatic cooking herbs and medicinal herbs can be divided into annual, biennial and perennial. Most amateur gardeners are primarily interested in herbs used as seasoning in cooking. Annual herbs in the culinary group are **basil, borage, chervil, summer savory, marjoram, anise** and **dill.** These can be sown outdoors during May, in the plot you have set aside for cooking herbs. Thin them out later on to a four to six inch spacing, according to how strongly they are growing.

Common basil

Summer savory

Anise

Marjoram

BIENNIALS

Parsley, caraway and **clary** are three very popular species among the biennial herbs. It is better to sow parsley seeds early in spring; during the winter you can keep them either inside the house or under the protection of a cold bed. Caraway is grown from seeds sown at the beginning of autumn, so that you get a crop of seeds the following year. It is better to sow clary in July, transplant it in the autumn, and use it the following summer.

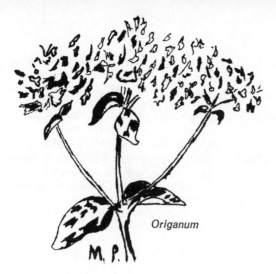

Origanum

THE BEST TIME TO HARVEST

The end of the summer is the perfect time to harvest several of these herbs. To get the best possible results, do this work on a sunny day, when the foliage of the plants is free of all traces of moisture.

As far as possible, pick your herbs during the morning, since the quantity of some of the volatile oils seems to diminish if they are picked at the end of the afternoon. Let me stress here that the aroma and the taste of **sweet basil, summer savory, marjoram** and other dried herbs depend above all on how you go about picking and preserving them.

The best time for picking herbs which are grown for their leaves is when they are in full flower. Cut them early in the morning, immediately after the dew has disappeared.

Lay the cut leaves out in a row along the edge of the bed rather than gather them into a pile, which would make them spoil very quickly. When you harvest the leafy stems of perennial herbs such as **rosemary, sage** and **winter savory**, only take the top half of the plant. If you remove more than that, you risk causing the destruction of the plant by frost during the coming winter.

Annual herbs such as **sweet basil** and **marjoram** will give a second crop if you cut them so as to leave a three- or four-inch stem on the plant.

Furthermore, since herbs tend to look alike after they have been dried, you should take care to separate and label each different species as you cut it.

PERENNIALS

Chives, horse-radish, mint, sage, tarragon, fennel (which is often treated as an annual plant) and **thyme** are excellent perennial herbs for the kitchen.

Horse-radish is difficult to transplant, and you would be better advised to sow it right where you want it to grow. Tarragon, thyme and mint multiply better by root division than by taking cuttings.

Your herb garden requires ordinary daily attention, such as weeding, cultivating and disbudding or clipping, depending on the requirements of each individual plant.

It is equally possible to grow some of your favourite herbs indoors during the winter. Early in the autumn, before the hard frosts set in, transplant little cuttings of **chives, parsley, chevril, mint** and **lemon-balm** into pots. Keep them in a sunny window, or underneath fluorescent lighting. However, remember that mint gives better results if it is taken indoors after the ground has frozen — for it needs this 'cold treatment' if it is to grow properly inside the house during the winter months.

Harvesting Aromatic Herbs

Many amateur gardeners grow aromatic herbs in order to use the leaves or the flowers or the seeds as seasoning. If you are lucky enough to be growing these plants in **your** garden to be used later to bring out the taste of your favourite dishes, the beginning of September is the right time to capture all the flavour and aroma of your herbs.

HARVESTING THE CROP

If you wish to dry aromatic herbs to keep them through the winter, you should harvest them when they are at the peak of their flavour, and in the best possible condition to be preserved. Since aromatic herbs owe their flavour primarily to the vegetable oils contained in little glands in the leaves or in the seeds, they should be picked when they are at their peak.

The harvesting of leaves should be done just before the plant comes into flower, while seeds should be harvested as their colour is turning from green to brown, before they fall. Remember that their essential oils can easily be lost if the harvesting, the drying process and the preserving are not carried out under the most favourable conditions.

THE DRYING PROCESS

Herbs which have been properly dried before being stored will keep well. Spread the herbs out on metal grills, or tie them in bundles and hang them up. Tender herbs such as **basil** and **mint** must be dried quickly in order to avoid discoloration and mildew.

The best way to dry herbs is to tie the leafy stems together in bundles, which are then suspended from a cord running across the room just below the ceiling. Protect them against direct sunlight, to avoid discoloration, and make sure there is enough ventilation to speed up the drying process. Incidentally, any empty room, or even an attic, will do for drying.

Never use an oven to dry herbs. Overheating during drying can seriously reduce the culinary and aromatic value of herbs. There is, however, a quick method, which involves drying the herbs in the oven at 250°F with the door left open. It must be carried out carefully, to avoid evaporation of the essential oils and discoloration of the leaves.

Basil

After seven to ten days, when the foliage is dry and crisp, take down the bundles you hung up to dry. Strip the leaves off each species and put them into separate containers. Whole leaves keep their flavour longer. So it is necessary to avoid crushing them before you are ready to use them. The dried leaves can be kept in hermetically-sealed jars or wide-mouthed bottles, to keep all moisture out and avoid any loss of the essential oils. If you use glass bottles, make sure they are not exposed directly to the rays of the sun. This will prevent their becoming discoloured. It is also advisable to keep these containers in a dry place.

HARVESTING AND USE OF HERBS

Here are some tips on the harvesting and use of aromatic herbs, the result of experiments carried out at the Kentville Research Station in Nova Scotia under the direction of Mr. E. W. Chipman, a professional horticulturist.

Anise: Pick this herb when the seeds are beginning to turn brown. The seeds, which taste of liquorice, are used to give an aroma to pastries.

Sweet Basil: The leaves should be harvested at the beginning of the flowering season. Cut the plants to within four to six inches of the ground. The leaves, either fresh or dried, go well with meat and vegetables.

Borage: The young leaves taste like **cucumber,** and are used in salads and marinades.

Coriander: Harvest the seeds as they begin to turn brown, and before the seed-case has split. These seeds are used in pastries.

Dill: Cut these plants when the first seeds have ripened. Use the leaves and the seeds in marinades.

Summer Savory: This herb should be harvested when the flowers are still in bud. Dry the leaves and the fresh stalks, then grind them to powder and sift them. Use for seasoning poultry-stuffing, meats and vegetables.

Caraway: Cut the umbels when they begin to turn brown, and let them dry. Use them to give an aroma to biscuits and other foods of that type.

Parsley: The leaves are generally cut as required, and used fresh. Use them as a garnish and seasoning for meats, vegetables and salads.

Balsam: Use the leaves to add fragrance to tea, soups and salads.

Chives: The tender leaves of this little plant have a delicate oniony flavour. Use them for salads, meat and vegetables.

Sweet Fennel: Pick the young shoots before they have flowered, and eat them like celery. The seeds can be used as seasoning.

Garlic: Garlic is harvested in the form of bulbs or 'heads', composed of small sections called 'cloves'. Use the cloves to season meats, vegetables, sauces and salads.

Horehound: This plant is used in moderation in salads, and to add fragrance to confectionery.

Hyssop: The upper leaves are used sparingly in salads.

Marjoram: Harvesting of this popular aromatic herb is carried out when the buds are formed. Use the leaves for seasoning meats and poultry.

Peppermint and **Green Mint:** If these leaves are to be dried, they should be harvested immediately the plants begin to flower. Use the leaves, either fresh or dried, in drinks and sauces.

Sage: Harvest this herb before it flowers. Cut six or eight inches off the top of the plant, then hang the leaves up or spread them out on a grill to dry them. Use for seasoning meats and stuffing.

Oregano: This herb is used for seasoning pâtés and pizza. It is very popular in the preparation of Italian dishes.

Sorrel: Fresh leaves are used sparingly in salads and soups.

Thyme: This is another very popular aromatic herb. Harvesting may be done while the plants are in full flower. Mix the leaves with other herbs to season meats, vegetables, soups and sauces.

SOME NECESSARY PRECAUTIONS

Mint and **parsley** lose their flavour during the drying process, unless a saline solution is used as a fixative. Use a teaspoonful of common salt per pint of water, and bring to the boil. Strip off the leaves and dip them for two or three seconds in the boiling salt water. Then shake the leaves to rid them of excess moisture, and lay them out on a grill to dry.

Tarragon also loses its flovour when it is dried. Therefore, it must be preserved in vinegar. Crush the leaves, put them into a jug and cover them with boiling vinegar. Then put the lid on the jug, and seal it tightly for a period of ten days. Note that the leaves must be completely covered by the vinegar, and that the jug must be shaken twice a day during the soaking-period to make sure the tarragon is properly infused. at the end of the ten days' soaking, strain off all the vinegar through a piece of muslin, then preserve the **tarragon** in sealed pots.

Pimpernel, sweet basil, mint, marjoram and **savory** are excellent in summer salads, to which their subtle flavour adds a little extra touch.

OTHER PRESERVING METHODS

In certain Mediterranean countries **sweet** basil is preserved for the winter. Several layers of fresh herbs are placed in pots. The leaves stay fresh and green, and can be used as needed. Other herbs are dealt with in the same way.

Many species of herbs, including **fennel, anise, caraway, coriander, cumin** and **sesame,** are grown for their seeds. The seeds are harvested as soon as they begin to turn brown, and the stems are showing signs of drying out. To avoid losses caused by the splitting of the seed-cases, cut the umbels directly into the containers. In order to avoid mildew, the seeds should be thoroughly dried on a fine-meshed grill before being stored.

ROOTS USED FOR SEASONING

Two herbs grown for their roots are **angelica** and **lovage.** They should be dug up for drying in the autumn, when they are in the dormant states. Prepare the roots for preservation by washing them and scraping them thoroughly, then cut the thicker ones lengthways.

Spread them out in a thin layer on a mesh screen in a well-ventilated room, and change their position once a day. The roots dry slowly, and it will take up to six weeks before you can put them into containers to store them. Before you do this, check how far they have dried out by bending them. If they are really dry, they will snap. When they are fully dry, store them in hermetically-sealed containers.

Blueberries In Your Garden

Many amateur gardeners grow **blueberries** in their garden. These plants are not very demanding. All you need do is give them an acid oil, rich in organic matter, and they will grow into fine plants that bear tasty fruit in summer. Blueberry plants will give pretty white flowers in profusion in the spring, and striking foliage in the autumn — both of which are definite assets to the appearance of your garden.

Rosemary

Blueberries grow well wherever the climate is suitable for growing apple-trees. They are fairly new additions to the list of cultivated plants — they were regarded as 'wild' until some fifty years ago. Since then they have come to be regarded as an important fruit-bearing species. Their popularity as garden plants has grown considerably, thanks to the selection of superior varieties which grow better and give an abundant crop of fine, delicious fruit.

Improved varieties such as **'Jersey'**, **'Rancoco'** and **'Rubel'**, produce splendid crops from the third or fourth season after planting. The plants bear fruit for from ten to twenty years.

SOIL AND PLANTING

Growing blueberries is relatively simple, provided that you give them the proper oil — i.e., acid (a pH value of 4.8 is regarded as the optimum), rich in humus, sufficiently moist and well drained.

The best time for planting is early in autumn, as soon as dormant plants are available, or in spring. The best plants are those which are one or two years old. Owing to their long life-span, and their eventual size, you should plant them three or four feet away from each other. If you prefer to plant them in rows, space the rows six to eight feet apart. Also, you should grow at least two varieties, to ensure good pollination. Although it is not necessary to give the soil any special preparation, it is a good idea to work a little sawdust or peat-moss into it before you do your planting.

The better varieties of blueberry yield a splendid crop of fine, delicious fruit.

MULCHING

Because of the nature of their root-systems, you must make sure that your blueberry plants are set at the right depth. If they are planted too deeply, their growth will be affected.

As soon as you have planted them, spread a mulch of organic matter in a circle two feet in diameter around the base of each plant. If you are planting in rows, spread the mulch between rows. Furthermore, the mulch should be thick enough to control weeds, and to ensure this you should add a little more at the end of each autumn.

SAWDUST

Several materials can be used as mulch. But sawdust is certainly one of the best — and it makes no difference whether it comes from hard wood or from soft. Incidentally, sawdust has no effect on the reaction of the soil or on its pH, although the bacteria in the soil use the nitrogen in the sawdust. For this reason, it is advisable to add nitrogen to the soil. If you are unable to obtain sawdust, then peat-moss, pine needles, straw or other organic matter should be used.

Among the many advantages of mulching, some of the most significant are that it helps conserve moisture and control weeds, thus doing away with the necessity for frequent weedings. In addition, a mulch helps the plants to get properly rooted — with the result that they give more abundant crops with larger fruit. On this subject, you should know that a six-year series of experiments on growth showed that plants grown with a sawdust mulch gave one-and-a-half times more fruit than the others.

FERTILIZING

Blueberries produce much more fruit when they are fertilized, especially with nitrogen-rich fertilizers. Apparently, the soil in mountainous regions provides enough of the principal fertilizing elements, with the exception of nitrogen. In this type of soil, blueberries prefer to use nitrogen obtained from an ammoniac source rather than that obtained from nitrates.

For soils with a pH vaulue greater than 5, the experts recommend ammonium sulphate as the source of nitrogen. In addition to providing nitrogen, this sulphate also tends to bring the acidity of the soil to the correct level. The quantity of this fertilizer required varies according to the age of the plant. For plants with mulch, apply ¼ lb.; but as the plants mature increase the quantity gradually until each plant is getting about one-half pound each growing season.

The best time to fertilize is early in spring, before the year's growth gets under way. The treatment should cover an area slightly larger than that described by the ends of the branches. Since ammonium sulphate is soluble, it is not necessary to work it into the soil. However, when the soil is relatively acid, with a pH value less than 5, any form of nitrogen suits the micro-organisms in the soil, which readily transform 'nitrate' nitrogen into 'ammonium' nitrogen. For light soils, an occasional application of a complete chemical fertilizer such as 6-9-6 is recommended.

A SERIOUS PROBLEM

One of the major problems that amateur gardeners have had to solve in growing blueberries at high levels is chlorosis, or yellowing of the foliage. Besides affecting the colour of the leaves, chlorosis stunts the growth of the plants, weakens them and prevents them from bearing fruit. In really serious cases, or if the condition persists for a long time, the eventual outcome is the death of the plant.

Chlorosis is caused by an insufficiency of iron, and is apparently due to the blueberry plant's inability to use the iron present in the soil. Indeed, it is quite common to find other plants growing very successfully in soil in which the blueberry suffers from chlorosis. This problem made it difficult to grow blueberries in mountainous soils until the discovery in 1950 of iron compounds which could be assimilated in the soil. These compounds form a quick and long-lasting solution to the problem of chlorosis. One application of two or three ounces for each plant affected will make every symptom of chlorosis disappear within less than thirty days. The effect of the treatment lasts two or three years.

PRUNING

Annual pruning is recommended, since well-pruned plants not only look better, but also yield abundant crops of fine large berries. A blueberry plant produces large fruit-buds on its young shoots, while below these buds, on the same shoots, there are smaller leaf-buds.

During the first two years after planting, prune back the flower-buds to obtain bigger and more productive plants. During succeeding years, when the plants are well rooted in, remove some of the flower-buds every spring. This will maintain normal growth and a uniform production of good large fruit.

Since the best fruit is borne on the strongest shoots, make sure you get rid of any weak, short, flimsy shoots or branches. When a plant bears a good number of buds, prune the strongest fruit-shoots by removing some of the flower-buds from them.

Few indoor plants can rival the beauty and charm of the episcias. These tropical plants attract and hold one's attention by their brilliant flowers and their leaves, which display a great variety of colours, shapes and textures.

CHAPTER 14

GROWING PLANTS INDOORS

THE AESTHETIC VALUE OF PLANTS

During the summer season, how pleasant it is to see the profusion of green and flowering plants which fill our gardens! In the winter, the beauty of these plants is sadly missed. However, the lack of green plants outside may be at least partly compensated for by growing plants indoors.

Of course, the space restrictions in most modern homes will not allow a large number of plants to be cultivated inside. However, you will discover that there are some very interesting combinations of plants which require similar conditions for successful growth in the home.

Scattering potted plants about a room in a haphazard fashion can destroy the otherwise attractive effect which may be created by massing them together in one area of a room. An arrangement of plants may be combined with pieces of sculpture, lamps or other decorative objects to create a striking effect in a room. The use of decorative containers, elegant plantstands or hanging baskets can enhance the appearance of your plant arrangement as well.

Plants are popular with professional interior decorators and are almost always used in display homes and offices. A group of ferns in a window, a potted palm in a bare corner, vines around a library window, several plants grouped together on a stand — are all tricks used by decorators to beautify a room. Regrettably, however, the professional decorator is usually more interested in the decorative effect than in the life span of the plants he or she chooses. This often results in the death of some of the less hardy plants in the group — and disaster to the effect created by their presence!

THE IMPORTANCE OF LIGHT

If you want to keep your plants for a good long time, the very first step is to find out what their conditions of growth are in the surroundings you have chosen for them. It is not very difficult to do this. You begin by determining how much light is available, because certain plants grow better in full sunlight, while others prefer a shaded light. Generally speaking, flowering plants need the sun, but you will get better results with leafy plants if you grow them in the shade or in a place where the sun's rays are filtered through curtains. For example, some plants which are easy to grow indoors, but which need a lot of light are: **episcia,**

*Philodendron and Mexican breadfruit are special favourites among apart-
ment plants. These leafy plants are easy to grow, and have a splendid
decorative effect.*

begonia, African violet, crown of thorns (Euphorbia splendens), **coleus,
gloxinia, geranium, kalanchoe** and **shrimp plant** (Beloperone guttata).

Other plants grow quite happily indoors during the winter, provided
that you put them in a spot that does not receive too much sun. These
include: **philodendron, aspidistra lurida, chlorophytum, dieffenbachia, dracaena, creeping ivy, fern, ficus,** and **wandering Jew** (Tradescantia fluminensis).

ARTIFICIAL LIGHTING

Outdoors, plants receive light from all directions at once, while indoors
they are only lit from one side. This means turning them frequently to
avoid their becoming deformed.

In this respect, artificial lighting is a very valuable aid, in addition
to creating some charming light-and-shade effects in the foliage. You
should note that a plant which needs a lot of light will not survive in semi-
darkness for very long. Furthermore, any sudden change of lighting or
temperature can have a serious effect on a plant. Thus, leaves and buds
may drop off when the plants are moved indoors from the greenhouse
in winter, unless they have been insulated with paper.

Plants react badly to a sudden loss of light and moisture, which usually
happens to them when they are moved inside from a greenhouse. Even
multiple waterings are not very helpful in this event.

If you cannot find space in front of any of the windows of your house,
you should use some form of artificial lighting. There are fluorescent tubes
specially adapted to growing plants indoors available now, and these
allow you to put flowers in the gloomiest corners — on the shelves of
your library, say, or even in cupboards. Lighting systems mounted on
special stands can be raised or lowered to suit the height of the plants.

The light-source is usually placed some twelve to fourteen inches above the top of the plants. You can buy complete outfits — a flower-box on a stand, complete with fluorescent tube above. 'Do-it-yourself' experts will prefer to build the stand themselves, to suit their own particular needs. You can also buy transparent boxes or tanks provided with fluorescent tubes, in which the correct humidity for any given species of plant can be maintained all the time. We shall look at this matter of artificial lighting more closely later on in this chapter.

WATERING

Although indoor plants are, generally speaking, very resistant, they cannot survive prolonged neglect. They need regular watering, adequate fertilizing and all the usual attentions.

There is nothing complicated about watering. All you need do is touch your finger to the surface of the soil. If the soil is beginning to dry out, water it thoroughly with warm water until it is completely soaked, and water starts trickling out from the drainage hole at the bottom of the pot. You need not water again until the surface of the soil again feels dry to the touch. Remove any excess water from the saucer underneath the pot, if it has not been absorbed within half an hour.

Since excessive watering is one of the chief causes of loss of plants, it is inadvisable to remove several plants from their individual containers and group them into one box or one common pot, with a view to creating a decorative effect.

Certainly few plants require exactly the same conditions, watering and lighting all the time. Thus, one plant will eventually dominate, while the others will tend to wilt and lose their looks. It is better for each type of plant to have its own container. This is a more flexible arrangement, which enables you to place plants individually wherever you want them, and thus avoid the impression of a flower-show exhibit of plants put together quite haphazardly on the spur of the moment. What you must try to get across instead is a reflection of your own good taste, your sense of harmony and your willingness to experiment in matters horticultural. There is a very wide variety of plants with flowers or foliage of the most striking colouring, which grow well either in full sunlight or in the shade. If you have a window that catches the sun, there are a great many indoors plants you can grow successfully.

On the other hand, there are plenty of plants that do very well in places where there is not much light at all. Some of these are **waxplant** (Hoya carnosa), **tradescantia, dracaena,** and **scindapsus** or **pothos.**

Every now and then these leafy plants can be replaced temporarily by **chrysanthemums, azaleas,** or **cyclamens** in pots. For those with a taste for research and experiment, I suggest that you try **oxalis, anthurium, spathiphyllum** and some of the **bromeliads** from the **pineapple** family.

If a plant is doing well, thanks to your care, it is certainly worth while keeping it, even though you are perhaps not getting the full benefit from it. Quite possibly the appearance of a plant, or even just the colour of its foliage, may be enough to interest you. On the other hand, you may prefer instead to group several plants of the same species together, to produce a pleasing mass effect. On this subject, it is worth mentioning that if you have your plants on stands of different heights, you can give them more light, more air, and a better appearance generally, than if you merely set all your pots at the same height.

Plastic pots and earthenware pots call for quite different methods of watering. The plastic containers tend to keep their moisture longer, since their walls are impervious to water and water-vapour, whereas the earthenware type allow water to evaporate through their pores.

One kind of pot is no better than the other. The important thing is that the pot should have a hole in the bottom for drainage, so that the roots never suffer from a lack of oxygen.

FERTILIZING

Fertilizing cannot really be described as a problem. Just follow the instructions printed on the container — and remember it is important **not** to use larger quantities of fertilizer than those suggested by the manufacturer.

Plants which need full sunlight for their growth should be fertilized once every 15 days. Those that grow in less well-lit places don't need fertilizing so often, once a month will be sufficient, even once every two months in winter.

NEED FOR MOISTURE

The principal problem you have to face in the growing of plants indoors is lack of moisture. However, there are several methods of effectively combatting the harm caused by the dry, overheated air of our houses.

It is not easy in our overheated homes to provide our plants with the moisture they need. The ideal would be to maintain the indoor temperature constant at 65°F in winter — but of course that is impossible.

One very popular method of maintaining ideal conditions for plants indoors is a flat dish of water with the bottom covered with little pebbles, on which the potted plants stand. Another way of decreasing the dryness of the air in winter is to put containers full of water on your radiators. However, a humidifier is much more effective, since it automatically maintains a degree of humidity that suits both the occupants of the house and their plants. If you are already using fluorescent tubes to provide the light your plants require, here's a little trick to increase the humidity around them. Take a large piece of plastic sheeting, or a large plastic bag, and enclose everything in it — lighting strip, and container. This 'tent' will keep the humidity in, and maintain a steady temperature.

Very fine effects can be obtained by growing philodendrons on pieces of bark, bits of driftwood, stakes covered with sphagnum moss, and other artistic supports of that nature.

Generally speaking, there is no need to transplant your house plants during the winter, since their growth tends to be fairly moderate. Furthermore, they can be placed quite close to one another, provided that their leaves do not actually touch. This grouping of plants has the advantage of increasing the local humidity where they are standing, as a result of evaporation of water-vapour from the soil and from their leaves. Obviously, the trays with the water and the pebbles in the bottom will increase the humidity still more. But equally obviously this does not remove the need for watering.

DISEASED PLANTS

Any plant that is in a healthy state after about a month in a dry room can be classed as a success. On the other hand, that does not do away with the necessity of getting rid of wilted, diseased or abnormal specimens without the slightest hesitation. You should not waste time on imperfect plants. It is very much better to go out and buy some new ones — it will prove much cheaper in the long run. Unfortunately, many people hate to discard plants, even when those plants are clearly beyond saving, simply because the plants were gifts. They rarely stop to consider that the person who gave them the plant has probably forgotten the incident entirely — and probably did not expect the plant to live for very long in any case.

Perserverance is an admirable quality, but it is better not to waste your energies and patience on a plant which often is of no particular interest, and which is merely taking up precious space. It is much better to buy an interesting new plant — perhaps one a little out of the ordinary — and quite often this course will be less expensive, too.

If you can properly appreciate the aesthetic value of plants in a house, and if they really give you pleasure, then it is in your own interest that this pleasure should be as complete as possible. Let me advise you, therefore, to remove all wilted, sickly plants without a second's remorse, and to replace them.

When we talk about the 'upkeep' of plants, what we really mean is an extension of the care we normally lavish on them. Among other things, it means removing leaves and flowers which have faded and started dropping, and it means driving stakes to support plants before they have begun to droop too much. I would also recommend that you turn your plants regularly, so that they do not get light from one direction only, which causes uneven growth.

Some Useful Tips To Help You Grow Indoor Plants

Those who grow plants indoors do not do so merely because they like the foliage, shape, colour or smell of the flowers. The real reason is the challenge of trying to save plants which, generally speaking, will not survive and grow normally without special care, since they are being grown in artificial surroundings.

Most of our house plants came originally from the jungle, the marshes, plains or mountains. Their survival depends on an equilibrium between air, water and the nutritive elements in their soil or other growing medium.

The general interest that we show in plants, whether they be grown outdoors or indoors, is by no means accidental. This is why the plastic philodendron will never be able to replace the genuine article. Living plants appeal to our sense of the marvellous, to our natural curiosity and to our capacity to accept responsibility.

You hear a great deal about people with 'green thumbs' who are always lucky with their plants. Nothing could be further from the truth — there is no such thing as 'luck' with plants. Just give them what they need, and they will grow wonderfully well. Give them just a little less than they need, and they may not survive. Deprive them of most of what they need, and they will surely die. In brief, success in growing a plant quite simply means understanding what it needs.

When we move our garden plants indoors, we do so in order to continue admiring them. To admire them, we have to look at them, of course. You must look at your plants very thoroughly. If a plant seems a bit droopy, or if it is discoloured, or if its leaves or flowers are not normally shaped — then there is definitely something wrong. It is up to you to keep your eyes open, to notice what state your plants are in, and to find out the cause if anything is wrong. It is much better to carry out this task yourself than to entrust it to others.

WATERING

If the leaves are soft, it may simply be because they need water. However, you must determine why. There is nothing complicated about this. Just push your finger into the soil up to the first joint. If it comes out dry, then the plant needs watering. On the other hand, if you can feel moisture, the problem could be too much water round the roots. The roots may be saturated with water, and beginning to rot — which means they can no longer absorb the water from the soil and feed it to the leaves.

Do not hesitate to up-root the plant by pulling it right out of its pot in order to get a good look at the roots to see if they are too dry, too wet or diseased.

WATCH YOUR PLANTS CAREFULLY

If the problem is an insect such as the mealy-bug, turn the plant upside down and submerge it completely in a bucket filled with a solution of Calathion. Finally, you must inspect your plants closely, handling them if necessary, to find out what is affecting them. If you are at all serious about growing plants, then you must develop your powers of observation. This is where the real joy of gardening lies — in integrating yourself with Nature — so you may have a better idea what to expect.

FACTORS FOR SUCCESS

The needs of a plant are not always the same, nor are they definite. You will understand them better if you have a basic knowledge of the principles of horticulture.

As far as soil is concerned, if you know what degree of air, water, and nutritive elements the roots need, then you will know what sort of soil is reuired for potting purposes. The key to success is drainage. The soil must be sufficiently porous to get rid of any surplus water and admit the oxygen needed by the roots. To maintain the necessary porous quality, you may add some inorganic matter to the soil — such as sand, bits of broken pottery, ground ashes, vermiculite or perlite. On the other hand, I should mention here that organic matter such as vegetable soil, compost or peat-moss is also necessary to provide the nutritive elements and the general medium required for satisfactory root-growth.

Generally speaking, the following medium suits indoor plants very well: mix 4 parts of loam, 2 parts of peat-moss or compost, 1 part of dried cow-dung (or the equivalent), 2 parts of coarse sand and some gravel or small pebbles for drainage purposes. For each bushel of this mixture, add one half-litre of powdered bone-meal and one quarter-litre of a complete chemical fertilizer such as 6-9-6. For **begonias, African violets, gloxinias** and other plants which prefer a woody soil, use two or three times the quantity of organic matter.

For **cactuses** and succulent plants, which need a rough, rugged soil, use two or three times the quantity of inorganic matter.

In the case of **azaleas** and **gardenias,** use acid soils and peat-moss, and treat them with an acid chemical fertilizer. The few plants which do well in alkaline soil, such as **'Martha Washington' geranium**, need a soup-spoonful of ground lime added to each six-inch pot.

Rex begonia (shown on the left) is an excellent house plant, which is available in several combinations of attractive colours. Vulcan kalanchoe (on the right) bears bright scarlet flowers in great numbers: these flowers make the kalanchoe one of the most decorative of indoor plants.

POTTING

Always use clean containers provided with a good drainage hole in the bottom. This hole should be covered with a layer of potsherds or coarse gravel.

Then add a layer of peat-moss or leaves, to stop the soil leaking out of the drainage hole or blocking it. Then add your soil, up to about ½ an inch below the lip of the pot. The soil should be tamped round the roots, and you should water it thoroughly to get rid of air-pockets. To compensate for the shock of transplanting, it is essential to keep your plants well away from draughts, and to provide them with excess moisture (for this, you can cover them with a plastic bag at night-time). Water them sparingly, and do not give them any fertilizer, at least for a period of se weeks, until the new roots have begun to grow and the plants are pro settled in.

WATER CAREFULLY

A good watering is one which keeps the soil sufficiently damp without drowning the roots. Waterlogged soils are deprived of air, and the roots are likely to die from lack of oxygen. When you water a plant, wet the soil all the way down to the bottom. Then do not add any more water till the soil has dried out. Succulent plants and **cactuses** come from desert regions, and can stand a much greater degree of dryness round their roots before they get their next watering than can plants grown in moist soil, such as **ferns** and **African violets.**

The only valid rule for watering is to keep a close watch on things, and to use your own judgment.

Plants like **bonsais,** the little dwarf trees, with their roots in relatively shallow containers, may need watering once or twice a day, while plants in large containers may be able to last up to two weeks between waterings.

FERTILIZERS

There are several excellent brands of fertilizer especially made for house plants. However, it is essential that you follow the maker's recommendations exactly. Thus, if a plant requires such-and-such a quantity of fertilizer, you do **not** do it twice as much good by doubling that quantity — quite the opposite, in fact. Remember, do not expect these fertilizers to solve all your problems for you when you are growing plants indoors. Fertilizing will not help a plant that is being attacked by insects or diseases or which is receiving too much water or is not draining properly.

INSECTS AND DISEASES

Diseases are less frequent in indoor plants than they are among greenhouse plants, because the atmosphere inside the house — which is usually drier — prevents the growth of microscopic fungi and bacteria. The appearance of powdery mildew and bacterial spots is normally due to an excess of moisture.

Rotting of the roots can usually be attributed to faulty drainage and excessive watering. The only satisfactory remedy is to correct these harmful conditions.

However, leaf spots and fusarium-type leaf rot may well be caused by too low a humidity — especially during the winter months when houses are artificially heated.

The most harmful insect pests are greenflies, scale insect, mites, mealybugs and whiteflies. Except for mites, all these insects are killed by spraying with, or immersing in, a solution of a Malathion-based insecticide. To put a stop to mites, whether they be the common red spider variety or the **cyclamen** mites, spray or soak the plant in a solution of Karathene, or Dimite or other equivalent product.

The essential thing in the war against insects is to act the minute you discover their presence. **Don't** wait till your plants are completely overrun. As you have already learned from your gardening experience, one of the basic principles of gardening is foresight.

The Best Soil Mixture

It is easy to grow plants indoors. Except for the really fragile varieties, plants will often accommodate themselves to inadequate conditions. There is, however, one basic factor which will not only help you to succeed, but also to achieve success in a measure which will really surprise your family and your friends. Use the best soil available. It must be sufficiently porous to allow surplus water to drain away, and admit the oxygen needed by the roots.

THE PROPER MIXTURE

Most of the ills that affect indoor plants stem from a poor soil, which is badly drained and possibly acid. This is due to the fact that a great many people think that house plants can accommodate themselves to any soil, or at least a soil that comes from the garden, even if it is poor in organic matter and fertilizing elements.

Generally speaking, though, garden soils are **not** suitable for growing plants in containers indoors. Also, in most cases, they do not have enough humus in them to retain moisture. However, taking into account the fact that plants grown in pots are in a medium very different from their natural medium, it is absolutely essential to put them into a soil which contains the special elements which can compensate for this radical change in surroundings.

The first requirement for these soils is to be able to drain easily, so that they do not become acid. This is why the ideal mixture contains coarse sand or gravel, and vermiculite or perlite — substances which are more or less inert, which permit the roots to spread out, and which let the air penetrate freely. Furthermore, it is essential that the medium should contain some humus, to retain moisture in sufficient quantity for it to be assimilated by the roots of the plants. Humus is provided, either by farm fertilizer, (manure, well-rotted leaves, compost) or, failing any of these materials, by peat-moss.

VARIOUS FORMULAS

Many horticulturists have obtained good results with mixtures consisting of half peat-moss and half sand, perlite or vermiculite. Other professional gardeners produce some very lovely plants in their greenhouses using nothing but ground sphagnum moss. These are mediums which suit the majority of indoor plants very well. However, since there is no

Dieffenbachias are tall, upright plants with magnificent oval leaves. They prefer a porus vegetable soil, which drains off quickly. Plants like Dieffenbachia amoena, shown below, must be watered twice a week.

earth in them, regular treatments with a liquid fertilizer are necessary — formula 20-20-20, for example, using one soupspoonful per gallon of water, every two weeks.

You can supply the necessary humidity to your plants by placing the pots in flat trays filled with pebbles and water.

A GOOD ALL-ROUND MIXTURE

As I mentioned earlier, an excellent mixture for indoor plants is four parts garden loam, two parts compost or peat-moss, one part dried cow-dung or other manure, and two parts coarse sand.

To each bushel of this mixture, you should add one half-litre of pow-dered bone-meal and one-quarter litre of a complete chemical fertilizer say, 5-10-15. Some plants, **gloxinias, begonias** and **African violets** for example, prefer a more woody soil. For these, you should use two or three times the amount of organic matter. Other plants, such as the **cactuses** and succulents, need a rugged soil. For them, use double or triple the amount of coarse sand. As for **gardenias** and **azaleas,** they should be grown in a mixture of acid soil and peat-moss, and treated with an acid fertilizer. Not too many plants grow well in alkaline soil, but the few that do, such as the **'Martha Washington'** variety of **geranium,** should have a soupspoonful of powdered lime added to each six-inch pot.

You will also find mixtures on the market especially prepared for growing plants indoors. They are ready for immediate use; and most of them have been sterilized to make them even safer to use. Incidentally, if you prepare your own mixture, I would recommend that you give it partial sterilization, either by heating it or by chemical fumigation. In this way you will destroy any harmful bacteria, larvae and eggs of insects, and any weed seeds that may be contained in the soil.

WATERING

Watering plants is really a very simple matter — though for many people it seems to be a fearsome task. Let me say at once that there are no hard-and-fast rules that apply to all house-plants. Each plant has differ-ent needs. It is important to water properly. All you need do is touch your finger to the surface of the soil. If you can feel that it is beginning to get dry, the time has come to water. You do not need to water it again until the next time it feels dry to the touch. Now, **how** you should water your plants?

FROM ABOVE, OR FROM BELOW?

Should you water them from above the pot, or irrigate them at the surface of the soil? Research into this question has shown that it really does not make much difference either way. I personally would advise you to make a change, if you always irrigate your plants at the surface of the soil. Watering from above washes away any accumulation of salt, which can be harmful to certain plants such as **African violets** and **gloxinias.**

When you water from above, you should use water which is at room temperature. It is essential that the water be able to make its way through the soil in the pot, and that all surplus be drained away. If the water stays on the surface, it means either that the soil is too hard-packed ,or that there is no drainage. If this happens, you must change the soil in the pot and replace it with a porous mixture and you must also provide proper drainage by covering the holes at the bottom of the pot with broken pottery shards or gravel, to stop the holes from beccomming blocked. In addition, proper drainage will enable you to avoid any inconvenience resulting from excessive watering.

If you are using a mixture with a good proportion of perlite, vermiculite or sand in it, it is practically impossible to over-water, since the water makes its way very rapidly through this material.

FREQUENCY OF WATERING

Far too many people water their plants too often. Some of them even keep their plants in a pool of water all the time, in the hopes of ending the watering problem once and for all. Such practices are definitely harmful to the plants.

The leaves of your plants are a sure guide as to how often you should water. Plants with large thin, soft leaves use more water than those with hard, waxy leaves. The **sanseviera**, for example, can live a long time without water. On the other hand, the **coleus** wilts very quickly if it does not receive sufficient water. I advise you to check your plants every morning, and not to let them wilt. Take care, however, not to over-water them in a misguided attempt to avoid letting the leaves get too dry.

Well-established **African violets** (Saintpaulia species) — for example, those in four-inch pots filled with a peat-moss compost and kept at normal temperatures — do not need watering more often than once every four days.

Plants with fleshy leaves, such as **aloes, crassulas** and the various types of **cactus,** will stay healthy without any water for as long as four to six weeks. On this subject, you should know that desert **cactuses** benefit from a rest-period if you leave them without water from December to the end of March.

Leafy plants such as **dieffenbachia, philodendron, scindapsus** or **pothos, aglaonema, aphelandra** and **peperomia** need water every three days if they are planted in the vegetable soil that they prefer.

Some Suggestions To Add To The Variety Of Your Plants

The middle of March is the time when many amateur gardeners check over their indoor plants in preparation for the coming of spring. Take the opportunity of getting rid of any of yours that are wizened or half-dead. It really is not worthwhile trying to revive plants which are not doing well — especially when you can get good replacements at quite reasonable prices. It will also give you a good opportunity to try out new varieties and thus to increase the pleasure you get from your hobby.

EPISCIAS

If you have any **African violets** that are looking sickly, now is the time to replace them. Look for some of the new cultivars with fringed or lacy edges, or perhaps some of the characteristic varieties with leaves resembling **holly** or oak. Wherever you are, you are likely to find some **African violet** fancier with his head buried in the catalogue of new varieties, hoping to find something good available at his local gardening centre.

In both Canada and the United States, indoor plant lovers have been so taken with the **African violet** that for almost twenty years they have tended to neglect several interesting relaed species. It is only recently that articles devoted to **episcias** have started appearing in the **African violet** periodical reviews. Sometimes known as **flame violets,** these plants look quite like the **African violet** and require the same sort of attention while they are growing, although they are less demanding concerning surroundings and general upkeep.

Their flowers are reddish-scarlet, or bright yellow, and they have very attractive foliage. Certain varieties have upstanding stems so heavily laden that they form a sort of drapery of green that is ideal for a window-sill or a fire-place. Unlike **African violets,** they do just as well in a sunny window as in the shade. Two of the most recent introductions are **Episcia melittifolio,** with pretty pink flowers on rapidly-growing plants, standing very straight, with no stolon; and **Colombia orange episcia,** an early-flowering variety, with orange flowers standing out against a foliage of smooth, even green.

SMITHIANTHA

Another close relative of the **African violet** is the **smithiantha,** one of the **gesnerias** almost unknown until about ten years ago, but which now receives its due measure of attention. This plant makes a beautiful effect with its tube-like flowers spotted with yellow, orange and white set against a background of velvety bronze foliage.

All its hybrids are easy to grow from tubers shaped like catkins. Plant them in a mixture of peat-moss and sand, which you must keep moist all the time, and fertilize them every two weeks, with a few weeks' rest after they have flowered. If you give them a longer rest-period and lower the temperature while they are growing, they will flower at different times of the year.

CLIMBING PHILODENDRONS

Climbing philodendrons belong to the **araceae** or **arum** family. They are easily grown, withstand wretched lighting conditions quite cheerfully,

Smithiantha is an excellent indoor plant for winter flowering.

and can go a long time without attention. The foliage is slightly variable in shape, but is almost always green or partly green. However, there is one red-leaved species — **Philodendron mandaianum** — which puts some colour into a dark corner of any room.

ANTHURIUMS

Apart from the **calla** itself (which can be grown outside, if special care is taken), the most important members of the **calla** family are the **anthuriums.** Many species exist, all of them very pretty with their decorative spathes — (often loosely described as 'flowers', as are the bracts of **poinsettias).** These spathes are leafy organs of various colours. In the absence of showy flowers, they attract insects to the real flower, which is called the spadix.

One of the more striking examples is **Anthurium andraeanum,** which comes to us from Colombia. Its spathes are pink, white, coral or red, according to the variety. **Anthurium scherzeranium** comes from Costa Rica and has reddish-scarlet spathes enveloping a spadix twisted into a spiral shape. This species offers many multi-coloured varieties, one of the most notable of which is **'Gold Charm',** which has white spathes and golden fruit.

These plants love the heat, and can stand a certain amount of shade. But they do need a lot of moisture. Plant them in peat-moss, **osmunda fern** root or coarse sphagnum moss, and feed them every two weeks with a weakish solution of fertilizer. You will be able to buy them at a nursery or garden supply centre.

There is an amazing choice of plants available at gardening centres these days. For example, you might find a **staghorn fern** (Platycerium bifurcatum), a rare fern, with fronds that look rather like the antlers of a stag. It needs a great deal of moisture, and you are well advised to water it every day with a vapour-spray. It is not an easy plant to grow, but modern houses usually provide enough light for it, and if you water it frequently the chances of success are not too bad. The best medium in which to grow a staghorn fern is a block of peat-moss fixed to a strip of bark, without any other form of soil. Remember, it is essential to maintain a high degree of humidity for this plant.

A species that has become much more common in gardening centres is feather palm (Chamaedores elegans "Bella"), a miniature palm native to eastern Guatemala. Its slender fronds end in a handsome crown of little feathery leaves. This species is notworthy for its early flowering.

You might also find some **Solomon Island ivy-arum** or **'devil's ivy'** (Scindapsus aureus), as well as some graceful plant such as **Thytis afzellii,** a native of Sierra Leone and Liberia. This is a climbing plant with clinging rootlets. Its arrow-shaped leaves, on long stems, are most decorative.

Artificial Lighting

A good many people limit the number of plants they grow indoors to fit the space available near the windows. However, thanks to artificial lighting, it is perfectly possible to give plants all the radiant energy they need, and thus to grow as many of them as you wish inside your house or apartment.

You can use ordinary incandescent lamps if necessary, but they put out more heat than is desirable. To obtain high-intensity light without too much heat, it is better to use fluorescent tubes. In certain cases, both these sources of light may be used together.

PHOTOSYNTHESIS

Since light plays an essential role in the growth of plants, the process by which carbohydrates are formed from carbon dioxide (CO_2) and water, in the presence of light, is called 'photosynthesis' — (from the Greek 'photos', the genitive of 'phos', which means 'light'). Light is the principal source of energy for plants. However, they do not all have the same need for light; some of them like full sunlight, while others prefer the shade. However, all of them absorb carbon dioxide, water and certain mineral salts. Thanks to the light of the sun, or to artificial lighting, they synthesize these basic materials into living organic matter and oxygen — indeed, under the action of light, plants actually release oxygen to the atmosphere.

During the night, photosynthesis stops, and the plants then absorb oxygen and release carbon dioxide.

THE LIGHT SPECTRUM

As you know, when light passes through a prism it is broken up into different colours — red, orange, yellow, green, blue, indigo, violet. There are other rays, which are invisible — such as infra-red, ultra-violet and gamma. Normal growth and development in plants are conditioned by the amount of red and blue and ultra-violet light the plants receive, as well as by the intensity and duration of the lighting.

DURATION OF LIGHTING

Plant physiology specialists have discovered that artificial lighting can be used to stimulate flowering or to retard it. For some time plant specialists have been using this discovery to control growth in a large variety of plants such as **chrysanthemums, China asters, poinsettias, tuberous begonias, tomatoes, coleus** and **tulips.**

Usually, ordinary incandescent lamps are used for the purpose, both outdoors and in the greenhouse. These lamps provide the low levels of lighting which are adequate for the task, they are inexpensive, and the light they give is rich in the infra-red rays to which plants are sensitive.

CYCLIC LIGHTING

The perennial **chrysanthemum** is a 'short-day-long-night' plant which will not flower in 'long-day short-night' conditions. **Chrysanthemum**-growers

A flower-stand fitted with fluorescent tubes and reflectors is an excellent way to grow indoor plants. The artificial lighting also produces a very pleasant decorative effect.

make use of this characteristic if they wish to retard the flowering of their plants. Rather than prolong the day, by adding several hours of artificial lighting after dusk or before dawn, all they do is interrupt the night for a period of four hours. This makes the night seem short to the **chrysanthemums,** which go on producing foliage, rather than flowering. **China aster** (Callistephus chinensis), on the other hand, is a typical 'long-day-short-night' plant.

You can also make 'long-day' plants bloom before the normal time by prolonging the duration of the day. Even feeble intensities of light will bring flowering on. The reverse is also true. **Poinsettias,** for example, need a full twelve hours of darkness during the twenty-four if they are to flower. Experiments have shown that one single minute of light in the middle of each period of darkness is enough to stop them from flowering. Again, **tuberous begonias** will only flower if they are given short periods of darkness (less than twelve hours) but they need **long** periods of darkness to produce a plentiful supply of tubers.

TWO TYPES OF LAMP

There are two types of lamp that can be used for plants. The first is the ordinary incandescent lamp, of various sorts — such as 'cold white', 'daylight' and 'natural white'. These all produce different intensities of red and blue light.

Fluorescent lamps have a greater luminous efficiency than incandescent lamps — i.e., they emit more lumens per watt of power consumed, and with less heat. Furthermore, the average life of a fluorescent tube is around 12,000 hours, as compared with only 1,000 hours for an incandescent lamp. 40-watt fluorescent tubes are the ones most frequently used in growing plants indoors. Several brands are available, the best-known being 'Plant Light' and 'Plant-Gro'.

Unless the plants you want to grow are not sensitive to the length of the day, the lamps should be used for twelve to fifteen hours out of every twenty-four. They can be switched on or off automatically by means of a time-switch. Using both types of lamp together will produce optimal growth and flowering. On this point, I can tell you from personal experience that excellent results can be obtained either by using two 40-watt fluorescent tubes, or by combining two 40-watt tubes with two ordinary incandescent lamps. For plants which need plenty of light — such as **orchids, geraniums** and **bromeliads** (the **pineapple** family) — you can even use three lamps of each type to obtain better growth. A point which must not be overlooked is that the light should be **reflected** onto the plants — which is why the installations available on the market all include a reflector.

MINIMUM REQUIREMENTS

The minimum lighting needed for indoor plants calls for 20 watts per square foot of surface, when a fluorescent tube is being used. Thus, an area four feet by two feet (eight square feet) calls for 160 watts of fluorescent lighting, or four 40-watt bulbs each four feet long. The supplementary incandescent lighting for this area would be about one fifth, or 30 watts — say, four 7-watt bulbs. Such an installation is quite suitable for growing several kinds of indoor plant. You can increase the lighting, of course, but if you **decrease** it you limit your choice of plants to those that do not need much light. The type of installation, and the kind of light-bulbs or fluorescent tubes you put in, will depend on what sort of plants you want to grow. Furthermore, since the lighting-effect is strongest directly beneath the centre of the lamps or tubes, and gets weaker toward either end of the tube, it is possible to place your plants selectively, according to their need for light. Finally, your lamps and tubes should be adjustable, so that you can vary their distance from the plants between, say, six and fourteen inches.

A VAST CHOICE OF PLANTS

Here is a list of some of the many plants which can be grown in artificial lighting:

Weak lighting: aspidistra, dieffenbachia, dracaena, ferns, philodendrons, peperomia, sansevieria.

Medium lighting: African violets, anthuriums, rex begonias, cissus, episcias, schefflera, syngoniums.

Strong lighting: certain begonias, gloxinias, impatiens, orchids, geraniums.

Plants can also be classified according to the duration of lighting over the 24-hour period that suits them best — 'short-day-long-night', 'long-day-short-night' or 'neutral':

'Short-day' plants (10 to 14 hours of light): **poinsettias, pinks, chrysanthemums, Christmas begonias, kalanchoes, Christmas cactus.**

'Long-day' plants (14 to 18 hours of light): **calceolaria, cactuses,** succulents, **orchids, bromeliads.**

'Neutral' plants (12 to 16 hours of light): **roses,** certain **begonias, African violets, geraniums, coleus.**

The period of darkness is the crucial time for most plants. A little light — even a few minutes only — during the 'darkness' period can adversely affect the flowering process or even stop it completely. **Poinsettias** are excellent examples of this sort of plant.

Although lighting plays a highly important role in the normal growth of indoor plants, there are other essential conditions. For example, the humidity should be between 40% and 60%, and the temperature and air circulation should be suitable for the plants you are growing — and for the soil and the fertilizers you are using — if you hope to obtain the best possible results.

GROWING PLANTS IN THE BASEMENT

Many garden-lovers grow a large variety of plants successfully, thanks to artificial lighting installations. Some of them who enjoy 'do-it-yourself' projects have built their own systems, while others have preferred to buy their installations ready-made at their local gardening centre or nursery.

These indoor gardens can be set up anywhere in the house, basement, playroom, kitchen, hallway, and so on. Several amateurs have even installed trays and fluorescent tubes in sets of shelves, or on the book-shelves in their library.

In my opinion, the ideal answer is to set up a permanent installation in a corner of the basement, where you can grow a great variety of plants as well as seedlings, cuttings and so on.

The simplest set-up for the basement consists of hanging fluorescent tubes from the ceiling-joists and standing the plant containers on the floor. However, it is much easier to see your plants and to handle them if they are standing on tables, or some form of table-high support.

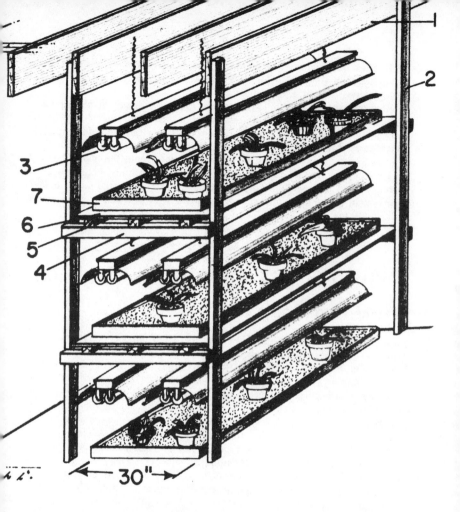

Above is a cross-sectional sketch of a fluorescent lighting system for growing plants, installed in a basement. The plants are grown on three different levels. Each section is four feet long, and is lit by four-foot fluorescent tubes set in pairs in holders fitted with reflectors. Essentially, the system consists of a wooden H-type framework standing on the floor and fixed to the ceiling-joists (1). The uprights (2) are two feet by four feet, as are the crosspieces (4). The longitudinal supports (5) are two inches by two inches, and three of them are used to carry a shelf made out of ¾" plywood (6). Flat metal trays (7), some thirty inches wide and filled with gravel, stand on the plywood shelves and the potted plants are placed in these trays. The lighting-fixtures (3) have reflectors twelve inches wide, and are held up by chains, thus allowing their height above the plants to be adjusted as required.   (Sketch: Sylvania Electric)

Trestles and planks may sound a somewhat makeshift answer — but it is a sensible suggestion for someone who wants to try out this method of growing as cheaply as possible.

Another system — a bit more elaborate, but still not at all expensive —consists of H-shaped frames standing on the floor and fixed to the ceiling-joists at the top. These frames are fitted with longitudinal ruuners, which carry three shelves made out of ¾-inch plywood. Fluorescent tubes are fixed above these shelves, to throw light down onto the plants beneath.

To stop any water getting into the lighting system, metal trays are normally used to catch the surplus when you water. Furthermore, a layer of gravel in these trays underneath the plant pots provides a good source of humidity for your plants.

Growing African Violets
With The Aid Of Artificial Lighting

SPECIAL FLUORESCENT TUBES

If you are an amateur gardener who has tried almost everything in the field of growing indoor plants, but has not yet discovered the many advantages of artificial lighting, let me suggest that you specialize in **African violets** (Saintpaulia species). As a start — if you are any sort of a 'do-it-yourself' person — you should build yourself an installation which will allow you to grow African violets without having to rely on natural sunlight. Smething about 7½ feet long by 3½ feet wide makes a good start, using two 40-watt fluorescent tubes — ('Gro-Lux', 'Wide Spectrum' and 'Plant-Gro' are all suitable types). The important thing is to provide the plants with conditions resembling as closely as possible those that they would encounter in a greenhouse — i.e., a closed environment in which the temperature and lighting may be adjusted without trouble.

A simple plywood box 3 feet high, 3 feet wide and 4½ feet long is quite satisfactory for growing plants in a basement. However, one of the sides must be removable, to let you get at the plants, and also for ventilation purposes. The lid of this box carries four 4-foot fluorescent tubes on its underside, or two twin-tube fixtures. These tubes are hung on little chains so that they can be raised or lowered as required, with their distance above the tops of the plants variable between six and fifteen inches.

READY-MADE FLOWERBOXES

You will also find ready-made flowerboxes on the market, which are provided with adjustable fluorescent tubes and a metal tray to hold the

This photograph gives some idea of an interior garden laid out in a basement. A great variety of plants can be grown there, thanks to artificial lighting provided by fluorescent tubes. A room such as this can be laid out to accommodate rooting of cuttings, forcing of bulbs, and indoor preservation of special plants during the winter, as well as the growing of general garden plants. (Photo: Sylvania Electric)

pots. All you need do to give the plants the necessary humidity is to lay a thin bed of vermiculite or peat-moss on the metal tray and enclose the whole thing in a sheet of plastic or a large plastic bag. This 'cocoon' will seal the humidity in, and also maintain a uniform temperature around the plants. If you have plenty of space available — whether upstairs in the house, or on the basement or cellar — you can have several installations, either separate or stacked one on top of another. In the latter case, assuming a total height of six feet, the bottom shelf should be ten inches off the floor, and the others should be spaced twenty inches apart.

TEMPERATURE

Granted that the first essential is a suitable degree of artificial lighting, you must not neglect the temperature of the surrounding air. Fortunately, African violets do very well in the same temperature and humidity conditions that human beings require. The ideal is a temperature-range of 72° to 75°F by day, and 62° to 65°F by night. It is not easy to maintain these temperatures in winter-time, either in the house itself or in the basement, and it is possibly even more difficult in summer, when the danger is that the temperature will go too high during the day, and not cool off enough at night. Extremes of temperature may make the buds burst open in certain varieties, so it is a wise move to hang a thermometer near your African violet plants.

HUMIDITY

Controlling the humidity is more difficult than controlling the temperature. Without a control device, the humidity will be too low in winter and too high in summer. You can increase the humidity in winter by regular watering of the vermiculite or peat-moss in the trays inside the boxes with the artificial lighting. The level of the water must not be higher than the bed of material covering the bottom of the tray, so that the pots are not actually standing in water.

In summer, when the humidity is at its highest, let the trays dry out. Too much humidity can bring on mildew. However, this can be held in check by adequate ventilation (keep a small fan running all the time), and by using an appropriate fungicide. Though high humidity is harmful, it is much less so than too low a humidity. If you find the humidity is too low during the winter, and the material in the base-trays — the vermiculite etc — is not putting out enough humidity for the plants, you can improve matters by covering the whole installation with a 'cocoon' of polyethylene.

POTS AND SOIL

Plastic pots are best for African violets. Clay pots may possibly be harbouring diseases and insect pests and it is almost impossible to get rid of them even if you use boiling water, the best fungicides and the most effective insecticides. As for soil, there seem to be as many formulas for soil mixtures as there are African violet fanciers! Whatever you use, the soil **must** be porous and able to retain fertilizing elements. One good mix consists of equal parts of peat-moss, vermiculite, garden loam and wood-charcoal (No. 10). You could add a bit of fertilizer to the mix, some powdered bone-meal, say, or some dried blood, or superphosphate, etc. For those who have neither the time nor the facilities to prepare their own soil mix, it is easy enough to find an appropriate mixture at a local nursery or gardening centre. Before you begin potting, remember to place some broken potsherds at the bottom of the pots, or some gravel or, best of all, a mixture of equal parts of crushed eggshells and wood-charcoal (No. 3).

WATERING

Watering must be carried out properly, and at the surface of the soil. Each plant should be watered according to its needs, for some of them dry out more quickly than others. Never water your plants really thoroughly, except when you know you are going to be away for a few days. Root rot will not be any problem if you are careful not to water too lavishly. It a plant seems to be too dry, it is a good idea to take a close look to make sure that its roots are not cramped. If they are, you must transplant it into a bigger pot.

During the dry periods that you may encounter in winter, I advise you to use a vapour-spray in the space above the plants. If you have used a porous soil mix, as I suggested earlier on, you will be able to re-pot any of your plants several times over — even if they are in full bloom — with very little risk of their wilting. When the soil mix is dry enough, turn the pot upside down and tap the bottom gently, the plant will come out easily enough, without disturbing the root-system. Take a pot of the next size — **larger** of course — and press some suitable soil-mix around the inside of the wall. Then put the plant in, and stamp exerything down gently around the roots. Finally, give it a good watering, until the water starts coming out of the drainage-hole at the bottom of the pot.

A well-potted African violet will produce plenty of flowers, as well as lovely foliage. The pot must let the roots have the room they need. It must also provide effective drainage, and to ensure this, the holes in the bottom must be covered with bits of broken potsherd. One other point to remember is to fill the pot with earth only up to about ¼ inch below the rim. This makes it easier to water.

FERTILIZING

Plants grown under artificial lighting are not affected by the seasons. It is summer all year around for them. By the same token, when you have worked out a fertilizing programme, you must stick to it. It does not really matter what make of fertilizer you are using, what counts is the dosage. The ideal is a phosphorus-rich fertilizer, with a formula close to 20-20-20, say, and containing some trace-elements.

All African violets need plenty of fertilizer. Treat them at least once a week, watering them with a solution of one teaspoonful of fertilizer per gallon of water that has had the chill taken off it (room temperature). Whenever growing African violets is being discussed, the question of the pH value of the soil is bound to come up; that is, the degree of acidity. The pH scale runs from 0 to 14: 0 represents the highest degree of acidity, 7 is the neutral point, and 14 is the peak of alkalinity. The pH value of soils can vary from 3.5 to 10. The soil best suited to African violets is slightly acid, with a pH value of 6 to 6.5. Amateur gardeners who plan to prepare their own soil mixes will find it useful to get themselves some soil analysis equipment. Nurseries and garden supply houses sell some very handy kits for the purpose.

INSECTS AND DISEASES

Insects and diseases are the major enemies that attack African violets, and unfortunately they are fairly numerous. Powderey mildew and root rot are the most common diseases. Powdery mildew appears as a superficial white powder (actually a form of fungus), usually on the upper part of the leaves. This disease is promoted by an over-high humidity coupled

The basement is the ideal place for growing many indoor plants during the winter, even though there is usually very little sunlight there. It is not difficult to install artificial lighting and it is easy to regulate the temperature and humidity as well.

with sudden drops in temperature. Prophylactic measures consist of avoiding excessive humidity, and spacing the plants far enough apart to ensure a good air circulation around them. The best treatment is to dust the affected plants with finely-powdered sulphur.

Root rot is usually caused by fungi and bacteria in the soil. Rotting of the stem is also due to a fungus or to bacteria. The flowers and leaves above the area of rot will fade and wither.

These diseases, which are caused by organisms in the soil, can be warded off by avoiding excessive watering and by using sterilized soil.

There are two types of insect to worry about: red spider mite and thrips.

The two-spotted or common red spider is particularly annoying because it is rather difficult to get rid of. It is a mite scarcely visible to the naked eye and which varies in colour from yellow to green or red. This insect is one of the worst enemies of indoor plants. It spins a fine web, which it uses as food. Light infestations are fairly easily dealt with by frequent spraying of the undersides of the leaves and a strong breeze. Against heavier infestations, try dusting two or three times with a solution of Malathion, or a preparation with a derris powder base (rotenone), at intervals of about four days.

Thrips cause the flowers to fall soon after they have bloomed.

Flat mites and **cyclamen** mites are two other tiny pests which sometimes infest African violets. The flat mite's favourite feeding-ground is the underside of the leaves, where it produces the same sort of indentations as the red spider mite. Use the same counter-measures against this pest as against the red spider.

The **cyclamen** mite can destroy plants, if there is a really heavy infestation. It feeds almost exclusively on the tender tissues of new leaves and buds, and on flowers. The affected leaves lose their shape and curl up, while the petals of the flowers become streaked. You can destroy this pest and prevent serious damage by regular dustings with derris powder every two or three weeks. The best way of putting a stop to an infestation is to immerse the plant, still in its pot, in hot water (110°F) for fifteen minutes.

Propagating
African Violets

Taking cuttings is the easiest and also the most practical way of propagating African violets. Obviously, there is more involved in this method than just plucking a leaf and sticking it into a glass of water! But all the same, the process is relatively simple.

Basically, it consists of taking cuttings and letting them take root in a four-inch pot filled with vermiculite or perlite. No matter what material you use, the method is always the same — just take the cuttings and bed them down inside the pot.

HOW TO GO ABOUT IT

Remove some young leaves from the centre of your African violet plants — young ones are the most vigorous, and will be the quickest to take root. Use a sharp cutting-instrument — a knife, scapel or razor-blade — to cut the petiole or leaf-stalk 1½ inches from the base of the leaf. Push this petiole deep enough down into whatever you have chosen as the growing-medium to leave the leaf resting on the surface. Water thoroughly as soon as you have planted all your cuttings.

MOISTURE IS ESSENTIAL

From then on, water the pot from time to time to maintain an adequate degree of humidity without, however, letting the growing-medium become swamped. The new plants should make their appearance after about three weeks.

You must leave the plantlets enough time to develop a good set of roots before you pot them out individually.

Remember, too, that fluorescent lighting on the cuttings stimulates the growth of their root-system.

Cuttings of African violet leaves do not need any particular attention, except for occasional sprinklings with a sprayer. This piece of equipment can be very simple — just an ordinary bottle sealed with a cork with several holes in it — that is, something like the "watering-bottle" a woman uses to sprinkle her clean laundry before she irons it. Excellent little sprayers are available in the shops and are not at all expensive. You can use one not only for sprinkling your cuttings with water, but also for spreading insecticides, fungicides or soluble chemical fertilizers, and it will last for many years.

The really important thing — and I feel I should stress this once again — is that you must provide enough moisture for your cuttings and the growing-medium you have put them in, without swamping them.

TRANSPLANTING

Transplant your cuttings as soon as shoots begin to appear around the base of the young plants. Put the rooted cuttings into little pots no bigger than three inches in diameter. If you use larger pots, there is a risk that

If African violet fanciers want to increase the number of their plants as rapidly as possible, the most practical way is to take cuttings and let them root themselves in a pot filled with perlite or vermiculite.

some of the cuttings will not survive. To get the best possible results, fill the little pots with a soil mixture consisting of equal parts of garden loam, peat-moss and coarse sand.

Some Easily-Grown Plants

It is **really possible** to grow plants indoors without a great deal of trouble? Yes, it is — provided that you choose the right kinds of plant to grow. Generally speaking, that obviously means plants which do not need a great deal of light or humidity (though if the truth be told, **most** plants can be grown indoors in the modern houses of today, thanks to systems of artificial lighting and efficient humidifiers).

Nowadays, even those without any experience can grow many different plants indoors including tropical and sub-tropical varieties. Here are a few examples I've chosen from among the best-known plants of this kind:

GREEN PLANTS

Indoor plants with decorative foliage are mostly tropical in origin, and usually require warm, moist surroundings, somewhat diffusely lit. This sort of plant has become very fashionable over the last ten years or so. The most popular plants of all are those which can withstand the relatively unfavourable conditions of our homes (high temperature and insufficient humidity). The choice is further influenced, not so much by the beauty and the colour of the plants, as by the way they suit the style of our furniture. I shall just mention a few varieties of green plants here which are fairly tough and require a minimum of attention: **aralias** (especially **Aralia Sieboldi), Aspidistra elatior, Aucuba japonica, Chaemadorea elegans 'Bella'** (known as **'Neanthebella'** at the florists'), common **coleus** (Coleus blumei), **Crassula arborescens, dieffenbachias, rubber plant** (Ficus elastica), **English ivy** (Hedera helix), **philodendrons** and **sansevierias.**

These plants seem to be able to take almost anything except over-watering and over-fertilizing, both of which make the foliage wilt, or turn yellow, or show other adverse signs. If you let them have plenty of light, they will go on growing for years.

ARALIAS: of all the large family of **aralias,** the one that is grown most indoors is **Aralia Sieboldi.** This plant is particularly suitable for some unusual fancy container. It adapts itself to temperatures ranging between 50° and 80°F, and grows just as well in the shade as in the sun.

Dracaena warneckii is a magnificent plant, with leaves reticulated in green and white. *(Photo: Lemoine Tropica, Montreal)*

ASPIDISTRAS are typical of this type of plant. They come from the rain forests of the tropical regions where everything is always damp, and they grow in the under-growth, among the fallen leaves and mosses, on the trunks of trees or in the crooks of huge branches. **Aspidistra larida** is unsurpassed for its ability to accommodate itself to unfavourable conditions. Beware of the red spider mite if you are growing **aspidistras.** This insect can destroy a plant very rapidly.

GOLD-DUST TREE (Aucuba japonica variegata) is one of the toughest of indoor plants. It can survive in places where most others would give up and die. Although cool spots suit it best, it can withstand quite high temperatures.

317

COLEUS BLUMEI is a very rapid grower. It needs a minimum temperature of 60°F, and plenty of light and humidity. In winter-time, if you do not take the precaution of putting the pot in a sunny window or under some fluorescent tubes, the colour of the leaves dulls, and the plant wilts and loses its looks.

CRASSULA ARBORESCENS is a long-established plant that you can rely on. Its fleshy leaves are a handsome jade-green, and are borne on good solid stems. They are very hardy, and can withstand nearly every condition they are likely to meet in your home, without damage.

DIEFFENBACHIAS are big, upstanding plants with rich green oval leaves, dappled with big spots of paler green. Their native habitat is the undergrowth of tropical forests. Inside the house, they will only flower if they receive lots of diffused light. Even if they do not get as much humidity in our houses as in their native surroundings they grow well, provided that you give them the type of soil that suits them, and a fairly high temperature. You should note that excessive dryness and shade will make the lower leaves go yellow and drop off. In addition, **dieffenbachias** do not take well to over-watering, and it is of absolutely prime importance to make sure that the soil drains well. Also, if a plant grows too tall and gangly, it is a good idea to cut off the top part and let it take root in sand or some other rooting-medium, such as vermiculite. Air-layering is a good method of obtaining a new plant.

RUBBER PLANT (Ficus elastica) is always popular. It needs warmth, and must be watered with care. If it gets too little water, the lower leaves will drop off; but the same thing will happen if you over-water on a badly-drained soil.

ENGLISH IVY (Hedera helix) will withstand nearly every condition it is likely to meet indoors, and can survive even if you set it up in hallways or other draughty places. It can even be grown in water. But if you do grow it in soil, you must not water it too often — too much water can give it root rot.

The best known of the climbing philodendrons is the one with the heart-shaped leaves, Philodendron cordatum.
(Photo: Lemoine Tropica, Montreal)

PHILODENDRONS are for the most part climbing or creeping plants. Sizes and shapes of philodendron leaves vary considerably, from the little creeping plant up to the really outsize specimens. The best known of the creeping **philodendrons** is the one with the heart-shaped leaves, **Philodendron cordatum** or **oxycardium.** It prefers good strong sunlight (which should be filtered, however), and a warm environment.

Philodendron hastaum has arrow-shaped leaves, and needs support from a stake because of its weight. These upstanding **philodendrons** are fairly new. **Philodendron wendladi** is a very vigorous plant, and it has the advantage that it grows wider than it does tall.

SANSEVIERAS, which are sometimes called **snake plants** or **boa plants** because of the markings on their leaves, are among the most tolerant of indoor plants. They will adapt to any condition you care to name — sun, shade, irregular watering, fluctuations in temperature, etc.

Other undemanding green plants

Here are some other plants of the same sort, which are very attractive, and make few demands: **aglaonemas, scindapsus** or **pothos, scheffleras, dracaenas, peperomias** and **chlorophytums.**

AGLAONEMAS are very handsome indoor plants that stand tall and straight. The best known is **Aglaonema modestum.** These middling-sized plants are very tolerant, and can put up with the lack of light and the dry warmth of our houses. All they ask is a temperature above 50°F. **Aglaonema modestum** can actually be grown quite well in water — but you must change the water frequently.

SCINDAPSUS or **POTHOS** is a climbing plant from the South Seas. **Scindapsus aureus** is known as **Solomon Island ivy-arum** or 'devil's ivy'.

It looks rather like **Philodendron cordatum**. The types I recommend that you try are the ones strongly marked with big spots and streaks of yellow and cream. You must make sure to give them a diffuse light, and to keep them in a warm spot — 70°F or more. You should also note that over-watering does them harm.

DRACAENAS were very popular in bygone days, and are now coming back into fashion. These plants come in all sorts of shapes and sizes. Generally speaking, **draceanas** stand humidity and varying light conditions better than **dieffenbachias** do. **Dracaena warneckii** is a magnificent plant with leaves streaked with green and white. There is no doubt as to its decorative value.

PEPEROMIAS are small plants which go very well in Chinese style gardens. One of the prettiest of them all is indisputably **Peperomia sandersii**. This has grey-green leaves with a most distinctive silvery sheen.

FLOWERING PLANTS

The easiest flowering plants to grow indoors are **fibrous begonias** (Begonia semperflorens), **sultana** or **patience plant** (Impatiens sultana), **African violets** (Saintpaulia species), **episcias, clivias, Beloperone guttata** and **achimenes**.
FIBROUS BEGONIAS which started off in the flowerbeds and were potted at the end of the summer will continue to flower after they have recovered from the shock of being transplanted. You must cut them back every now and then to keep their compact shape.

EPISCIAS are plants with red and yellow flowers, which grow under a hotter sun than **African violets,** but which call for almost the same sort of treatment otherwise. A characteristic of these plants is their exotic foliage, which reflects sparkling metallic glints, like jewellery. The foliage is the main attraction of most of the **episcias,** but certain species have flowers which are just as eye-catching for their brilliant colouring. Since most of them are creeping plants with delicate and decorative foliage, they are often described as '**flame violets**' or '**yellow African violets**'; but really they are not like the **African violet** at all. **Episcias** can be propagated just from the leaves alone, in the same way as the saintpaulias.

CLIVIAS are bulb plants with persistent leaves shaped like whips. The red or reddish-orange flowers are carried in bunches at the top of tall-standing stems. These plants require a cool spot during the entire year. At the beginning of spring, when the new shoots appear, the temperature can be somewhat higher (60° to 65°F) and the waterings more frequent. **Clivias** will flower year after year in the same soil, if you let them rest for a month after each flowering.

ACHIMENES can be started off at the beginning of February by planting the little tuberous roots that look like caterpillars. They come into flower in spring and autumn.

AFRICAN VIOLETS (Saintpaulias) need a good open soil, rich in organic matter. If they are to flower well, it is absolutely essential to let them have enough light — but don't overdo it, for if they get too much the leaves turn yellow. As well as filtered light, they need a fairly high degree of humidity. Watering should be carried out with room temperature water.

BELOPERONE GUTTATA or **shrimp-plant** has handsome green foliage, and its flowers are enclosed in bracts which resemble shrimps both in shape and colour — hence the name. It prefers heat and bright light.

Rex Begonias –
Excellent Indoor Plants

Among the big family of **begonias,** the group of **rex begonias** with their decorative foliage is unquestionably the most popular. These plants are magnificent, and outstandingly decorative, mainly because of their beautiful particoloured leaves and their great variety of shades.

Many people think — quite wrongly — that rex begonias cannot be grown successfully in the greenhouse. From my own personal experience, I can assure you that over thirty-five varieties can be grown as indoor plants quite easily.

CERTAIN REQUIREMENTS

Although these begonias have certain special requirements, growing them inside the house is relatively easy. Nevertheless, it is of the utmost importance to remember that they are tropical plants, and that if they are to grow normally and look beautiful they need conditions that resemble those of their natural habitat as closely as possible. They need light, fairly high humidity, warmth, draught-free ventilation and a soil rich in organic matter and kept well watered.

WARMTH AND VENTILATION

When growing rex begonias indoors, the first thing to do is to lay down a proper set of rules. In winter-time, the room temperature should never exceed 75°F during the day, or 65°F at night.

Proper circulation of air in the room where you have your begonias is an essential factor for success, since the circulation of air around the plants helps prevent the development of grey mould and other diseases. On this subject, I suggest you open the windows a little, at the top, for about fifteen to twenty-five minutes each day — being careful, however, to avoid draughts.

Rex begonias only attain their full degree of beauty and perfection if they are grown in conditions which suit them. For example, you cannot transplant a magnificent specimen from a warm, damp, well-lit greenhouse to a gloomy corner of a room where the air is too dry, and expect that plant to retain its beauty. If it is subjected to that sort of treament, it's leaves will turn brown and wither, and its stems will grow disproportionately long in their search for light. The end-result will be a sickly plant without the slightest trace of good looks.

Although they do produce flowers, rex begonias are grown more for their foliage. Consequently, they do not need to be in full sunlight. However, if you want handsome plants that grow normally, with their leaves on short stems, you must set them near a well-lit window. If there is not enough daylight coming in, then give them artificial light from fluorescent tubes.

WATERING AND POTTING

Adequate watering is essential if you want to have top-quality plants. Besides, everybody who has any success with begonias keeps the soil damp all the time, because he knows that rootlets tend to dry out — and that affects the growth of the plan. On the subject of watering, let me stress how important it is to have the water at room temperature. Furthermore, your soil **must** be well-drained. You should saturate it, let it dry out, and then water it again.

Rex begonias have to have enough space for their roots. If you put them in pots that do not give them enough room, they will lose their vigour as a result of insufficient humidity. Plants grown in pots tend to be a bit too small anyway, and to shed their leaves. I would advise you to re-pot your begonia plants three or four times a year. Let me also say here that a soil rich in organic matter is absolutely essential for the production of good-quality plants.

IDEAL CONDITIONS

There are two ways of ensuring that rex begonias get the most favourable conditions for normal growth when grown indoors.

The first is to grow them somewhere where they will get enough light — either natural or artificial, where they will be warm, and where you can control the humidity. A humidifier is a very useful piece of equipment for this purpose. You can also stand your pots in a flat tray or a flowerstand, first covering the bottom with gravel or peat-moss soaked in water. Evaporation will then give your plants the humidity they need.

Rex begonias are grown chiefly for their magnificent foliage. Here are three examples which show very clearly what a great difference there is between the leaves of the several varieties.

The second method consists of growing your begonias in ideal conditions similar to those you would arrange for them to have in a greenhouse. This involves using a decorative cabinet equipped with an artificial lighting system and provided with sliding glass doors, if you want to have your plants in the living-room. For plants grown in a basement, a simple plywood box is all you need. What it amounts to is providing a closed space where you can easily regulate the temperature and humidity and control the light.

The dimensions of the cabinet or the box should be as follows: 3 feet high, 3 feet wide, and 4½ feet long. One side should be removable to allow for ventilation and to let you get at the plants. Four 4-foot fluorescent tubes, or two twin-tube fixtures, should be installed under the lid of the cabinet or box.

There is a new piece of equipment available which you may be able to find at your nursery or garden supply centre. This simple but effective device consists essentially of a metal frame carrying fluorescent tubes which can be moved up and down, with a tray for the pots, and the whole thing is enveloped in a "cocoon" of polythene.

323

INTERIOR DECORATION

The possibilities of using rex begonias to liven up the interior of a house are very numerous. Thus, a chimney-piece can be nicely set off by a background of conifer branches and one single begonia plant with silvery or silver-green foliage. Or why not stand a decorative tray full of water in the centre of a table, put a bowl upside down in the middle, and stand a begonia plant on it, so that the foliage is reflected in the water? For a permanent decoration, choose a suitable shelf — perhaps even a book-shelf in the library — and equip it with fluorescent tubes. Make a tray to fit, out of thick aluminum foil, and stand it on the shelf. Cover the bottom of this tray with a layer of vermiculite or damp peat-moss, and place your begonia pots on it.

Begonia plants in a tropical fish tank, or a small plant in one of those oversized brandy balloons, also make pleasing decorations.

VARIETIES

There are a great many varieties of rex begonia. Here are some of the better-known among them: **'Merry Christmas'**, which has leaves covered with geometrical stripes in red and green and silver; **'Mikado'**, which has leaves of various shades of purple and iridescent silver-green; **'Iron Cross'**, which is pea-green, with a mahogany-coloured Germanic-looking cross in the centre; **'Black Night'**, which is a deep chestnut studded with pinkish spots; **'Helen Teupel'**, which has silvery leaves ornamented with markings in deep red; **'Oregon Sunset'**, which has crinkly leaves coloured just like maple leaves in autumn.

Gloxinias Are Very Decorative

Mid-January is the perfect time to start growing **gloxinias.** The tubers — which are imported — are in plentiful supply at that time, so the prices are very reasonable. These lovely plants produce an abundance of trumpet-shaped flowers, carried on strong stalks which spring from a large rosette of leaves. They are available in an assortment of colours which range from white, through pink and crimson, to purple. You can also find mixtures of these colours in the same flower.

KEEP THEM INDOORS

Gloxinias are at their peak in spring and summer, and flower often for several weeks. You should never plant them in a garden. Keep them indoors or on a protected balcony during the summer. Their hillock of big velvety leaves forms a wonderful background for their magnificent flowers — each of which can grow more than 5½ inches across.

These superb plants come from the same family as African violets. They are very easy to grow indoors — which gives them a marked advantage over quite a few greenhouse plants which do not make very satisfactory house plants. Even the least experienced amateur gardener can grow these plants without trouble, if he pays due regard to certain essential requirements.

RICH, POROUS SOIL

The first essential is to use good-quality soil for your gloxinias. A suitable mixture is one generous part of peat-moss, one generous part of good garden loam and one part of sand. The tubers should be planted individually in **azalea** pots — (which are a little more shallow than ordinary pots). Put them into these pots — either the five-inch or the six-inch size

Gloxinias, with their big multicoloured trumpet-shaped flowers set off by beautiful velvety foliage, must be numbered among the most interesting plants grown indoors in winter.

— just as you would other tuberous plants, and provide them with satisfactory drainage by laying some small pebbles or potsherds at the bottom
of the pots. The tubers should be set so that their upper surface is level
with the surface of the soil — which should be about ¾ to 1 inch below
the top of the pot, to allow for watering. If you cannot tell which is the
upper surface of the tuber, start off by letting it sprout in a damp mixture
of peat-moss and sand, keeping an eye open for shoots to appear. As
with most other plants, gloxinia shoots come out of the upper surface of
the tuber, and the roots are at the bottom. Some tubers are rounded at
the bottom, with the upper surface slighly concave.

POTTING AND WATERING

After potting the tuber, give the soil a thorough watering. After that,
until the plant has started growing, water sparingly and only when the
soil feels dry to the touch. When the growth gets properly under way and
the plant is well covered in foliage, water it enough to keep the soil
permanently moist.

Note that you use only a little water at the start, and increase the
amount as the plant grows larger. Don't forget to watch the drainage. You
want to keep the soil damp, not waterlogged! Furthermore, as with
African violets, you must avoid wetting the foliage and the coronas. Leaf
spot is another thing to avoid, though it is much less frequent in gloxinias
than in African violets: it is caused by cold water, so the answer is quite
simple. Water the plants carefully, with room temperature water and keep
the moisture off the foliage.

FERTILIZING AND LIGHTING

As soon as the flower buds appear, apply a liquid fertilizer. You will
get excellent results from a good general-purpose fertilizer — something
like 20-20-20, say — used at a strength of one ounce per gallon of water.
You can also use liquid commercial fertilizers, provided that you follow
the maker's instructions to the letter. To get the results you hope for,
you must fertilize at regular intervals.

The most important factor in growing gloxinias is lighting, without any
doubt. These plants grow well indoors provided that they are near a sunny
window. If there isn't a satisfactory source of light, the stems grow weak.
However, you should avoid direct sunlight. It should be filtered through
a curtain for example. If you are using artificial lighting, put your pots
twelve to fifteen inches beneath the fluorescent tubes. If you are using
incandescent lamps, however, I advise you to increase this distance, for
that type of light can damage the plants. Gloxinias can stand more light
than African violets, but after the spring is over they need more shade —
or at least some filter between themselves and the burning heat of the
midday sun.

When they are in flower, gloxinias need a fairly high temperature at night — 65° to 70°F — and something a bit higher than that during the day, with a humid atmosphere and good ventilation. If the night-time temperature falls below 60°F, the plant will stop growing entirely. My advice is to maintain a minimum of 70°F during the day, in winter-time, if you are growing your gloxinias in a basement under artifical lighting.

AFTER FLOWERING

Once the plant has come into flower, a cooler temperature will prolong the flowering-period. When the flowers have all fallen, gradually reduce the waterings until the leaves wither and die. Most types of gloxinia need to move into their dormant state gradually like this, after their flowering's over.

When the leaves have withered, put the pots in a cool spot (50°F), and leave them. Don't water them. Usually, a rest period of six to ten weeks is sufficient. If new shoots form earlier than this, pot them out and let the plants develop normally.

PLANTING THE TUBERS

The usual practice is to let your gloxinia plants become dormant late in the summer, then you let them stay like this until January or February. At that time, the tubers are removed from the earth and placed in damp vermiculite or in a mixture of peat-moss and sand, as recommended for tuberous begonias. If you buy bulbs, treat them also in this way. To get the tubers to "take", the temperature must be around 70° to 75°F. When the leaves and roots are sufficiently well developed, re-pot each tuber individually, covering it with a very light layer of earth. Keep only a few of the strongest stems at this time.

PROPAGATION

Unless they become diseased, or you neglect them, your old bulbs will stay in good condition for several years. New plants can be propagated by leaf cuttings, or by the rooting of newly-planted tuber stems. Leaf cuttings are an easy and effective method of propagation. All you need do is cut the leaves while the plants are in full flower, then place the cuttings in a glass jar filled with water, or on a bed of ground sphagnum moss. They put down roots in a very short time, and when the tubers appear, all you have to do is put them into 4-inch pots.

Finally, the old tubers can be divided as soon as they begin to grow. Cut them with a very sharp knife, leaving at least one shoot on each piece. Then plant them out in little pots.

SEEDING

Gloxinia seeds sown in winter or in spring will produce plants ready to flower in six to eight months. It is preferable, however, to use cuttings or to buy new bulbs if you want to increase the number of your plants. It is not really very easy to grow gloxinias from seed, inside the house.

Furthermore, seed does not produce the true varieties. And the seeds themselves are so delicate that you have to handle them with the greatest of care. However, if you **do** try seeding, the ideal formula is a good mix of sand, soil and peat-moss. Use this to fill a pot up to about one inch from the top, and lay a bed of sphagnum moss on top of it. Sow your seeds onto the sphagnum moss, then stand the pot in a basin of water until the sphagnum moss becomes damp. Then cover the moist seed-bed with a cone-shaped cap of polythene film, which will keep it moist until the seeds sprout.

Aralias And Primulas

Generally speaking, amateur gardeners seem to prefer flowering plants, because their gay colours somehow make the house look "warmer" during winter-time, and also because the flowers stimulate their sense of the aesthetic. All the same, green plants with decorative foliage are really just as interesting to grow. Not only are they necessary to highlight the effect of the other plants, but they grow very well in places that do not receive much light, that is, where most flowering plants cannot manage to survive — or at least find it impossible to show themselves at their best.

ARALIAS — VERY GRACEFUL PLANTS

Among these green plants — most of them tropical in origin — why not grow the ones that are the most "unusual", with foliage so "different" that it must inevitably catch all eyes? **Aralias**, from the big family of **Araliaseae,** are perfect examples of "unusual" plants: they have a rare grace all their own.

They grow like dwarf shruby trees, and have tough, leathery leaves that are usually finely serrated, giving them an appearance of lightness which is often almost ethereal. Several species have the pleasant habit of producing new little shoots all along the stems or the main trunk.

If the humidity inside your house is high enough, the leaves of your aralia plants will stay fresh and green all year long. One excellent way of providing these plants with sufficient humidity is, as with so many other indoor plants, to put the pots in a tray with a layer of gravel in it covering the bottom. All you need do is keep this layer moist by watering it regularly.

A POROUS SOIL

Aralias prefer a light, porous soil, which must be kept moist all the time, without being drenched. They also like the warmth of modern houses, and a room that gets a bit of sunshine.

Among the most popular species in the **Araliaceae** family are some of the **dizygothecas** or 'false aralias' **Dizygotheca elegantissima** the leaves example, and **Dizygotheca veitchii.** These two little shrubs are very much alike. Their stems bear slender, finely-divided leaves, with long folioles, narrow and dentated. In **Dizygotheca elegantissima** the leaves are streaked with red; in **Dizygotheca veitchii,** they are streaked with white. To get the best effect in each case, I advise you to group three or four plants together in one pot.

Another popular member of the **Araliaceae** family is **Fatsia japonica.** This is a hardy species with upstanding stems ornamented with large palmate leaves — either plain green, or streaked with white or yellow.

PRETTY PRIMULAS

In January, the cold still reigns supreme outdoors, and the sun's feeble rays are hardly noticeable across the snow-covered countryside.

Indoors, however, there is every promise that the sun will soon regain its strength ,and that everything will turn green again. There is no more sure way of rekindling your optimism and giving yourself a forestate of spring than by growing **primulas.** These pretty indoor plants, so proliferous with their flowers, are easy to grow and it is worth noting that if you want to brighten up the interior of your house, primulas cost a great deal less than cut flowers, and are not so hard to grow as forced bulbs. Their delicate charm will captivate you, so that you will never want to be without them in your home.

In winter-time, the delicate charm of primulas in our houses holds out the promise of a radiant spring.

NEW PLANTS

Generally speaking, you should buy your primulas while they are in flower. You can prolong their flowering - period without harming the formation of new flower-bearing stems, if you take certain precautions. These plants need thorough waterings, plenty of light, and fertilizing with c h e m i c a l fertilizers about every ten days.

When they have finished flowering, you can put the pots down in the cellar, or in some other cool spot, until the spring. At the beginning of summer you should plant your primulas out in the garden, where they will flower again.

PROPAGATION

New plants are easily obtained from seeds. The only equipment you need is some trays filled with sandy soil covered with a thin layer of finely-ground sphagnum moss. Sowing should be carried out between January and March.

Cover your trays with a sheet of glass or plastic. Avoid putting the containers in too sunny a spot, to prevent evaporation. After the seeds have sprouted, remove the cover gradually, and at the end of three weeks, plant out the seedlings individually in three-inch diameter pots. Make sure that the corona of each little plantlet is exactly at the level of the soil.

When these little pots become too full of roots, you will have to re-pot the plants into four-inch pots, which are more suitable for flowering purposes. The soil for this final potting should be porous, and rich in organic matter.

THE BEST SPECIES

FAIRY PRIMULA (Primula malacoides) is noteworthy for its big rounded leaves with their floury-feeling backs. The flowers range from mauve to deep purple.

TOP PRIMULA (Primula obconica) is the most frequently-grown species. It has large, rounded, velvety leaves. The flowers are pink, red, purple or white with yellow centres.

CHINESE PRIMULA (Primula sinensis) is fairly sensitive to changes in temperature during its flowering-period. Its pinky-lilac flowers are extremely elegant. This primula has very velvety leaves.

KEW PRIMULA (Primula kewensis) has spatula-shaped or oval green leaves, which look as though they have been dusted with flour. Its many flowers are a brillant yellow.

JAPANESE PRIMULA (Primula japonica) is one of the most handsome and most vigorous species of all. It grows equally well indoors as in the rockery. All the flower-buds should be pinched off after the first year, and some of them during the second winter.

The ABC's Of Growing Ferns

Growing ferns indoors is relatively simple, if you follow certain basic principles, and take into account the fact that these are typical plants that grow in shaded undergrowth. Therefore, the first thing you must give them is a filtered light, like that in their natural habitat. With experience and practice, you will be able to adapt the following advice to fit each individual case.

DRAINAGE

Adequate drainage is one of the most important requirements of these plants. To improve drainage in a pot, enlarge the hole in the bottom, then cover the hole with some potsherds.

Whatever the size of the pot, cover the bottom with ½ an inch of gravel, then ¼ of an inch of clean sand, and then add a layer of sphagnum moss ½ an inch thick

POTTING

There are two kinds of fern; the ground ferns, which grow in the soil, and the epiphytes or "aerial" plants, which grow on other plants.

The ground ferns, such as the **pteris** the **nephrolepsis** and the **cyrtomium,** use a soil mix containing ⅓ sandy loam, ⅓ peat-moss, and ⅓ coarse sand. Add a pinch of dried cow-dung or some similar organic fertilizer. Mix well, then water the mix and let it stand for a week. You can also buy soil mixes ready for potting, but whether you use one of these or prepare your own, it is essential not to pack the soil too tightly in the pot.

The epiphyte or "aerial" ferns, such as the **davallias, platycenums, aglomorphias** and some of the **polypodiums,** should be potted in the same way. In their case, avoid heavy soils. Instead, use a coarse, porous mix consisting of ½ a part of ground conifer bark, ¼ of a part of loam and ¼ of a part of clean sand and dried manure. Wrap the roots carefully in sphagnum moss, using a wooden rammer to pack the moss in tightly against the wall of the pot. Don't cover the stem or the rhizome with earth. It is very important that the root system should be disturbed as little as possible during the re-potting operation. If the roots have been disturbed as a result of dividing the plant, remove some of the fronds (the "leaves" of the fern) to restore the balance between roots and foliage.

Ferns suitable for indoors are very easy to grow, provided that you give them a diffuse light similar to that in the shady undergrowth of their natural habitat. *(Photo: Lemoine Tropica)*

WATERING CALLS FOR JUDGMENT

Keep the soil moist, but not soaked, for otherwise the air will be completely driven out, fermentation will set in, and the roots will rot. This risk is always present during the cold days of winter.

To determine whether your watering practices are correct, use the following method of assessment. Before each watering, take a pinch of earth between your thumb and forefinger. If you find your fingers wet, then cut down on the watering.

With temperatures above 75°F — especially in summer — ferns that that are growing properly will probably need water every day.

Remember, too, that heavy, clayey soils retain water longer than others, and don't drain as easily. On the other hand, sandy, porous soils require more water, due to their superior drainage.

HUMIDITY

As you know, humidity is the result of water-vapour condensing in the air. It is expressed as a percentage, running from total absence of humidity, (0%) up to saturation (100%). The warmer the air, the more humidity it can absorb. As a result, more water-vapour is needed to maintain the same degree of humidity when the temperature goes up. A relative humidity of 70% is ideal, though ferns will grow quite well at a lower humidity. A simple and effective method of increasing the degree of humidity is to place your pots in a tray with a layer of gravel covering the bottom.

If there is a reasonably satisfactory circulation of air in the room, you can also spray the fronds lightly every now and then. Dishes filled with water on the radiators or the furnace are equally useful for keeping the humidity of a room sufficiently high. Another method is to cover the earth in the pots with a layer of damp sphagnum moss. However, the most effective way of getting a normal degree of humidity in an apartment in which you are growing ferns is to install a humidifier.

Whether the room where the ferns are is well-lit or gloomy, insufficient humidity reduces the quantity of water in the foliage — which will wilt and go brown, and ultimately bring about the death of the plant. Young fronds are particularly vulnerable to a lack of moisture, and certain ferns are more subject than others to damage from insufficient humidity. The fronds will also go brown if the soil is short of water.

LIGHT

Ferns need light, just like any other plant that manufactures its own sustenance through the phenomenon of photosynthesis. Several ferns simply won't grow in a really gloomy location.

Filtered artificial lighting is advisable if the natural lighting is 50% below normal. However, too much sunlight will turn the fronds of certain ferns yellow, while young fronds in other varieties will turn brown and die. However, even if your windows are on the south side of the house and the sun shines in through them all day long, you can still grow ferns there, provided that the rays of the sun are adequately filtered — by using blinds, for example.

Certain varieties such as **cyrtomiums, Tsus sinense** and **polystichums** do well in the winter sun, but they will not survive if they are exposed all day long to the hot sun of summer. **Nephrolepsis** grows well under a strong light — but not in the sun's rays.

However, if the humidity is high enough, and the temperature is not over 70°F, most ferns can stand a certain amount of sun.

RE-POTTING

The best time to re-pot your fern plants is early in spring. However, if you take care to disturb the roots as little as possible, ferns can be re-potted at any time. Creeping ferns can be divided and re-potted in the spring, without any trouble.

When there is no more danger of frost outside, potted ferns will benefit from spending the summer in a nice shady spot in the garden. Bury the pots up to the rim, or take the plants out of the pots and plant them in the soil in a nice shady place; then when autumn comes, you can re-pot them.

FERTILIZING

Ferns need fertilizing. In any case, all growing plants can make good use of soluble nutritive elements, for the fertility removed from the soil by rain and watering needs to be replaced. The best method of fertilizing ferns can be expressed in two words: **little** and **often.**

You can even fertilize them daily, if you use a weak enough solution. The best way to get good results is to use a solution, half the normal strength, of a nitrogen-rich liquid fertilizer, every two weeks. Don't fertilize young plants. or plants which have just been potted.

TEMPERATURE

Temperatures between 50° and 75°F are ideal for growing ferns, though most of them can handle a somewhat wider spread. When the temperature is high, try to increase the humidity. Avoid exposing indoor plants to bad weather.

INSECT PESTS

Domestic ferns are subject to attack by several insects: the most common are scale insects, mealybugs and greenflies.

The male of the fern scale insect is white and thin, while the female is bigger, and pear-shaped. However, you must be careful not to make the very common mistake of confusing the sporangiums (or spore-cases) of the fern, which are located on the back of the fronds, with scale insects.

If you find scale insects on several fronds, use a solution of Malathion diluted to half-strength, and apply it with a small brush or a spray. Remove any fronds that have been too badly affected. This same treatment will also help you control mealybugs and greenflies. Never use any products with an oil base. The best temperature for spraying is 70°F.

OTHER TIPS

Do not let your potted fern wilt — but don't let them the become waterlogged either. It is necessary to fertilize every two weeks. Don't try to grow ferns entirely in the shade — but don't keep keep ferns that like a bit of shade out in the sun all day. Take all possible care with the roots when you are transplanting. Finally, do not pack your ferns so close together that they are starved for air and moisture.

Growing Cactuses And Succulent Plants

Of all the indoor plants which prefer heat, and grow well when they are put in a sunny window, **cactuses** and succulent plants are well up among amateur gardeners' favourites.

There are few house plants which give as much satisfaction with strictly minimal attention. All you need do is give them plenty of sun and warmth, and the barest minimum of care — and they will grow, slowly but surely, year after year.

Growing cactuses and succulents will be a source of happiness for you — they are full of pleasant surprises! You will find they come in every shape you can possibly imagine. Some of them are downright amusing, others are quite surprising, while some are even rather **odd!**

There are few plants as fascinating to grow as cactuses. These plants are extremly varied — in shape, colour and flowers. The illustration above shows some of the more popular species: Trichocereus, Cereus, Echinocactus, Ferocactus cactiformis, Gymnocalycium fredericki, Opuntia erinacea forma ursina, Haworthia fasciata, Echinopsis calochlora, Mamillaria plumosa.

IDEAL PLANTS FOR CITY-DWELLERS

Even though you may be able to spare very little space for growing your cactuses and succulent plants, you can put them almost anywhere, and in any sort of soil. Provided you don't water them too much, and let them have plenty of light, either natural or artificial, these plants are perfectly happy in a decorative flowerbox or on a coffee-table.

These are the ideal plants for city-dwellers, since there is no difficulty in growing them. They also have the inestimable advantage that during the summer holidays you can leave them for a good long time without having to water them.

Nevertheless, if you intend to go in seriously for this sort of operation, then you must give the plants a little more attenion. Their main requirement is excellent drainage. This is a point which cannot be stressed too strongly or too often.

You must remember that these plants come from regions where humus is very rare, where the soil is poor and gravelly and full of rocks, where sudden rainstorms flood everything, but don't leave any water in the soil because it drains away so quickly. Thus, the ground is very soon just as dry after a rainstorm as it was before. Furthermore, in cactus country a leaden sun blazes down pitilessly onto the plants, day after day. They get a brief respite during the night, when the temperature drops suddenly, and they profit from this, and absorb the light dew which forms at these times.

POTTING AND SOIL

When potting a succulent or a cactus, use the smallest pot possible. Earthenware pots ("clay" pots) are preferable, because they are porous. If you must use a pot larger than two inches in diameter, use one of the shallow pots — the sort used for growing azaleas. This will give the plants plenty of horizontal space to spread their roots, which will help them support a good heavy above-soil growth — ordinary pots sometimes have a tendency to overturn, especially with a heavy plant above the soil.

The pot must also be a good-quality one, since the plant will probably be staying in it for a long while.

You can buy ready-made soil mixes from gardening centres and nurseries and major florists. However, if you prefer to prepare your own mix, here is a formula that many amateurs have used successfully; two parts coarse sand, two parts good loam, one part mixed earthenware shards, wood charcoal and crushed eggshells, and one part humus or leaf-compost. For each bushel of this mixture, add two cups of bone-meal and ½ a cup of powdered limestone.

Before putting your soil mix into the pot, cover the bottom with a mesh made out of plastic or some other rust-proof material. The object of this mesh is to stop worms, snails and earwigs from getting into the pot during the summer, when your plants are out in the garden.

Put some potsherds over the drainage hole, to keep it from getting clogged. Then add a bit of earth, then put the plant in and spread the roots out — if they are not already encased in earth — before you cover them with more soil. While you are doing the actual potting, remove all broken roots.

RE-POTTING

If you have to move one of your plants into another pot, try to keep some soil around the roots when you move it into its new home. Then pour the earth into the pot, around the outside of the plant. It is important that the soil you use for re-potting should be fairly dry. Thus, it will be easy to spread it around and to pack it down after you have put the plant into the pot. (Remember here that the base of the stem should be just above the level of the soil.)

Another little tip for dealing with cactuses. Hold the plant in your left hand — preferably gloved, to avoid being pricked by the spines or needles — and pack the soil round its roots with a blunt-nosed dibble. Leave a one-inch space between the surface of the soil and the top of the pot. To make sure that the earth packs down normally, and to remove air-pockets, tap the side of the pot lightly.

A GOOD SOAKING

After you have done your potting or re-potting, put the pot to soak in a pan of water. When it has absorbed enough water, take it out of the pan and dry the outside with a cloth. After a couple of days, put the pot out in the sun, and then water it every now and then, or you can give it a good soaking once a week. Whichever method you decide to use, make sure that the pots are draining properly. It is very important to let the soil dry out completely after each watering, and never let your plants spend a night in waterlogged soil — otherwise there is a risk they might start to rot.

AIR IN THE SOIL

Roots need air if they are to remain healthy. That is why you must not overwater your plants, and why it is preferable to use a clay pot rather than a stone or plastic container. Make sure also that the degree of humidity of your soil does not remain constant all the time, for that tends to increase the soil's acidity.

SOME FINAL TIPS

During the short, cold days between the beginning of December and the middle of February, let your plants rest, and hardly water them at all. After mid-Feruary, start watering them again, and give them a boost in March with a dose of a soluble fertilizer such as 'Plant-Treat' (20-20-20). In this way, your plants will start flowering in April, and some species will go on flowering right up till the autumn.

If you put your cactus and succulent plants outside for the summer, make sure the pots are not resting directly on the ground and protect them against the rain. The best spots to keep them are in covered porticos, or up against one side of the house where the eaves will give them partial protection against the rain and other elements.

If you follow the advice given above, you should not have any problems with your cactuses and succulents.

Stapelias – Unusual Plants

Are you looking for something really out of the ordinary in indoor plants? Then interest yourself in **stapelias** — a plant which looks like a cactus without any prickly spines, with flowers that resemble starfish. Among these xerophilous plants (which means 'dryness-loving') there are some astonishing species of rare beauty.

Stapelias are remarkable upstanding succulent plants, with quadrangular fleshy stems which carry very decorative flowers. They are not at all demanding, and are easy to grow indoors.

SUCCULENT PLANTS

Although stapelias are succulent plants, they are by no means static. It is true that most succulents have no leaves — (at least, not what one usually thinks of as "leaves", and one is inclined to believe that they are inert. Indeed, it is very difficult for the untrained eye to notice any growth progress at all. So it is always surprising when these plants, which seem so lifeless, suddenly break into flower.

Stapelias belong to the big family of **Asclepiadaceae** or **milkweeds,** which are latex-producing plants. Stapelias are upstanding plants, with opposed leaves on fleshy, quadrangular stems, and they produce strange-looking but very decorative flowers. Their extraordinary stems are really quite striking. Together with the star-shaped flowers with their various colourings and markings, they put the stapelia in a category of its own.

There are many kinds of stapelia, but most of them are more likely to be seen is botanical gardens than in the amateur gardener's home. Admitedly, most of them produce flowers that give off a very nauseating stench — which is doubtless why they're called carrion flowers! However, the best-known species, and the one most popular as an indoor plant, the **variegated stapelia** (Stapelia variegata) is much less offensive than the others. In fact, its odour can only be detected at very close quarters.

In this close-up photograph, a stapelia plant displays its strange stems and flowers, which are shaped like starfish, with various colours and markings.

EASILY GROWN

Like all succulents, stapelias are quite easy to grow. For normal growth, they need a well-drained bed. A good soil mix for them is made up as follows: one part of garden soil, one part of pulverized brick, one part of sand and one part of peat-moss. To give this mix the necessary nutritive elements, add one soupspoonful of superphosphate to each bucket of mixture.

Stapelias need plenty of light. Put them near a window which gets the maximum possible amount of sunlight. You can also use artificial lighting provided by fluorescent tubes.

WATERING AND INSECTS

These plants don't require much water. A good soaking every month is enough for them, especially in winter. However, if you have placed any plants near a warm air duct, they will need watering more frequently — say once a week.

Happily, insects are not much of a problem in the growing of stapelias. Nevertheless, when you get your first plants, examine them carefully with an eye for the possible presence of mealy bugs and scale insects. If they are harbouring these insects, wash them well, then plunge them into a solution containing a soupspoonful of nicotine sulphate per gallon of water. Alternatively, you could use one of the modern insecticides on sale at nurseries and gardening supply centres.

THE PRINCIPAL SPECIES

Among the many species of stapelia, three are particularly noteworthy:

GIANT STAPELIA (Stapelia gigantea). This has large brown, velvety flowers which fully justify the designation "giant" — for they reach a diameter of twelve to eighteen inches. The large buds which form before the flowers break out look just like balloons, and make a most fascinating spectacle. When the flowers open, they are flat and wheel-shaped. They are very hairy, and pale brownish-purple in colour, streaked with crimson lines.

VARIEGATED STAPELIA (Stapelia variegata). This is the species most usually grown as a house plant. It comes in various shades of red, purple and brown, and is very mottled and speckled.

NOBLE STAPELIA (Stapelia nobilis). This species produces remarkable flowers, pale yellow and red in colour, which look quite like the flowers of the **giant stapelia.** They are easily grown from seeds or cuttings. To produce a new plant from a stem-cutting, simply choose a stem which can be cut off right down at the base. Let it dry in a sunny window for about ten days, then stick it into damp sand. It will put out roots in three weeks' time.

MIXED SEEDS

Nurseries and garden centres usually offer a "general mixture" of succulent seeds (among which **stapelias** will be represented). To obtain the maximum possible success with these seeds, you should sow them on ground sphagnum moss — just as you would for annuals.

Prepare a mix of equal parts of sand and soil, and cover it with a ½-inch layer of ground sphagnum moss. Sow the seeds, then cover them with a thin layer of ground sphagnum. Then put the container (either a box or a tray) in a well-lit window. Water as for annual plants, making sure that the sphagnum moss stays damp until the seeds sprout. To ensure this, you may have to give the container a bit of shade.

Plants For Christmas

GIFTS WHICH ARE ALWAYS APPRECIATED

One of the most satisfying pleasures of the familiar Christmas festivities must surely be the giving and the receiving of plants as gifts.

At the beginning of December, amateur gardeners descend in droves on the florists' shops and nurseries as though drawn by some irresistible magnet. This seasonal attraction is in fact completely natural — for not only do plants make excellent gifts, they have a special value all their own as part of the Christmas decorations.

To keep your plants looking attractive as long as possible, you must give them the appropriate attention, as well as providing them with surroundings favourable to their normal growth.

Whether your plant is an **azalea,** a **poinsettia,** a **cyclamen** or some other species, there are certain questions you must always ask yourself concerning the attention it should be given. Much will depend, for example, on where you grow your indoor plants. In most houses, the temperature is around 70° to 72°F during the day, and drops to 65°F at night-time.

CHOOSE WISELY

You should bear in mind that most of these Christmas plants flower only once a year, while others flower but once, and then never again.

Thus, you must exercise some care in the choice of the plants you propose to give as Christmas gifts. The first thing to consider is the conditions that exist inside the houses where these plants will be growing. Obviously, you must choose plants that will do well in those conditions.

For example, it would be wrong to give a **cyclamen** (which needs a coolish temperature) to someone who lives in an over-heated apartment On the other hand, this plant would do perfectly for somebody else whose house can offer a cool corridor, an unheated room, or a porch where the temperature is only 65°F during the day and drops to 50°F at night. Remember, in caring for a clcyamen, that the prime factor to be considered is the temperature.

THE PROPER TEMPERATURE

Temperature plays a very important role in the normal development of a plant. However, you must not go to the lengths of sacrificing the comfort of those who live in the house for the well-being of your plants. Provided you give them enough water and light, most plants will last a long time, even if the surrounding temperature is up in the 70°F range. It will be easier if the plants were well prepared before they were taken out of the greenhouse by a slight drop in temperature lasting several days. Such plants will last much longer.

THE IMPORTANCE OF LIGHTING

The next thing to watch is lighting. Nearly all plants given as Christmas gifts are either in full flower or covered with buds, and they don't need any sun to bring them into flower. However, if the plant is being kept, with a view to its flowering again the following year, then its preference as to lighting must be taken into account — that is, does it require

December is the ideal time to visit your florist's or nursery where you can pick up a great variety of indoor plants which will make excellent presents for Christmas and New Year's Day. Of all the various attentions they require, the most important is to keep the soil in the container damp. The next is to remove flowers as they wilt. In this way, you can keep your plants in flower till after the holiday is over. (Photo: Malak, Ottawa)

343

a lot of light, or very little? A cool, sunny window is ideal for **azaleas, cyclamens** and **Christmas begonias.** In contrast, a shady window is the place for a dish-garden, and for plants grown for their foliage — **(dieffenbachia, philodendron, ficus, rex begonia, caladium,** etc.). However, it is worth noting that even though **poinsettias** prefer a well-lit spot, it is quite possible to keep them in a room where they are not receiving direct sunlight.

WATER FREQUENTLY

Most plants sold at the florists' or the gardening centres have a well-developed root-system that fills the container. In consequence, they need watering frequently — as often as every two days, possibly. Apart from this, it is not really possible to give any hard-and-fast rules about watering.

Generally speaking, you should keep the soil slightly damp — taking due account of the fact that more plants are killed by too much water than by dryness.

Several plants will be in decorative containers — dish-gardens, for example. Such containers are almost invariably non-porous, and they don't have any drainage hole in the bottom to let the water out — which means you must be very careful how you do your watering.

WATCH THE HUMIDITY

It is very important remember that inside the house your plants are not living in the same conditions as when they were in the greenhouse. Some of them will have been grown in a cool atmosphere, while others will have been used to higher temperatures. The humidity inside a greenhouse is relatively high, while the reverse is true, generally speaking, inside a house. You can provide your plants with the necessary humidity either with a humidifier or by standing the pots in a flat dish with the bottom covered by a layer of gravel soaked with water.

The Highly-Popular Poinsettia

The **poinsettia** (Euphorbia pulcherrima) has been **the** Christmas plant **par excellence** ever since the American Ambassador to Mexico, Mr. Joel Robert Poinsett, introduced the plant into the United States in 1830. The poinsettia — which has become almost as much a part of the Christmas scene as the traditional Christmas tree — has been considerably developed since those days, especially during the last two decades.

The bracts which form the ornamental part of the plant are now larger, and certain new varieties have been introduced which last longer. New colours are slowly replacing the traditional red and green with pastel shades. These cultivars, in white, creamy rose and salmon, last longer than the reds and blend in perfectly with the Christmas decorations. Among the many new varieties, the following examples are worthy of note: **'Annette Hegg'**, with numerous bright-red bracts; **'Eckespoint Cl'**, with its superb involucre of deep-red bracts; **'Mikkel Pink'**, with clear salmon-pink bracts; and **'White Ecke'**, with its heavy, creamy white bracts.

POINSETTIAS LOVE THE SUN

If you are lucky enough to be given a poinsettia for Christmas — or better still, several poinsettias! — **don't** banish them to a corner of the living-room, with the intention of getting rid of them as soon as the leaves start to fall. On the contrary — put them in a sunny window and look after them properly.

There are certain stages that poinsettias must go through during their growth-cycle. Once you understand these stages, there no reason why you shouldn't be able to keep your plants for several years. However, many people find it hard to think about gardening when the ground's covered in snow and the windows are all a-glitter with frost. Yet how could there be a better way of linking autumn and spring, and forgetting the rigours of the winter season, than growing poinsettias in your home?

TEMPERATURE AND HUMIDITY

First of all, you should know that poinsettias bought for Christmas have only just come out of the greenhouse, and they will be seriously affected if you don't provide them with the same conditions to grow in. "Suitable temperature" is the first rule to remember. The best temperature lies between 60° and 65°F. In addition, a fairly high degree of humidity is necessary. If the temperature is higher or lower than those given above, the leaves will turn yellow and drop off. However, if you give your poinsettias the care they need, they will stay beautiful till the end of February, and even into March, which is when they start going dormant.

At that time, gradually cut down on the watering until the soil goes dry. Then put the plants down in the cellar and let them stay there, dormant Stop watering completely now: and in a few weeks the stems will dry out.

RE-POTTING

Towards mid-May, bring the plants into the daylight again. Then prune the dead stems back to the third dormant bud. After that, re-pot the plants in good garden loam enriched with well-rotted cow manure or compost. Choose a sunny spot in the garden and bury the pots in the soil, right up to the top lip. Water them every morning. You will find, to your pleasure, that poinsettias grow rapidly in spring. After a few days, the buds will swell and split.

The poinsettia is the ideal plant for the holiday season. It is very decorative, and it requires only the minimum of care. It is very easy to keep it in flower for several weeks, and even to make it flower again every year for several years.   *(Photo: Malak, Ottawa)*

Fertilizing is an important factor in growing poinsettias. Thus, every three weeks, feed each plant a soupspoonful of a complete fertilizer.

It is very important that the soil around the roots should always be damp. Therefore you should cover the soil with a thick mulch of lawn clippings or some other material — such as peat-moss, for example. This stops the soil from drying out too much between waterings.

Poinsettia plants are vigorous and grow rapidly, provided that you give them the necessary attention. If you let your plants grow haphazardly, they wil not produce many flowers and their stems will be too long. To avoid this, you must pinch off the first shoots as soon as they are six inches long. Do the same thing with the second set of shoots. After that, let the plants grow freely. Trimming off the shoots like this gives you compact, tufty plants which will flower nicely at Christmas.

GOING BACK INDOORS

Before the first frosts arrive, at the end of September, dig up your plants — still in their pots —and start gradually taking them back indoors. For the first three days, only take them into the house for the night. Then begin lengthening their stay indoors until you are no longer taking them out at all. They will be completely acclimatized to their surrounding by that time.

Put them near a sunny window, on the southern side of the house if possible. Water them plentifully, to maintain a high degree of humidity all the time. Fertilize them every three weeks.

If the plants are to be in flower at Christmas, you must not let the buds appear before mid-October. Insufficient lighting will make your poinsettias come into bud far too soon. The solution is to give them plenty of light during the day (though too much light will retard the arrival of the buds). One other precaution, keep them away from artificial light during the budding and flowering periods.

Sometimes the Christmas decorations — bouquets for the dining-table or garlands round the fireplace — have some cut poinsettias among them. However, poinsettias are not usually used in floral arrangements, since they tend to wilt almost as soon as they've been cut.

There **is** a method of preventing these flowers from wilting, however, provided you have the time and patience to carry it out.

If you want to use them as cut flowers, cut them at least twenty-four hours in advance. Put the cut stems through holes pierced in a big sheet of cardboard, and immerse the ends in boiling water for a full minute. This makes the milky sap coagulate, which prevents the flowers from withering. Poinsettias treated in this way will last for several days. Another method of preserving poinsettias as cut flowers is to singe the cut ends of the stems in a flame. Then plunge them into cold water and leave them there until you're ready to use them.

How To Look After Christmas Plants

There is no reason why plants given or received at Christmas-time should last only a few short weeks. It is perfectly easy to prolong their life for several months — if not for years. Many of them can be kept flowering for three and even six months, and most of them will get through the summer easily enough, to give flowers and fruit once again the following winter.

These plants make certain common demands, and in addition each has its own particular requirements. Let's deal first with the common demands.

A COOL SPOT

It is essential to put these plants in a cool spot, though they must be kept clear of draughts. A stream of cold air coming from a window or an open door will make the buds fall off and the leaves turn yellow. On the other hand, the direct heat from a fireplace, or a constant air temperature above 72°F, is as good as a death warrant for nearly all these plants.

Put them near windows, where the air is cool, and take the precaution of slipping a sheet of cardboard or a newspaper between the glass and the plants, to prevent their being hit by frost.

If they have spent the day in one of the warmer rooms in the house — the living-room, for example — then you should remove them in the evening and put them in a cooler place for the night (though you must **not** expose them to the cold). The garage might be suitable, perhaps, or anywhere else where the temperature's a bit lower.

ADEQUATE HUMIDITY

The humidity must be kept at 50% or higher. Succulents such as **kalanchoes** and **cactuses** can get by well enough with a lower degree of humidity, though the shock that other plants experience in an over-heated room will hit them just as badly if the atmosphere is too dry. Further, you must remember that all these plants have just come from the moderate temperature and the high humidity of a greenhouse.

As soon as you receive the plant, remove the aluminum foil wrapping from around the pot and stand the plant in a tray lined with gravel — but don't force the pot down into the gravel. Then pour water into the gravel, without covering it completely. The water that evaporates from the tray becomes a constant source of humidity. You can also spray warm water over your plants, using a little household sprayer. You can put the bigger plants in the kitchen sink when you spray them, to avoid drops of water on the furniture, drapes and walls. The water should not be allowed to touch the flowers — otherwise they will be spotted. Spraying helps the growth of the buds and the foliage considerably, even though the extra humidity it provides does not last very long.

SUFFICIENT LIGHTING

Put your plants near a sunny window, or under a source of artificial lighting.

Generally speaking, open flowers will last longer if they are not exposed to the sun's rays or to light reflected by the snow. Plants with many buds, however, **do** need plenty of sunlight. A compromise solution in their case is to put them near a source of diffuse light until the flowers wilt, then remove the flowers and stand the plants in full light to encourage the opening of the buds. In any case, whatever the situation, the winter sun is not likely to prove too hot, even for open flowers.

FRESH AIR

Plants need a change of air from time to time. To change the air in the room without letting them get too cold, all you need do is to open a window or a door a little in the room next door, and then open the communicating door an inch or two between the two rooms. Plants will last much longer in a place where the air is changed every now and then.

All the same, it is absolutely essential to avoid direct draughts.

WATERING

You must water your plants regularly and carefully. Most plants should be watered in the morning — just enough to keep the soil slightly damp. Don't let the soil get either too wet or too dry.

For shrubs, a deep watering is the only answer. Once a week, when the soil is fairly dry, stand the pot in a bucket filled with water up to about an inch below the rim of the pot. When the soil has absorbed enough water by capillary attraction to make the surface go damp (this could take over an hour, depending on the size of the pot), take the pot out of the bucket, spray the leaves, then let the shrub dry out a bit before putting it back in a well-lit spot.

A Jerusalem cherry plant, with its bright orange berries and its handsome, shiny leaves of lovely deep green, is always a much-appreciated present at Christmas-time. It needs very little heat, but you must keep the soil damp and remember to fertilize it. (Photo: Malak, Ottawa)

SPECIAL REQUIREMENTS

POINSETTIAS: in the old days, a poinsettia plant only lasted seven to ten days. Today, its beauty can grace your living-room for three full months in the year — sometimes even five — thanks to the selection of new hybrids.

Put your poinsettias near a sunny window, preferably on the southern side of the house. Water them frequently, to keep a high degree of humidity all the time. Fertilize them every three weeks. Spray the foliage with water once a week, to keep it damp. If little shoots appear beneath the flowers, cut them off at once. The bracts will wither very quickly if you don't remove these shoots.

CYCLAMENS prefer a climate which is not merely cool, but actually on the cold side. Sad to say, one very seldom finds a healthy specimen in a living-room — but it would be wrong to blame the florist for this. Most failures with this plant are due to inability to withstand heat. If you grow it under plenty of light, at a temperature between 55° and 65°F, in well-watered soil, it will produce little shoots for four months or more. Spray it with water once a day, and fertilize the soil with a liquid fertilizer every two weeks.

Stand the pots in a tray of gravel soaked in water, thus providing the necessary humidity as the water evaporates. Use warm water when you water your cyclamens — they cannot stand cold water.

Gradually cut down on the watering after the plant has finished flowering. In August, re-pot into fresh soil.

AZALEA and **HIBISCUS:** these plants grow well in a cool spot, at a temperature of around 50° to 60°F. They spend the summer out in the garden. The hibiscus stands the heat better, and will flower several times during the year, provided you place it near a sunny window.

During their active period, fertilize them once a week, following the manufacturer's directions closely. Thin them occasionally, to preserve their shape. Both azalea and hibiscus require watering in depth.

CHRYSANTHEMUMS: most potted chrysanthemums are greenhouse varieties, and are not suitable for the garden. To make them last as long as possible, you must keep them in a room where the temperature is not too high, with some sun during at least part of the day, and give them plenty of water.

The plants will retain their beauty for three weeks, or even longer, depending on the number of buds they have, and on the conditions under which they are growing. They should be put somewhere where the temperature doesn't go above 70°F — though 60° would be preferable.

Water them deeply. Cut back the stems to a height of two inches after they have finished flowering. Then take the plants down to a cold cellar or a garage where the temperature stays above freezing-point. Water the soil often enough to keep it from drying out completely. Bed them out in the garden late in spring.

KALANCHOES: these succulent plants come into flower several times right up until May, provided you give them plenty of sun and fresh air. Let the soil dry out between waterings, except when the plants are in flower. Kalanchoes do not require the same humidity as other plants — in fact, if the atmosphere is too humid or they receive too much water, they will develop mildew in the form of a whitish powder on their leaves. Any plants so infested should be cleaned with a little powdered sulphur. If your kalanchoes are growing somewhere where it is too hot, and there is no fresh air, you are likely to find the leaves becoming infested with white flies. In this event, clean the plants with a swab of cotton wool soaked in alcohol.

If you cut off the first crop of flowers very close to the stem when they wither, new flowers will appear soon afterwards.

SMALL-FRUITED PLANTS

Of all the fruit-producing indoor plants, two of the most popular species are the **Jerusalem cherry** (Solanum pseudocapsicum), a decorative little plant adorned with small scarlet or orange berries, and the **ornamental peppers** (Capsicum species).

JERUSALEM CHERRY: Unfortunately, the dry atmosphere in most houses makes the leaves and fruit of the Jerusalem cherry fall. Although they are quite hardy indoors, these plants cannot stand a great deal of heat. Their fruit will last longer in an unheated room. Keep the soil damp, and water them with a diluted fertilizer such as 'Plant-Treat' (20-20-20), every two weeks.

ORNAMENTAL PEPPERS These produce little red or yellow fruits which will last a good long time if you keep the plant at a temperature of 60° to 65°F during the day, and 45° to 50°F at night. The soil must be damp all through, for the foliage and the fruit fall very quickly if the roots go dry. The same thing happens if there is a leaking gas-jet anywhere in the house. It is not worthwhile to keep these plants and try to grow them for more than one winter. Jerusalem cherries go rather gangly, and lose their looks completely, while ornamental peppers are really only annual plants.

HOW TO MAKE YOUR CHRISTMAS PLANTS LAST LONGER

Among the various plants you might receive as Christmas gifts, there are several which can easily be kept to flower again during future winters. Some examples worthy of note are **poinsettias, azaleas, chrysanthemums, kalanchoes** (Kalanchoe blossfeldiana), **Jerusalem cherries, Christmas pepper** (Capsicum frutescens) and **cyclamens** (Cyclamen indicum).

We have already discused how to go about making **poinsettias** last.

When an azalea plant has finished flowering, the advice of most florists is to keep it in a well-lit spot and continue to water it from time to time. As soon as there is no longer any risk of frost outside, transplant it into one of the beds in the garden. This plant will flower again the following winter.
(Photo: Malak, Ottawa)

AZALEAS: with the proper care, you can make your azaleas flower again each year. After it has flowered, put the azalea plant in a cool, sunny place, and water it regularly. At the end of May or the beginning of June, transplant it into the garden. Bury the pot in the soil, right down to the rim, in a partly-shaded spot which is sheltered from the prevailing wind. Water regularly all through the summer to prevent the soil from drying out. Fertilize with soluble fertilizers such as 20-20-20. At the end of June, trim off any shoots that have grown too long, and strip the buds from the other stems, to force increased production of branches.

Azalea plants must be brought indoors before the frosts set in. Put them in an unheated porch, or in a room where the temperature will be between 40° and 50°F at night, and will only rise 5° to 10° higher during the daytime.

As the green buds start appearing on the plants, cut down on the watering, and stop fertilizing.

In mid-December, put the potted azalea in a warmer room, near a sunny window, and begin fertilizing again. Now the temperature should be about 60°F at nights, and from 70° to 75°F during the daytime. Note that if the temperature is too high, there is a risk that the buds will dry out and not open at all.

CHRYSANTHEMUMS: most chrysanthemums grown indoors in pots are greenhouse varieties, and do not do very well if they are planted out in the garden when they have finished flowering. With some difficulty, they can usually be persuaded to flower for a second time indoors.

If a number of plants have been grouped into a single pot, they should be taken out individually and re-potted, each in its own separate pot, and then cut back to one inch above the soil.

New shoots will appear if the plants are set near a sunny window and given a thorough watering.

At the beginning of June, choose a sunny spot in the garden and dig the plants in. Water regularly, and fertilize every two weeks with a soluble fertilizer. As soon as the stems are six inches tall, remove the buds, and continue this disbudding process till the end of August. Then bring the plants back indoors and put them in a sunny window, where the temperature won't fall below 60°F. When buds begin to show, drop the temperature to 55°F at night. By day, try to keep it between 65° and 70°F.

To encourage large flowers, take all the buds off each shoot except the central one — unless you are dealing with a **pompon** variety, in which case let the buds remain. Like **poinsettias,** chrysanthemums need short days if they are to produce buds. Treat them as **poinsettias,** as far as the duration of lighting is concerned.

KALANCHOES: these are small succulent plants with small red flowers bunched together in tufts at the tops of the stems. The flowers last longer than those of any other Christmas plant.

They prefer a temperature of 60°F at night, and 70° to 75°F during the day.

While they are actually flowering, put them near a really brightly-lit window. At all other times they should be in a reasonably sunny window. They can be propagated by means of cuttings, or they can be grown from seeds.

The pots containing the new plants are put outside during the summer. They must be protected against the direct light of the sun, which is too strong for them. The plantlets should have the appopriate buds nipped off to give them a more compact shape.

To ensure that the 'mother' plant (the one you received as a Christmas present) will flower the following year, you must do three things: (1) Bury the pot in the soil outside for the summer. (2) Nip off buds as necessary, to make the plant more bushy. (3) Remember to water it regularly.

FRUIT-BEARING PLANTS: ornamental peppers and **Jerusalem cherries** need plenty of light and a lowish temperature — say 45° to 50°F at night, and 60° to 65°F during the day. Furthermore, the soil must be kept moist all through, since the flowers and fruit fall rapidly if the roots are allowed to dry out.

It is easy to grow new plants from the seeds contained in the little fruits. These seeds should be sown in June.

CYCLAMENS: it is very difficult to make cyclamens flower again outside the greenhouse. However, there is no reason why you should not try. When the plant has finished flowering, gradually cut down on the watering. In due course, (early in the spring) re-pot the corm in a loam rich in organic matter and containing 25% perlite.

The upper half of the corm should be left protruding from the soil. During the summer, put it outside to grow — but don't let it be exposed to the direct rays of the hot midday sun. Water it frequently, and fertilize it every two weeks with a soluble fertilizer.

Bring the pot back inside before the cold weather sets in in the autumn, and put it in a cool but sunny window.

Watch out for a destructive insect, the strawberry mite, which makes the leaves of the plant curl up. Every plant with curled-up leaves must be burnt, unless you want to run the risk of the other plants becoming infested — especially your African violets, which are particularly vulnerable to the attacks of this insect.

How To Control Harmful Insects

With the approach of spring, many amateur gardeners who grow indoor plants learn — perhaps for the first time — that there are such things as insects. Although insects that attack house plants are fairly rare — at least, compared with the number of plant pests outside — people often tend to become upset when they encounter them. If you do happen to notice insects on your plants, try to avoid using methods of extermination which are likely to do more harm to the plants than to the insects!

TINY FLIES
(which are NOT harmful insects)

You must not believe that all those insects you see hovering around your indoor plants are automatically dangerous parasites. Most of the time they are more than likely to be tiny flies, which appear after the plant has been watered. They are quite harmless to living plants, since they live on decomposed organic matter in the soil. Far from being a cause for alarm, their presence is actually a good omen.

It is usually a sign that the soil contains a satisfactory proportion of organic matter, and is well suited to the production of healty plants capable of resisting harmful insects.

It must be admitted, however, that these tiny insects multiply very rapidly, and have an annoying habit of lighting on the walls — thus making their presence only too obvious. The best way of getting rid of them is to water the soil thoroughly with chlordane. Use a level teaspoonful of sluble chlrdane pwder (50% strength) to a pint of water.

SPRINGTAILS

It is appropriate to add here that among other similar insects are the springtails — little jumping insects, white in colour, which also feed on organic matter. They show up on the surface of the soil or in the water in the saucers set underneath the pots.

You can rid yourself of springtails with chlordane. Use this insecticide in the same way as described above for getting rid of the flies. Malathion is also very effective. Mix ½ a teaspoonful of the concentrated 50% emulsion in a pint of water.

PARASITES

Here is a brief list of some of the parasites that attack indoor plants, followed by a résumé of the most effective methods of getting rid of them:

SCALE INSECTS (which are related to the mealybugs): these insects have a scaly-textured shell and, like the mealybug, they can withstand most dusting preparations.

APHIDS: black, red or green aphids or "plant lice" are frequently seen on indoor plants.

RED SPIDER MITE: this little mite, which resembles a tiny spider, weaves its web on the backs of leaves and on the stems. The dry atmosphere of our houses suits it perfectly. Once it has managed to establish itself, it multiplies rapidly.

SPECIAL INSECTS: I should mention here that quite often certain groups of plants have a special insect that seems to have chosen them as its own private province. Thus, one particular mite is the special pest of the **cyclamen** and the **strawberry** bush. There is another mite that preys on **African violets;** the scale insect attacks ferns; and the black vine weevil eats into **cyclamen** roots. If you are growing these plants in large numbers, it is sometime necessary to give them special treatment.

CONTROL OF PARASITES

To control these various insects, the first thing to do is to use a stiff brush on the plants, which will get rid of scale insects and mealybugs. Then give them a good washing under the tap. The day after you have washed the plants, dust the leaves and the stems with the insecticide recommended for the particular pest you are trying to destroy.

If the plants are infested with **mealybugs** or **scale insects,** spray them with a solution of Malathion — one teaspoonful per gallon of water. Or if you prefer you can wash the leaves with a solution of nicotine and soap, made by mixing 1¼ teaspoonfuls of nicotine sulphate with ounce of soap in a gallon of water. (Let me advise your to dissolve the soap in a little hot water first). There is also a commercial preparation of nicotine sulphate available, which has an oil in it and which is a very effective treatment against these insect pests. Once again, I must stress that it is always most important to follow the manufacturer's recommendations faithfully when you use an insecticide. Incorrect use of these powders and solutions could damage your plants.

The best way of getting rid of **red spider mites** is to use a commercial miticide. You will find this sort of preparation on sale in nurseries, garden supply centres and at the plant department of most large department stores. The most common form is an aerosol container that sprays the chemical straight onto your plants. Red spider mites can also be flushed away by a strong jet of water — either from a hose-pipe or from a syringe. However, this latter method can only be used somewhere where you don't mind a lot of water on the floor, or splashes on the walls — the garage, for example, and of course it is quite suitable outside, when the temperature permits.

You can rid your plants of **aphids** by spraying them all over with a solution of Malathion, or of nicotine sulphate mixed with soap — you can even dip them into this latter preparation, if you like. This solution is prepared in the same way as the one I described above, for getting rid of scale insects and mealybugs.

WHERE DO THESE PESTS COME FROM?

There is one fact you must remember when you find insects attacking your plants. These insects do not breed in a house that has no vegetation inside it.

There's only one way in which these parasites can enter our homes — and that is on the plants themselves. You must also pay very special attention to any new soil you bring into the house. Soil bought from a nursery or garden supply centre or in a shop, is usually sterilized, and free of parasites. However, that is not the case with soil that comes from the garden. It can contain an incredible number of parasites or their eggs.

ESSENTIAL PRECAUTIONS

Prevention is always the best rule in gardening — and that applies to indoor gardening as well as outdoor. Keep an eye on your plants, examine them as often as you can. Every now and then put them in the bath-tub and give them a good shower. This will greatly improve their health, and so will spraying water over their foliage. Another thing — dipping them

356

in a bucket of insecticide is often just as effective as spraying them —
for this method ensures that the whole plant gets covered with the
insecticide. Remember, too, that the water used for spraying or notering
should always be at room temperature.

Give Your Indoor Plants
A Holiday

Just like greenhouse plants, your indoor plants will benefit from some
time outdoors during the summer months. Furthermore, they can add
considerably to the beauty of the garden.

As soon as the temperature at night gets warm enough — over 55°F,
let's say — you can move your plants out of the house into the garden
without danger. After only a few weeks, you will notice the beneficial
effects on your plants from this holiday in surroundings where they are
enjoying plenty of humidity and an optimum amount of sunlight. All the
same, if your house plants are to get the full benefit from their time in
the open air, it is essential that you should know exactly what the basic
requirements of these plants really are, and you should ensure that those
requirements are properly satisfied. Let me stress, for example, that
somewhere facing north or east, protected from too much light, and
sheltered from strong winds, is the most suitable sort of location.

Incidentally, **sansevierias** like a bit of sun, while **begonias** require more
shade. Remember, too, that if you cannot provide effective protection
for delicate broad-leaved plants such as **philodendrons, rex begionias,
dracaenas,** and **dieffenbachios,** it would be much better to keep them in
the house.

ESSENTIAL PRECAUTIONS

By now you will have realized that there is no question of just putting
your potted plants outside and leaving them there. These plants need care
and attention all through the summer. If they are really to benefit from
their stay in the open air, it is essential to take certain precautions. To
ensure the success of house plants when you take them outside, you must
proceed as follows:
1. Eliminate all plants which are no longer healthy or attractive including those which have grown too big and can not be pruned effectively.
2. Prune those plants that need it, to improve their symmetry or reduce
   their size.
3. Re-pot any plants that need more space, and put them in bigger pots.
   Remember to check to see if there are any insects on the plants,
before you dig the pots into the ground.

If you find insects — or if you even suspect they might be there — put the pots to one side and spray the plants with water or an insecticide. Remember to spray the backs of the leaves, too — that is especially important. Don't forget that it is much easier to deal with any parasites **before** the pots are buried in the ground.

GROUP YOUR PLANTS

To make it easier to maintain your plants, it is better to group them by species in various different flowerbeds that offer different conditions. Full sunlight for the ones that can stand it — **(succulents, cactuses, amaryllises,** and **geraniums).** Partial shade for **azaleas, Christmas cactus** and **orchid cactuses;** and more shade, generally speaking, for plants with fine foliage like **begonias, philodendrons,** etc. You will find conditions like these near a tree or a tall leafy bush (the foliage mustn't be **too** thick, of course) or near a building. If you do not have a suitable place for these plants on your property, you can spread them out among the flowerbeds generally, or among your shrubs.

This dracaena plant (Dracaena warneckii) has been planted outside in a shady spot sheltered from the prevailing wind. It will be in excellent condition when the time comes to take it back indoors for the long winter months.

WATERING AND DRAINAGE

Potted plants set in the soil, or in a trench of peat-moss or sand, must be watered. Note that the rims of the pots should be a little higher than the surface of the ground, and that for proper drainage their bases should be resting on clinkers or gravel. If you install the pots in that way, the plant roots will not try to creep out over the rim of the pot, or out through the drainage hole.

To stop the plants from growing in the same direction all the time — that is, towards the sun — you should give the pots a half-turn in the ground every now and then.

FERTILIZING

It is sometimes necessary to fertilize plants during the summer, especially if they are growing strongly. Use either a dry or a liquid chemical fertilizer for this.

Remember to follow the manufacturer's recommendations exactly, when you use the fertilizer.

A BENEFICIAL STAY

There is no doubt at all that any plants with fine flowers or foliage, which you do not actually need for the interior decoration of your house, will benefit from this sort of open-air summer holiday. Their time outdoors will help them get through the long months inside the house more easily.

In conclusion, let me stress that you must remember the right date for taking your plants back indoors after their holiday in the garden. This is usually done just before the first light frost, usually towards the beginning of September in Eastern Canada. Your local expert will advise you as to the proper date for your own region.

Bringing Your Indoor Plants Back Inside

When the chrysanthemums begin to flower, the time has come to prepare for the return of your indoor plants after their holiday outside in the garden.

During the summer months, the heat and the humidity and the long hours of sunshine have more or less reproduced the growing-conditions of the tropical countries where many of these plants originated. So you should not be in the least surprised to find that if you have watered your plants regularly, and looked after them properly, they are full of vigour around the beginning of September.

The beginning of September usually coincides with a change of temperature. The nights grow longer and colder — in some areas there may even be frost. These cold nights, replacing the warm nights of summer, are a warning to plant-lovers that winter is at hand.

BEWARE OF THE COLD

This change of temperature, coupled with the shorter days, induces a state of dormancy in house plants which are still outdoors — and this at the very moment when we want to be admiring them in all their splendour. Furthermore, fragile tropical plants like **peperomias, philodendrons, anthuriums** and several of the **gesnerias,** suffer damage during cold nights.

Even if these plants do not die after one or two drops in temperature down to around 40°F, they can well lose all their decorative value.

Knowing the natural habitat of your indoor plants will help you decide which of them should be the first to be brought back inside. Indoor plant lovers who know about these things will bring in the plants that come from rainy tropical forests first of all. They will let plants from the high plateaus of Mexico and from southern China stay out in the garden for a few more days.

If you are not too well informed about the backgrounds of your plants, and do not know which to choose, you should bring them all back into the house before the first frost.

MANY ADVANTAGES

Bringing your plants indoors early in the autumn not only protects them against low temperatures and prevents them from going dormant too soon, but also helps to minimize the harmful effects of the contrast between the high humidity they enjoyed during the summer months, and the much lower humidity of the artificially-warmed air inside the house in winter.

As the nights get cooler during the month of September, the furnace stays on longer and longer; and this brings the humidity down gradually, day by day, thus giving the plant cells sufficient time to adapt to the changing situation.

On the other hand, if the plant stays out in the garden until such time as the furnace is on continuously, the sudden change in the condition of the air surrounding them from humidity to dryness, can make the foliage and the floral buds drop off suddenly, and most of them will not be replaced until the beginning of the new year, when the new shoots make their appearance.

This dracaena (Dracaena 'Janet Craig') spent the summer in a shady place in the garden, sheltered from the wind. It is now in excellent condition, ready for the long winter months back inside the house.

(Photo: Lemoine Tropica)

THE IMPORTANCE OF LIGHT

The change of season brings an inevitable slow-down in the growth of all your plants, however much care you have lavished on them. The principal source of energy needed for their development is no longer fertilizer — it is light.

Without light, there is no growth. Plentiful light is also the principal factor on the production of flowers, except in the case of a few plants like **poinsettias** and **chrysanthemums,** which flower only when their days are shorter than their nights.

361

THE DORMANT STATE

As a matter of fact, plants stop growing almost completely during November and December, with their very short days. During this period many plants are totally or partially in the dormant state.

To stop plants from wasting away, you must provide them with light by putting plants which are in flower near a window on the south side of the house, as well as giving them enough humidity. Even so, this only maintains the status quo. The plants will not look any better much before the beginning of January.

ARTIFICIAL LIGHTING

Fortunately, there's an excellent substitute for sunlight — artificial lighting. With special fluorescent tubes — 'Go-Lux', 'Plant-Grow' or 'Optima', for example — you can increase your plants' health and growth, which in many cases would otherwise disappear. You no longer have to limit yourself to window-sills to give your plants enough light during the winter. You can provide yourself with lighting appliances consisting of one, two or even four fluorescent tubes, at quite reasonable prices. These installations are big enough to stimulate the growth of **African violets, begonias, episcias, gloxinias** and other similar plants.

Also, since plants grow quickly in summer and slowly in the autumn, you should pot and prune your indoor plants as early as possible.

Experienced amateur gardeners usually proceed as follows. When they take their house plants outdoors in June or July, depending on the temperature, they transplant them into bigger pots (usually one size larger) and give them a very close pruning. This procedure gives the plants a new, bushier shape, which will be well established by the autumn.

MOVING-DAY

When the day arrives to take the plants back into the house you should follow these steps. First of all, examine the leaves carefully, then the flowers and the stems, to investigate the possible presence of aphids, scale insects, red spider mites and other harmful insects. A good watering with an all-purpose insecticide containing Malathion will kill most of these parasites.

Since this type of insecticide is poisonous to warm-blooded animals, it is advisable to carry out this spraying out of doors. If you have to spray inside, you should use an insecticide containing pyrethrum and rotenone instead.

SNAILS AND EARTHWORMS

Snails and earthworms are two more enemies of your indoor plants. Snails are usually found underneath the pot, sometimes in the drainage hole, or on the underside of the rim of the pot. They hide during the

This is an amaryllis (Hippeastrum) which has been outside in a semi-shaded spot since the beginning of the summer. In September, before the frosts set in, it should be put somewhere dry and sheltered from the cold, and watering should be discontinued. When the foliage turns yellow, cut the leaves off close to the bulb and let the pot stand undisturbed for about three months. Then you should get the bulb ready for flowering during the Christmas season.

daytime, but in the evening they slither out, to bore holes in the leaves and stems.

Many indoor plant fans do not need to worry about snails, since their gardens are too dry for these parasites. But if your indoor plants are in flowerboxes filled with peat-moss or earth when you put them outside for the summer, or in pots standing on a bed of wet pebbles, then you may find when you bring them in again that you have also brought in snails and earthworms.

How can earthworms damage indoor plants when the latter are back inside the house? Although they do not feed on the vegetable tissues of the plant, earthworms move about in the soil, and thus spoil the direct contact between the plant's rootlets and the soil particles.

You can easily detect their presence by the droppings they leave on the surface of the soil. To get rid of them, take the plant out of the pot, tapping the pot as you do so. Then comb through the soil with your fingers. Another method consists of watering the soil with a solution made from a teaspoonful of mustard powder, or from potassium permanganate in sufficient strength to colour the water pink. Either of these solutions will bring the worms up to the surface of the soil.

An electric mini-tractor has been a long-felt want in the sphere of gardening equipment. This new tractor, the 'Elec-Trak', is powered by six batteries, which can be recharged very simply by plugging in to the ordinary 110-volt domestic supply. Some forty different attachments or accessories can be hitched on, for various gardening tasks throughout the year. This new product also marks a big step forward in the fight against pollution.

CHAPTER 15

MISCELLANEOUS

Flowers To Dry
For Floral Decorations

If you are among those who would like to make up winter bouquets from dried flowers, you have only to visit your garden supply centre and get yourself some seeds of flowers that are easy to dry. You will have no trouble in finding the sort of seeds you need to carry out your project.

Let me say here that most of these flowers are very interesting to grow, not only for the effect they produce after they have been collected, but also for the comments they occasion. The petals of these flowers consist of fibres which are so rigid that they appear to be artifical, and it is difficult not to be surprised when you learn they are natural after all.

SEEDS

Every plant in this category — except sea-lavender — can be grown from seed sown directly into the bed where you want the plant to grow. Sowing should be carried out as soon as the soil is sufficiently thawed and dried out in the spring. As for sea-lavender, it grows better if it's sown indoors at the start — or if you buy it as a plant from a nursery or gardening centre during the planting season.

TRANSPLANTING

I must warn you that certain plants are not very easy to transplant. Therefore, it is preferable to sow them sparingly right where you want them to grow, and to thin them out later on to one plant every six inches, It is also important to remember that if you intend to use them as cut flowers, you must leave eighteen inches between rows. On the other hand, if it's merely a matter of beautifying flowerbeds or borders, 6-inch spacing all round is sufficient.

The immortelle is perhaps the most popular of all the plants grown for the production of flowers for drying.

THE BEST PLANTS

In order to make a success of your flower-drying operation, I would advise you to cut the flowers to be dried when they are at their peak — that is, before they are too far advanced. While they're drying, keep them standing upright in vases, bottles or other empty containers.

Here is a list of the best annual flowers for drying — which also happen to be the easiest to grow. Not only are they used for making winter bouquets, they're also an excellent decorative element in flower-beds of annual flowers, where they can be used to mark the borders.

IMMORTELLES

There are the classic **immortelles** (Helichrysum bracteatum 'Monstrosum'), which are grown in great numbers, and then dried and coloured. They are extremely easy to grow from seeds sown directly out of doors.

Immortelles are available in several distinct colours — such as bronze, bright yellow, pure white, deep red, scarlet and pale pink, or in various combinations of colours.

SEA-LAVENDER

Like **immortelles,** these annual plants of the **Limonium** family are grown mainly for the production of cut flowers — though they grow well and make a very good showing on sandy slopes. Seedsmen stock three main species **notch-leaf sea-lavender** (Limonium sinuatum) is the commonest, and the easiest to grow; the flowers it produces are yellow, pale blue, or pink. Next comes **Suworow's sea-lavender** (Limonium suworowii); not only is its name somewhat difficult to pronounce, it is also a bit more demanding than the others. Sow it in boxes, during May, then transplant it later on. It produces long, slim, twisted spikes loaded with pink flowers which make a remarkable effect in bouquets of dried flowers. Finally there is **Algerian sea-lavender** (Limonium bonduellii), which looks like **notch-leaf sea-lavender,** but only produces yellow flowers which are bigger and much slower-growing.

CELOSIA

There are two types of **celosia** grown in our gardens. One looks like a cockscomb — and indeed is commonly known by this name; the other resembles a tuft of feathers, with delicate plumy inflorescences.

Both types are excellent flowers for cutting and drying for use in winter. Among the best **cockscombs** the following are worthy of mention: **'Fireglow',** with big orange crests carried on strong stems; **'Toreador',** a very bright red; and the enormous flowers of the new **'Empress'** types (**'Golden Empress', 'Crimson Empress', 'Rose Empress'** and **'Orange Empress').** Even though you can to some extent succeed in producing **celosias** by sowing them outdoors towards the end of April, they produce their crests or their plumes more quickly if you sow them indoors six weeks previously, and only move them outside when there is no longer any risk of their being damaged by frost — say during the first week in June, for Eastern Canada. They develop poorly if their growth is arrested — by leaving them in the pot too long, for instance, and not transplanting them soon enough.

GLOBE AMARANTH

The **globe amaranth** (Gomphrena globosa) has been considerably improved in recent years, to the point where there is a great variety of colours to choose from today. There are also several compact dwarf forms which are very useful as border plants in light sandy soils. Naturally, you must expose them to full sunlight, as you do all the other flowers for drying, and they grow better in poor soils. The **'Dwarf Buddy'** variety is the best for use as a border, while the mixed strains are preferable as flowers for cutting.

ACROCLINIUMS

These exquisite annual plants produce flowers for drying which resemble **daisies** — white, pale pink and deep pink. They provide the smallest flowers for permanent winter bouquets.

MOLUCCA BALM

This interesting annual plant (Molucella laevis) is only grown for floral decorations. It's not very decorative growing in the ground, and unless you remove the leaves when the flowers open, it loses the full value of its lines and natural curves. You can dry it in the same way as the others, and use it in winter bouquets.

OTHER SPECIES

I should also mention one or two other species which are worth looking for in the catalogues — for example, the **xeranthemums** with their silky white or pink flowers; the pink **'Swan River'**, variety of **Mangle's Sunray** (Helipterum manglesii); and **silver cockscomb** (Celosia argentea 'Childsii').

How To Preserve
Autumn Bouquets

Dried grasses, flowers, branches and leaves, arranged in winter bouquets, can be put in all sorts of places where fresh flowers couldn't live.

It is easy to preserve them. The first thing to do is to bundle them up in fairly tight little bunches, with all the heads together. Do not make the bunches too large or they could go musty. Before you hang each bunch up, wrap it in a sheet of paper — but don't fold the paper over the flowers. This wrapping is a protection against dust, and stops the stems from getting broken. The little bunches should be hung up in a dry, airy, darkish place, so that they will keep their beautiful autumn colouring.

IRONING

To preserve leaves, it is absolutely essential to iron them. The iron should be only just warm, and you should use it delicately on both sides of the leaves. Then dip the long branches into a glass jar — (preferably tall) — filled with a mixture of ⅔ glycerine and ⅓ water. The end of the stem should dip about 2 inches into this mixture, which replaces the sap of the branch. On morning, you will see little drops forming at the end of the leaves, then you must seal the end of each stem with wax, to make sure that this artificial sap is retained in the branch.

If you have picked any tiny flowers from the grass family, you can start arranging your bouquet immediately by sticking each of the stems into a piece of styrofoam, for example, or some of those little porous coloured rocks that are used to decorate aquariums — or even a sponge. Note that if the flowers are small enough, all bouquets can be dried in this way. If you have been given a small "country style" boquet as a gift, you can preserve it for a long time, using the same method as for the leaves — (⅔ glycerine and ⅓ water). Let the bouquet soak up the mixture. It is not necessary to seal the stems, but let the bouquet dry out in a dry, airy, darkish spot. Then remove any flowers and branches which are not up to standard, and rearrange the bouquet if necessary.

If you like the idea of a bit of a sheen on the flowers, spray them with an aerosol bomb of colourless varnish.

COLOURING

You may want to colour a bouquet of dried flowers. If so, prepare a few little dishes of ordinary househould dye, and spray the colours on. If you can possibly avoid it, do not dip the bouquet into the liquid — this will make the flowers soggy. To colour each delicate flower, use just a little pinch of dye — don't drown it! The best colours are made from ink (which comes in all sorts of shades), mercurochrome or methylene blue. You have probably already realized that this colouring job is better done out of doors, or in the bathroom!

Let me suggest an amusing little experiment — pick some flowers, grasses, or gramineous flowerlets, and add a little ink, or mercurochrome, or methylene blue (which is used for painting sore throats) to the water in the vase. The coloured water will rise into the flower by capillary attraction, and will appear in the petals.

FLORAL ARRANGEMENT

Here's another original arrangement for you to try — you will have pretty little green plants all winter long.

Pick some pine cones, and put them in the oven to make them open up quickly. Once they're open, put a little earth in the cavity behind each 'scale', then plant seeds of **wheat, rice, lentil,** or **millet** — you will find all these in the shops that sell health foods). You could even put a few **ivy** cuttings in. Moisten the soil every day. Group several fir cones together in a flat dish, and you will have a pretty little garden that's very pleasant to look at whenever the weather's dull.

Gardening Equipment

Most town-dwellers who are enjoying the pleasures of gardening for the first time never fail to be somewhat surprised by the difficulties they encounter in carrying out the chores inherent in plant-growing. They are anxious to give their plants and lawns all the necessary attentions; but they find it difficult to make a choice from all these tools and instruments and equipment and machinery. Which tools are really useful and effective? Which should get priority? Which really save time and trouble? These are the sort of questions the amateur is faced with.

It is quite obvious that your task will be much easier and more agreeable if you have the proper tools for the work you are trying to do. However, that does not mean to say that you must spend a lot of money on them.

The essential thing is to choose sensibly, to suit your real needs and your financial resources — that is to acquire the equipment which can really make your task easier, so that gardening is always a relaxation for you, and not just another chore.

ESSENTIAL TOOLS

Without any doubt, the most important tool for gardening is the spade. You can use it for many different tasks — digging, levelling, transplanting and so on. Then comes the garden fork, which is useful for digging, especially in heavy soils. You really cannot do without it when you want to dig up bulbs, onions or potatoes, and it is also indispensable for transplanting trees and large herbaceous plants.

It is an excellent substitute for the manure-fork, too, if your garden is too small to warrant your buying one of these.

The soil around bushes and in borders and flowerbeds should be friable and free of weeds. The hoe is the perfect tool for these two purposes. There are dozens of different kinds, provided with either three or four tines. They are easy to use, and very effective.

Whether it's a garden of ornamental plants, or a simple kitchen-garden, there are certain tools you cannot do without — a trowel, a hand hoe, a roundended shovel, a scraper and a garden rake. A garden fork is essential when you have to break the soil up. However, if the area to be dug is at all large, you should hand all the hard work over to a motorized rotary tiller — a "rototiller" or "power tiller". This type of machine digs the soil and does an excellent job of hoeing all through the season.

Without doubt, one of the most important pieces of garden equipment is the wheelbarrow. You should note that the little two-wheeled handcarts are easier to handle than wheelbarrows, and you can transport heavy loads in them just as easily as you can light ones.

Some indispensable tools for keeping your garden beautiful. The photograph above shows several gardening accessories which can be easily handled by a woman: secateurs for trimming rose bushes, shrubs, flowers, etc.; shears for hedges; grass shears with swing-blade; and garden hoe.

THE UPKEEP OF THE LAWN

Not surprisingly, one of the most difficult problems in gardening is the upkeep of the lawn. If the grassed area of your garden is 500 square feet or less, a hand-mower is quite adequate. For anything larger than that, you should use a power-mower. There is a vast choice of these instruments, of many different makes. They run from the small rotary mower, with either an electric or a gas-powered motor, up to big mowers mounted on small tractors. These mini-tractors have a large assortment of accessories which enable you to do such varied jobs as mowing the lawn, digging, hoeing and getting rid of snow.

A good pair of lawn clippers is an essential tool for doing the edge of the lawn. Modern lawn clippers are easy to use compared with the old-fashioned type, which called for strong muscles on the part of the gardener who was using them. The high-quality tempered steel blades of today's clippers can be sharpened, and they keep their edge for a good

Effective upkeep of the lawn calls for the use of a spreader which lets you sow seed and distribute fertilizers and additives with speed and precision.

long time. More and more, both professional and amateur gardeners are turning to electric edge-clippers — which are to hand-clippers what the power-mower is to the hand-mower. In fact, they clip the grass all around the edge of the lawn and around the flowerbeds in much the same way as the rotary mower does its work on the main body of the lawn.

You must also remember that a grass-rake is a tool you will need, to collect the grass clippings from the lawn, and to clean up your property in general.

Bamboo rakes are very popular for this sort of work, since they don't damage the lawn. A steel rake with flexible teeth lasts longer, but you must be more careful how you use it. If you have really large areas to deal with, it is better to use a mechanical lawn-sweeper — it will only take you one hour to do a job which would take you six hours by hand. There are some models which can be attached behind a rotating-cylinder mower drawn by a tractor. This combination lets you mow the lawn and sweep it simultaneously.

If you are going to do it properly, the upkeep of a lawn requires the use of a spreader which lets you sow seed and distribute fertilizers and additives with speed and precision.

THE LAWN-ROLLER

Although you only use your lawn-roller once or twice a year, it is a piece of equipment every amateur gardener must have if he takes his hobby at all seriously. There is always the possibility, if you are lucky, that some generous neighbour will lend you his roller every now and then, which will save you some expense. However, I must stress that experience has shown that you cannot have a nice lawn without rolling and aerating it.

The best type of roller is made of thick steel which can be filled with water or sand, and with rims which let you fit aeration bars.

The roller is used in the spring, before the lawn is mowed for the first time, and after you have finished cleaning it up after the winter to get rid of all the rubbish (bits of stick, stones and gravel). Rolling should be carried out with as heavy a roller as possible. The object is to flatten out the surface of the lawn again after the effects of frost and thaw and the irregularities left by earth-worms and (sometimes) by field mice or moles.

The roller also serves to tamp the grass-seed down into the soil after you sow a lawn.

AERATION BARS

When the soil is so tightly packed that water and fertilizers only penetrate a little way into the soil, if at all, you must aerate your lawn. The best way is to use a roller fitted with aeration bars which drill little holes into the ground, thus permitting air and moisture to circulate freely around the roots. This treatment produces a strong, healthy crop of grass, which smothers couch-grass and other weeds.

WATERING SYSTEMS

Hoses and sprinklers are indispensable to the normal upkeep of a lawn, especially during dry periods. Hoses have been much improved over the past few years. Rubber hoses are much lighter than they used to be, and more supple, while plastic ones are much less stiff, can withstand blows better, and are less affected by changes of temperature.

For some time flat hoses have been available on the market. These assume a cylindrical shape under the effect of water pressure. They are easier to coil up, since they are very supple and take up less space than cylindrical hoses.

The problem of watering large areas of grass has been solved, thanks to the sprinklers that are used on golf courses. These adjustable devices can cover a wide circle, or just an arc of the circle, as desired. If you must put a sprinkler near the street or the house, for example, this type of control is absolutely essential.

Ready to maintain a handsome lawn. This young lady won't have any trouble keeping her grounds in excellent condition. In addition to a scuffle hoe, which is used for cutting roots and weeds, she has a good garden rake, a grass rake, a lawn aerator, a garden hose and an electric rotary mower with a bag for collecting the clippings.

THE OSCILLATING SPRINKLER is very fashionable nowadays. It too covers a large area, and distributes the water with great precision. However, you must realize that neither the oscillating sprinkler nor the pulsating variety covers the required area all at once — they cover different portions of it in succession, moving back and forth from the central point. Therefore, the water can penetrate into the soil while the sprinkler's slowly spreading water over another section of the ground that has to be covered. This also avoids loss of water by run-off from the surface.

PERFORATED TUBULAR SPRINKLERS are plastic tubes pierced with numerous little holes arranged in a scientifically-planned pattern over the whole of their surface. They are very effective for delivering water onto hedges, borders and flowerbeds. However, to obtain the full advantage of their extremely fine spray, you must leave them in the same spot for quite a long time. This also applies in the case of canvas hoses, and these latter have the further disadvantage that they don't function very well if there are any sharp bends, or any marked unevenness of the ground.

CRAWLING SPRINKLERS are excellent for watering large areas, because they move slowly and spread water uniformly. Certain models switch off automatically when they have watered the required area.

ROTATING SPRINKLERS of several different types are also available — several of them with adjustable jets. They are suitable for small areas, and deliver a lot of water in a short time.

BURIED SPRAYERS This is a watering system which is sure to become more and more popular in the future. It consists of spray nozzles set permanently in the lawn at ground level, and connected to the water-supply by a network of underground pipes.

The system usually includes a time switch which provides for automatic operation. It waters the whole lawn simultaneously and provides the same amount of water all over.

ROOT IRRIGATORS not only provide the root systems of trees with a sufficient amount of water, they are also an excellent means of feeding the trees with essential nutritive elements.

SECATEURS

The normal upkeep of trees and shrubs calls for a certain minimum of tools. Secateurs are high on the list of these essential tools. In addition, if you have a hedge, you will need a pair of hedge-shears. On this subject, I should mention that electric hedge-clippers make the task of trimming your hedges much easier and quicker. Don't worry about the electric cable — with a little practice on your part it soon stops getting

Trimming is one of the attentions a hedge simply must have if it is to remain an ornament to your garden. Hedge shears with tempered steel blades give a clean, even cut, and thus avoid damaging the branches of the bushes.

in your way, and you find you are no longer afraid of cutting it accidentally. One word of warning — if you plan to buy this type of instrument, it is better to choose the model with the larger gap between the teeth — this causes the least damage to the branches of the bushes.

Though not actually essential, there are some tools which are useful for special cases. These are branch-cutters, which look something like secateurs with large blades and long handles, and can deal with branches up to two inches in diameter; and pruning-saws, which are used for bigger branches, and have thin blades with special teeth, so that they can get into cramped places and cut green or dead wood with equal ease.

Saws with adjustable telescopic handles and pruning-hooks mounted on long poles are two other very practical pieces of apparatus for cutting high branches.

OTHER TOOLS

A few words should also be said about the various tools necessary for the elimination of weeds. Reaping-hooks and scythes are excellent for cutting long grass in places which are too cramped to let you use a rotary motor-mower, or even a hand-mower. Note also that a pruning-knife is an excellent tool for cutting long grass and brushwood with stems up to about one inch in diameter.

CONTROL OF INSECTS AND DISEASES

The fight against insects and plant diseases calls for only a few pieces of apparatus. A special applicator that fits onto the end of the garden hose provides an effective and rapid method of spraying insecticides, fungicides and herbicides. The water pressure in the hose is enough to produce a suction and thus pick up the chemical compound held in the reservoir of the applicator, so that no pumping is required. The concentrated chemicals are diluted by the water. Several gallons of chemical can be sprayed in this way, without the operator having to carry a heavy reservoir filled with a diluted solution, and spraying it by hand.

SPRAYERS

For those whose property is fairly small, a very useful piece of equipment is a compressed-air sprayer with a 3-gallon capacity reservoir and a variable-power atomizing nozzle. This apparatus can be obtained either in "backpack" form, or mounted on a shoulder-strap.

If your garden is very small, you can use a much smaller model, with a reservoir that holds only a pint of liquid.

In every case, try and choose a sprayer which produces a fine mist at the nozzle.

Dusting equipment for insecticides and fungicides is also used frequently.

For small areas, you can buy small models with a capacity of from five to eight pounds. They have a hand-crank and a flexible tube which allows you to spread the chemical exactly where you want it.

PROPER CARE OF TOOLS AND EQUIPMENT

Let me remind you here that the good gardener — even if he is only an amateur — takes proper care of his equipment and gardening tools.

He checks them over and drys them carefully before storing them. The good gardener also has a place to keep his equipment when he is not using it — somewhere where he can find it again easily. It can be a corner of the cellar, a workshop, or a special shed near the garden. The time you spend putting your gardening equipment into order is not wasted at all — quite the contrary!

New Insecticides To Replace DDT And Other Chlorinated Hydrocarbons

It is very common these days to say that we live in a world of change. Yesterday's stock of knowledge is continually being replaced by the new discoveries of today. In all the history of the human race, never has the evolution of ideas and knowledge been as rapid as it is today, or so widespread. Every day scientific research and technology are discovering facts which were hitherto unknown to us. The inevitable result is that one of man's greatest aptitudes, the power of adaptation, is tested to the limit. Changes occur with such rapidity that many people find themselves totally unable to accommodate themselves to them, and in many cases anxiety and fear follow in the wake of new knowledge. Only too often, some of us are led by our emotions to react in an absurb and unexpected fashion, to draw hasty conclusions, to adopt a negative attitude in the face of progress. In many cases people do not understand, or — worse still — do not **wish** to understand, that certain decisions, even though they may appear outwardly to be wrong, are in fact progressive, and will contribute to the improvement of the general lot of mankind.

TIMES CHANGE

This is exactly the situation that prevails in the world of pesticides. The virulent controversy centred on the use of DDT is a perfect example.

As a result of this controversy, we have become suspicious of almost every pesticide. However, we must **not** allow ourselves to be gripped by panic, draw false conclusions and take unfortunate decisions simply because one particular group of pesticides has had some unforeseen and accidental side-effects. We must **not** generalize and think that every chemical pesticide has the same disadvantages.

The use of the chlorinated hydrocarbon known as DDT is now outlawed, or hedged around with crippling restrictions, in almost every country in the world. How has this come about? After having been the miracle insecticide since 1942, after having saved countless thousands of lives by effectively protecting crops against the depredations of a host of insect pests and saving vast forests from destruction, DDT has suddenly fallen under suspicion. This wonderful product has all at once become Public Enemy No. 1, both for men and for animals, Why? DDT's long persistence, now recognized as a scientific fact, has attracted the attention of researchers, who have made the somewhat frightening discovery that it accumulates, directly or indirectly, in vegetable tissues, in animal tissues — and in human tissues.

CONTROL MEASURES

Use of DDT or other chlorinated hydrocarbons such as aldrin and dieldrin has, for several years, been forbidden on crops intended for use as animal feed.

Within Canada, the Food and Drug Office has established very rigorous limits concerning the residual effects of these chemical compounds. Strict surveillance of foodstuffs is maintained, to check their retention of pesticides, and every food product is immediately banned if it is found to contain a higher proportion of pesticide than is permitted.

The violent reaction against DDT and similar products stemmed from the realization that the prolonged residual effects of these pesticides were responsible for contamination of the air and water. The damage caused by this contamination to animal life — particularly fish and birds — has been studied in depth. But quite apart from the fact that the survival of our fauna is of prime importance, and all our efforts must be devoted to this end, there are other and even more serious dangers — namely the persistent and cumulative residual effects of the toxic products which are found in the soil and in the water. Physical deformities have already been clearly established among young fish and birds, and although there is as yet no proof that DDT can present any mortal danger to mankind, equally it has not been proved that this particular compound will not produce similar physical deformities among future generations.

It will readily be agreed that the situation is disturbing, and these fears for the future have contributed in large measure to the decision to ban DDT — or at least to limit its use to specialists under the very strict surveillance of the competent authorities.

REPLACEMENT INSECTICIDES

How do matters stand today? What substitute products have been provided to help us control insect pests in our gardens? The ban on the use of DDT, aldrin, dieldrin and heptachlor should present no problem to amateur gardeners, for very effective replacement insecticides exist, some of which are listed overleaf. On this subject, let me stress that more detailed information is readily available from the Federal Ministry of Agriculture, from your corresponding Provincial Ministry, from your local Botanical Gardens and from reputable seed suppliers and nursery-gardeners. Whatever you use, I would advise you to pay particular attention to the instructions on the label which pesticide manufacturers put on every container.

REPLACEMENT PRODUCTS FOR DDT
AND SIMILAR COMPOUNDS

Insects
> Whiteworms, maybugs, greyworms, wireworms, earthworms, ants, elm bark beetles, leaf-eating caterpillars, mosquitoes.

Former Product	*Replacement Product*
Aldrin	**Chlordane**
———	**Thiodan, Methoxychlor, Sevin, Abate, Baytex,**
DDT	**Diazinon, Malathion**

Note that the use of lead arsenate is still permitted.

I must stress that the table above merely indicates the existence of certain replacement insecticides: furthermore, I have only mentioned a few insects. However, my object is not to give a complete list of insect pests, or the chemical compounds intended to eliminate them. Nor does the table list the necessary precautions to be taken when using the various replacement insecticides mentioned. For further instructions, and fuller information in general, you should read the special brochures put out by the various levels of government, seek the advice which is readily available to the public at Botanical Gardens and obtain descriptive literature from the manufacturers themselves. Here again let me stress how important it is to read the labels on the containers of the different pesticides.

Further changes are to be expected in this complex sphere of chemical compounds intended for use against insects that are enemies of plants. The amateur gardener should take an interest in the new pesticides that are being discovered, and in the research being carried out in the field of toxicology into residual effects and metabolism. This will give him more confidence, since he will realize that all these complex problems are very thoroughly analyzed by highly qualified experts before any new pesticides can be approved and obtain the requisite government seal permitting it to be offered on the open market.

Be Careful When Using
Anti-Parasitic Preparations

During the summer months you will need to use some form of anti-parasitic preparation, whether an aerosol spray against flies or mosquitoes, or a herbicide for use against dandelions. Never forget that these preparations are poisons, and must be handled carefully.

Before their approval under the terms of the law on anti-parasitic preparations, these products underwent numerous tests. Their effectiveness for their specific purposes is guaranteed, and they are quite harmless if you use them exactly in accordance with the instructions.

Read the label of a new product every time you use it — in fact, read it twice. Take all the precautions recommended, especially as regards the interval of time to be left between the last application and the collection of the crop, if you are using one of the products intended for use on foodstuffs.

Use the recommended product, and measure out the requisite quantities carefully. Too much can be harmful, and too little will be useless. Never measure out anti-parasitic preparations with kitchen utensils, and mark the pots and pans you use for this purpose so that they are never used for anything but these chemical compounds.

Keep the preparations in hermetically-sealed containers — never in bags, boxes, bottles, cups or open cartons without identifying markings. If the label's been lost or torn, it is better to destroy the whole packet rather than to guess at the contents.

All these chemical products should be kept in a locked room, where children cannot get at them. Never use the containers once they are empty. All paper bags should be burnt, and glass or metal ones should be buried somewhere where they cannot contaminate any water. You should also destroy any weeds, etc, that have been killed by these preparations — never throw them into the kitchen garbage.

Never smoke while you are using anti parasitic preparations. Wear protective clothing and avoid breathing in any of the powder or the fumes that may be given off. If you get any on your skin, wash it off at once with soap and water and take care to give your hands a thorough washing before you eat.

Keep your children and household pets away from the scene of operations, and try to keep the stuff off other growing things.

Mulches Are Extremely Useful

Most amateur gardeners, however limited their experience, are aware how useful mulches are in the garden during the very hot days of summer. Everyone knows that mulching makes it easy to retain the humidity of the soil, and at the same time to cut down the work of hoeing and weeding.

Furthermore, the organic matter in the various mulches gradually improves the humus content of the soil and also increases its capacity for water retention. Again, in hot weather, mulches effectively reduce the temperature of the soil and stimulate plant growth.

MULCHING MATERIALS

There are several materials which may be used as mulch. Most of them are quite inexpensive, very easy to find, and are easy to spread over the surface of the soil — usually in layers two to four inches thick around the plants. The best-known mulches are rotted leaves, sawdust, buckwheat scales, peat-moss, shredded bark, wood chips, straw, cocoa-bean husks, hay and grass clippings.

Wood chips and sawdust — which can be obtained easily enough from sawmills and carpenters' shops — make excellent mulches. All the same, there is one precaution you must take when using them. Before you spread them on the soil you should apply a fertilizer rich in nitrogen. Without this, the bacteria which decompose the mulching material must borrow the nitrogen necessary for decomposition purposes from the soil. This loss of nitrogen results in a decrease in the number of flowers, which are also smaller in size.

Shredded bark from pulp and paper mills makes an excellent mulch. In Eastern Canada, cocoa-bean husks seem to be one of the easiest materials to find. You should have no difficulty in discovering which is the commonest material in your own region.

Among other available materials I should mention corn cobs, buckwheat scales, peat-moss and bark fibre. Peat-moss needs extra nitrogen from an application of chemical fertilizer, but that is not the case with cocoa-bean husks or corn cobs or buckwheat scales. However, wood chips also need an application of some fertilizer rich in nitrogen, to avoid depletion of the nitrogen in the soil.

THE USEFULNESS OF COMPOST

Every amateur gardener should have his own compost heap. It should contain plenty of leaves, for these are one of the most economic forms of materials for mulches. It is easy to keep a compost heap damp — just cover it with a sheet of polyethylene. This ensures rapid decomposition, without any odour becoming noticeable.

Black polyethylene sheeting is sold as mulch, and if there is no other material available at a reasonable price, you should be prepared to use it. This sheeting cuts down the work of weeding and removing grass, and preserves the humidity of the soil. However, it does nothing to improve the quality of the soil since it has no nutritive elements or organic matter to add to it.

REALLY HOT WEATHER

Mulches can be spread any time during the summer, but the best time to use them is before the really hot weather sets in. You can spread your mulch as soon as you have enough suitable material. It can be something as simple as a shovelful of the rotted leaves which collect under trees, or it can be any organic material from around your summer cottage — grass clippings, say, or even dried weeds which haven't had time to produce their seeds.

Most soils need humus, and the only way of providing them with this humus is in the form of organic matter, such as exists in the fibrous materials I've listed above.

DURING THE HOLIDAYS

July and August are the two summer holiday months. Many amateur gardeners think they have solved all their problems if they have hoed out all the weeds from their flowerbeds and borders before they leave for the lake or the sea or the mountains. However, I would advise you to spread a mulch, which will stop the weeds from growing back and will also keep the ground moist until you return. Of course, you must take care to water the garden thoroughly and fertilize it before you leave.

If you have a kitchen-garden, and plan to be away for a few days, you needn't worry any longer about weeds or a possible lack of water. Give it a good hoeing, and then stretch a sheet of black polyethylene as mulch between the rows of vegetables. This precaution stops most weeds from germinating, and keeps your kitchen-garden clean and tidy untill the end of the season.

Many amateur gardeners have a mini-tractor nowadays as part of their equipment — it makes the upkeep of their land much easier. The large variety of accessories available help to make the mini-tractor even more effective for motorized tasks, and enable it to carry out a whole host of jobs, both gardening and otherwise.

Antirrhinums or
snapdragons:
F-1 hybrid
'Madam Butterfly'
with double
azalea-type
flowers

Border of
'Floral Carpet'
snapdragons

Celosia: 'Flame of the Forest', with plume-feathered flower-spikes, 30''

Celosia: 'Golden Triumph', with plume-feathered flower-spikes, 24'' - 30'' (annual)

Petunia: F-1 hybrid grandiflora 'Chiffon Cascade' (annual)

'Bridal Bouquet':
100% double flowers

'Crusader': grandiflora

'Blue Mantle': F-1 hybrid
grandiflora

'Candy Apple': F-1 hybrid
grandiflora

'Dorothy Favourite': 100% double
'Victorious' flowers

Zinnias:
F-1 hybrid
'Torch'

Zinnias:
hybrid
pompom
'Cherry
Buttons'

Verbena:
hybrid
'Blaze'

Apples: 'Quebec Belle'
variety, which lasts until july.
Looks like the 'Delicious'
variety and tastes like
the 'Spy'

Red currants:
'Red Lake'

Raspberries: 'Newburg'   Strawberries: 'Red

CHAPTER 16

CALENDAR OF WORK

January

In January, the main activity of an amateur gardener is of course growing indoor plants. However, even if it is too early to be thinking yet about the spring and the work outside in the garden, it **is** the right time to be planning next season's gardening programme. The most important thing right now is to draw out on paper where you want your flowerbeds and borders to go, so that you can settle exactly where you are going to plant shrubs, herbaceous perennials, annuals and other plants, when spring finally arrives.

NURSERY CATALOGUES

Most plant nurseries send out their catalogues in February and March, so that's the time to write to request your copy. The majority of these catalogues are sent out free to anyone who asks for one, but even if you must pay for them, it will not be very much — and it is certainly well worth the cost. You simply cannot afford to be without this reference material when planning your garden.

In addition, most nursery-gardeners offer a complete choice of woody plants such as ornamental trees and bushes, fruit trees and bushes, as well as wide range of conifers, vines, and so forth.

FORCING BULBS

If you potted any spring bulbs in the autumn or at the beginning of winter — **narcissuses, daffodils** or **tulips** — with a view to forcing them, and they have been in the cold for the last six to eight weeks, now is the time to put them in a warmer spot for a week before you expose them to light and heat in your windows. Place paper cones over the young shoots from the hyacinth bulbs. This will make the flowers grow taller than the leaves. However, you must leave a small hole an inch across at the top of the cone.

During January you should also inspect the **dahlias, cannas** and any other tender bulbs you may have stored away. If they have dried out, water them to bring them back to life. Throw out any bulbs that show any signs of rot.

Dwarf shrubs that have been kept in the cold for forcing — **deutzias, astilbes** and **spiraeas,** for example — can now be moved into a warm room. It is also time to start bringing the **hydrangeas** back to life, so they will be in flower for Easter. You should also start potting your **gloxinias** and **begonias** at the beginning of the month.

Remember, too, that the month of January is the right time to start a dish-garden, or one of those glass display-cases known as "terrariums".

This pot of mixed flowers cannot fail to please any gardener who is fond of lovely plants. The pot contains caladium, begonia, poinsettia and a chrysanthemum. When spring comes, you can transplant them all separately into the garden, then bring the whole thing together again as an interior decoration the following winter. *(Photo: Malak, Ottawa)*

POINSETTIAS

The **poinsettias** you got for Christmas will last longer if you put them near a warm sunny window that's sheltered from draughts. Make sure the air around them is kept nicely humid — but do not actually stand the pot in water. **Poinsettias** don't take temparature-changes too well, especially sudden cold spells, which make them shed their leaves rather easily.

During the winter, the air inside a house tends to get a bit dry, and the plants suffer as a result. You should, therefore, change the air in your rooms from time to time.

HUMIDITY IS ESSENTIAL

In addition to fresh air, plants also need humidity. Furthermore, some humidity is better for **your** health, too — and it also reduces your heating costs. Besides the use of humidifiers and dishes with water in them, one effective way of supplying your plants with sufficient humidity is to put them in the bath or the sink every now and then and give them a good spraying.

In the middle of the winter, while your plants are dormant, they need very little attention. Water them when necessary, but don't give them any fertilizer — this could stimulate their growth too much. Remove all dust from the foliage, and give it an occasional spraying — (except for **African violet,** which shouldn't have their leaves watered). If you discover any insects such as scale insects, aphids, mealybugs, etc. spray the plants with an insecticide.

SALT AND ICE

It cannot be denied that salt is an excellent material for removing ice from sidewalks, entrances and flights of steps. But if your plants are to survive, it is essential that this compound (whether calcium chloride or sodium chloride), should **not** be allowed to come into contact with the lawn, the flowerbeds or your woody plants.

When spring comes, you do not want to be required to repair burnt areas on the lawn, or face problems of spoilt or stunted growth in your flowerbeds, or damaged trees and woody shrubs. Therefore, you should use salt very sparingly. Preferably, use a complete chemical fertilizer such as 6-9-6 to melt your ice.

Snow provides a protective cover for your plants. The low temperatures of January and February, coupled with the alternate frosts and thaws of early spring, are the main causes of damage to your beds of herbaceous perennials. Lay some branches of **cedar** or other conifers over these beds, so that the snow will build up and protect them.

DAMAGE CAUSED TO
WOODY PLANTS BY SNOW

As far as possible, you should remove the snow from your conifers. Conifers weighed down by snow after a snowstorm may look very beautiful, but you must remember that several branches may be broken under the weight of the snow — which is often quite considerable. It is better to remove this snow without delay, before it gets hard. The best tool for the job is an old broom that has become soft from long use.

It is particularly important to clean off conifer hedges, because the snow tends to force the individual bushes apart.

Make good use of any fine weather to remove dead or diseased wood or any branches that aren't growing too well from your ornamental trees. Don't forget to protect any raw surfaces more than an inch in diameter with a coating such as 'Braco', or 'Mastic Pelton', since this speeds up the healing process.

February

The early days of February always seem to produce a special sort of weariness all of their own, as the winter seems to go on and on for ever. The happy days spent in the garden the summer before are nothing but vague memories now, and the garden, which looked so beautiful with all its bright summer colours, is merely a spread of white with the monotony broken only by your conifers — if you have any — or by the bare branches of deciduous trees. If the snow is not too thick, you may also be able to see the bare branches of the shrubs.

INSPECT YOUR INDOOR PLANTS

You must not neglect your indoor plants, which help you to forget the miseries of the cold season every day. Examine them one after the other to make sure that at least their basic needs are being satisfied. In this way you may determine whether the leaves are falling off or turning yellow, and which of the plants has failed to flower, or is infested with insects.

Humidity is a constant problem inside a house or apartment in winter, unless you keep a humidifier going, or otherwise ensure that the plants receive enough moisture. Spraying the foliage is an excellent method of providing indoor plants with the necessary humidity.

If you have plants which need a fair amount of sunlight, and the dark days of February do not supply it, try fluorescent lighting. You will be surprised and delighted by the results.

The new varieties of cyclamen with fringed flowers are simply superb. To prolong the life of these plants indoors, keep them in a cool, well-lit place. Do not water the leaves, and only water round the edge of the pot. This reduces the risk of the main stem, buds and leaves becoming withered.
(Photo: Malak, Ottawa)

February is the time to remove any dead flowers from your **African violets** (to stimulate growth), and to fertilize these plants with a water-soluble fertilizer such as 'Plant-Treat' (20-20-20), for example. You should also get rid of any **'Paperwhite' narcissuses** which have finished flowering.

But there is no need to throw away the **poinsettias** which looked so beautiful during the holiday season. Let them dry out until the end of April, and then cut back the stems to make the plants produce new shoots. Later, when there is no further risk of frost, you can plant them in a semi-shaded spot in the garden. Bring them back into the house in mid-September so that they will be in flower for Christmas.

TAKE CARE OF THE TENDER BULBS

Inspect the **dahlia** tubers you stored away in the cellar in sand or vermiculite. If they have dried out, sprinkle them with water, then bury them again as they were before. Also take the opportunity of examining your **gladiolus** corms, and throw out any of them that show the slightest signs of rot. Also see whether any of the corms have started sprouting. If they have, it means that they are too warm, so move them somewhere where it's cooler.

CHOOSE YOUR SEEDS FROM THE CATALOGUES

When you receive your catalogues from the nursery or gardening centres, make your choice of seeds and bulbs and plants as soon as possible, so that you can be sure of getting the ones you need for your garden at the right time. Now is the time, too, to sow your perennials, biennials and hardy annuals. If you want to have **asters** flowering early in the garden, you should sow them indoors in mid-February, in seed-boxes.

Pot your **begonias** and **oxalis** bulbs, then bury the pots in a box of damp sand and store them in a cool place. When the plants start growing, move them into the light. Water them lightly, until a good strong root-system has developed.

PLANNING NEXT SEASON'S GARDENING WORK

Even though there is still another month before you must make up your mind definitely about the plants you want to have in your garden and around you property, it is by no means too early to start thinking about your spring planting programme. In fact, it is better not to wait till spring arrives — you will have plenty of other things to think about then. Proper planning of the coming season's gardening work means that between now and the end of March you should devote every spare moment and every spell of good weather to the task.

SOWING ANNUALS

Proper planning does not, of course, mean that you should throw yourself headlong into projects such as sowing annuals. As you know, most annuals germinate very quickly. If you do your sowing too early, before very long your windows will be cluttered up with boxes full of growing plants, and you will have nowhere left to put anything else. Worse still, there is a serious risk of these plants "growing proud" — i.e., becoming very tall and weak — unless you give them plenty of light.

If you plan to keep rapid-growing annual plants for more than eight weeks before you transplant them, March 18 is about the earliest date you should think of sowing them — at least, in Eastern Canada.

Although the beginning of February is still too early to plant most flowers and vegetables, it is by no means too early to start buying and setting up the necessary equipment you will be needing for sowing.

A heated basement is the ideal place for doing your sowing, even if sunlight is very scanty there — perhaps even non-existent. All you have to do is install a fluorescent lighting system and your sowings will be successful — even annual species that are slow to germinate. It is also possible to buy equipment fairly cheaply which will give out an excellent substitute for daylight.

One important point — install a separate electric outlet for your fluorescent tubes. Next, if you do not already have an old rectangular table, you should buy one in a junk-shop. Make sure that its legs are firm, and that it is high enough for you not to have to bend double when tending your plants. If you plan to do a lot of sowing, you will probably want to get yourself a second table.

Another point you must not overlook is the width of the table. This must be matched to the beam of light thrown by the fluorescent tubes above it, so that all the plants are properly lit.

It is not a bad idea to have a table that is longer than the tubes, you can use the extra space to store potting-soil, peat pots, labels, packets of seed, and so on.

Drive some nails into the ceiling joists and hang the reflectors from them on chains at either end. This will enable you to raise or lower the fluorescent tubes as needed.

If the temperature falls below 60° F at night, you can avoid your seeds and plants being affected by the cold by adding one or more 60-watt incandescent bulbs to your fluorescent lighting system. Hanging between the reflectors, these bulbs warm the surrounding air — and they consume much less current than an electric heater.

I must stress here that unless you have a greenhouse or fluorescent lighting, February is about your last opportunity for sowing the following seeds, which are very slow developers: **pansies, annual phlox, coleus, begonias, lobelias,** and **centaureas.**

HOTBEDS

Amateur gardeners who have hotbeds should lift the frames to warm up the beds.

At the end of the month, warm the beds still further by adding two feet of manure. When the soil temperature in the hotbed falls to 90° F, sow the **tomato** seeds. When the temperature drops to between 70° and 80° F, sow **onions, peppers, aubergines** and so forth.

A FORETASTE OF SPRING

To give yourself a foretaste of spring, pick some branches or stems from early-flowering woody plants — either trees or shrubs — and force their growth indoors.

Among the species that you can persuade to cover themselves in foliage flowers are the following: **pussy willows, forsythias, apple trees, plum trees, spiraeas, cranberry bushes, flowering wild quinces, cherry trees** and **serviceberries.**

Cut these stems to the required length, and put them in a vase full of water. Place the vases near a well-lit window in a warm room, where the stems will get at least three hours sun per day.

Many people use the special flower preservatives on sale at florists' shops. These help preserve the stems, and cut down the time required for forcing.

CHECKING YOUR TOOLS

February is also the time to start getting ready for your spring planting programme and your work outside in the garden. While there is still not too much work to be done, you should take the opportunity to check over your tools and equipment, and to repair them if necessary.

Give yourself a foretaste of spring by forcing stems or branches of early-flowering woody plants such as the serviceberry.

From now on, your lawn-mower must be kept in first-class condition. If you find that any adjustments or repairs are needed, you still have plenty of time to get them done. Furthermore, if you must take any of your equipment to a garden tool specialist at the hardware store to have it attended to, make sure you choose a time when he's not too busy, so that he can give you all the time necessary to ensure that you get satisfactory service.

People usually put off doing the preliminary chores for next season's gardening far too long. There's so much time available in February, but they don't make good use of it.

PRUNING TREES

February is a particularly suitable time of year to prune your deciduous-leaved trees. There are of course no leaves left on these trees, and as a result it's very easy to choose which branches to get rid of and which to keep.

The pruning of ornamental trees, fruit trees and shrubs should begin during the second half of the month. Cut out all surplus branches which might spoil the normal development of the plant, also any branches that are diseased or damaged.

If you are dealing with a young tree that is sufficently developed, do the job properly and keep only those branches which will give the tree the required "framework".

BEFORE THE END OF FEBRUARY

It is very important to prune **beeches, hornbeams** and **sugar maples** before the end of February, since they lose a good deal of sap when they're pruned or trimmed. Although this loss of sap is not necessarily fatal to them, it often leads to the loss of several branches, which spoils the look of the tree and lessens its vitality.

Before launching an attack on the branches, I would advise you to plan the task carefully. Your trees are very valuable assets, and it is better to proceed cautiously and make sure you have a valid reason before you remove a single branch — much less two or three.

If you have big trees to deal with — (especially if the branches that have to be removed are high) — then it is worth your while to hand the job over to specialists. These men have the necessary equipment, and it will take them only a few minutes to do what would mean hours of work for you — not to mention the possible risk of incurring serious wounds.

This sketch shows an apple tree which has been properly pruned from the start. It has developed a solid framework, its branches are well spaced and at a convenient height for picking the fruit. Spraying against insects and diseases is very much easier with a tree like this.

WHY PRUNE?

Apart from the necessity of getting rid of dead, damaged or rotten branches, you should prune your ornamental trees to help them achieve a solid framework capable of successfully resisting the assaults of violent winds and surviving storms. One of the main objects in triming young trees is also to give them the shape you want them to have. If you carry out your pruning properly, you can trim the branches the way you want them to go and thus give the tree the desired shape.

FORKS NEED ATTENTION

Weak forks should be eliminated without any hesitation. The sort of fork shown here is produced when two principal stems branch off from the central axis and grow upwards parallel to the trunk. If you are unlucky enohgh to have two main stems, and you let them both grow, the time will eventually come when they will split apart where they join — which means the loss of a tree which is often of considerable ornamental value to your property.

To avoid this, you should only let one principal branch grow. However, if you are dealing with a tree which has already achieved some considerable size, all you need do is couple the two main trunks firmly to each other by bolting them together. In this event, you should us a long steel bar, threaded at either end; this bar is passed though holes drilled through the twin trunks, and nuts are screwed on tight at the end. Unless you have

Weak forks must be eliminated without the slightest hesitation. The sort of fork depicted above is the result of two or three principal stems branching off from the central axis and growing upwards parallel to the trunk.

the necessary equipment yourself, it's best to leave this work to specialists.

BIG BRANCHES

I cannot stress too strongly how careful you must be when you prune the larger branches. They should be cut off level with the trunk, or with the branch that carries them. Start by making a saw-cut underneath, a few inches from the main trunk or branch. Then use the saw on the upper side, two or three inches from the trunk, until the branch falls away. Finally, cut off the resulting little stump flush with the trunk. Note that the initial cut underneath the branch is inended to stop the bark being torn downwards along the trunk of the tree.

All cuts bigger than ½ an inch in diameter should be protected with a special coating such as 'Braco' or 'Mastic Pelton', which seals the wound hermetically, and hastens the scarring process.

Note that in the case of two branches which cross, the less important one should be removed. If there is a branch growing more quickly than the rest, cut it back to make the tree look more symmetrical.

FRUIT TREES

The objects of pruning fruit trees are to develop a solid framework with regularly spaced branches to ensure a height that makes it easy to gather the crop, and to eliminate excessive growth. Another equally important reason for pruning a fruit tree is to let the air circulate freely between the branches and to make it easy to spray insecticides and fungicides.

On apple trees, and on many species of ornamental tree, you can often see vigorous young shoots on the branches, sticking up like the thongs of a whip. These are suckers, which should be cut off level with the trunk.

Besides these suckers, don't forget to remove any branches which are tangled together, or diseased, or too badly damaged to be healed. If you want your apple trees to yield plenty of fruit, you must also cut new growth back to 1 or 2 buds, which encourages the production of shoots. A well-pruned fruit tree grows more strongly and can easily bear the weight of its crop.

The branches of this tree have collapsed as the result of a storm. Because a weak fork was not done away with soon enough, the tree has been completely ruined, and will have to be cut down and replaced.

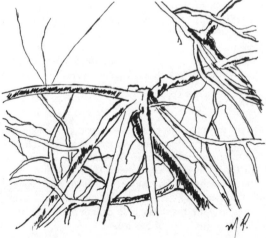

396

March

PREPARING FOR SPRING

March is the time when Mother Nature gives us a foretaste of the coming spring, with beautiful floral displays from the plants indoors.

If you took the necessary precautions during the previous autumn, your shrubs should certainly have managed to get through the winter without too much damage. Now you must make sure that they're in first-class condition for the start of the growing season. If the wind has removed the mulch of rotted leaves which was protecting the roots, replace it without delay in order to keep the ground frozen below the roots. One or two hours' work can save you expense — sometimes quite a lot of expense, for replacing shrubs is never cheap.

PRUNING TREES AND SHRUBS

Now is the time to press on with your pruning — the deciduous-leaved ornamental trees and the summer — and autumn — flowering shrubs. Prune vines now, too, and fruit trees, before the buds start swelling with sap.

The following woody plants, which came into bud in the autumn, shoudn't be pruned until they have finished flowering: **deutzia, forsythias, Japanese quinces, spiraeas** and **diervillas.**

The same goes for **maples,** which must not be pruned at this time of year, to avoid their losing too much sap.

DORMANCY SPRAYING

This is the right time for "dormancy" spraying, before any growth has begun — once it has, there is a risk of damaging the tender young leaves.

Dormancy spraying is done at the beginning of spring, to control destructive insects and any micro-organisms of plant diseases that have survived the winter. These micro-organisms can attack several types of fruit trees, bushes and ornamental trees during the months of March and April — **lilacs, junipers, elms, ashes, willows** and **pear trees** all fall prey at one time or another. Scale insects, for example, can damage woody plants by sucking out the sap, thus making the shoots and branches dry out.

Spraying with dormant oil spray should be carried out before the new season's growth commences. The temperature must be above freezing-point, and you should be satisfied that it will stay between 38° and 40° F for the next six or eight hours of the day.

Use only the special emulsified oils recommended for spraying trees and shrubs.

You must remember that this type of product is a poison, which must be handled with care. Make quite sure, too, that the particular spray you are using is suitable for the woody plants you plan to spray. For example, you should **not** use oily sprays on thin-barked trees such as **beeches, sugar maples, Japanese maples,** trees of the **nut** family and the following conifers: **Douglas fir, American larch** or **tamarack, cypress, pine trees** and **yew.**

SNOW MOULD

After the snow disappears in March, you may find whitish circular patches with a pinkish edging on your lawn — often as large as one foot in diameter. These are caused by snow-mould, which is the commonest of all lawn diseases. This particular infection is especially prevalent in lawns which contain **ryegrass, meadowgrass** and **fescues.**

Snow-mould is caused by poor drainage of the soil, by applying nitrogen-rich fertilizers late in autumn, or by prolonged dampness of the soil in spring. To ward off the disease, you should apply a mercurial fungicide to the lawn at the end of the autumn.

Unfortunately, this isn't the only disease that attacks lawns. There are several other diseases, such as **Kentucky bluegrass** leaf spot, **'Merion' bluegrass** rust, and powdery mildew. These lawn infections cannot be cured merely by resowing the affected areas. Nor is fertilizing a satisfactory method of treatment. The nutritive elements in fertilizer encourage a thicker, more vigorous growth of grass, but they also create conditions which favour the spread of dieseases. Thus, fungicides are the only answer.

Among the fungicides available for the prevention and treatment of various lawn diseases, two of the most effective are 'Acti-Dione RZ' and 'Merfusan', 'Acti-Dione' is an antibiotic fungicide of proven effectiveness in the control of most lawn diseases. However, it's important to make up a fresh solution every time you need to use it. 'Merfusan' is used as a preventative against lawn diseases and can be applied in spring, summer or autumn.

MULCHES, SEEDS AND CUTTINGS

Don't remove the mulch from flowerbeds of perennials, especially if they are growing in heavy soil.

Sow **tomatoes, cabbages, lettuce, peppers,** etc. now. Mid-March is also the right time for sowing slow-growing annuals in seed-boxes.

These annuals include **asters, heliotropes, ageratums, lobelias, petunias,** potted **pinks, salvias** and **zinnias.** Towards the end of the month you can carry on with sowing **fairy primrose** and **cyclamens.** Now is also the right time to start growing **tuberous begonias.**

If your indoor plants such as **dracaenas, palm trees** and **rubber plants** (Ficus elastica) seem to lack vigour, or are too big for their container, repot them.

March is also the appropriate time for **dahlia** cuttings. All you need do is plant the tubers in a bed of damp peat-moss. Let the shoots grow a few inches tall, then cut them and put them in a dish of coarse sand. Be sure to leave one shoot on the tuber, with two pairs of eyes on the end of it. This way, new shoots will appear, and enable you to take more cuttings.

With the end of the winter, many garden equipment shops offer snow-blowers at reduced prices, to make space for summer equipment such as lawn-mowers. If you get too much snow to shovel easily, this offers an excellent opportunity to buy a machine cheaply which will be very useful to you the following winter.

Put up nesting-boxes at the end of the month and go on feeding the birds as you've been doing since the onset of the cold weather.

April

THE FIRST WORK OUTSIDE

The temperature's getting warmer all the time now. During the last two weeks in April Nature really reawakens. It's the beginning of spring — and the beginning of work outside in the garden. For example, it's time now to uncover the **rose** bushes. However, you must proceed in orderly fashion: thus the first step is to remove the boards, or the branches, or the leaves which have protected the bushes throughout the winter. Next, clear away part of the mound of earth you built up around each bush. Later on, clear the bushes completely with the help of a rake.

PERENNIALS, KITCHEN-GARDENS, AND LAWN EDGES

April is the time to turn over the soil in your beds of perennials. The best way of going about this is to break the earth up with a digging-fork, to a depth of about one inch near the plants, going progressively deeper as you get further away from them. Don't forget to cut back the shoots of your herbaceous perennials down to ground level, and to take out the more obvious weeds with a fork.

Before you begin to dig, it is a good idea to spread a complete fertilizer such as 6-9-6, using three pounds per 100 square feet, so that it gets worked nicely into the soil.

If you are one of the lucky ones with a kitchen-garden, let me remind you that if you didn't dig it over in the autumn, you should do so now.

You have no doubt noticed that at this time of the year the edges of your lawn are often in poor condition. If you want a nice clean edge, use corrugated border-strip made of galvanized iron or plastic. This border-strip has the great advantage of doing away with the need to clip the edges of the lawn. Furthermore, it's very easy to install — all you need to do is drive it into the ground. But don't use a hammer on it directly, or you will knock it out of shape — put a block of wood over it to spread the load, and hammer the wood instead.

CLEANING THE LAWN

As soon as it is physically possible — that is, immediately after the snow's all gone — clear the lawn of the rubbish that has accumulated on it — sticks and stones and bits of brick and gravel and so on. A week or so later, go over your lawn with a rake with good solid teeth. This will get rid of all the old dead grass. Then sow grass seed on any bare patches (using a high-quality mixture containing **bluegrass, fescue** and **bent grass**), and rake lightly a second time.

This is also the time to roll the lawn — though you must be careful not to over-compact it — to get rid of worm-casts and little lumps of earth.

NEW LAWNS

New lawns sown towards the end of the previous summer need special attention at this time. Briefly, the main, and most important precaution is to walk as little as possible on a newly-sown lawn. If you walk on it too much, you will break the young blades of grass which are about to sprout and not a single blade will make its way through the surface crust. This is a very common mistake made by inexperienced gardeners, who feel they have to keep checking the thickness of the grass by visual inspection.

INDOOR PLANTS

Many indoor plants like to take a little holiday outside. The mere fact of getting them outside will often release precious space inside the house — for some of these plants take up a great deal of room — and give you a welcome opportunity of rearranging your furniture. Nevertheless, you must bear in mind that indoor plants require some form of protection at all times. The best method of providing this is to build a framework

400

over them. There is nothing really complicated about it — all you need do is stretch a skin of polyethylene over a wooden frame made from "two-by-twos". However, you must make quite sure that the whole thing is really airtight. In addition, to enable you to water the plant, you should fit a movable panel, which you just raise up as necessary.

According to the specialists at the Institute of Plant Research, if you want to ensure that your plants are effectively protected against the frost, you should cover the framework on cold nights with strips of burlap or an old blanket, up to about May 24th. Also note that ventilation is not a problem with this type of framework. No special measures are needed (unless the temperature rises to unusual heights) because the polyethylene allows air to pass through.

For the first two or three days after you've put your indoor plants into the framework, make sure they are getting enough shade, especially if the weather's hot and sunny.

FIRST SOWINGS

Once you have dug over your garden and satisfied yourself that the soil is friable and properly drained, you can start sowing the first seeds in your kitchen garden without further delay. Sow **beetroots, carrots** and **parsnips** first. These vegetables will not be harmed by light frosts, and they won't begin to germinate for several weeks in any case.

On this subject, **parsnip** seeds just sit there in the ground for almost a month before the slightest sign of growth becomes visible. If conditions are favourable, you should take the opportunity at this time of sowing the seeds of some slow-growing flowers such as **lupins, sweet peas** and **delphiniums.**

BUYING ROSE BUSHES AND SHRUBS

Mid-April is the best time to buy your **rose** bushes and shrubs from the nursery. Take advantage of the fact that this is when the choice is best and buy your plants right now. However, if you are not completely ready to do your planting, or if the weather is too cold, dig a trench along the south wall of your house, or in some sheltered sunny spot, and trench your plants in temporarily. After all, the fresh air of your garden offers these plants a far better atmosphere than the dry, stuffy interior of some shop can ever do.

A judicious choice of **rose** bushes and shrubs is not a very complicated matter. All you need do is choose plants which don't yet have any long shoots. Trenching them into your garden presents no real difficulty, either. Dig a trench about 18 inches deep, and stack the earth from the excavation along one side of the trench to form a sort of berm. Put the plant roots carefully into the bottom of the trench, so that the plants themselves are resting against the berm. Then fill in with earth from another trench dug parallel to the first one.

May

The arrival of the month of May is the signal that spring is really with us at last. At the beginning of the month, the **apple** trees come into flower, and leaves appear on the **maples. Darwin tulips, irises, poenies** and **bleeding hearts** (Dicentra) beautify the flowerbeds and the surrounding greenery, while the hedges and thickets of pea trees (Caragana arborescens) are covered with pretty yellow flowers like butterflies.

A FAIRYLAND OF COLOUR

The woods and the fields have already started to become a fairyland of colour, with pink **azaleas,** white **trilliums, lady's-slippers, bird's-foot, lupins, may-apple** and **mountain-laurel** — to mention only these few plants.

May is the month for colours, for scents — and for gardening. Already there are several important tasks to occupy amateur gardeners.

INSECTS AND DISEASES

Remember that Mother Nature does not limit her activities solely to encouraging the lush growth of plants! From now on you must be on guard against insect pests and microscopic funguses, which can cause countless problems throughout the summer.

There is no insecticide or fungicide, either in liquid or in powder form, that can really be classed as 100% effective against all forms of either of these two types of infestation. However, several mixtures exist which enable you to control these enemies of your plants completely, and

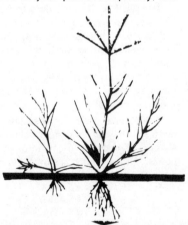

You can prevent crabgrass appearing in your lawn by applying a special anti-crabgrass chemical fertilizer early in the spring.

At the beginning of May you should protect your rose bushes against rose scale insects, which suck the sap of the plant. You will know they are there if you find round white blisters on the stems.

Scales on the bark of the trunks or the branches of white pines, Austrian pines or Mugho pines, indicate presence of pine-needle scale.

put a stop to their depredations. It is most important, however, that you always stick to the manufacturer's instructions when you use these products.

NEW LAWNS

Mid-May is a good time to lay a lawn. If you have decided to sow rather than to sod, choose your lawn-seed carefully.

Never use any of the mixes that contain a high percentage of meadow grasses — **timothy** or **orchard grass,** for example. Cheap mixtures never really turn out to be a bargain. In fact, while one pound of **Kentucky bluegrass** contains some two million seeds, the same weight of **ryegrass** has less than 250,000 seeds in it. When you are sowing a lawn, I would advise you to buy the best mixture — you will always get your money's worth.

IMPROVING YOUR LAWN

When it is a question of improving an existing lawn, you can mix your lawnseed with a chemical fertilizer and spread the mixture in one single operation, using a spreader. Use 4½ pounds of a top-quality mix, with thirty-four pounds of 6-9-6 fertilizer, for every 1000 square feet of surface — alternatively, you can use twenty pounds of 12-4-8 fertilizer for the same area). If conditions are favourable, the new grass should appear in about two weeks. For shaded areas, it's advisable to use a seed-mix consisting mainly of **creeping red fescue.**

If you did not fertilize your lawn at the beginning of spring, there is still time to do it now. To inhibit the germination of **crabgrass, foxtail,** and **cockspur grass** among your lawn grasses — **(bluegrass, fescue, rye-grass,** and **bent grass)** — a complete fertilizer, 6-9-6, containing the anti-**crabgrass** compound "Tupersan", should be applied at the biginning of the month.

THE LEAF MINER, AN INSECT TO BE DESTROYED

Be prepared to do battle with the leaf miner, a powerful enemy of your garden plants. A properly-planned spraying programme is the chief contributing factor in a successful campaign against those destructive insects the **honeysuckle** leaf miner, the **birch** leaf miner, or the **holly** leaf miner.

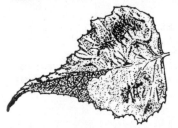

To deal with the birch leaf miner effectively, use a systemic insecticide which penetrates into the plant for fuller protection.

To enable you to pick the best moment to do your spraying, examine the leaves carefully every two days. The slightest little swelling on the leaves indicates the presence of this insect pest. Use systemic insecticides against it. These soak into the plant and give it better protection.

SCALE INSECTS

If you notice tiny scales on the bark of the trunks or the branches of your **white pines, Austrian pines** or **Mugho pines,** the plants have pine-needle scale. This may be treated with applications of "diazinon" or "Sevin-50", or with a systemic insecticide such as "Cygon 2E".

PROTECTING YOUR ROSE BUSHES

From now until the autumn you should protect your **rose** bushes against insects and diseases. To this end, use a mixture of the insecticide "Cygon 2E" and the fungicide "Phaltan", or a special product such as "Rose Bush Powder", which contains two insecticides — "Malathion" and "Sevin" — and a fungicide — "Phaltan" — which suppresses leaf spot and mildew. Begin spraying and powdering as soon as the leaves appear on the bushes, and continue all through the season, with a week between each application.

404

PLANTING CONIFERS

Although the month of September is a better time to be planting conifers, you can in fact plant them now, in May.

Whatever you are planting — trees, shrubs, conifers, or deciduous-leaved woody plants — it is essential that the soil be properly drained. You can satisfy yourself on this point by filling the hole you've dug for the planting with water, and noting how long it takes for this water to drain away. If there is still water in the hole after several hours, choose somewhere else to do the planting, or drill some holes to let the water get down through the impermeable bed beneath.

If you have any **apple** trees on your property, or any other species which are growing slowly because their roots are too close to the surface, one possible reason is a clayey sub-soil. Drill some holes six inches apart using an iron bar or an auger, and pour some agricultural chalk into them. This will eventually allow the roots to get down deeper into the soil.

Lilacs and other spring-flowering shrubs should be pruned immediately after flowering. To keep these plants growing strongly, you must cut out some of the old wood every year.

PRUNING SHRUBS

Lilacs and other spring-flowering shrubs should be pruned immediately after flowering. To maintain rapid growth in these plants, you must remove some of the old wood each year.

Thus, cut out two or three of the oldest branches from the **lilacs**, to stimulate the growth of the new shoots at the base of the plant. The same treatment works equally well with other species besides **lilac philadelphus**, for example, or **deutzia** or **beautybush.** Keep the most vigorous of the new shoots, and cut out the weakest ones in June or September.

The panicle of peeges hydrangea (Hydrangea paniculata grandiflora) is the hardiest and most striking of the hydrangeas. Its large clumps of flowers produce a very beautiful effect in August and September. This hydrangea is equally suitable for shrubberies or as a flowering hedge.

You can also prune shrubs which flower at the end of the summer, such as the **panicle hydrangea.** Hardy, fast-growing shrubs like **dogwoods** can stand a thorough pruning — almost down to the ground. This will stimulate them to produce long new shoots.

To ward off and control infestation by insects, apply a systemic insecticide on the shoots and branches of your shrubs.

LIGHT AND INDOOR SOWING

Light is essential for the normal development of young plants. If you have done your sowing in boxes indoors, put them near the sunniest window — otherwise the plantlets will be tall and feeble. You could also install a fluorescent tube 12 inches above the boxes, and leave it on for twelve hours a day. This will give you straight, sturdy plants.

Fragile young plants need acclimatizing gradually. Put them in a cold frame before you plant them out in the open ground. All the same, you should watch out for frost until the end of May.

OUTDOOR SOWING

If you are sowing seeds of annuals straight into the beds or borders where you intend them to grow, rather than scattering them at random, try to sow them in separate rows two or three feet apart, depending on the final size of the plants. You should also label each row, to identify the contents. Leaving a good space between them makes it unnecessary to transplant them later on.

Now is the time to sow your annual vines. Not only will these add colour to the garden, they will also form a valuable windbreak.

Sow semi-hardy flowers and vegetables at the beginning of the month, and tender plants at the end. Once there is no longer any risk of frost, plant **tomatoes, peppers** and **cucumbers**, and other fragile vegetables and flowers.

TOMATO PLANTS

Transplant **tomatoes, cucumbers** and **melons** into the garden — remember to cover them with those little caps called "Hot Kaps", or with some similar protective device. These "Hot Kaps" are almost as good as a little private greenhouse for each individual plant, they give protection against frost, rain, wind, dryness and the attacks of insects.

Your **tomato** plants will need protection for some ten to fifteen days, depending on the temperature and the date of sowing — at any rate, until they're growing nicely. To toughen the plants, tip the little caps so as to leave the southern aspect exposed for a few days before you finally remove them.

SOIL SUBSTITUTES

Professional flower-growers often prefer to use soil substitutes, because they need less care. Whether you do your sowing in a seed-box or in a pot, the lower half of the seed-bed should be a mixture of two parts of garden soil, one of peat-moss, and one of sand. Passing this mixture through a sieve with a ¼-inch mesh gives you a really top-quality seed-bed.

HERBACEOUS PERENNIALS

Towards the end of the month, sow your herbaceous perennials in a shaded cold frame, or in the open ground if they're protected by some sort of screen. You must bear in mind, however, that even though growing perennials from seed is the quickest and easiest way of producing a large number of plants of the same species, it won't necessarily give you plants which are identical with any given variety within that species.

During the month of May you should split the old clumps of your late-flowering herbaceous perennials as soon as the new growth starts appearing. However, there are certain exceptions to this rule: **irises** should **not** be divided until July or early August, **Oriental poppies** should wait until August, while **peonies** should not be done before early September.

If you want to propagate species with more or less woody stems, such as **chrysanthemums, purple loosestrife** or **phlox,** take cuttings when the new shoots are four to six inches tall.

Plant several cuttings in a 6-inch flowerpot, spacing them an inch apart from each other. Stand this pot in a flattish dish filled with water, keeping the level of the water two or three inches below the bottom ends of the cuttings.

The cuttings must also be protected against direct sunlight.

Big **peony** plants — especially those of the "double" varieties — need some form of support. You'll find that nurseries and gardening centres carry thin steel hoops that are ideal for this purpose. Make sure, however, that you put these supports in before the wind and the rain have snapped any of the stems.

BULBS

Fertilize your spring-flowering bulbs just before they come into flower, or while they are actually in flower. This strengthens them for next year's flowering. Work a good complete fertilizer for vegetables into the soil — say three to five pounds of 5-10-15 per 100 square feet of surface.

Do not cut the leaves off any bulbs that have finished flowering, and don't fasten them together in any way — it is absolutely essential for these plants to have their foliage exposed to the sun, so that they can manufacture the nutritive elements necessary for the formation of flowers next spring.

From about the middle of the month, you can plant tender bulbs — that is, the summer-flowering bulbs — such as **gladioli, montbretias** and **tiger-flowers.** These bulbs all require the same sort of conditions — the most important being a well-drained soil and sunlight.

In Eastern Canada, gladioli corms should not be planted outside before the second half of May. Gladioli need a good, rich, well-drained garden soil. Plant them in rows in a nice sunny spot. (Photo: Malak, Ottawa)

Plant **cannas** and **tuberous begonias** at this time as well, and remember that while **dahlias, montbretias, tiger-flowers** and **cannas** prefer to be in the sun, **tuberous begonias** and **caladiums** are shade-loving plants.

A word of caution about **dahlias** — note that when you divide the tuft you must make sure that some of the old stem, with a bud or an eye on it, remains attached to one or more tubers, for buds will not appear on the tubers themselves.

THE IMPORTANCE OF MULCHING

A good digging-over is especially important when the surface of the soil dries out after a shower of rain. Use your spade to mulch the soil, and also as a means of getting rid of weeds.

The moisture introduced into the ground by spring showers can be preserved by a mulch — which, again, is also a method of preventing the spread of weeds. There are several materials you can use for this purpose — peat-moss, for example, sphagnum moss or straw.

Dahlias require a high degree of humidity, and a rich, well-drained soil. Each tuber must carry part of the old main stem with an eye or a bud on it. Planting can be carried out after the middle of May. The tubers are set individually in a trench six inches deep, and you must ensure that the buds are pointing upwards. It is a good idea to drive a small stake into the ground about three inches away from the stem. Later on, when the time comes to put in a support for the plant, this stake serves as a marker, so there is no danger of damaging the plant. (Photo: Malak, Ottawa)

Wood chips are becoming more and more popular, because they do not stick together in a lump, and they let the rain get through into the soil. This material has another important advantage, too, in that it does not rob the plants of any nitrogen. Buckwheat scales are one of the best of all mulches, because they let water penetrate easily into the soil, and at the same time prevent any loss of water from the soil by evaporation. This material is very much in demand nowadays as a mulch to conserve moisture in flowerbeds and borders.

June

June is one of the most active months in the year for the amateur gardener. There are many tasks to keep him busy all through the month, both in the garden and on the rest of his property.

LAWNS

Do not mow a newly-sown lawn unless the grass is very strong and thick. Scatter handfuls of granular fertilizer over it, or water it lightly with a liquid fertilizer, in order to provide the grass with the nutritive elements it needs.

To destroy the common weeds in the lawn, use 2,4D amine. Spray it on while the grass is growing. The temperature should be at least 65° F, and the weather fine.

(Incidentally, make sure you never use the same spray to apply insecticides and herbicides.)

WATERING

The arrival of June serves to remind us of one of the very elementary but very important requirements of our plants — water. It is impossible to over-emphasize the value of a thorough watering, properly carried out. Remember, too, that it is mainly the roots of the plant that need water and that you must wet the lawn to a depth of at least four inches. When you water flowerbeds of annuals and perennials, you must let the water go at least five to six inches down into the soil, while for shrubs, the requisite depth is at least twelve inches.

PLANTING

The second half of June is the ideal time to plant **broccoli, cabbage** and late **cauliflower.** It is also the ideal time to sow your **rutabagas.**

To keep the garden looking neat, remove all dead flowers spring-flowering bulbs — **tulips, daffodils, narcissuses,** etc.

Plant all varieties of dahlia bulbs now. Later on, you will have to provide the big stems of these plants with some support.

You can also plant **gladioli** now, and **tuberoses** (Polianthes tuberosa).

INSECTS AND DISEASES

Dust pesticide onto your conifers and rose bushes. The best way of fighting insects and diseases is to use an all-purpose pesticide containing a mixture of insecticide and fungicide. This type of product will give good results, provided that you use it regularly and in accordance with the manufacturer's recommendations.

Make a note of the bare spots in your flowerbeds, where your bulbs have flowered, so that you can fill in the gaps during the autumn. Suitable plants for filling in these gaps are **petunias, myosotis** and **anlyssums,** which are often used in **rose** beds, planted between the bushes. They remove only a very small amount of the nutritive elements contained in the soil.

Check your **hollyhocks** to see if they have been affected by rust.

Go on sowing your perennials, so that they will be ready for transplanting into their permanent beds at the beginning of the autumn. After they have flowered, take cuttings from the following perennials, **rock-cress** (Aubrieta), **sandwort** (Arenaria), **snow-in-summer** (Cerastium), **candytuft** (Iberis) and **stonecrop** (Sedum).

The auger is the ideal tool for taking samples, if you want to have your soil analyzed to find out if it is deficient in nutritive elements. This analysis enables you to feed it with the appropriate fertilizer and so provide the elements that all plants need for normal growth.

TREES AND SHRUBS

You can plant deciduous-leaved trees and shrubs up until June 15, provided that you take all the necessary precautions.

Shrubs and conifer bushes are very easy to plant if you keep a ball of earth around the roots.

This month, sow the seeds of biennials and perennials such as **campanulas, digitalis, hollyhocks** and **wallflowers.**

Remove all the old dead flowers from the **lilac** and **rhododendron** bushes — but do not, of course, take all the branches off with them.

Wash your **birch** trees over with the systemic insecticide 'Cygon', to ward off attacks by the leaf miner.

After the flowering season — that is, at the end of June or the beginning of July — you should trim your hedges of deciduous-leaved shrubs such as Japanese barberry (Berberis thunbergii), pea tree, cotoneaster, hawthorn, privet, honey-suckle, mock orange (Philadelphus), currant bush, Chinese elm, or downy viburnum. An electric hedge-clipper, like the one being used by the young lady in the illustration below, not only makes it easy to keep your hedges in good shape, but can also be used to trim the grass alongside borders and walls.

PRUNING YOUR SHRUBS

As soon as the early-flowering shrubs are in bloom, they should be pruned. The new wood for the following year will grow during the summer. Shrubs in this category include some of the **spiraeas, dogwoods** and **forsythias.**

Towards mid-June, start trimming any hedges which began growing early in the spring.

Now, too, is the time to cut back the principal stems of conifers, while the wood is still soft and green. Leave a stump at least an inch long, to allow a new shoot to form. Don't remove the topmost shoot of the shrub until the conifer has grown to the desired height.

PUTTING YOUR HOUSE PLANTS OUTSIDE

A good many house plants profit enormously from a spell outside during the summer.

Choose a cool day for their move outside, a day without sun. Dig the pots into the soil right up to the top, this will avoid any loss of moisture by evaporation through the porous walls of clay pots. Put a small stone or a bit of slate underneath each pot as you dig it into the ground. This will not spoil the drainage — and it will stop earthworms from getting inside the pot.

July

THE BEST MONTH OF ALL FOR GARDENING

July is the best month of all for gardening. However, even though the gardens is clad in all its glory at this time, it is also a fairly critical period for your plants, for several tasks have to be carried out at the same time. Furthermore, these tasks are essential not merely for the healthy development of the plants, but also for the general appearance of the garden.

Many amateur gardeners succumb to the temptation to carry out these summer tasks right at the beginning of the month, thinking that the garden will then manage to keep itself in good shape right up to the end of the summer holidays. This is absolute nonsense, of course, as you will see from the following list, which describes just a few of the many gardening tasks which demand attention during July.

WEEDS

A good thorough hoeing at this time is an absolute necessity — it will do away with weeds before they have gone to seed, and thus prevent them from multiplying. After you have hoed your ornamental plants very thoroughly, lay down a mulch (such as peat-moss) to retard the growth of weeds and also to conserve moisture until your return from holiday. Naturally, your flowerbeds and borders must be well watered and fertilized before you apply the mulch. In the case of vegetables, spread a sheet of black polyethylene between the rows to act as a mulch after you have finished hoeing. This precaution stops most weeds from germinating, and keeps your kitchen-garden neat and tidy till the end of the season.

CARE OF THE LAWN

July's really hot mid-summer weather is a very difficult period for a lawn.

Too many people tend to cut their grass too short, with the result that it gets burnt by the heat, and is then invaded by **crabgrass.** Unless you have applied a pre-emergence anti-crabgrass preparation, this weed pest will compete with your lawn grasses for the available moisture and nutritive elements in the soil. Destroy it at once with an appropriate herbicide.

One good thorough watering a week which gets right down into the soil, is much better for a lawn then several light, short ones.

Next, set your mower to give a cut two inches high, and leave the blades set at this height until the end of August. Another important thing to remember is watering. You **must** get the water deep down into the ground. One really thorough watering once a week does more good than several light, short ones.

TREES AND SHRUBS

July is also the month to check the growth of the trees and shrubs. If the new shoots on the trees are less than six inches long, it means the soil is probably deficient in nutritive elements.

Start planning now to fertilize late in autumn, with a special fertilizer called 'Hibernal' (3-6-12 Mg. Bo.). Never fertilize in July, for this could encourage a late growth in your woody plants, and the new shoots will only be damaged by the cold.

TRIMMING CONIFER HEDGES

Before leaving for holidays at the end of July or the beginning of August, you must find time to trim the new growth in persistent-leaved hedges — except for **cedar,** which should be trimmed in autumn. If you wait to carry out this task until you get back from your holiday, there will be so much growth that it will not be easy to prune, and once done, the hedge will stay brown and uneven. Naturally, if the hedge is not yet as tall as you want it to be, you should give it a light trimming only, and cut off just the tips of the new shoots; but if it is high enough already, you can take the new shoots off at the base.

If you have not managed to get rid of **birch** leaf miners, carry out a second spraying, either with an insecticide containing 'Malathion', or with a systemic insecticide such as 'Isotox'.

ROSE BUSHES AND PERENNIALS

The best way of keeping **rose** bushes and perennials free of diseases is to spray them regularly. You can combat both insects and diseases at one and the same time by using a mixture of the systemic insecticide 'Isotox' and the fungicide 'Phaltan'. This latter product is particularly effective against black spot, which may attack rose bushes during this month. Alternatively, use a fungicide containing sulphur and fermate.

Prune climbing roses as soon as they have finished flowering, to encourage the growth of new branches and buds during the following season.

DAHLIAS AND POPPIES

If you want really big flowers on your dahlias, now is the time to remove unnecessary buds, so that all the energy of the plant is channelled towards the one terminal bud.

If you are thinking of dividing your Oriental poppies, do this at the end of the month, or perhaps a little later, early in August — whenever the new foliage appears. Prepare the soil by treating it with a complete fertilizer. When you do the division, make sure that each portion has two eyes on it — otherwise that particular new plant won't flower for two years or more.

CHRYSANTHEMUMS AND PEONIES

Chrysanthemums should be cut back at the beginning of the month, and then again during the first week of August. This encourages the formation of several shoots, and eventually the appearance of a good number of buds in September.

Water your **peony** plants if the weather stays hot and dry, and give them a dose of powdered bone-meal. This fertilizing will give you a magnificent crop of flowers the following year.

RELOCATING LILY-OF-THE-VALLEY

Once the **lilies-of-the-valley** have stopped flowering, you must decide whether or not they need relocating. If the plants have not been moved for several years, they may well have grown so thick that they are stifling themselves. If this is the case, then it is imperative to relay this carpet of greenery somewhere else. This should be done at the beginning of July, if possible. If you do have to relocate these plants put them somewhere in the shade. Work the soil over thoroughly, and add about five pounds of a complete fertilizer (6-9-6) per 100 square feet of surface. If the soil is poor in organic matter, add twenty pounds of peat-moss per 100 square feet of surface. This can be done at the same time as you add the chemical fertilizer.

Water thoroughly, and the new plants will be ready to give you a rich carpet of flowers the following year.

PROTECTING YOUR IRISES

Here are a couple of tips about **irises.** First of all, the old flower-bearing stems should be cut back right down to the leaves they spring from.

Next, July is the appropriate time to deal with an iris borer. You can get rid of this pest quite simply when you dig up the rhizomes that need dividing, merely by throwing away any of them that are infected. Remember that unless you get rid of the iris borer, the plants can become infected with soft rot.

HEALTHY PLANTS

If any of your plants are not growing as strongly as they should be, spray their foliage with a completely soluble fertilizer such as 20-20-20.

Furthermore, remove all dead flowers, to ensure the maximum possible crop among your annuals and perennials.

As soon as the **delphiniums** have finished flowering, cut them back to just above the leaves — unless you want to collect the seeds. If the leaves are looking unhealthy, cut the stems near the soil to give new shoots a better chance of growing and producing a second crop of flowers in the autumn. In addition, dig in a little complete chemical fertilizer around the base of each plant. This will help the production of further flowers in the autumn.

INDOOR PLANTS

If you didn't repot your indoor plants when you brought them outside for their "sumer holiday", now is the time to do it. However, this does not mean that once you have installed them in some suitable area in the garden you can just abandon them to their fate — far from it!

It is a good idea to check and see how they are doing every now and then. Water them when necessary, and examine each plant carefully for insect pests. You must also turn the pots round a little in the ground from time to time. This prevents the roots of the plants from driving down into the soil beneath the pot. If you do not take this precaution, you may have to break these roots off in the autumn, and this is a shock to the plant.

As for the plants that are still in the house, put them in the bath just before you go off on your holidays, give them a good watering, and then cover them with a piece of polyethylene sheeting. In this way they will stay humid enough for at least three weeks, and since most bathrooms are reasonably well lit, the plants will not suffer too badly from lack of light.

August

THE GARDEN AT THE PEAK OF ITS BEAUTY

Like July, August is a very hot month, and it is a splendid time to take a summer holiday. However, any amateur gardener who stays at home rather than going away for his summer holiday, will see his garden reach the peak of its beauty and colour, with **phlox, gladioli, dahlias** and all the annuals in full flower.

Many of those who do go away are reluctant to do so for more than a few days at a time, for fear of finding their flowers and vegetables all withered away or seriously damaged on their return. August is generally very hot and characterized either by extreme dryness or by an excess of humidity, and damage to plants is very common, either from mildew or from the attacks of mites.

PRECAUTIONS WHILE ON HOLIDAY

I feel I should take the opportunity here of giving a few words of advice to every amateur gardener who is going to be away on holiday, so that he can look forward to finding his plants full of vigour on his return.

Here are a few precautions you must **not** neglect. Before you leave, give the flowerbeds and the kitchen-garden a really thorough watering. Then, before the ground is fully dry, spread a mulch (peat-moss, pine-needles, etc.) around the rose bushes, flowering plants, vegetables and shrubs to conserve the moisture in the soil. Also, remember that plants which are supported by stakes should be tied as high up as possible, so that the stems will not be broken during summer storms.

Another thing to do before you leave is spray your plants with a mixture of insecticide and fungicide. This particular precaution is especially important for rose bushes, dahlias and chrysanthemums.

Furthermore, there are certain attentions which are absolutely essential for house plants which have had their pots buried up to the top in the soil outside. Water each plant thoroughly, then wrap it in a piece of polyethylene sheeting and put it in a cool place, such as the cellar or the garage, where it will get plenty of light but be out of the heat of the sun.

ESSENTIAL WORK

For those who want to restrict themselves to the bare minimum, gardening work during August is reduced to general maintenance — hoeing, watering, staking and control of insect pests and plant diseases.

However, for most amateur gardeners who are really interested in their garden and are prepared to devote the necessary time to it, August represents an opportunity to pay special attention to their plants.

This is the right time of year to examine the perennial flowerbeds carefully. They probably have one or two bare patches in them, and perhaps they are lacking in symmetry or colour here and there. Once you have carried out your inspection, you can decide straight away which plants will have to be replaced next month, rather than waiting till the last minute before making up your mind. Write the names of the plants you are

During the month of August there must be no let-up in the fight against insect pests and plant diseases. If your plants are affected, spray them at once with the appropriate insecticide or fungicide.

going to replace on large markers, and then stick them in at the places which need improving. However, if you are going to replant a whole bed, I would advise you to make a scale drawing and use it as a working-plan when the time comes.

ADEQUATE WATERING

Plants need a lot of water during hot summer days. Lawn-watering is not too difficult a task nowadays, what with the multitude of automatic watering systems available. Watering flowerbeds, hedges, trees and shrubs needn't be an irksome task, either. Apart from certain types of automatic watering device, you can provide your plants with the necessary water by piercing holes in an empty tin can and fixing it over the end of your hose, or by using a perforated tubular attachment on the hose.

THE ADVANTAGES OF A MULCH

Besides being very beneficial to your plants, a mulch will spare you hours of hoeing and weeding. All you have to do is choose the right mulch for your plants. Factors to be taken into account when making your choice are the colour of the mulching material, its capacity for absorbing water, and whether or not it bunches together, or hardens on the surface.

TREES AND SHRUBS

It is time once again to check trees and shrubs. Examine the new shoots. If the shoots on the trees have grown less than six inches, then very probably the soil lacks fertilizing elements. In this case, you should plan a treatment for late autumn, using a special complete fertilizer such as 'Hibernal' (3-6-12 Mg. Bo.). Fertilizing in August is not recommended, since it could bring on a late growth which would be liable to damage by the frost.

For conifers, use a complete fertilizer with an acid reaction.

RENOVATING A LAWN

Mid-August is the best time to put down a new lawn or to rejuvenate an old one. If you are going to sow new grass, you must prepare the soil by a good digging-over. Do this a week or two in advance, so that it has time to settle. Sow your grass seed after August 15th or at the beginning of September. Use a seed mix suitable for your local conditions. Almost certainly, this means a mix containing at least 70% fine permanent grasses.

The treatment or rejuvenation of a lawn should be carried out between mid-August and mid-September. Essentially, the process involves incorporating organic matter enriched with fertilizer into the soil.

FERTILIZING A LAWN

During the really hot days of summer, you can let your grass grow a little longer than usual. **Bluegrasses** and **fescues** grow slowly in very hot weather, anyway. If the blades are left a little longer than normal, they will provide the roots with better protection against the sun.

If you have already treated your lawn with a synthetic urea-based fertilizer such as 6-9-6 or 12-4-8, you do not need to add any further fertilizer now. However, if you have not done this, use a nitrogen-rich fertilizer now, either organic or inorganic.

Water the lawn thoroughly, unless it is a very wet summer and there are frequent lengthy rain falls.

ROSE BUSHES

Rose bushes need constant care. Never neglect watering combatting insects and diseases, removing dead flowers and weeding.

Tie new stems to trellises or other supports. Be constantly on guard against infestation by insects, and diseases such as black spot and mildew.

Prune your climbing **roses** as soon as they have finished flowering. This will stimulate new growth for the following year.

CONIFERS

The period between the last week of August and the end of September is the best time to plant conifers. Their annual growth is over then, and the warm soil encourages the rapid appearance of new roots.

Water your conifers thoroughy, both trees and shrubs. Do this once a week until the autumn rains.

PERENNIALS AND BIENNIALS

Your small perennial and biennial plants should be large enough by now to be planted out into flowerbeds.

Before you transplant them, it is a good idea to take an overall look at the colour scheme for the various beds and borders, to make sure the new plants will fit in. When you plant them, give them enough space to let them develop normally.

LILIES, POPPIES AND OTHER HERBACEOUS PLANTS

Madona lilies and **Oriental poppies** should be planted any time now, from the end of the month up to October. Division and transplanting of your **poppies** can be done as soon as the foliage goes brown. It is important to get this under way before new shoots start appearing in the autumn.

Note that garden centres and nurseries usually deliver new plants in August. So if you only have the old style of **poppy** in your garden, with the usual reddish-orange flowers, why not order some of the new varieties now?

Work a chemical fertilizer into the soil before you do any replanting. When you have divided the roots, make sure they are all healthy and growing well — otherwise the plants will not give any flowers for two years or more.

The time is also ripe to divide other herbaceous plants such as **bleeding heart** (Dicentra), **bugloss** (Anchusa), **basket-of-gold** (Alyssum saxatile compactum), and **phlox.** After you have transplanted the new plants, remember to give them a thorough watering. If the sun is really scorching, I would advise you to protect the plants during the first couple of days after you have planted them, in order to let them get properly rooted in.

DAHLIAS

As noted earlier, if you want to have giant **dahlias** next year, you must nip off unwanted buds, so that all the plant's energy is directed towards the terminal flower-bud. If you have not done this, do it now.

PHLOX AND TUBEROUS BEGONIAS

August is the month for **phlox,** but it is also the time when mites and mildew make their appearance on these plants. You can put up an effective fight against both these insects and the disease, with the aid of a product containing an insecticide and a fungicide as well — such as "Captan" or "Ferbam". Remove all dead flowers before their seeds fall to the ground. If you do not take this precaution, you will get new plants with flowers that do not look like those of the mother plant.

Tuberous begonias are also in full flower now. You will get excellent results if you take one or two precautions. Do not water them too much, or give them too much fertilizer, protect the plants against violent winds, and grow them somewhere where they will get the benefit of filtered light and a good circulation of air. You should note that these plants do best if they are given a light dose of suitable fertilizer every three weeks.

PEONIES AND IRISES

Water your **peonies** in dry weather, and fertilize them with bone-meal. This will make your plants produce good healthy buds for the following season.

The best time to plant, transplant, or divide your **peonies** is at the end of August or the beginning of September. **Peonies** should be transplanted or divided whenever the necessity arises. If the plants are not flowering any longer, or hardly at all, or are producing flowers which are smaller than usual, the time has come to divide the root-clumps.

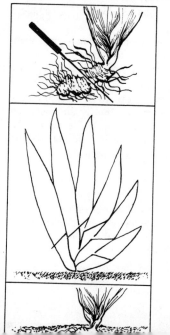

Dig up clumps of irises to divide them, and to get rid of the iris borer and fungus rot. Kill the borers, then divide the clumps, getting rid of any parts affected by rot before you plant the bulb cuttings — each of which should carry two or three 'fans' of leaves with roots attached. Add some bone meal to the soil, and don't plant irises too deep.

423

As a general rule, **peonies** should be divided and transplanted every five to eight years.

The months of July and August are the best time for planting **irises.** Do not, however, plant them too deeply. As for dividing **irises,** this should be done when they begin to flower less well than usual, or when the root-clumps start invading their neighbours' territory.

After you have divided the clumps, take the opportunity of cutting out any parts affected by rot.

LILY-OF-THE-VALLEY

I advise you to inspect your bed of **lily-of-the-valley** after the plants have flowered. If the bed is crowded and the plants seem to be too thick, choose a nice semi-shaded location and make a new bed.

Add five pounds of a complete fertilizer (6-9-6) per 100 square feet of surface. If you find the soil lacking in organic matter, mix twenty pounds of peat humus in with the fertilizer and the soil. Divide your plants, and plant them at least four inches away from each other. Water them thoroughly. If the bed's not too thickly populated, give it a dose of a complete fertilizer, and water it again.

GENERAL CARE OF CHRYSANTHEMUMS

Take care to install supports for your **chrysanthemums** before they topple over. Now is also the time to give them a dose of a complete fertilizer, to increase the size of the flowers.

If you have not already pinched your **Chrysanthemum** buds — and even if you did it early in July — you should carry out this operation without further delay. This will give you leafier plants, which will yield a good crop of flowers in September.

After a few years, you will find that the roots have become very numerous, and that the flowers are getting smaller. This is an indication that it is time to dig the rhizomes out of the ground and divide them. The old part, in the centre, can be thrown away, and you should replant the outer, and younger, portions of the rhizomes in fresh ground.

INSECTS AND DISEASES

With the hot days of summer, the number of red spider mites increases in the most surprising way. A new generation comes into being every five or six days when the temperature stays above 80° F, and each new generation is capable of reproducing itself ten days later.

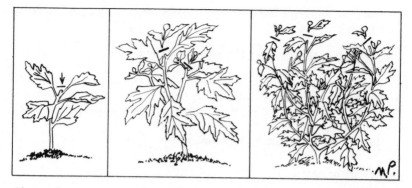

Chrysanthemums grown from cuttings are naturally tall, single-stemmed plants. To correct this fragile form of growth, pinch off the terminal bud (see left-hand diagram) to force the growth of lateral shoots. Then, 20 to 30 days later, cut the ends of the stems to obtain a leafier plant (see centre diagram). Repeat this operation a second time (see right-hand diagram) and the plants will become still bushier.

On certain trees such as the **maple** and the **elm,** and on many shrubs, aphids can do a lot of damage during the hot days of August. Spraying with 'Malathon' will hold them in check. For black spot on your **rose** bushes, you should apply 'Phaltan', which is a very effective fungicide. Always use it in strict accordance with the manufacturer's instructions. To deal with mildew, the recommended treatment is either 'Captan' or microfine wettable sulphur.

It is a sound idea to examine your trees and shrubs and the plants in your flowerbeds every now and then to make sure they are not infested with plant bugs or mites. The warm days of August encourage these destructive insects to multiply in large numbers. You can detect the presence of plant bugs on the underside of the leaves. Mites, however, are too small to be seen with the naked eye. An effective method of detection consists of shaking a branch of the tree over a sheet of white paper. If there are mites present, some of them will drop off onto the sheet of paper, where they show up as tiny little black dots moving about.

To control these destructive insects, start spraying your plants immediately, twice a wek. Effective insecticides include products based on 'Malathion' or on methoxychlor, or on a mixture of both.

BUYING SPRING BULBS

This is the perfect time of year to order new bulbs — **narcissuses, tulips, daffodils, crocuses,** etc. — ready for planting in the autumn. This is when the nurseries and gardening centres offer the widest choice — so don't wait!

MULCHES FOR TOMATOES AND MELONS

I would advise you to lay a mulch around the **tomato** plants, not only to conserve moisture, but also to prevent the soil from dirtying the tomatoes. If your plants are not supported on stakes, a good clean mulch will protect the fruit quite effectively.

Take the same precautions for **melon** plants.

INDOOR PLANTS

This is a good time to inspect your house plants and see if they need repotting. If so, you should give them a special soil mixture when you repot them. The following formula suits the majority of indoor plants: 2 parts sand, 2 parts leaf-mould, 2 parts compost, 2 parts peat humus, and ½ a part of dried manure or powdered bone-meal. Mix all these ingredients carefully.

On the other hand, indoor plants which are "on holiday" out in the garden need attentions which go beyond a little occasional watering.

Give them small amounts of fertilizer every ten to fourteen days. Keep a sharp eye open for the presence of insect pests, and remember to turn the pots in the soil occasionally.

DEAD FLOWERS

The appearance of your garden will be considerably enhanced if you remove all dead flowers from **zinnias, African marigolds, petunias, phlox,** and other annuals and perennials. Otherwise, they tend to look neglected, and they yield smaller flowers as well.

PICKING HERBS

Most pot herbs should be picked when the plants come into flower. If there is any earth on the leaves of herbs such as **mint, sage, thyme** or **rosemary,** wash them, shake the excess water off, and then hang them up to dry in some dark, well-ventilated spot.

Herbs used as seasoning, such as **caraway, anise, dill,** and so forth should be picked when they begin to change colour — this is the sign that they are ripe.

Also, remember to pick the flowers you want to dry for indoor winter bouquets, namely **zinnias, sea-lavender, amaranths, celosias** and **immortelles.**

September

With the coming of September, the garden is truly at its best. The annuals are in full flower, the lawn unfolds like a magnificent green carpet while the **chrysanthemums,** now at the height of their glory, present a riot of colour — red, gold, purple, orange and white. As autumn approaches, the **rose** bushes are in full flower again, the **delphiniums** are parading their beauty for the second time and the **phlox** seem to dominate the whole garden with their glorious display of colour.

THE BEST MONTH FOR GARDENING

For a good many amateur gardeners, September is the best month of the year — for now they have the satisfaction of seeing the results of all their planning and labour during the spring and summer, and can feast their eyes on the floral beauty all around them.

For most people, September means the end of the summer holidays. It is also the time to inspect the garden thoroughly and to correct any slips you made during the summer months. Fortunately, the temperature this month is just right for the various gardening tasks required.

RENEWING THE LAWN

From the end of August until mid-September is the ideal time to sow a new lawn or to renovate an existing one, either by sowing or by using sod.

For a lawn exposed to the sun, you should use a seed-mix containing a preponderance of **Kentucky bluegrass.** For shaded locations, a mix with **red fescue** predominating is recommended.

Now is also the time to get rid of weeds with a herbicide. In addition, renewing a lawn involves the application of humus and organic fertilizers, or a complete chemical fertilizer.

Whether you are renovating an existing lawn or laying a new one, you must do the job as quickly as possible, since the roots of the new grass must be properly developed before the frost comes along.

You must bear in mind that in order to obtain a fine lawn you have to prepare the soil properly, drain it adequately, fertilize it, and use high-quality seed or sod. The very fact that your lawn needs putting back into good shape probably means that one or more of these essential requirements was neglected at the start.

DIVIDING PERENNIALS

Many perennials can be divided during September. As examples, the list includes **bearded irises, bleeding hearts** (Dicentra), **Oriental poppies, yellow lillies** (Hemorocallis) and **peonies.**

To deal in more detail with **peonies** — the end of August and the beginning of September are the best times to divide these plants, because the new clumps then have plenty of time to get well estabished, and will flower abundantly during the following season.

When you plant the new clumps, make sure their eyes are not more than two inches below the surface — otherwise you risk not getting any flowers for several years. **Peonies** need a soil rich in organic matter (well-rotted manure, peat-moss, leaf-compost, etc), enriched with powdered bone-meal. Prepare the soil properly, and **peonies** will flower for several years.

Although the best months for planting **irises** are July and August, there is still time at the beginning of September to divide clumps of **bearded iris, Japanese iris** and **Siberian iris.** During the first few days of the month you can also plant clumps of **Spanish** and **German iris.**

BORDERS OF PERENNIALS

Examine all perennial borders and flowerbeds carefully. If you have not made any changes in them for several years, it may perhaps be necessary to do so now. You may decide, for instance, that such-and-such a border should become a flowerbed, or vice versa. Very probably the root-clumps of **phlox** and **hemerocallis** and **large-flowered oxeye daisies** have spread widely and the clumps are ragged at the cente. Mix some powdered bone-meal into the soil before you replant after dividing them, and water them after replanting.

PHLOX, CHRYSANTHEMUMS AND OTHER PLANTS

Phlox should be cut after flowering, then treated with a chemical fertilizer in either solid or liquid form.

As for **chrysanthemums**, if you give them certain attentions now, they will reward you with a most magnificent display of flowers. First of all, you can transplant them — even if they are already in flower — to anywhere in the garden where they will show to better advantage. You must water them well, and cover them with a mulch in the autumn to protect them against the cold during the winter — for their roots are fairly near the surface.

The root-clumps of hardy **asters** can also be moved now. Inspect the plants at the same time, and if you find any insects on the foliage, dust an insecticide over them.

Any **lily-of-the-valley** plants that are producing a lot of foliage but no flowers should be divided. When the leaves are dry, treat the plants with a solid fertilizer in order to obtain a nice crop of flowers next spring.

CLEANING UP YOUR ANNUALS

September marks the start of the autumn clean-up period. Take out all the annuals which have finished flowering. You will then be able to take a closer look at those annuals which are still in full flower, such as **calendulas, "Ten Weeks" stock** and common **morning glories.** As you admire them, you realize that **morning glories** are extremely interesting plants. The flowers remain open all day if the weather's cool — as cool, say, as during the stormy days at the beginning of the summer.

Young annual plants (1) such as lantanas, calendulas and petunias, can be potted (2) and taken into the house where they will stay in flower for several weeks.

As long as **lantanas, calendulas, geraniums** and **petunias** are still in flower, why not take the opportunity of putting the smaller plants into pots? Then you can take these young plants into the house, where they will stay in flower for a few more weeks. However, you must carry out this potting during warm weather, and water the potted plants thoroughly. This makes it easier for them to adapt to conditions indoors — where you must take care to put them somewhere that gets the sun.

AROMATIC HERBS

Some of the aromatic herbs, such as **rosemary,** can be dug up now and repotted inside the house. Two more herbs that grow equally well indoors are **parsley** and **chives,** which are so useful in the kitchen.

To propagate your geranium plants, take some cuttings three or four inches long (1). Strip the leaves from the base of each cutting, which should then be coated with a hormone preparation to reduce the danger of rot (2). Place the cuttings in a container full of sand kept damp by water filtering through the wall of a clay pot (3).

USE OF THE GREENHOUSE

For those of you who have greenhouses, the time has come to sow annuals which will give flowers from December through to the spring. Sow some **sweet peas**, for example, or **French marigolds, nasturtiums** or **schizanthus.**

GERANIUM CUTTINGS

It is easy to propagate **geranium** plants by by taking cuttings, in order to have some plants to grow indoors. Use a sharp knife or a good pair of scissors, and take some cuttings three or four inches long.

Next, strip the leaves from the base of each cutting, to lessen the shock of transplanting and avoid the risk of rot. Then the base of the cutting should be coated with a preparation of vegetable hormones such as 'Seradix B', to hasten the root-growing process, and to reduce the danger of rot. Put each cutting into a bulb-bowl or an **azalea**-pot, using sand as the rooting medium. Bury a 3-inch clay pot in the sand, with its drain-hole plugged. Fill this pot with water, which will then filter continuously through the wall of the pot, thus keeping the sand damp. Once the cuttings have been potted they should be kept in the shade for several days, and then exposed gradually to the sun.

PLANTING LILIES

Lilies should be planted in September or October. If you want to achieve success growing these splendid flowers, give them a well-drained, sandy mould, and make sure to plant the bulbs before the first frost. **Madonna lilies** should be planted as early as possible in September. I would advise you to prepare the soil well before you do any planting. Fertilize it with well-rotted manure, compost or peat-moss, and a complete chemical such as 5-8-10, using one pound of fertilizer per 100 square feet of flowerbed.

PLANTING CONIFERS

From the end of August to the end of September is the best time to plant conifers, but certain precautions are necessary if you hope to succeed with an autumn planting — for this season is usually very short, especially in Eastern Canada. Plants put in the ground during this period have very little time to form new roots after they have been planted.

Here, very briefly, is how to go about planting conifers: Dig a hole two feet wider and eight inches deeper than the ball of earth surrounding the roots of the conifer. Put the ball of earth — still in its jute sacking — into the hole, with the top of the ball about an inch below the surface of the soil.

Fill in with good rich loam to within four inches of the top. Water thoroughly, so that the new soil soaks up as much water as possible. Then complete the filling-in, leaving a slight depression all round the stem of the plant. I must stress again that watering is particularly important. To get through the winter properly, conifers need a bigger reserve of water in the autumn than do plants with deciduous leaves.

TENDER BULBS

The time is approaching for you to dig up the tender bulbs (that is, those bulbs which flower during the summer), such as **trigidias** and **tuberoses.** You must also lift your **tuberous begonias** and **caladiums** before the first frosts arrive. Your **gladioli, cannas** and **dahlias** can be lifted just after the first frosts.

Vermiculite and perlite are being used more and more nowadays for storing bulbs in winter.

COMPOST AND THE KITCHEN-GARDEN

Let me urge you to set up your own private reserve of organic matter for your plants — that is, a compost-heap. Use all your garden rubbish — plants, leaves, grass clippings and so on, as well as vegetable waste from the kitchen.

Choose an isolated corner of your property, far from the kitchen, as the site for your compost-heap — somewhere you can get at fairly easily with your wheelbarrow. It will help to conserve moisture if the site is somewhat shaded. The volume of the compost-heap varies according to the quantity of organic material it contains. A heap four feet wide by six feet long by four feet high will give you a surprising amount of the organic matter the soil needs so badly.

Start the heap off with a layer of rubbish about six inches thick, add a little complete chemical fertilizer (6-9-6, for example), water thoroughly, and cover with six inches of earth. Continue this layering process until the heap reaches a convenient operating height, and cover the whole thing with a final 6-inch layer of earth.

This makes an excellent source of fertilizer for your kitchen-garden, and humus for your soil. It enables you to improve the arable layer of your land and also to prevent erosion.

As soon as you have picked the vegetables, sow **rye**, which makes a useful 'green fertilizer'. The following spring, cut the cereal before it has grown too high, then dig the stalks back into the soil, and add five pounds of 6-9-6 fertilizer per 100 square feet of surface.

TAKING YOUR PLANTS BACK INDOORS

Cool nights are a warning that cold weather is on the way. So it is best to get your plants back into the house in good time — not merely to avoid early frosts but also to let plants which have become acclimatized to outdoor conditions get used to their new surroundings before the central heating is turned on.

It is easy to obtain new gloxinia plants. All you need do is cut off a leaf and place the stalk in water.

Fragile plants such as **oleanders, hibiscus** and **fuchsias,** which have been in pots or flower-stands, need a little time to reintegrate themselves into their winter quarters.

"Moving day" for your house plants involves quite a few tasks — such as washing out the pots, watering as necessary, repotting in certain cases, and even fertilizing. Remember that these plants are going to spend several months indoors, and that you must therefore supply them with a suitable soil, properly fertilized.

October

The cool, refreshing days of October are an invitation to amateur gardeners to get busy on the numerous tasks that await them in the garden and on their property generally. The lovely autumn foliage, the deep green of the lawn, the cool, damp soil, the clear blue sky above — all these tempt the gardener to stay outdours as long as possible.

PLANTING TREES AND SHRUBS

Autumn is an excellent time to plant trees and shrubs such as **lilac, ornamental apple trees, maple** and **philadelphus.** All deciduous-leaved trees or bushes should have lost their foliage and be in the dormant state before you plant them.

Most people look on the arrival of autumn as the end of work in the garden. In a sense, they are right — it is the time for gathering in the crops, and for cleaning up the garden. From another aspect, it is also the best season of all for gardening. Until mid-November, the temperature outside is generally quite comfortable, and rainfall is more regular and less violent than in summer. It is the right time for transplanting, for garden soil is at its best now for growing plants. Hoeing and mulching have made it nicely friable, and the warm temperatures of summer have helped to free the nitrogen and the other elements which work more slowly in the cold soil of the spring. Chemical fertilizers applied in autumn benefit the plants immediately because the bacteria in the soil have multiplied during the summer and are highly active at this time.

Most amateur gardeners are in fine form for work in the garden after the summer holidays and their weeks of exercise in the open air. Working on your property in the autumn is also easier and more pleasant than it was during the somewhat cool days of spring or under the blazing summer sun.

The autumn gives you more time to plan your garden or do your planting, whereas in spring everything has to be done as quickly as possible so that you are not defeated by the rapid growth of all the greenery, and the continuous procession of the many important jobs which have to be done.

In the autumn, nurseries and gardening centres stock a large variety of plants, which will brighten up your property. You will find that woody plants do not show any further growth at their extremities now, since next season's flowers and leaves are lying hidden beneath their winter buds. However, even though the extremities are no longer growing, many plants will still form new roots after being transplanted.

TRANSPLANTING

If you must transplant rose bushes, shrubs or vines where the roots have been cleaned of earth, it is essential to wait until the leaves have finished their work for the plant and have all dropped off. Your local landscape gardener will be only too pleased to show you how to move the various species of plants until the frost has got far enough down into the ground to bring your transplantation programme to an end for the current year.

Normal methods of transplanting should be followed in the autumn. Dig a hole twice as deep and twice as wide as the roots, then fill this hole with a good loam mixed with humus and sufficient fertilizer. You must also water the soil round the plants after transplanting them — not so much because the plants need water, but because this watering will tamp the soil down round the roots and get rid of pockets of air.

In any case, as you probably know, pockets of air can form along the roots of trees if their upper parts are disturbed by winter winds. Stakes or other forms of support will prevent them from being too badly shaken about by the wind.

FERTILIZING

Liquid fertilizers, which can be immediately assimilated by the plants, are ideal for stimulating the vigour of your plants, and they make the perfect complement for powdered bone-meal and other solid fertilizers. For their part, organic fertilizers applied in the autumn will decompose slowly in the soil and be ready to supply the necessary stimulation to the plants early in the spring. Where the soil is so light that chemical fertilizers may filter down past the plant roots, the fertilizers should be mixed with peat-moss, which will keep them close to the roots.

There are few gardens — at least in Eastern Canada — in which even the hardiest of plants will not have some buds damaged during the course of the winter. Continuing horticultural research is being carried out to find various ways to prevent this sort of damage to plants during the cold season. It is now established that plants suffer worse damage if they continue to produce tender young shoots right up until the frosts arrive. In view of this, it is obviously wiser to stop fertilizing the rose bushes and perennials late in summer.

Any autumn fertilizing should be delayed until the annual growth is over.

FERTILIZERS FOR WOODY PLANTS

The end of the autumn is the perfect time to fertilize trees and shrubs.

All growth at the ends of the branches and shoots has stopped, but the roots remain active until the soil freezes down to their level.

Autumn fertilizing can also be done with minimum loss.

Although spreading the fertilizer over the surface of the ground is a quick way of dealing with deciduous-leaved trees, it is the least effective method — and the most costly, since most of the fertilizing elements are washed away by the rain trickling over the surface of the ground.

The best way to do this is to put the fertilizer into holes drilled into the soil with an auger or an iron bar. Drill these holes in circles around the trunks of your adult deciduous-leaved trees, and place them from fifteen to eighteen inches deep, and space them no more than three feet from each other. You need one hole for every pound of fertilizer used.

Conifers and deciduous-leaved trees should be fertilized at the same time as the lawn, after a complete chemical fertilizer has been spread over the surface of the latter.

The fertilizer I recommend is "Hibernal" — (3-6-12 Mg. Bo.). This is an excellent preparation for trees and shrubs. It provides these woody plants with the nutritive elements they need, and helps to stop their bark from splitting during the winter.

PLANTING SPRING BULBS

Autumn is the time to plant bulbs — certain varieties of which represent the result of carefully-planned production programmes over two or three years. At the beginning of each autumn we receive important shipments of bulbs from Holland, Belgium, France, Italy and Japan. How successfully these bulbs will flower next spring depends on planting them now, in autumn, for this is the time of year when their roots should be developing in the ground.

To ensure a rich carpet of colour on your property next spring, plant your bulbs before the end of October. If you plant them as early as possible in the month, they will have sufficient time to develop strong roots before the ground freezes. Make sure the soil is properly drained, and add a little powdered bone-meal or superphosphate to give each bulb a good supply of phosphorus.

Crocuses, squills, chionodoxas, aconites, narcissuses and **tulips,** all grouped together in flowerbeds or borders, or dotted about in little clumps, will produce a great variety of colour on your property before most of your spring-flowering shrubs and trees have started to come into flower.

Take advantage of the vast choice of bulbs available in the gardening centres to get yourself a wide variety. Plant them without delay in a

To ensure a good variety of colour on your property in spring, plant crocus bulbs as early as possible in October. (Photo: Malak, Ottawa)

Successful flowering of hyacinth bulbs in spring depends on their being planted in October — for then their roots will have sufficient time to develop before the ground freezes. (Photo: Malak, Ottawa)

In the autumn, plant small bulbs such as crocus, winter aconite or bulbous iris. They will make their appearance very early in the spring, and will create a handsome carpet of colour. (Photo: Malak, Ottawa)

well-drained soil enriched with nutritive elements. Although you can delay the planting of your **tulips** until the end of the month, the smaller bulbs, such as **chionodoxas, crocuses** and **grape hyacinths** (to name but three), should be planted straight away.

FORCING BULBS

You can grow several kinds of bulbs indoors. It is easy to force **narcissuses, jonquils, hyacinths,** etc. Tender **narcissuses, crocuses** and **colchicums** can be planted in a bed of pebbles or vermiculite, with water barely covering the base of the bulbs. Most other bulbs grow better in soil.

After you have potted your bulbs, put them in a cool dark place until the roots are well developed and the foliage is starting to grow. Then move them into the warmth and the light.

STORING

The storing of summer-flowering bulbs calls for certain essential precautions. Immediately after the first sharp frost, remove the roots of the **dahlias** from the soil, without breaking the root-collars. Cut the shoots down to an inch in length. Let them dry in the sun for a few hours, dust

Plant your tulip bulbs with a trowel or a planter. Put them five or six inches down into the ground, and space them inches away from each other. To avoid creating a monotonous effect, do not plant them in straight lines.
(Photo: Malak, Ottawa)

them with a 'Malathion'-based insecticide, then store them away. Bury them in sand, vermiculite or perlite, somewhere where the temperature varies between 36° and 50° F.

Gladioli corms should be stored in the same way. However, remember to dust them first with a 'Malathion - based insecticide to get rid of any thrips that may be present.

Keep your **begonias** in a cool, dark place. If the frost has killed the shoots, take the tubers out of the ground and let them dry for a day or two out in the sun. Then lay them out on a dish and cover them with a layer of perlite or vermiculite.

When the foliage of your **caladiums** starts going yellow and then brown, take the bulbs out of the ground, clean them, and let them dry for two weeks somewhere sheltered from the frost: then store them at a temperature of 50° F in sand, peat-moss, sawdust or vermiculite.

CHRYSANTHEMUMS GROWN INDOORS

Certain varieties of garden **chrysanthemums** can be potted and taken indoors. However, you must keep an eye on the ventilation inside the house during the first few weeks, to make sure the plants have enough air and are thus able to acclimatize themselves easily to conditions indoors.

This is also a good time to visit the nurseries and gardening centres to see the latest varieties in flower. This sort of visit will let you decide which varieties to buy for your garden next spring.

Growing plants in containers is becoming more and more popular. Potted plants are being grown not only indoors or on the patio or terrace, but also in the garden. This form of gardening in containers is never dull, since the plants can be moved from one spot to another as necessary — either singly or in groups, and thus you can make all sorts of varied arrangements — by species, by colour or by size.

It is also an excellent way of maintaining the growth of your plants indoors, during bad weather. During October, you should be planning various new locations for your potted plants for the months to come.

INDOOR PLANTS

Once again, remember to air the house well during the first few days after you bring your plants back indoors at the end of their "summer holiday" outside in the garden. Water them carefully, and make sure none of them is infested with insect pests. If you give the foliage of your plants a good washing when you bring them back indoors, you should not have any serious problems with insects. I should stress that **philodendrons, ivies, dieffenbachias** and **dracaenas** need light, though not direct sunlight. Wipe over their foliage from time to time with a soft, damp cloth.

Do not wait until the last minute to buy new plants to decorate the inside of your house during the winter. As soon as the temperature begins to drop, and you find yourself working in the garden less frequently and for shorter periods, go out and get some new indoor plants which are interesting enough to hold your attention and inspire you to increase your stock of knowledge about the growth and upkeep of house plants.

AROMATIC HERBS IN POTS

Before the weather gets too cold, put some aromatic plants from your garden into pots, so you will have fresh herbs to season your dishes all through the winter. Try to pot some **chives, rosemary, marjoram** and **basil.**

WORK IN THE KITCHEN-GARDEN

Once you have gathered in all your vegetables, dig the soil over and plant **rye** to provide the soil with some humus, and to prevent erosion during the winter. In the spring, when the rye is from eighteen to twenty-four inches high, dig it into the ground.

As you know, even though October is traditionally the month for us to admire the beautiful colouring of the leaves on the trees, it is also a period in which certain gardening work **must** be done before the onset of winter. A few hours of work this month will give you weeks of pleasure in your garden next year.

UPKEEP OF THE LAWN

With all the tasks demanding the amateur gardener's attention during this month, it is easy enough to neglect the lawn. You should continue to cut the grass, with the blades of your lawn-mower adjusted to a height of between one-and-a-half and two inches. The lawn should not be too long when winter comes, for then there is a danger of the grass being crushed. As for newly-sown lawns or bare patches that have been re-seeded, I would advise you to water them during dry periods, so that the roots of the grass get well established before the arrival of the cold weather.

Lawn grasses will take every possible advantage of the autumn growth period if they are given a minimum of care. Even slow-germinating perennial grasses will spread a coating of green over the bare spaces which appeared during the summer and are spoiling the lawn. You can also get rid of weeds, right at the beginning of the autumn, by applying herbicides. It is important to carry out this treatment against weeds at the beginning of autumn so that the lawn grasses have sufficient time to recover their vigour properly before the arrival of the cold weather. How well your lawn will fight weeds next spring depends largely on the precautions you take this autumn to ensure that it has the necessary vigour.

Lawns benefit from an application of fertilizer during the autumn. If you really want a fine lawn next spring, treat it with a complete chemical fertilizer such as 'Hibernal' (3-6-12 Mg. Bo), for example, using two pounds per 100 square feet of surface.

This fertilizer, which does equally well for trees and shrubs, protects your lawn against snow-mould and winter damage. You will also avoid yellow or brown blotches on the lawn in the spring.

CLEANING UP YOUR PROPERTY

The autumn clean-up of your garden comes logically at the end of the gardening season. In temperate regions such as most of Canada, this means October.

The major task, quite obviously, is getting rid of the leaves. The basic principle here is not to let them accumulate on the ground. They can cause serious damage to a lawn if you do not get rid of them as soon as they fall. Above all, it is essential not to let wet leaves lie on the lawn, for they will choke the grass very quickly.

The leaves which form the thickest covering — and consequently the most harmful — are those of the **maple** and the **ash,** since they fall from the tree before they are completely dead, and are less likely to be blown away by the wind than are the leaves of the oak and the beech, which stay on the tree until they dry out completely.

Many people prefer to wait until all the leaves have fallen before they rake them up. This is not a good idea, for your lawn can be considerably weakened in a very few weeks by a heavy covering of leaves. Not only does this cause the grass to turn yellow, it can also create conditions favourable for diseases.

The best way of getting rid of dead leaves is to remove a load each week during the period that they are falling. This job is a nuisance, certainly, especially if you do it with a rake.

However, several models of rotary lawn-mowers are now fitted with a bag over the hole where the grass clippings come out. If you run your mower over the lawn, the leaves get chopped up by the blades, and are ejected into the bag.

THE LAWN-SWEEPER

The most commonly-used method of collecting leaves — though **not** the easiest — is to rake them together into piles.

The odour of burning leaves is a common reminder of the time of year, with thick columns of smoke rising into the air along every street. However, as the population grows, and air pollution continues to get worse and worse, many municipalities now forbid the burning of leaves. Even if it is not actually forbidden within your own municipality it is a harmful practice, and it should be discontinued everywhere. What you should do instead is either pile all your dead leaves onto a compost-heap and turn them into mulch, or let the garbage-men get rid of them. In any case it is easy enough to dispose of leaves fairly quickly by using large plastic garbage bags.

Whatever method you use to dispose of your dead leaves, you must first get them up off the ground.

The lawn-sweeper clears your lawn of fallen leaves and other debris far more quickly and with much less trouble than a rake. This simple, effective and practical machine is mounted on rubber-tired wheels, and can be either pushed by hand or drawn behind a small garden tractor. It sweeps the leaves up into a high-capacity collecting-bag. There are many different models, all of them extremely effective. The sweeper has a rotating brush which picks up the leaves and the grass clippings, and shoots them into the collecting-bag. Even if you are using a motor-mower which picks up the grass clippings as it mows, I would advise you to run over the lawn again afterwards with a lawn-sweeper, especially in autumn. Their fibre brushes do not damage the delicate young blades of grass, and their wheels make it easy to transport the load to wherever you have established a compost-heap or pile of mulch.

It should be noted that the three types of lawn-sweeper are not just for use during an autumn clean-up. They do a useful job all through the gardening season, and you can sweep your paths and terraces with them just as easily as you can the lawn.

BLOWERS AND VACUUM-CLEANERS

For some years special blowers have been on the market. These have the same effect as a an automatic rake — only they **push** the leaves into piles rather than pull them. They are very efficient machines.

There are also suction cleaners which work the same way as the ordinary household vacuum-cleaner.

The blowers which pile the leaves up into one big heap are used more on public property and on large private estates. Both blowers and suction machines have extension hoses which allow you to clean around thickets, trees and shrubs, and along wall-beds, either sucking up or blowing away the leaves and other debris that have accumulated there.

If you use either of these machines on crisp, dry leaves, the leaves will crumble — thus considerably decreasing their volume and making it much easier to bag and dispose of them.

The suction cleaner makes a better job of this particular aspect of the operation. I must stress that partly crushed leaves make excellent material for a compost-heap. To obtain the best results, place your leaves and other vegetable debris in layers, and then cover them with layers of earth. If the compost-heap is located in a sunny corner and kept moist, the process of transformation will take place quite satisfactorily. The compost should be piled above ground level, to facilitate the circulation of air and thus speed up the action of the soil bacteria which are responsible for the process of decomposition.

Remember that it is essential not to make the layers of leaves too thick, and you must intersperse them with layers of earth. Otherwise the leaves will all clog together and your compost-heap will be a failure.

THE MOTORIZED ROLLER

In a way, a compost-heap is like a very slow shredder, and the complete reaction can literally take years. By contrast, a motorized roller only takes a few minutes to transform heaps of leaves, grass cuttings and other vegetable debris.

The roller crushes peat-moss, compost, leaves, etc, and produces an excellent mulch around the base of trees and shrubs — thus conserving moisture, controlling weeds and gradually improving the composition of the soil.

A PROBLEM THAT MUST NOT BE OVERLOOKED

Cleaning the lawn in autumn should be one of the most obvious tasks, especially in view of all the dead leaves. It is important not to forget some other things which are not so obvious. Thus, the culm or haulm of the lawn is too often overlooked. (This is the dead matter that accumulates around the base of the blades of grass.) For a really good autumn clean-up, this dead matter must not be neglected. It is essential to get rid of it before it becomes a thick mat.

The best tool for the purpose, for large properties as well as small, is a good solid garden rake. Give the roots of your lawn a really good raking-over, then remove the debris — which by now has been brought up to the surface — with a flexible lawn-rake. Now air and water can penetrate into the soil once again, to help give your lawn renewed vigour.

WATCH OUT FOR WINTER DAMAGE

Nothing is more discouraging for an amateur gardener than to realize, when spring comes, how much damage has been caused by the winter. But you can —in fact, you **should** — take certain necessary precautions in the autumn which will prevent any winter damage. This damage to your plants ran be caused by dehydration, frost getting into the tissues of the plants, splitting of the stems from the effect of the cold, or broken roots caused by the soil heaving under the effects of alternating frost and thaw.

Dehydration or drying-out of plants is caused by the wind, a lack of water and too thin a covering of snow upon the ground. To protect your trees and shrubs against dehydration, give the plants a thorough watering late in the autumn, before the ground is too deeply frozen. Spread a mulch — peat-moss, straw, etc — over the surface of the soil, around the base of the plants. It is better to wait until the surface of the ground is frozen, so that field-mice won't make their nests under the protective covering of the mulch.

Some protection against the wind is equally necessary. Use screens of polythene sheeting — or preferably burlap. Snow-fences with a screen of burlap around them form an effective protection for young trees and shrubs against the sun and the parching winds. Burlap has the double advantage that it cuts out the rays of the sun and still lets the air circulate freely. This is particularly important for conifers.

There are also certain preparations based on synthetic resins — 'Wilt-Pruf' is one example — which you spray on the conifers at the end of October to stop evaporation, and on deciduous-leaved trees to protect their bark.

The use of these products on your conifers enables you to avoid dehydration caused by the sun's rays and the wind, and as a result you will not be troubled by yellowing or by falling needles during the following spring.

Snow-fencing and a screen of burlap will effectively protect your conifers (both shrubs and young trees) from sun and parching winds throughout the winter. Burlap has the double advantage of cutting off the rays of the sun while still allowing the air to circulate freely.

DAMAGE BY RODENTS

It is always a sad thing in spring to find you have lost a tree because the bark has been eaten away from the trunk by rodents (field-mice in particular). To avoid this, it is a good idea to surround the base of your trees (especially the younger ones) with a sort of "corset" made of galvanized steel wire with a ¼-inch mesh. It should be at least two feet high, or even higher, enough to bring it up above the level of the snow.

Make the "corset" loose enough round the trunk so you can leave it there for several years while the tree is growing. Take care to bend in the cut ends of the wire mesh, so that there are no jagged spikes left showing. The mesh should also be buried at least three inches deep into the ground.

To prevent your trees being stripped of their bark during the winter by rodents such as field-mice — as has happened to the tree in the illustration below — you should enclose the base of the trunk in a protective 'corset' made from mesh.

It is also possible to use plywood, aluminum, building paper, plastic strips or burlap. However, all these materials are less satisfactory and less durable than the wire mesh "corset".

Never use tar paper. This can reduce the trees' and shrubs' resistance to cold, and thus create favourable conditions for diseases. If you are using a material such as plywood or plastic strips, it is very important that you remove it at the beginning of spring, to prevent mildew and other diseases.

As we have seen, it is all very well to admire the beautiful colours of the leaves on the trees in October, but this is also the month in which certain gardening tasks **must** be done before the arrival of winter. A few hours work in the garden now will mean weeks of pleasure for you next year.

November

LAST WORK IN THE GARDEN

In November one realizes — mainly from the way the days keep drawing in —how quickly the winter is approaching. The plants have nearly all stopped growing, and most amateur gardeners have already turned their attention to their indoor plants. All the same, there is still some work to be done outside before you can forget all about your garden until next spring.

Even though a few hardy chrysanthemums and annuals are still bravely making a little show of colour here and there, gardens are bare now, and the time has come to finish off your last gardening tasks before it gets too cold to work outside.

REMOVE ANNUALS

The annuals should be torn up now, and any dead perennials cut back close to the ground. This precaution gives visible proof that you care about the appearance of your property, even though some gardeners deliberately leave the stalks and foliage on their plants, to catch and hold the snow during the winter.

However, this is not necessary if you put down a suitable mulch, especially around the chrysanthemums, which don't stand up to the winter too well because their roots are fairly near the surface of the soil.

One task you must not neglect is a general clean-up of your property — and clearing away dead leaves in particular. If you let them accumulate, they are likely to damage the lawn, and to become breeding-grounds for plant diseases and hiding-places for insect pests and rodents.

Apart from this clean-up, you should also carry out the following tasks: — prune trees and shrubs, protect plants against the winter, plant tulips, dig up the summer-flowering bulbs, prepare a compost-heap, check over your garden tools and equipment, get your snow-blower ready and other similar tasks.

PRUNING TREES AND SHRUBS

The chief danger for trees during the winter comes from the wind. Dead branches can cause considerable damage, or even serious accidents, if they're blown about by a strong wind. Furthermore, if the crown of a tree is too bushy, the wind can well snap it off. In both cases, the corrective measure is obvious — a careful pruning.

Dead or damaged branches on deciduous-leaved trees and shrubs can be cut off at this time of year. However it is essential to use the proper tools — which must be properly sharp, as well. Any cuts more than an inch in diameter should be covered with a protective coating such as "Braco" or "Mastic Pelton". Get rid of all dead wood, and thin out the crown of the tree so that the wind can blow through it easily.

If the tree is not too high for this work to be done from the ground, or standing on a solid step-ladder, you could take care of it yourself. (Incidentally, a tree-saw with a telescopic aluminum handle that extends from two feet to six feet is an excellent tool that will make this sort of job much easier). However, if you are dealing with large trees, in most cases it is better to leave this kind of pruning work to specialists.

Summer-flowering shrubs can be pruned now — hibiscus and tamarisk in particular. In addition, cut the dead wood out of all the shurby trees.

Newly-planted trees should be supported by stakes so that they will not be shaken about by the wind — which often results in the roots being displaced. As you know, it takes a tree a good two to three years' normal growth before its roots have "taken" properly.

PLANTING TREES

A tree that has been chosen with sound judgement, and then planted properly and given all the necessary attentions, adds more than any other plant to the beauty of the permanent layout of a property.

Trees are often planted as a frame for the house, or as a background. You should bear these two important roles in mind when you are planting your own trees. Find out how tall they will be when they have finished growing and determine their good points as well as their bad ones. In addition to the bigger trees which are essential to your decorative scheme, it is a good idea to have some smaller ones which provide a seasonal interest — some special flowers or fruit, say, or a beautiful autumn colouring, or some unusually-shaped stems and branches.

The source of the tree is important. As far as possible, should you decide to dig up some trees yourself out in the countryside, or from some waste ground, choose specimens with well-developed root-systems. Bear in mind that if you are taking trees from the wild, the smaller ones — say five feet tall or under — are much easier to transplant than the others. Trees taken from open ground can stand the sun better than those that came from a forest.

Trees growing in humid soils rich in organic matter usually have stronger root-systems than others. It is therefore important to dig them up carefully, so as to save as many of the roots as possible.

Make sure the roots don't freeze, or dry out, while you are transplanting the trees. It is better to move deciduous-leaved trees only in the dormant state.

Autumn is the ideal time for transplanting, because then the roots will be well established before the next year's growth starts in the spring.

LOPPING YOUR TREES

When you plant a large tree, you must lop some of the branches at the top, in order to balance the shortening of the roots. Any dead, broken or dangrous branches should be removed completely, and then the lateral branches should be pruned. Most specialists advise that the head of a tree should have at least a third of its mass lopped off at the time of planting. The best way to go about it is to make the major boughs smaller and shorter, and then to cut the lateral branches short. You should not, however, prune the main stem of the tree unless it has been damaged.

Obviously, a tree that has been transplanted with all its roots, without any of them having been broken or damaged, will need hardly any pruning at all. In short, the main object of pruning on plantation is merely to establish a state of equilibrium in the plant.

Soil drainage is important for trees. Unsatisfactory growth and a predisposition towards attacks by insects are often the results of bad drainage — which can be corrected by installing earthenware drain-pipes covered with gravel.

SUPPORTS

Trees which are moved with roots bared, or with too small a ball of earth around them — especially in the autumn — should be supported by one or more stakes to help them withstand the violent winter winds. The best way to go about it is to plant a stout cedar stake in the same hole as the tree, some six or eight inches away from the trunk. Then twist a length of hose-pipe around the tree in a figure eight and nail the two ends of the pipe onto the cedar stake.

PROTECTING YOUR PLANTS IN WINTER

As mentioned earlier, damage to plants in winter is usually caused by dehydration, frost getting into the tissues, splitting of the stems from the effect of the cold or broken roots caused by the soil heaving as the result of alternating frost and thaw.

The various methods suggested for protecting your plants during the cold season have only one purpose — to reduce temperature-fluctuations in the immediate vicinity of the plant, both in the soil and in the surrounding air. Mulches are extremely useful for this purpose. The ones most frequently used are peat-moss, buckwheat scales, ground corn-cobs or dead leaves.

MULCHES

There is no specific time to use mulches and other methods of protecting your plants against winter damage. Do not follow the calendar, what counts is the temperature, and especially the depth of frost in the soil.

When the frost has penetrated at least two inches into the ground, spread mulch to keep the soil-temperature steady. As you know, fluctuations in temperature may cause a thaw, and this in turn leads to heaving of the soil which can result in the roots becoming exposed to the cold, or being broken. You can use straw or hay as your mulching material. These are excellent, but they are not easy to find in the city. I would advise you to use dead leaves or peat-moss instead. It is important that the material you choose should be light, to avoid choking your plants. Some amateur gardeners prefer to use conifer branches, especially over their beds of bulbs.

PROTECTING TREES AND SHRUBS

To provide adequate protection for your trees and shrubs against dehydration or drying-out caused by the wind, lack of water or too thin a covering of snow on the ground, you should water them thoroughly in November, before the frost gets too far down into the ground.

When the surface of the soil has frozen, spread a mulch over it, around the base of the plants.

Shrubs, particularly conifers, need protection against the wind and the sun. Install screens of polyethylene or, better still, burlap.

Most trees withstand the weight of the snow quite well — although certain conifers may become so weighed down that their branches break. If you have already encountered this problem, and want to avoid it in the future, it is a good idea to wind some cord or strips of burlap around the tree to hold the branches close to the trunk. If you take this precaution before the first snowfall, the branches cannot be weighed down by the snow, and thus will not bend.

(Incidentally, while tar paper should never be used to protect smaller trees against dehydration and attacks by rodents, an exception may be made in the case of large trees. You will find that wrapping the trunk with tarred paper or strips of burlap serves the purpose very well).

PROPER PROTECTION FOR ROSE BUSHES

This seems a good place to recapitulate the method recommended earlier to ensure that various rose bushes — hybrid teas, multifloras and grandifloras — are adequately protected during the winter. First of all, prune all the branches to a height of eighteen inches. Then get rid of all dead wood, leaves and other rubbish. Then water each bush with a mixture of insecticide and fungicide.

As soon as the frost begins to affect the leaves of the rose bushes, cover the base of each plant with a mound or earth up to twelve inches high. Finally, when the frost is well down into the ground, cover the mounds with conifer branches, straw or some similar material to prevent erosion of the soil during the winter.

(1) Protect hybrid tea rose bushes with a mound of earth seven to ten inches high before the arrival of the frost. (2) Cover chrysanthemums with a mulch when the ground is frozen. (3) Pot amaryllis bulbs. (4) Tie cords around conifers to avoid damage from the snow. (5) Spread the young branches of climbing rose bushes out along the ground, and cover them with earth. (6) Bush off the leaves of African violets. (7) Decorate your window-boxes with conifer branches.

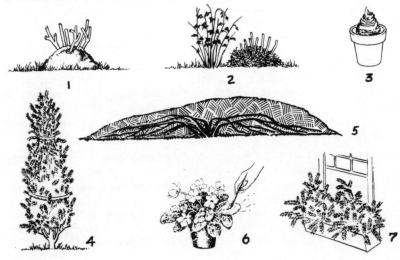

To protect climbing roses, detach them from their support, lay them out along the ground and cover them with earth or mulch. Then secure a sheet of waterproof building-paper over them.

Shrub roses should be dug up, laid on their sides in a trench dug specially for the purpose and then covered with earth.

FLOWERBEDS OF PERENNIALS

Once the soil has frozen, you must get on with the winter protection of your perennial beds. Pine needles are the best material to use for this purpose. Buckwheat scales also make an excellent mulch. However, it is not advisable to use the leaves from most trees — like the maple or the ash for example — since they tend to clog together under the effect of the autumn rains.

As you know, the object of spreading mulch on flowerbeds of perennials is not to protect the plants against the cold, but to **keep** them cold once the soil has frozen.

PLANTING TULIPS

Before the soil freezes is the time to plant those tulips which will bring so much pleasure next spring with their wonderful colours. Remember

There is still time to plant tulips before the ground freezes. They will give a wonderful display of colours next spring. The big flowers of hybrid Darwin tulips produce a striking effect near an ornamental apple-tree.

(Photo: Malak, Ottawa)

that tulips grow best in a sandy, well drained loam, which has been enriched with organic matter (well-rotted manure, etc) a few months beforehand.

A few handfuls of tulip bulbs, like those illustrated below, will liven up your property next spring. Plant them in clumps around the conifers, and along the walls of your house. (Photo: Malak, Ottawa)

When you do your planting, add five pounds of a complete chemical fertilizer (5-10-15) per 100 square feet, and to preserve the vigour of the bulbs, also work a little powdered bone-meal into the soil.

Tulip bulbs should be planted six inches deep, and the same distance away from each other.

STORING TENDER BULBS

Gladioli and other tender bulbs which you have recently dug up and have left temporarily in the garage or the basement should be cleaned off before being finally stored for the winter. Make sure that the tubers or bulbous underground shoots of tuberous begonias and caladiums are all removed.

You can wait till after the first frosts to do your cannas and dahlias. However, if the ground seems about to freeze up properly, it is better to lift them immediately — otherwise you may find it difficult to get them out of the ground.

Once you have lifted the root-clumps, put them in a cool, well-ventilated room or in the cellar, and leave them to dry for at least two weeks.

Put all your bulbs, tubers and rhizomes into a dish or a box filled with perlite or vermiculite.

Store your containers somewhere cool, dark and well-ventilated — the cellar, for example. You will find your summer-flowering bulbs in perfect shape next spring.

FINAL TASKS IN THE KITCHEN-GARDEN

Amateur gardeners who have any rhubarb plants in their kitchen-garden would do well to spread some well-rotted manure or some compost round these plants, so that the roots can store up the nutritious elements that will guarantee them a vigorous growth next spring.

Strawberry plants will give a plentiful crop next year if you protect them this autumn with a mulch of chopped straw or sawdust. Blackberry bushes, raspberry canes and currant bushes will also benefit from a mulch spread after the ground has frozen, either at the end of November or the beginning of December.

THE COMPOST HEAP

Nearly all organic matter is suitable for the compost-heap. However, you must not use any material tainted with a plant disease or an insect pest. Thus peony leaves, for example, even when they have been blackened by the frost, can still be full of gray mould, and once this fungus disease gets into your compost-heap it can ruin it completely.

You should burn all peony leaves, or send them out with the garbage.

Many gardeners do not know what to do with their dead leaves. Some burn them, some get rid of them with the household garbage, while others use them as a mulch. Too few people seem to realize the best use for them — as compost.

It is not enough to throw together a pile of vegetable rubbish, leaves and grass clippings and then just let the whole thing decompose haphazardly. The best times to start forming a compost-heap are obviously either in the autumn or at the beginning of spring, when it is easier for you to find a place you can set aside for this undertaking. The shaded area beneath a tree, where usually nothing will grow, is a good place to put a compost-heap. It will be sheltered there from the wind and the sun — which otherwise would probably dry it out too much.

Of course, a compost-heap should not be exposed to view. If you do not have a suitable tree to hide it behind, cover it over with a tarpaulin or a sheet of polyethylene. Naturally, the dimensions of the heap will depend on the size of your garden and the amount of vegetable rubbish you collect from it. For an ordinary garden, the maximum dimensions would be four to six feet wide by eight to ten feet long. Start the heap off by spreading a couple of inches of manure, compost, or good rich loam as the base, then add the vegetable rubbish (dead leaves, for example) as and when you have any.

You can also start your compost-heap with a layer of leaves twelve inches thick, with a layer of garden soil four to six inches thick on top (or you could use surface soil mixed with coarse sand, if the soil is heavy).

To make sure that all the various types of beneficial bacteria are present in sufficient quantity, and working well to decompose the material as quickly as possible, dust some very thin layers of good rich surface soil onto the organic material in your heap, put one of these layers of soil on whenever you have built the heap up another six inches. To speed up the decomposition process, and to improve the value of the compost as a fertilizer, spread a complete chemical fertilizer over each layer — 24-12-6, say, or one that is even richer in nitrogen. Continue in this fashion until the heap is as high as you want it to be. The top of the heap should be covered with eight to ten inches of earth, which will serve to keep in the various gases, formed by the decomposition.

Leave a slight depression on the top of the heap. This will help conserve moisture, which is essential for compost.

SHRUB CUTTINGS

It is easy to prepare cuttings from deciduous-leaved shrubs. All you need to do is snip off some shoots about nine inches long — for example, from weigelas, philadelphus or euonymus.

Tie these cuttings together in bunndles of twenty-four and bury them under eight inches of damp sand in a cold frame. In the spring, as soon as the soil conditions will permit, plant each of these cuttings deep in some semi-shaded spot. This will give you new plants at no expense at all.

CHECKING YOUR TOOLS AND EQUIPMENT

There is a saying that when the frost is on the pumpkin the time has come for the gardener to start checking over his gardening tools and equipment for the winter. Saws, shovels, picks, spades, rakes, secateurs, pruning-knives and lawn-movers all need cleaning and protecting against bad weather.

Above all, you must not neglect your pressure-spray, which has been so useful a weapon in the struggle against insects and diseases and weeds. To clean the spray, use a warm solution of a detergent containing ammonia. Inspect all parts and make sure they are in good working order. Give the moving parts a good coat of oil, and smear the valve with vaseline or some similar greasy preparation to prevent it from drying out.

This is the time to clean all your garden tools in order to prevent rust. Take the opportunity of tightening all loose handles and giving all metal surfaces a good stiff brushing before wiping them over with an oily rag. If any of your tools are rusty, use an anti-rust preparation.

Sharpen the blades of the lawn-shears and secateurs. The lawn-mover deserves special attention and don't forget to sharpen the blades and oil them carefully.

Garden equipment specialists also recommend that you should drain the gas-tank of your motor-mower, empty the oil out of the sump and clean the carburator. Also, remove the spark-plug and finish off with an overall inspection of the machine to make sure there are no parts broken or missing.

There is less work involved if you have an electric mower. It only requires cleaning the blades and their protective sheathing, and carrying out an overall inspection.

Whatever type of mower you have, it will be in much better shape next spring if you enclose it in a plastic bag before you put it away for the winter.

You needn't wait until all the leaves have fallen and winter is upon you before you get the snow-blower ready. It is a good idea to get this machine out of the garage or storage shed, give it a thorough going-over and get it working. It is much better to do this inspection **now**, without hurrying it, than it is to have to go at it feverishly in the middle of the first snow-storm and find that the carburator is not working, or that the spark-plug needs replacing, or that the drive-chain is broken.

Also, if anything does need repairing, the mechanics who specialize in the maintenance and repair of this type of equipment are more likely to be available now — before long, they will be swamped with work and you will have to wait your turn as patiently as you can.

HOW TO TAKE CARE OF INDOOR PLANTS

The house plants you bought recently should be sprayed, to maintain a humid atmosphere immediately around them. This will help them get used to conditions inside your house. However, it is unnecessary to take this precaution with succulent plants and cactuses.

Inspect your indoor plants frequently to make sure they do not have any mealybugs, whiteflies or aphids on them. Use "Malathion"-based preparations, in accordance with the manufacturer's recommendation. If you are using an aerosol bomb, do not spray from any closer than eighteen inches from the plant. This is to avoid any danger of burning from the chemical.

Water your plants whenever necessary, and make sure that each container has a proper drainage hole.

Whiteflies can very easily ruin all your plans for decorating the interior of your house with fine, vigorous plants.

You are indeed fortunate if you have not yet found any on your plants — for these insects multiply very rapidly, and will form colonies anywhere if you let them get established.

A 50 per-cent concentration of "Malathion" or pyrethrum, dissolved in water, will help to control them. Spray it on once a week. Be sure to spray underneath the leaves as well as on top. It is better to use a deodorized "Malathion" if you do not want the whole of the inside of your house smelling of the stuff.

December

December is a dreary month in the garden. For the past several weeks, Nature has been without her lovely garb; and there are only a few conifers here and there to brighten up the bare country-side.

Most amateur gardeners turn their attention indoors now, and grow house plants.

Even though the cold weather is already beginning to make itself felt, that does not mean you must retire finally inside the house and forget about what is going on outside until next spring.

CARE OF THE LAWN

As far as possible, you should avoid walking on the lawn, especially before the frost has got well down into the soil. In several places, especially where the ground is poorly drained, water accumulated from the heavy rains of autumn has a tendency to form pools, or at least to soak the soil and soften it up to the point where it is easy to damage the lawn merely by walking on it. Even if the soil is well drained, it is better not to walk on the lawn — and especially not to make a habit of walking in the same path. Before the snow finally covers the ground, remove any dead leaves which may still be lying on the lawn. These leaves can damage the lawn by cutting down the circulation of air and by causing mildew.

PROTECTING YOUR PLANTS DURING WINTER

Once the frost has got down into the ground, you should protect your deciduous-leaved ornamental woody plants (both trees and shrubs) and your conifers — especially those you planted during the past year. Surround

Screens of lathing covered with jute make an effective protection for any conifers you want to preserve from the parching winds of the cold season, and from the sun during the last weeks of winter and the beginning of spring.

their bases with a thick mulch of straw, peat-moss or some other similar material. When you are dealing with low shrubs with persistent leaves, such as the Korean littleleaf box (Buxus microphylla koreana), do not spread the mulch so close that it actually touches the trunk of the plant.

As for flowerbeds or herbaceous perennials, mulch should not be laid when it is raining or snowing. The plants should be dry, and the soil should be well frozen. I suggest that you use straw, oak leaves, maple leaves, or any other vegetable rubbish which will protect the plant without interfering with the flow of air. The same type of protection should also be given to beds of spring-flowering bulbs: tulips, hyacinths, narcissuses, winter aconite, crocuses, chionodoxas, daffodils, squills and grape hyacinths.

Now is also the time to protect the barberry or Japanese barberry plants with a small mound of earth round the base of each plant. The same treatment should be applied to tuberoses and hydrangea plants.

As mulches, use conifer branches, buckwheat scales, straw or peat-moss. Incidentally, tests carried out in various experimental gardens have proved that buckwheat scales may be one of the best mulches obtainable. It allows water to penetrate easily into the soil, and at the same time prevents it from being lost by evaporation.

PLANTS IN CONTAINERS

Box and hydrangea plants growing in containers must be stored for the winter in a cool dark cellar, well ventilated and sheltered from the frost. Water these plants occasionally.

Deciduous-leaved shrubs can be stored in a cold frame, but take care to ensure adequate ventilation to avoid mildew. Another way of guaranteeing their protection during winter is to take these plants out of their containers before the ground is frozen, replant them in some well-sheltered spot, and then spread a thick layer of mulch over the soil.

PERENNIALS IN COLD FRAMES

If you keep campanulas, daisies, pansies or other perennials in cold frames, watch the ventilation until the soil has frozen. Then spread a fairly thick layer of mulch, let the casing back down onto its base and cover the whole frame over with straw for the rest of the winter.

ICE-SALTING AND ITS EFFECT ON PLANTS

In many parts of Canada, ice is a real problem during the winter season. Salt (either calcium chloride or sodium chloride) is being used in ever-increasing amounts to make the roads safe for traffic. Salt is also used on private and public property to melt the ice on footpaths, alleyways, flights of steps and balconies, etc. This chemical compound does a splendid job, but its use also brings severe problems in its wake. It is extremely harmful to lawns and plants.

I would advise you to use a chemical fertilizer instead — a compound which is just as efficient in preventing people from slipping on icy surfaces and hurting themselves, and in stopping cars or other vehicles from skidding. For example, try spreading a nitrogen-rich fertilizer, such as urea (45-0-0), ammonium nitrate, or ammonium sulphate, using seven pounds per 100 square feet of surface. Alternatively, you could use a complete chemical fertilizer — 6-9-6, 12-4-8, or 7-7-7; here, the recommended spread is five pounds per 100 square feet.

These fertilizers are in fact salts, which will melt the ice quickly — and will also provide fertilizing elements for your plants.

Here is a suggestion that will bring a little life back to a drab December landscape — why not attract the birds, by putting food out for them? There are all sorts of things you can give them — bread, nuts, raisins, crumbs of cake or doughnut, fat, or simply mixed bird-seed. You will be surprised and delighted by the amount of activity that will cause!

FORCING BULBS

Bulbs that you potted earlier for growing indoors have put their roots down by now, and are ready for forcing. If you want some early shrubs, why not pot some now, and store them until the beginning of January when they will be ready for forcing? Suitable species are azalea, deutzia, forsythia, philadelphus or flowering almond (Prunus triloba).

If you have stored any dahlia tubers, now is the time to inspect them, so that you can detect any signs of softening or rot at an early stage. Cut out any affected areas with a sharp knife, and treat the tubers with a fungicide.

THE BEAUTY OF GLOXINIAS

If the sight of the gloomy winter landscape puts you in a bad mood when you look out of your windows, get some **gloxinias** and grow them indoors. Their great beauty may lead you to believe they are difficult to grow, but you are mistaken. While not actually to be classed as child's play, growing them presents no insurmountable problem. All you need do is take care of their essential needs. Just give them a humid atmosphere, a day-time temperature of 68° to 70° F, and protect them from strong sunlight. To get the necessary humidity, you can install a humidifier in the room or put a dish of water near the plants.

Gloxinias are sold either as tubers or as potted plants. They give magnificent flowers — red, pink, blue and white, and some plants produce flowers in which all these four tints are combined.

They make an excellent Christmas gift.

A MINI-GARDEN OF CACTUSES

Cactuses are some of the most interesting indoor plants to grow during the winter. Their needs are very simple: a sterilized earth-mix (which is on sale at gardening centres), and a light watering, every eight to ten days.

You can buy envelopes of mixed seeds, which you sow in a dish or a pot placed in a sunny window, or under a special lamp used for growing plants indoors. However, you must always be on your guard against ordinary household gas. If you use gas for cooking, do not put your cactuses in the kitchen. These plants plants die very quickly if there is the slightest trace of gas in the air.

If you are in a hurry to see the actual plants rather than wait to let them grow from seed, you can buy them at your florist's or local gardening centre — and you will be pleasantly surprised by the wide choice available there.

CHRISTMAS TREES

As the end of the year approaches, people often ask themselves whether it is better to buy a Christmas tree (either for indoor or for outdoor decoration) as early as possible, or to wait until the last week before Christmas.

Remember that the earlier you buy a tree, the longer it will have been since it was cut. Such trees will therefore be the first to dry out and lose their needles. Whereas if you decide to buy your tree later (when the choice will probably be much more limited, admittedly) you will at least have a fresher tree.

When you take your tree down after Christmas, instead of just throwing it out, why not use it as protection for flowerbeds and rose bushes?

CHRISTMAS GIFTS

As the holiday season draws near, you may find yourself wondering about gifts for the amateur gardener.

If you have friends or relatives who are interested in gardening, a nice indoor plant makes a gift that is always much appreciated. Tools such as electric shears, secateurs, garden scissors and so on are always useful.

There is also the whole field of garden equipment — lawn-mowers, rollers, rotary tillers, spreaders, mini-tractors and their accessories, and so on — if you are thinking of the more expensive sort of present.

Another excellent idea is a gift certificate at a nursery, florist's or a reputable seedsman, or at a gardening centre. This certificate enables the recipient to choose his own gift at the time that suits him best. Thus, if he has decided on trees, shrubs, perennials or annuals, he will use his gift certificate when the planting season comes along.

And then there are always new books about plants — what about one of those?

You must never forget that the true amateur gardener, the real horticulture **aficionado**, thinks about his plants the whole year through. During the winter, besides all the chores of looking after his indoor plants, he is busy preparing for next season's work out in the garden. Layout, revised versions of the layout, sowing programme, planting programme, and so forth are but a few of the various projects he will start putting into operation the following February and which will keep him occupied for several months to come.

However, there is no doubt that if you want an attractive garden you must plan ahead, and all planning worthy of the name, in gardening just as in every other sphere of activity, calls for serious preparation in which the basic element should be a solid background knowledge of the subject.

The festive season really gets under way when the family sets out to look for a Christmas tree. Choose a tree with a straight trunk, and plenty of branches to hang decorations from. Make sure it is not too dry. Stand the tree in a container full of water, adding water as necessary to keep it filled — but first remove a few inches of bark from the base of the trunk — this lets the tree absorb more water, which keeps it fresh longer, and lessens the danger of fire. (Photo: Malak, Ottawa)

INDEX

464

Printed by
IMPRIMERIE ELECTRA

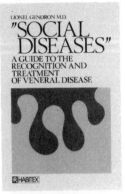

"SOCIAL" DISEASES

A Guide to the Recognition and Treatment of Venereal Disease

Dr. Lionel Gendron

—especially among the young. This book has been written so that the general reader may understand the causes, recognize the symptoms and appreciate the long-term effects of venereal disease.

122 pages, Fully illustrated

CELLULITE

Dr. Gérard J. Léonard

The author, one of the leading authorities on the subject in Canada, has written a book which will bring hope to all women who suffer from cellulite — hope founded on a scientifically based treatment which has been effective in reducing the problem.

224 pages, Illustrated

WAITING FOR YOUR CHILD

Yvette Pratte-Marchessault

From the first signs of pregnancy to a complete course of postnatal exercises, this straightforward and informative new book provides the answers to the many questions a new mother may ask.

192 pages, Fully illustrated with photographs and drawings

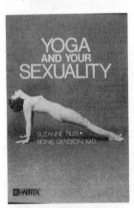

YOGA AND YOUR SEXUALITY

Suzanne Piuze and Lionel Gendron, M.D.

Two well-known authors combine their special knowledge and skills to describe a particular kind of mental and physical harmony — that of mind and sexual function. Physical function is explained, along with the principles of yoga as they apply to a healthy mind and body.

Fully illustrated 190 pages

VISUAL CHESS

Henri Tranquille

This book illustrates simple moves which occur in actual play and which are logical and easy to understand. Many celebrated attacks and defenses drawn from famous games are also included.

175 pages, Illustrated in two colours

INTERPRETING YOUR DREAMS

Louis Stanké

This fascinating new book, in a dictionary format, will help the reader understand the significance of his dreams and appreciate the activity of his subconscious.

176 pages